# iPhoto™ 2

## fast&easy™

# iPhoto™ 2 fast&easy™

Lisa A. Bucki

Premier Press™

**Publisher:** Stacy L. Hiquet
**Senior Marketing Manager:** Martine Edwards
**Marketing Manager:** Heather Hurley
**Associate Marketing Manager:** Kristin Eisenzopf
**Manager of Editorial Services:** Heather Talbot
**Project Editor:** Jenny Davidson
**Technical Reviewer:** Brian Proffitt
**Retail Market Coordinator:** Sarah Dubois
**Copy Editor:** Sandra Wilson
**Interior Layout:** Bill Hartman
**Cover Designer:** Mike Tanamachi
**Indexer:** Katherine Stimson
**Proofreader:** Sara Gullion



ISBN: 1-59200-071-1

Library of Congress Catalog Card Number: 2003104021

Printed in the United States of America

03 04 05 06 07 BH 10 9 8 7 6 5 4 3 2 1

Premier Press, a division of Course Technology
25 Thomson Place
Boston, MA 02210

*To Steve, Bo, and Rika, for all that they give me.*

# Acknowledgments

My thanks go out to everyone at Premier Press for again giving me the opportunity to be a part of this successful series. Like other *Fast & Easy* titles, this book results from outstanding contributions by a number of Premier Press team members. Thank you to Publisher Stacy Hiquet for her continued support of my writing efforts. Project Editor Jenny Davidson, Copy Editor Sandra Wilson, and Technical Reviewer Brian Proffitt deserve recognition for providing the editorial muscle and attention to detail to ensure this book's quality and timely publication. Thanks as well to the production team, Bill Hartman and Sara Gullion, and Indexer Katherine Stimson for producing the polished pages herein.

# About the Author

An author, trainer, and publishing consultant, **Lisa A. Bucki** has been involved in the computer book business for more than 12 years. She wrote *Mac OS X Version 10.2 Jaguar Fast & Easy*, *FileMaker Pro 6 for the Mac Fast & Easy*, *Adobe Photoshop 7 Fast & Easy*, *Adobe Photoshop 7 Digital Darkroom*, and *Managing with Microsoft Project 2002* for Premier Press. She also has written or contributed to dozens of additional books and multimedia tutorials, as well as spearheading or developing more than 100 computer and trade titles during her association with Macmillan. Bucki currently also serves as a consultant and trainer in Western North Carolina.

# Contents at a Glance

# Contents

# Introduction

This *Fast & Easy* book from Premier Press covers the newest version of iPhoto 2, Apple's powerful program for organizing and reproducing photos under Mac OS X. Even if you've just taken your first set of photos with a digital camera, don't be intimidated. This book zeros in on the key skills you need to know, making each skill accessible with concise steps and clear illustrations.

*iPhoto 2 Fast & Easy* teaches the steps that will enable you to navigate the iPhoto interface, import digital photos from a camera, and organize your images in albums. You will also learn to correct and arrange images, create books and slideshows, print your photos, or even order professional prints and photo books. To help you expand your skills even further, this book covers how to share photos with other users and how to save time by creating scripts.

If you want to build a robust library of your digital images, iPhoto 2 and this book provide everything you need.

## Who Should Read This Book?

This book is geared for novices who are new to iPhoto 2. Users of earlier iPhoto versions who have upgraded to iPhoto 2 also can benefit from this book, because it presents the features that are new in iPhoto 2.

Because nearly every step in this book includes a clear illustration, you won't have to struggle to learn a process or find the right tool onscreen. The non-technical language also helps smooth the transition from newbie to comfortable user.

With each task clearly identified by a heading, you'll also find it easy to use the table of contents to find the steps you need. So, whether you want to work through the book from beginning to end or find just the tricks that you need, this book will accommodate your style and enhance your results.

# Added Advice to Make You a Pro

Once you get started, you'll notice that this book presents many steps, with little explanatory text to slow you down. Where warranted, however, the book presents these special boxes to highlight a key issue:

- **Tips** give shortcuts or hints so you learn more about the ins and outs of Mac OS X Version 10.2.
- **Notes** offer more detailed information about a feature, food for thought, or guidance to help you avoid problems or pitfalls in your work.
- **Cautions** alert you to pitfalls and problems you should avoid.

Appendixes at the end of the book highlight additional topics: downloading and installing iPhoto 2, taking better photos, and connecting to and disconnecting from the Internet as needed. Finally, the glossary explains key terms that you need to understand to work effectively in iPhoto 2.

Whether or not you have used iPhoto before, you'll have fun as you dive in now with *iPhoto 2 Fast & Easy*!

PART I

# Introducing iPhoto 2

# 1

# Getting Started with iPhoto

Apple developed the iPhoto application to help you import, organize, print, and share your digital photos. The latest version, iPhoto 2, offers improved features such as the ability to correct scratches and other imperfections in digital photos. But before you can go there, take a few minutes to master the program basics. In this chapter, you will learn how to:

- Start iPhoto.
- Learn about the parts of the iPhoto window.
- Move between the different iPhoto modes.
- Get help in iPhoto.
- Quit iPhoto when you've finished working.

# Starting iPhoto

Starting the iPhoto application loads the program onscreen so that you can begin working. As when you start other Mac OS X applications, the iPhoto application's tools and commands become available only after you start the program.

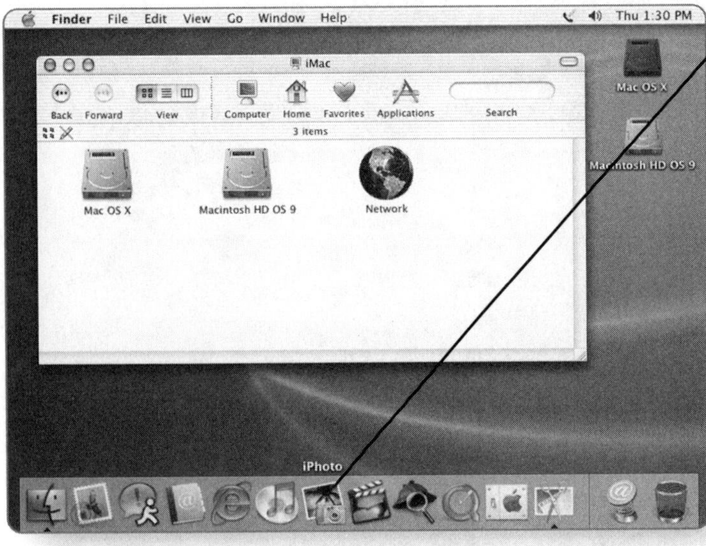


An icon for iPhoto 2 appears on the Dock by default, making startup quick and convenient. Click on the icon to launch iPhoto.

> **NOTE**
>
> The first time you start iPhoto 2, a Welcome to iPhoto message box opens. Click OK to continue. Then, a prompt to upgrade the existing *library* to work with iPhoto 2 appears. Click on Upgrade to convert the library and continue.

# Navigating the iPhoto Window

When you import digital photos, iPhoto places them in its *library*, or main photo catalog. From there, you can organize the photos into individual *albums* or groups. The iPhoto 2 application window offers a variety of controls that you can use to navigate between the library and albums, as well as organize, edit, view, and share your photos. While later chapters will teach you about various operations in greater detail, survey the controls now so that you can get comfortable in iPhoto.

> **NOTE**
>
> The first time you start iPhoto 2, it won't contain any photos. I imported some photos into iPhoto to help make the figures in this section a bit more clear.

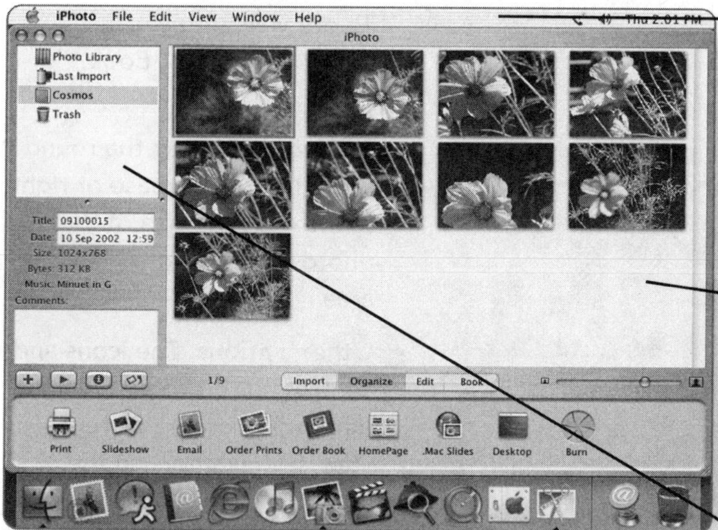


- **Menu bar.** The iPhoto menu bar loads when you start the program. The menu bar organizes available commands, with each menu listing several related commands.
- **Photo viewing area.** The photos in the photo library or selected album appear here. A blue outline appears around the currently selected photo.
- **Library list.** Shows the library, albums you create, and the Trash, which holds temporarily-deleted photos. Click on an item here to view its contents in the photo viewing area.

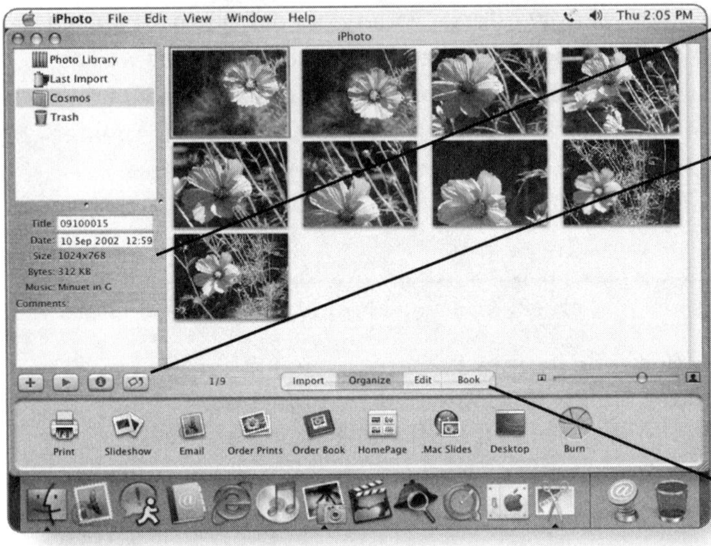


- **Information.** Lists details about the currently selected album or photo.
- **Add, Play, Information, and Rotate buttons.** Click on the desired button to add a new album, play the current album as a slide show, display or hide the current album or photo information, or rotate the selected photo by 90 degrees, respectively.
- **View buttons.** Click a button here to change to the desired iPhoto view: Import, Organize, Edit, or Book.

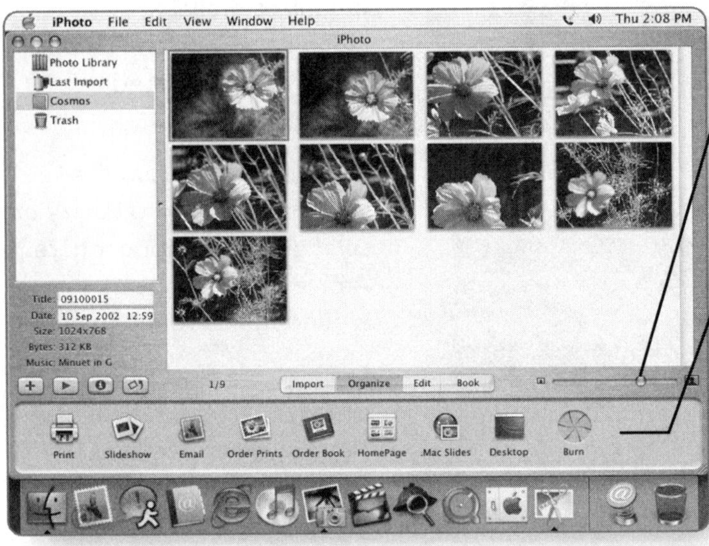


- **Size control.** Drag the round slider left to decrease or right to increase the size of the photos in the photo viewing area.
- **Other options.** The icons and controls in this toolbar vary depending on the current view. For example, in the Organize view, you can click on an icon to Order Prints of the selected photo or create a Web HomePage.

# Taking a Look at the Views

Each of the different views enables you to perform specific actions on the photos in your library or the selected album. Click on one of the view buttons just below the photo viewing area to change to the desired view. The following images show you each of the available views. Later chapters will describe in detail how to use each view to manage, edit, and print your digital images.

> **NOTE**
>
> The views are also called panes, as in "Book pane."

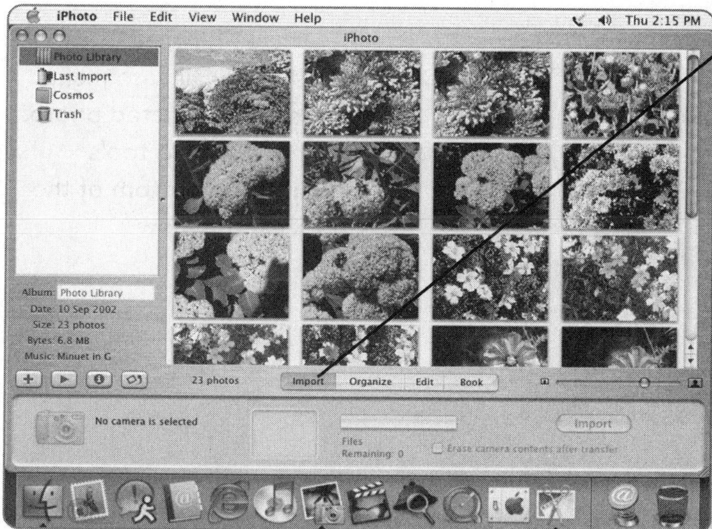


- **Import.** Choose this view when you want to import photos from a digital camera or disk. If you've connected your digital camera, information about the camera and its contents appears at the bottom of the iPhoto window.

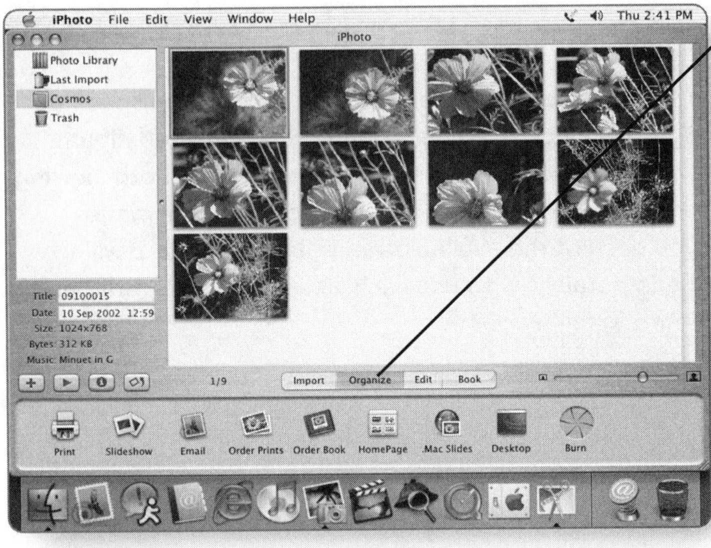


- **Organize.** In this view, you can change the order of the photos within the library or selected album. You also can use the icons at the bottom of the window to order prints and more.

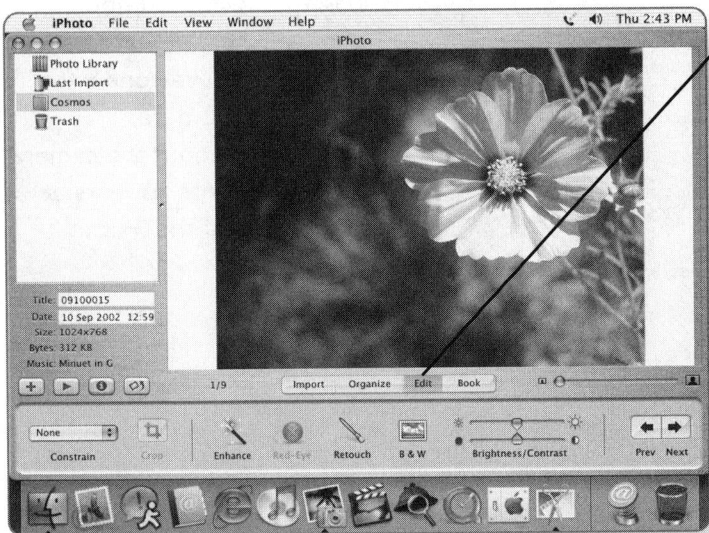


- **Edit.** Use this view to make changes to a selected photo. The photo editing tools appear at the bottom of the window in this view.

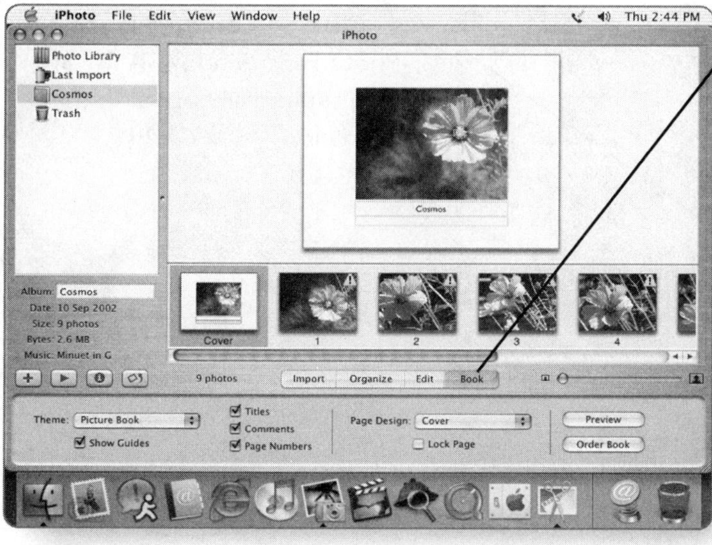

- **Book.** Work in this view to set up the photos in the current album as a book that you can print yourself or have professionally printed.

# Getting Help

Like many other applications optimized for Mac OS X, iPhoto 2 uses the Mac OS X Help Viewer to present help information. The Help Viewer works much like a Web browser. Click on topic links (formatted in blue and underlined by default) to navigate to the Help topic you need. The following steps show a basic Help navigation, but keep in mind that some Help Viewer links may take you to an online site or a search location.

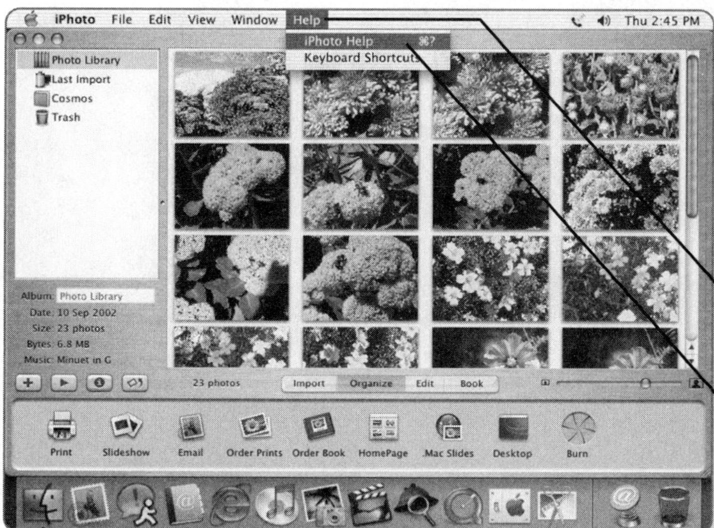

**1.** Click on **Help**. The Help menu will appear.

**2.** Click on **iPhoto Help**. Help Viewer will open.

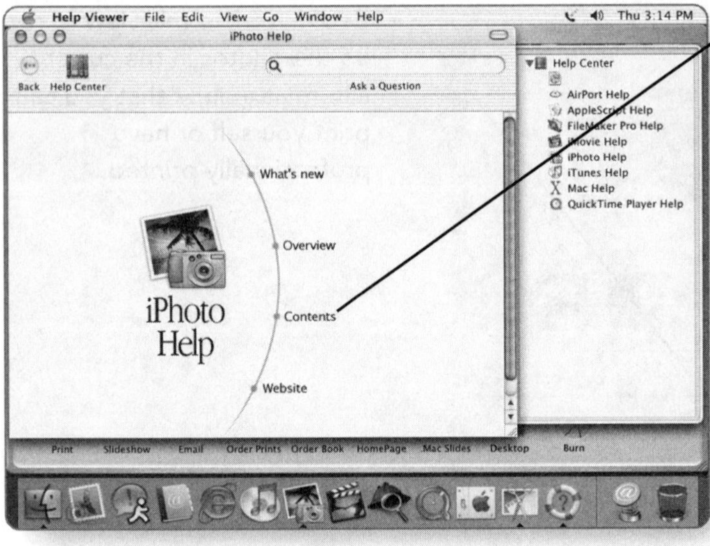


**3. Click** on **Contents** in the iPhoto Help window. A list of Help topics will appear in the left pane.

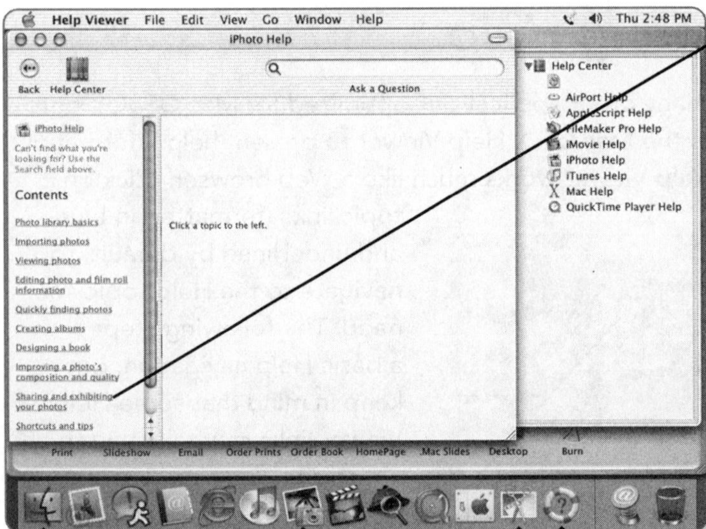


**4. Click** on the **topic you want.** A listing of more specific Help topics will appear in the right pane of the iPhoto Help window.

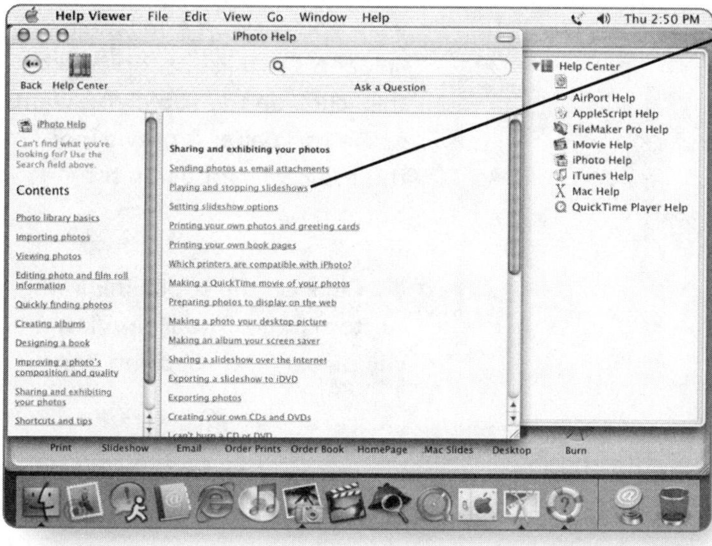


**5. Click** on the **topic of interest**. The topic will appear in the iPhoto Help window.

> **NOTE**
>
> When you select some Help topics, you may be prompted to connect to the Internet to download more information. Click OK to launch Internet Connect so that your system can dial your Internet connection. Appendix C, "Dialing the Internet If Needed," explains how to connect and disconnect.

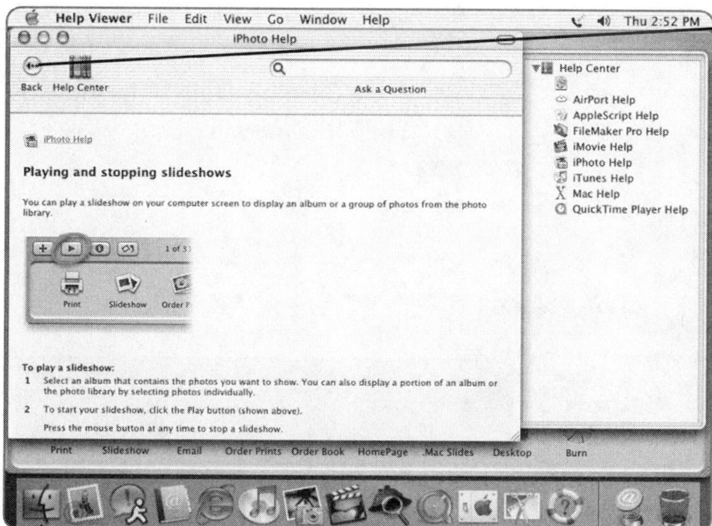


**6. Click** on the **back button** or other links as needed. The Help Viewer window will navigate to the appropriate page.

> **NOTE**
>
> Click on the iPhoto Help link at the top of any page to return to the initial iPhoto Help page.

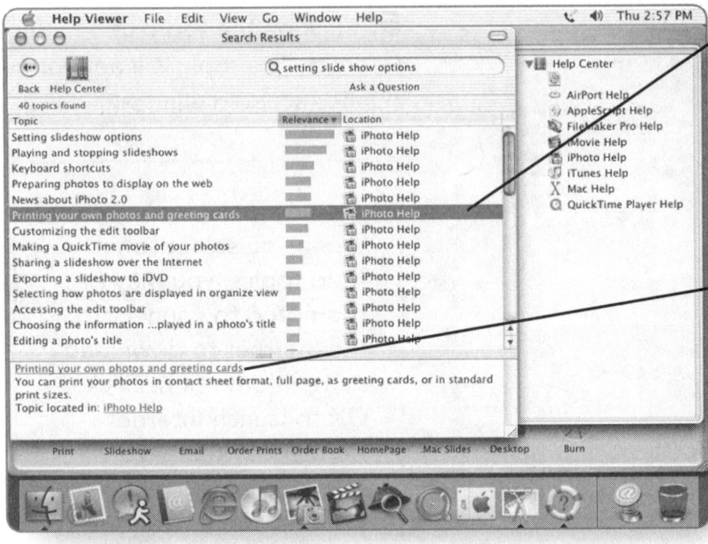

**7.** If you click on a Tell me more link and see a list of topics like this, **click** on the **topic you want** in the top pane. A preview of the topic will appear in the bottom pane.

**8.** **Click** on the **topic link** in the bottom pane. The Help Viewer will display the specified page.

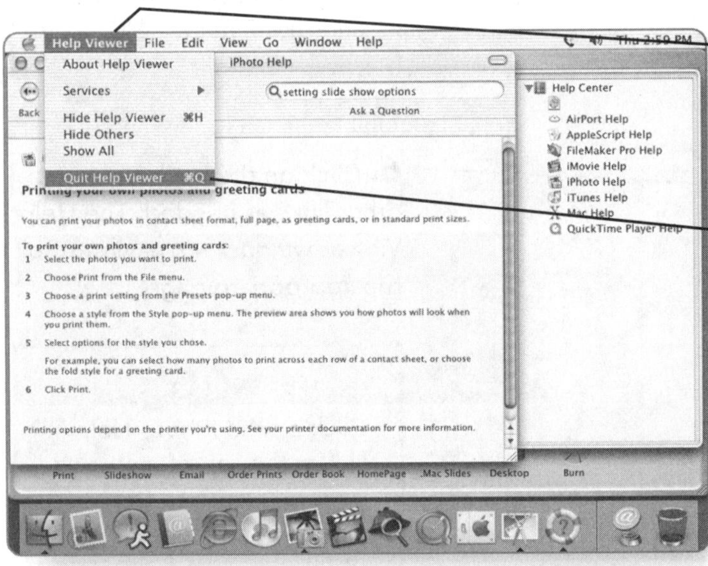

**9.** When you've finished viewing Help, **click** on **Help Viewer**. The Help Viewer menu will appear.

**10.** **Click** on **Quit Help Viewer**. Help Viewer will close.

# Quitting iPhoto

You can quit the iPhoto application at any time to finish working and free up RAM in your system. Note that there's no need to save your album files before quitting. iPhoto saves your albums automatically each time you make a change.

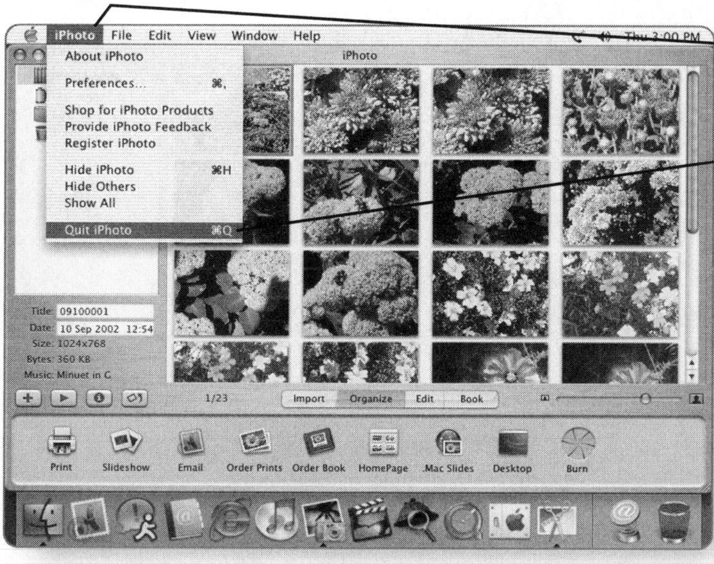


**1.** **Click** on **iPhoto**. The iPhoto menu will appear.

**2.** **Click** on **Quit iPhoto**. iPhoto will close.

# 2

# Importing Photos

Before you can use iPhoto 2 to organize your digital photos and create cool slideshows or books, you have to bring your digital images into iPhoto. This chapter focuses on getting that job done, showing you how to add digital images to the iPhoto 2 photo library and begin to work with the images once they're there. In this chapter, you will learn how to:

- Store and view digital photos in the photo library.
- Import digital photos from a camera or other digital media reader.
- Import digital photos from a disk or folder.
- Select and delete images in the photo library.
- View photo information.

# Understanding the Photo Library

The iPhoto photo library acts as a digital storage area and catalog of all the images that you've imported into iPhoto.

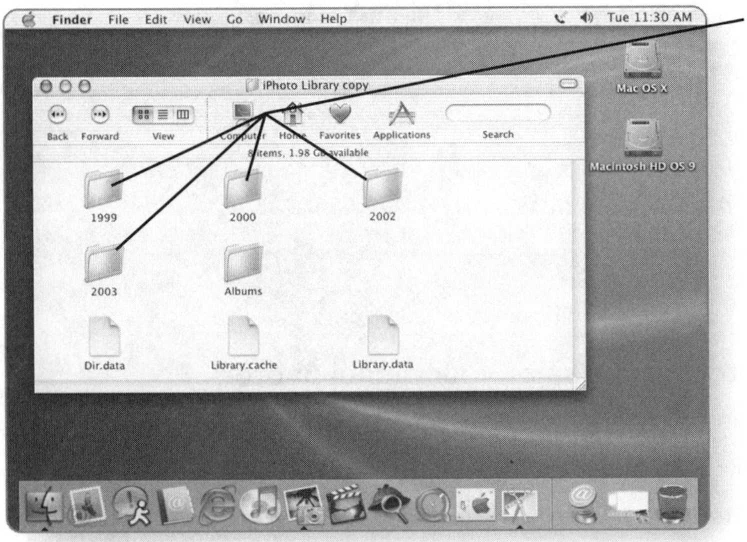


Importing a digital image into iPhoto automatically creates a copy of the image and places the copy within the photo library folder—the iPhoto Library folder within the Pictures folder of your Home folder—on your system's hard disk. iPhoto automatically creates subfolders within the iPhoto Library folder to organize photos by the date they were taken (year, month, and day). This illustration shows an older copy of my iPhoto Library folder, with subfolders for images from various years.

For each album you build, iPhoto creates a specific subfolder (using the album name) within the Albums subfolder of the iPhoto Library folder. The album subfolder identifies each image in the album via an alias or shortcut to the original image imported into the iPhoto Library folder. This technique enables you to include a particular image in multiple albums without having multiple copies of the image file consuming hard disk space.

**NOTE**

Chapter 13, "Archiving Your Photos," gives you a variety of techniques for working with library folders, including burning a library to CD-R and selecting a library folder to use in iPhoto

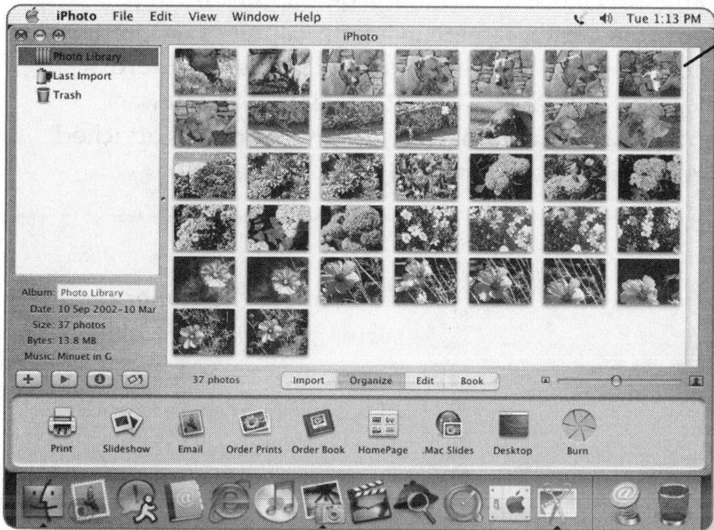


Within the iPhoto 2 application, all of the digital photos that you've imported show up in the photo viewing area when you have Photo Library selected in the library list at left.

# Importing Images from a Digital Camera

In most cases, you'll want to import images directly from your digital camera into iPhoto. Mac OS X Version 10.2 and iPhoto 2 directly support a number of digital cameras. (To verify whether your digital camera is compatible, see http://www.apple.com/iphoto/compatibility/camera.html.) Connect the camera to your system via the USB or FireWire port and turn it on. iPhoto will recognize the camera and launch so that you can download images from the camera to your system. Digital cameras typically save images in the JPEG and TIFF file formats, and iPhoto can easily import both of those formats.

> **NOTE**
>
> Mac OS X Version 10.2 also includes the Image Capture application for downloading photos. You can specify whether to launch iPhoto or Image Capture when you attach your digital camera in Image Capture's preferences. The first time you load images in iPhoto, a dialog box appears to ask you to verify that you want iPhoto to launch automatically when a camera is attached. Click on Yes to have iPhoto launch automatically.

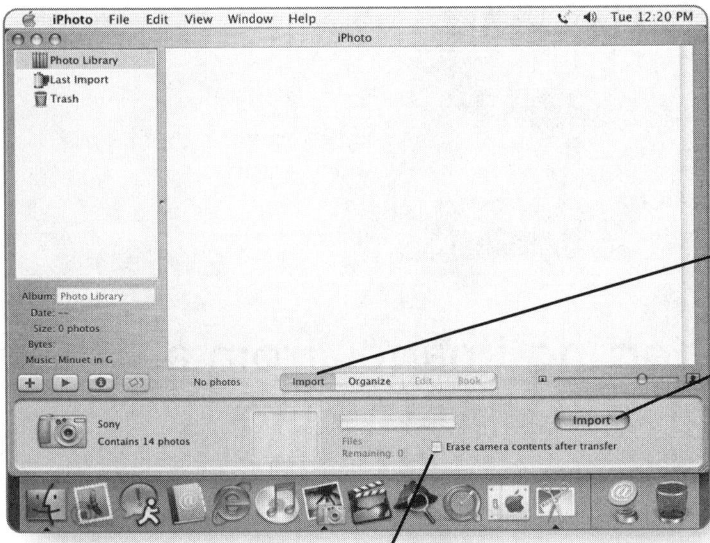


1. **Connect the camera** to the system, **turn it on** or plug in its power source, and **switch** to its **playback or transfer mode.** iPhoto will launch.

2. **Click** on **Import**. The Import view pane appears.

3. **Click** on the **Import** command button. iPhoto will import the digital images from the camera's storage, will add a thumbnail for each image into the iPhoto Photo Library, and will switch to the Organize view.

> **NOTE**
>
> Click on the Erase camera contents after transfer check box only if you want to delete the images from the storage in your camera after the import.

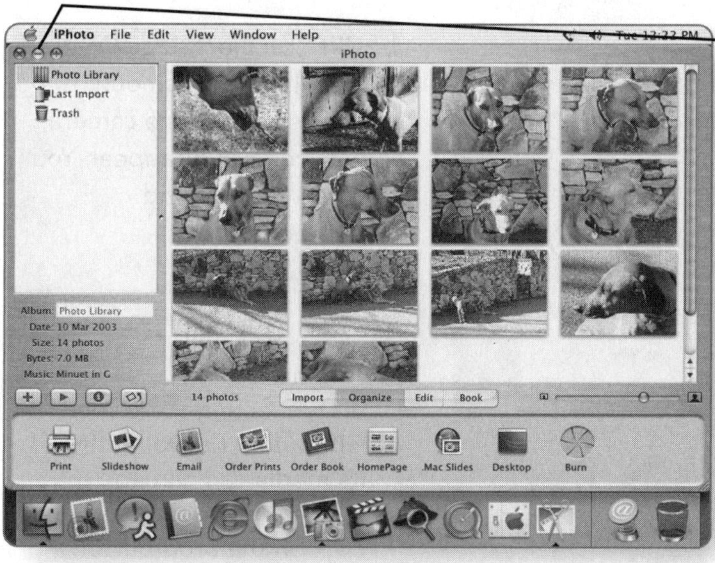


**4.** **Click** on the **minimize button** for the iPhoto window. iPhoto minimizes to an icon on the Dock.

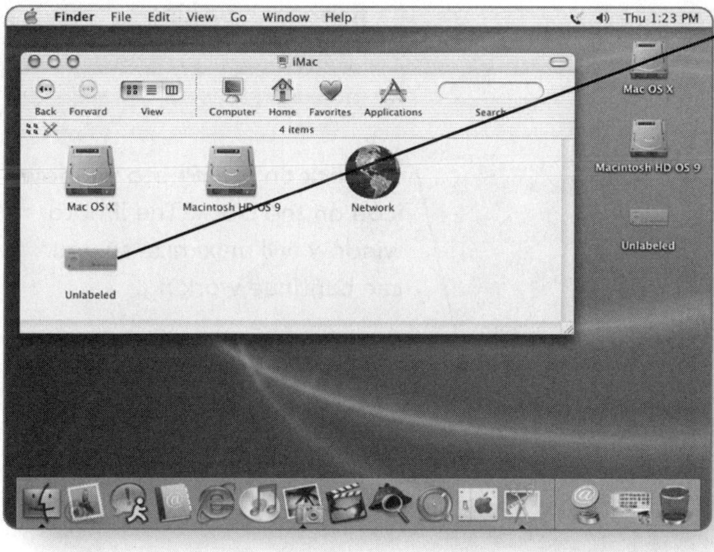


**5.** **Control+click** on the **storage media icon** for your camera. The contextual menu will appear.

> **TIP**
>
> Control+click, Command+click, or Shift+click means to press and hold the Control, Command, or Shift key on the keyboard, and then click on the desired object or icon onscreen.

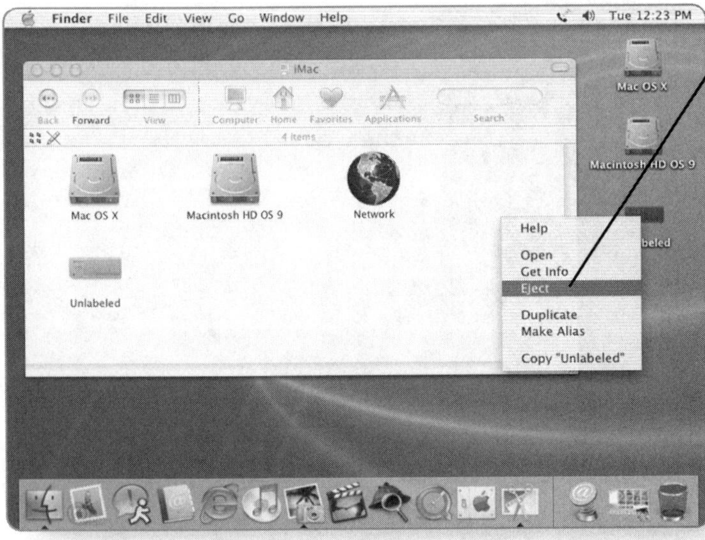


**6. Click** on **Eject**. Mac OS X Version 10.2 will dismount (disconnect from) the camera, and its icon will disappear. You may now turn off and disconnect the camera.

> **CAUTION**
>
> Turning off and disconnecting the camera without first dismounting its media can damage the media. You also should click on the Stop button in iPhoto before disconnecting the camera if iPhoto has not yet finished importing images.

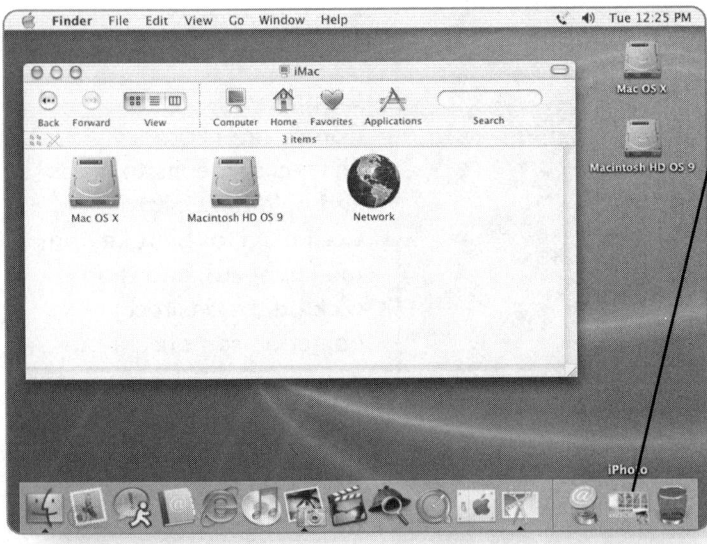


**7. Click** on the **iPhoto window icon** on the Dock. The iPhoto window will maximize so you can continue working.

**NOTE**

If you've had your images professionally processed by Kodak, inserting your Kodak Picture CD into the drive should launch iPhoto, so that you can simply click the Import button to import the pictures. If iPhoto doesn't automatically recognize an inserted Picture CD or if you've used another photo processing company to digitize your photos, use the process described in the next section to import the photos from the CD-R folder holding them.

## Importing Images from a Digital Media Reader or Disk

If your digital camera isn't compatible with iPhoto 2, you can connect a media reader to your Mac and use the reader to import digital photos from the storage medium (typically Compact Flash, smart media, or Memory Stick) used by your camera. Because readers work like a disk drive attached to your system, importing from a media reader works like importing from a disk attached to the system. iPhoto also can import images already burned to a CD-R or stored on another system on your network if you've previously copied the images or scanned and saved them there. No matter where the images to import are stored, the image files must be saved in one of the following file formats:

- BMP
- GIF
- JPEG/JFIF
- MacPaint
- PICT
- PNG
- Photoshop PSD (with or without layers)
- SGI
- FlashPix
- TIFF

Start the following import steps from within iPhoto.

**1.** **Connect the media reader** to the system, **turn it on** or plug in its power source if needed, and **insert the digital medium** that you previously removed from your camera. (Or, insert the CD-R holding your digital images.) Mac OS X will mount the media as a disk drive.

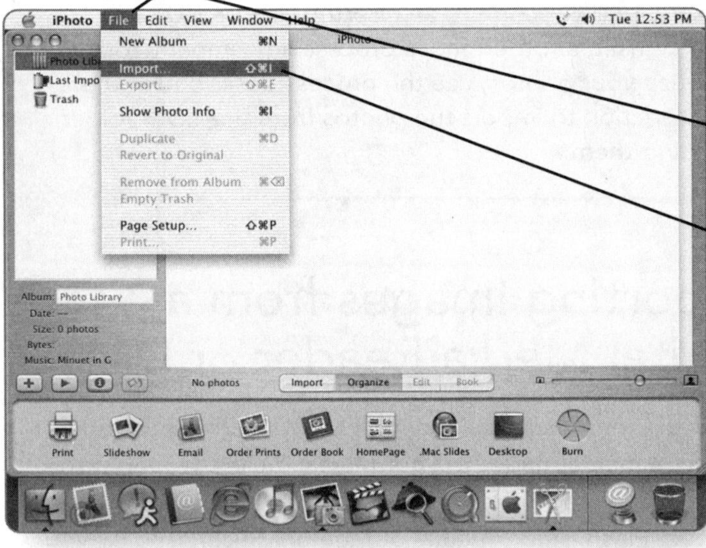


**2.** **Click** on **File**. The File menu will appear.

**3.** **Click** on **Import**. The Import Photos dialog box will open.

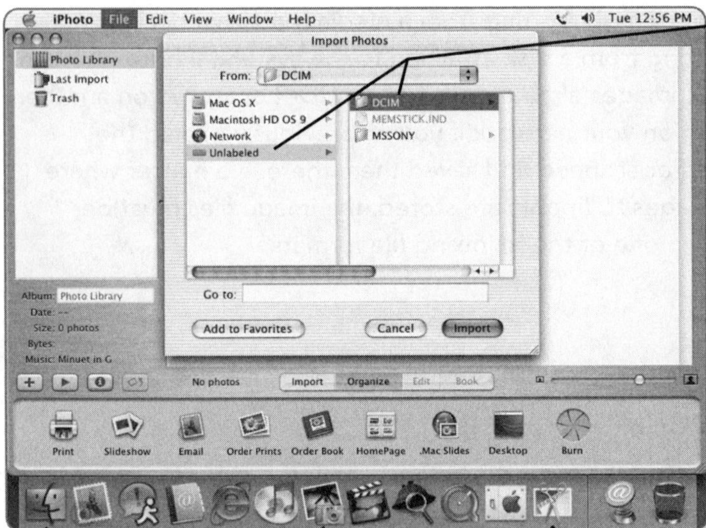


**4.** **Navigate** to the **disk and folder** that holds the photos to import. A list of digital images in the specified location will appear on the right.

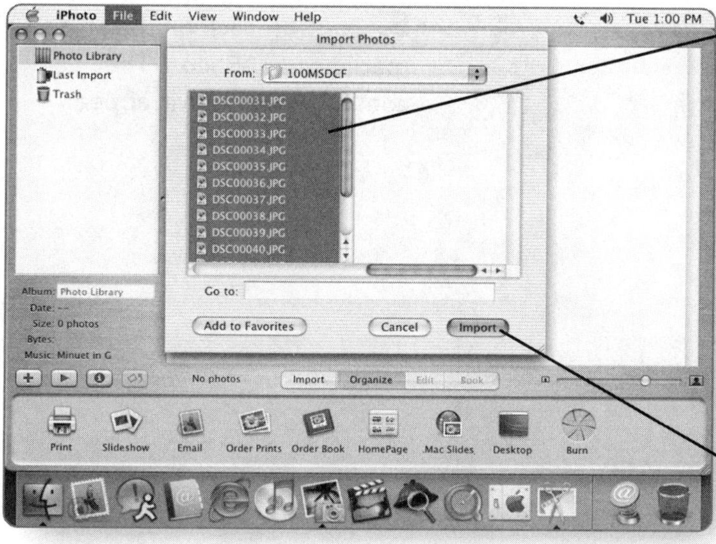


**5. Click** on **photos** to import. The photos are selected and a preview icon will appear next to each one.

> **TIP**
>
> Command+click or Shift+click to select multiple photos for import.

**6. Click** on **Import**. Again, iPhoto adds a thumbnail for each digital photo into the photo library, and copies the image files to your Mac's hard disk.

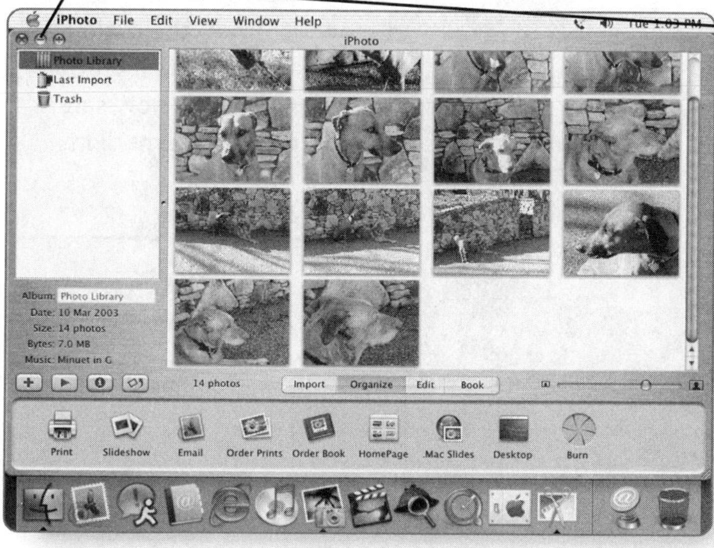


**7.** If you imported the images from a digital media reader, **click** on the **minimize button** for the iPhoto window. iPhoto minimizes to an icon on the Dock.

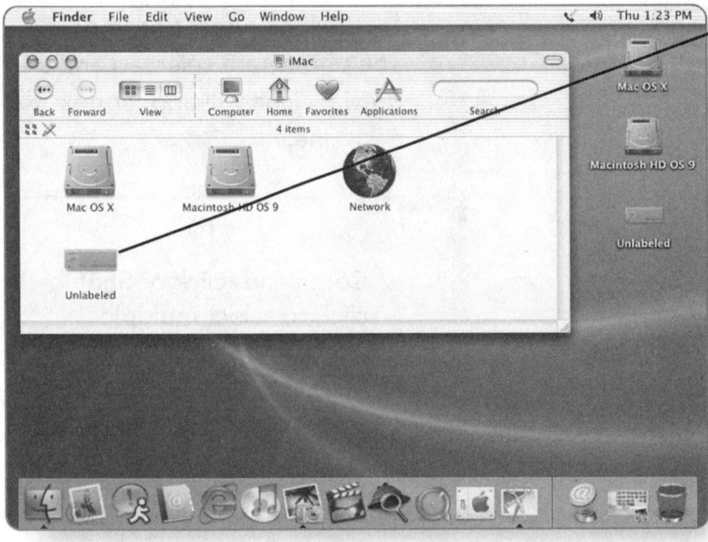


**8. Control+click** on the **storage media or CD-R icon**. The contextual menu will appear.

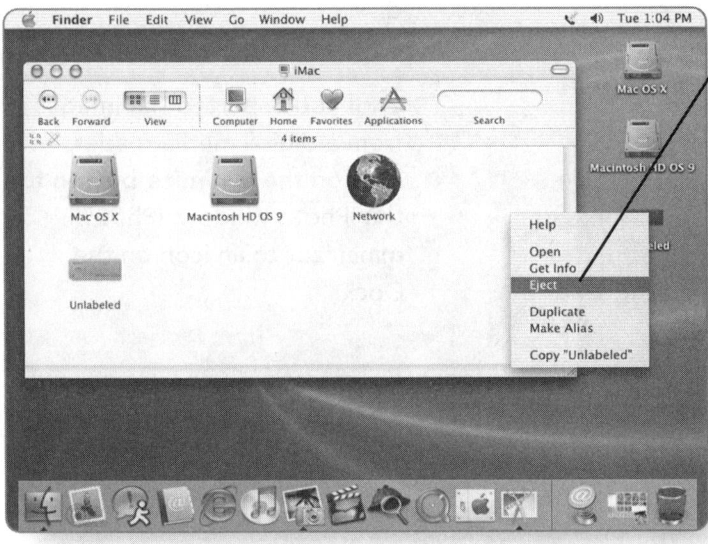


**9. Click** on **Eject**. Mac OS X Version 10.2 will dismount (disconnect from) the digital media reader, and its icon will disappear. You may now safely remove the storage medium from the reader.

> **CAUTION**
>
> Removing the card or stick without first dismounting it can damage the media.

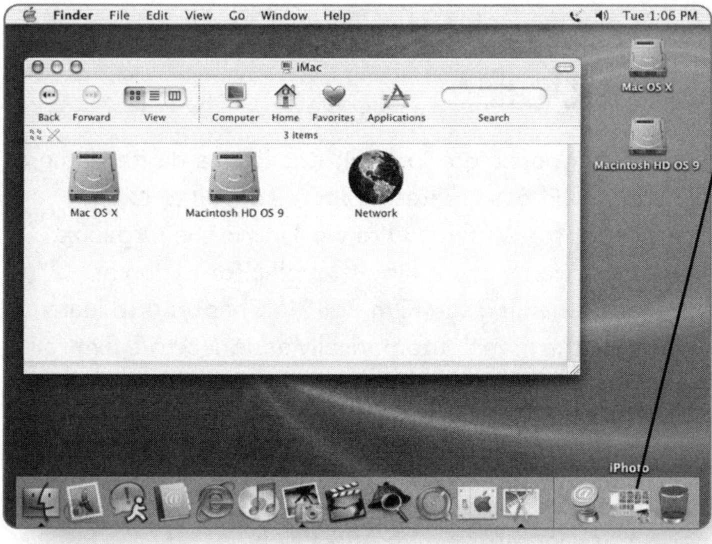

**10. Click** on the **iPhoto window icon** on the Dock. The iPhoto window will maximize so you can continue working.

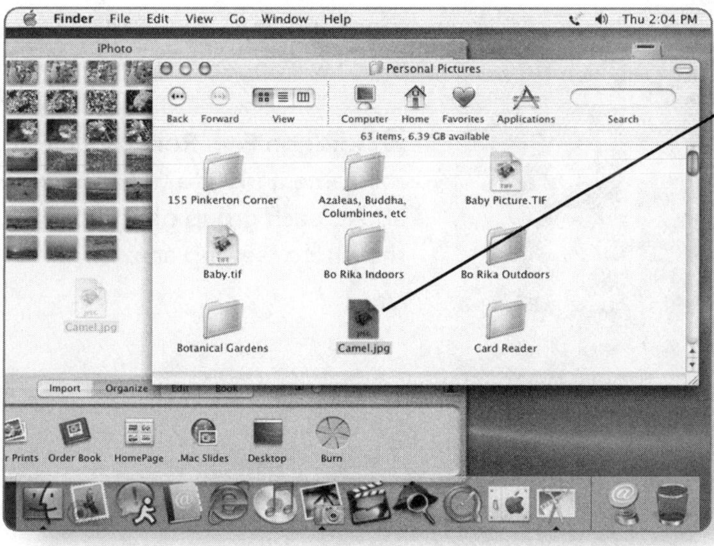

### TIP

You can use the Finder to import images automatically. Display the icon for the folder or image to import in the Finder. Drag the icon over the photo viewing area in iPhoto. iPhoto will import the selected image (or folder) as a new film roll.

# Viewing and Hiding Roll Information

Each time you import a group of photos from a digital camera or other source, iPhoto creates a *film roll* or *roll* to further organize the photos. When you're working in the Organize view (pane), you can view or hide the roll information as desired. See "Renaming the Film Roll" in Chapter 4 to learn how to change the name automatically assigned to a film roll.

> **TIP**
>
> Remember, click on the Organize button in the iPhoto window to change to the Organize view.

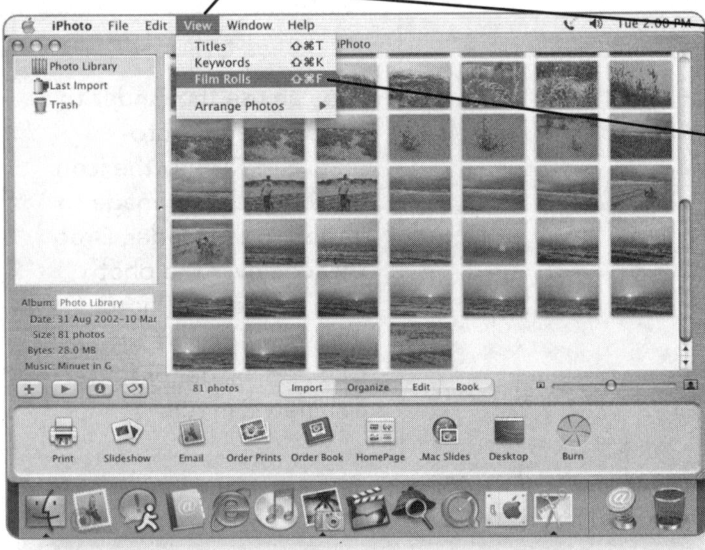


1. **Click** on **View**. The View menu will appear.

2. **Click** on **Film Rolls**. A film roll name and date will appear above each group of photos in the photo viewing area.

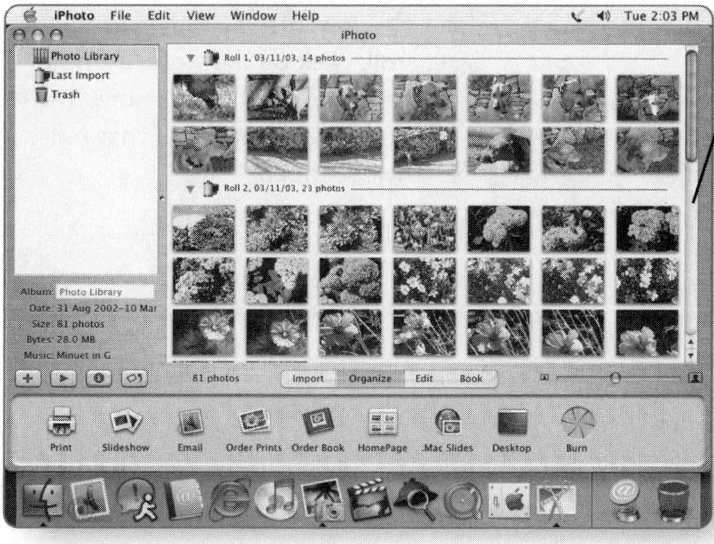


**3. Scroll** the **photo viewing area** as desired. You will see the film roll name and date above each group or roll of photos.

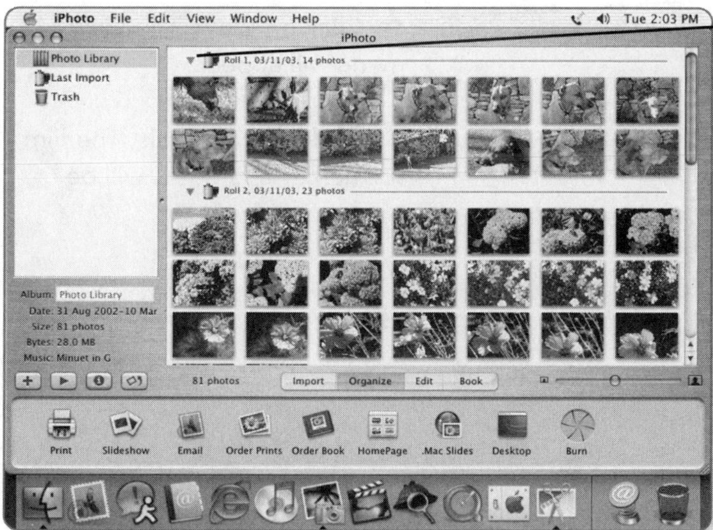


**4.** To hide (collapse) the images in a roll, **click** on the **down triangle icon** beside the roll name. The digital images within that roll will be hidden.

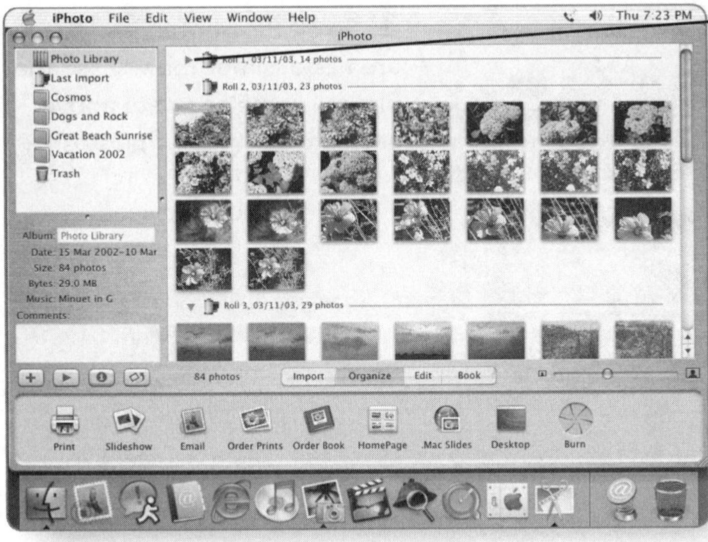


**5.** To redisplay the images in a roll, **click** on the **right triangle icon** beside the roll name. The digital images within that roll will reappear.

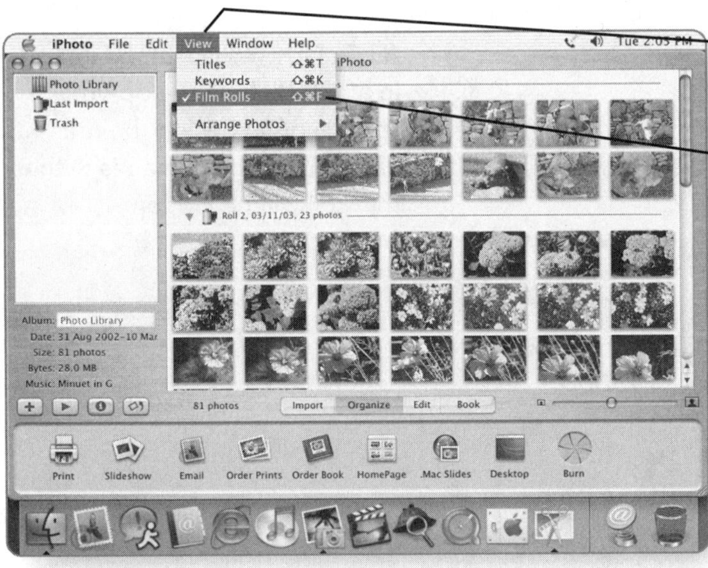


**6. Click** on **View**. The View menu will appear.

**7. Click** on **Film Rolls**. The film roll names and dates will be hidden.

# Selecting Images

To add images to an album or delete images, you have to select them in the photo viewing area. A blue highlight outline appears around each photo you've selected. Following are various techniques you can use to select and deselect photos.

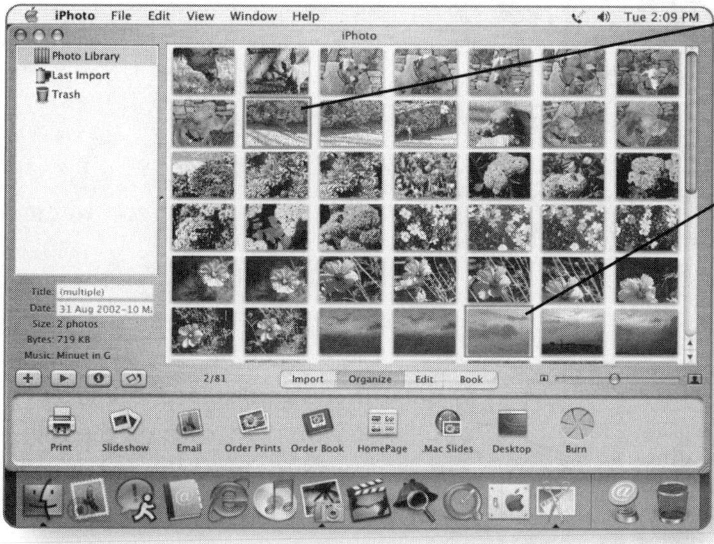


- Click on a single image to select it. You also can click on a single image to remove the prior selection.
- Command+click on additional nonadjacent images to select them. (Or, Command+click on selected images in a group to deselect them.)

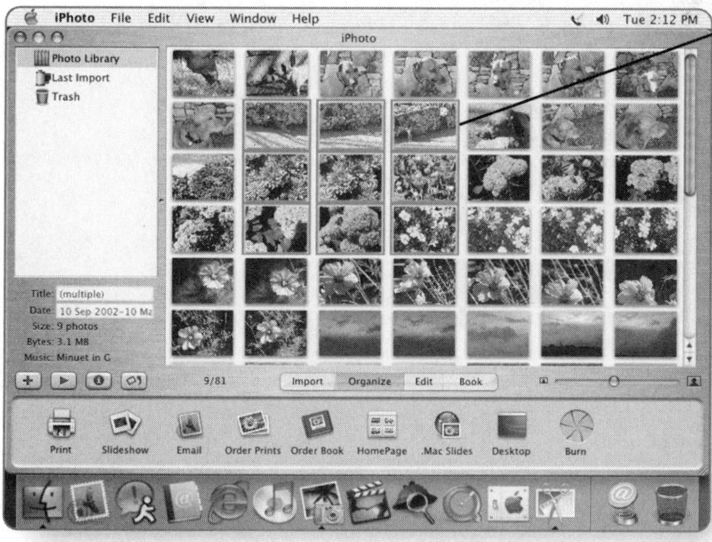


- Drag the mouse pointer over a group of adjacent images to select them. Or, click on the upper-left image in the group and then Shift+click on the lower-right image.

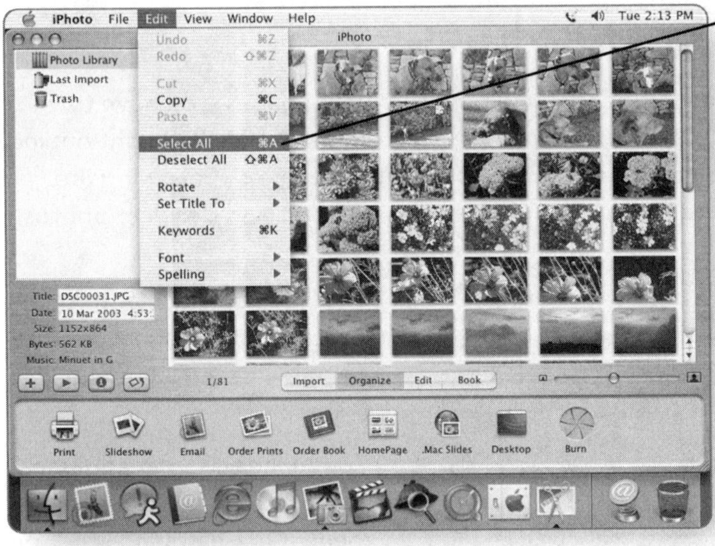

- Click on Edit, Select All (or press Command+A) to select all of the images.

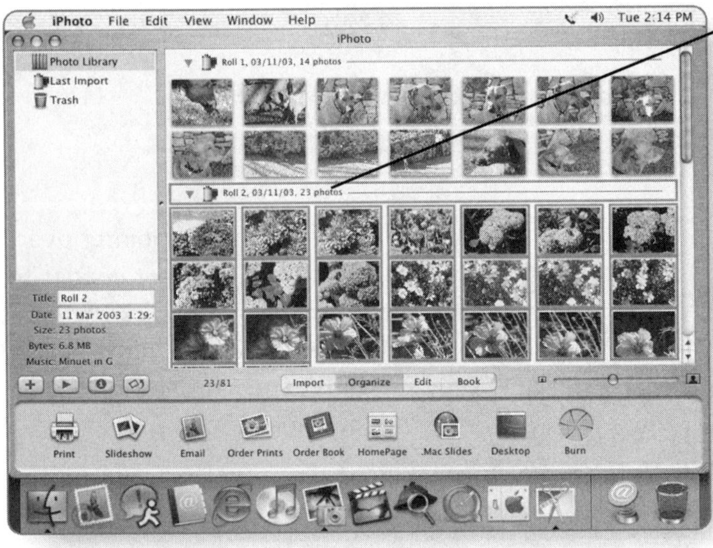

- If you've displayed film roll information, click on the roll name to select the entire roll.

# Deleting Images from the Photo Library

You can delete a selected image from the photo library, which also removes it from the iPhoto Library folder on your hard disk. You would use this procedure, say, if you see that a particular photo you've imported looks too blurry.

> **CAUTION**
>
> Deleting an image from the photo library also deletes the image from any albums in which you've placed the image. (Chapter 3 explains how to create albums.) Make sure you don't need the image in a particular album before removing it from the photo library.

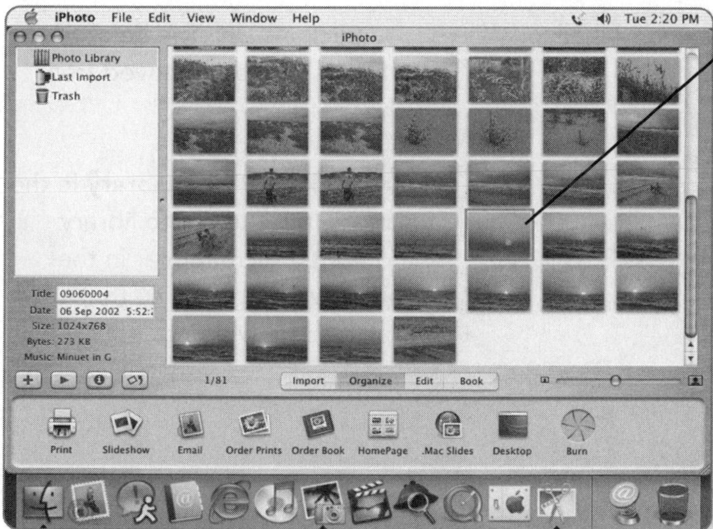


**1.** **Select** the **photo(s)** to delete. The selection highlight will appear around the photo(s).

**2.** **Press** the **Delete key** on your keyboard. The digital image will be moved from the photo viewing area to the Trash. (The Trash icon appears in the library list at left.)

> **TIP**
>
> You also can drag images from the photo viewing area over to the Trash icon. If you mistakenly delete a photo, press Command+ Z or choose Edit, Undo Move to Trash.

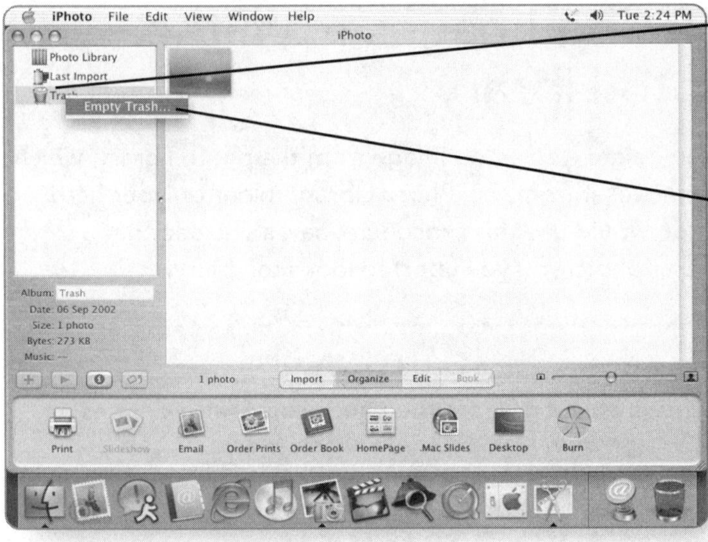


**3.** To make the deletion permanent, press **Control+click** on the **Trash icon**. The contextual menu will appear.

**4. Click** on **Empty Trash**. A message box will prompt you to confirm the deletion.

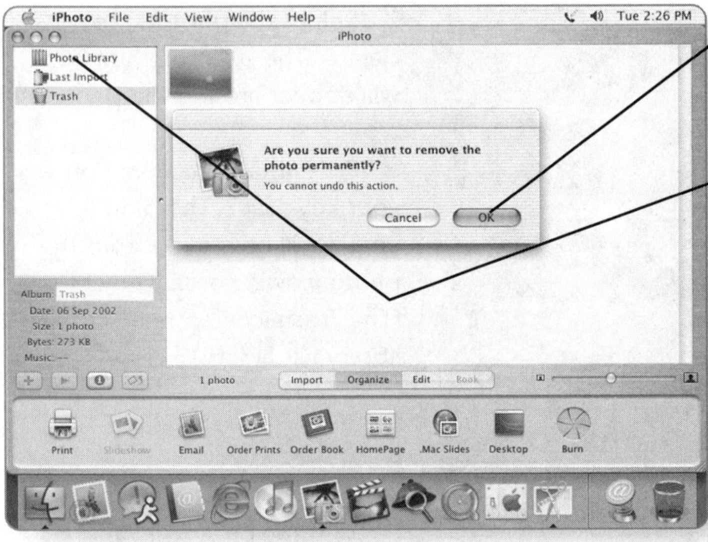


**5. Click** on **OK**. The deleted photo(s) will be removed from the Trash.

**6. Click** on **Photo Library** in the library list. The photo library contents will reappear in the photo viewing area so that you can resume working.

### NOTE

If the Trash contains multiple images that you'd like to undelete, click on Trash in the library list, select the images to undelete in the photo viewing area, and drag the images to the Photo Library icon in the library list. Or, choose File, Restore to Photo Library to restore the selected photos.

# Viewing Photo Titles and Info

You can view two types of photo information in iPhoto. Chapter 4, "Working with Photo Information," explains how to make changes to photo title information. This section only explains how to view and navigate the available information.

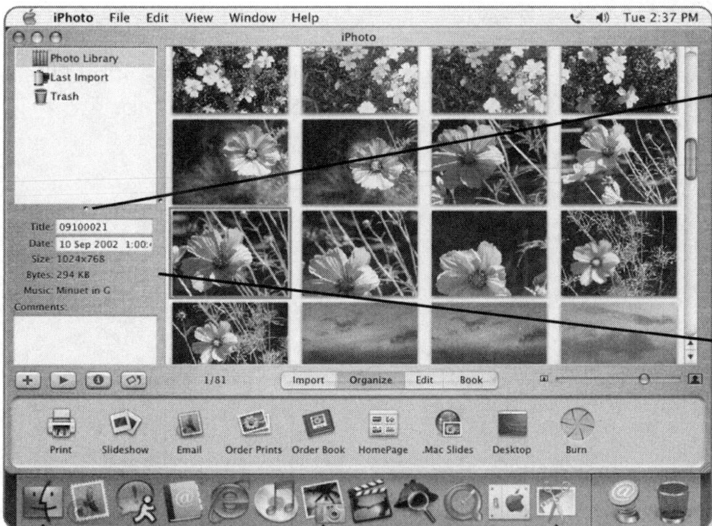


### TIP

Drag the lower border (near the dot) of the library list up to provide more room for the displayed information.

- To view basic photo info about a selected photo—such as its Title, Date, and Comments—look below the library list. If you can't see the desired information there, click on the Information button to cycle through the available types of information.

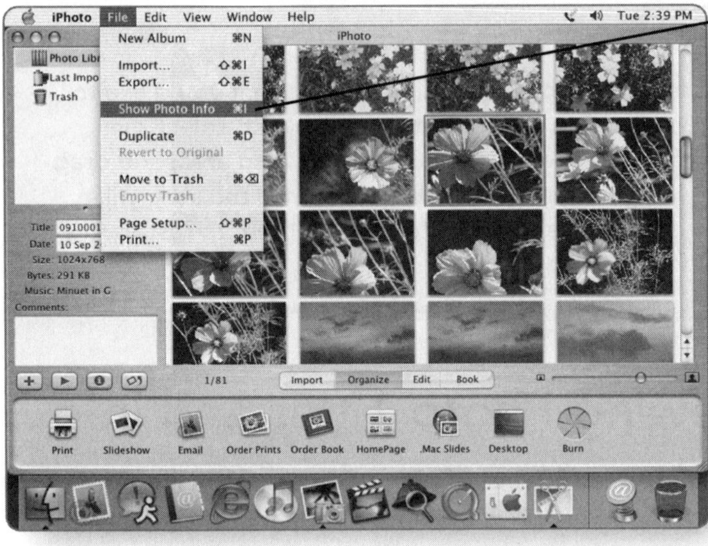


- Most digital cameras store certain details about each image with the image file, such as the type of camera used to take the image and the exposure settings used. To display this information in the Photo Info window, choose File, Show Photo Info.

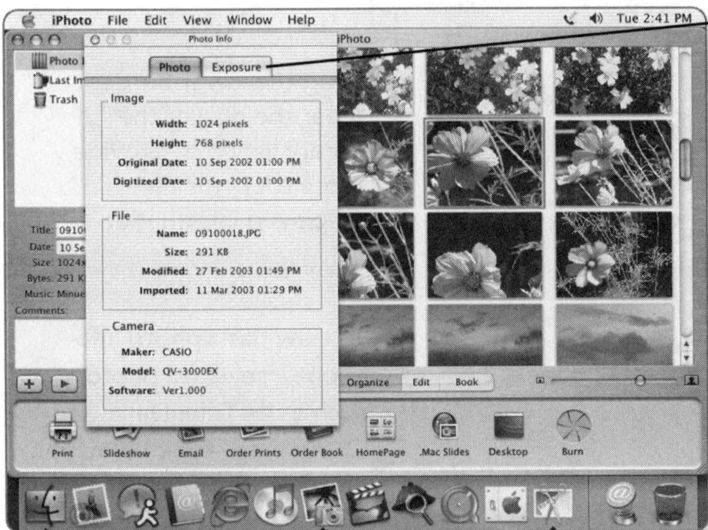


- Review the information on the Photo tab, and then click on the Exposure tab.

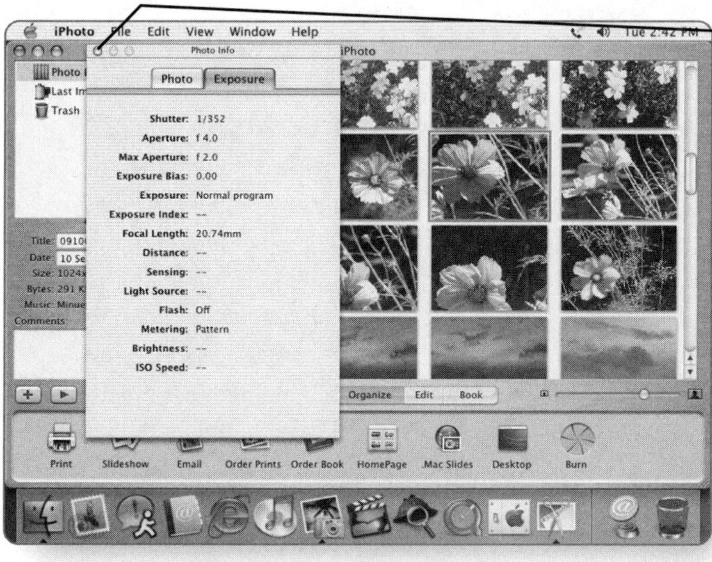


- Review the information on the Exposure tab, and then click on the window Close button to close the Photo Info window. The information on the Exposure tab is called *EXIF data*.

### NOTE

If you really like a particular digital photo that you've shot, then it pays to be aware of the exposure settings used for that image. If you later want to produce another great image of a similar subject under similar lighting conditions, you can manually select the same exposure settings (assuming your digital camera features a manual mode).

# 3

# Creating and Managing Albums

To do anything fun like create a book in iPhoto, you have to understand how to organize digital images. iPhoto enables you to place photos from the photo library into digital albums. Once you have grouped photos in an album, you can arrange them into any order you prefer. In this chapter, you will learn how to:

- Create an album and add photos to it.
- Select an album to view its contents.
- Specify the order of the images in an album.
- Make a copy of a photo in an album.
- Remove a photo from an album (but not the photo library).
- Play an album as an onscreen slideshow.
- Change the display size of photos in an album.

# Creating an Album and Adding Photos

Over time, your photo library will grow to dozens—if not hundreds—of photos. iPhoto enables you to organize photos from the library into individual albums. Each album can hold a collection of photos with a particular theme, or simply a selection of photos that you want to print, view as a slideshow, or publish online at a particular time. Adding a photo to an album does not remove the photo from the photo library. The photo remains available in the library so that you can add it to other albums.

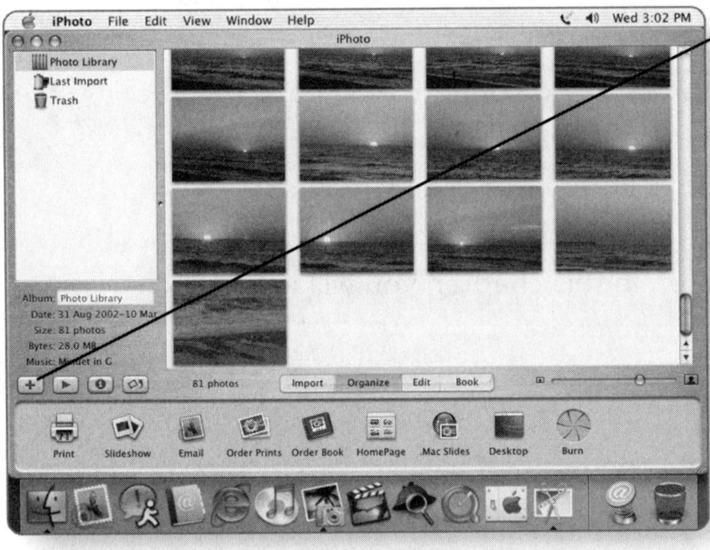


**1. Click** on the **Add button**. The New Album dialog box will open.

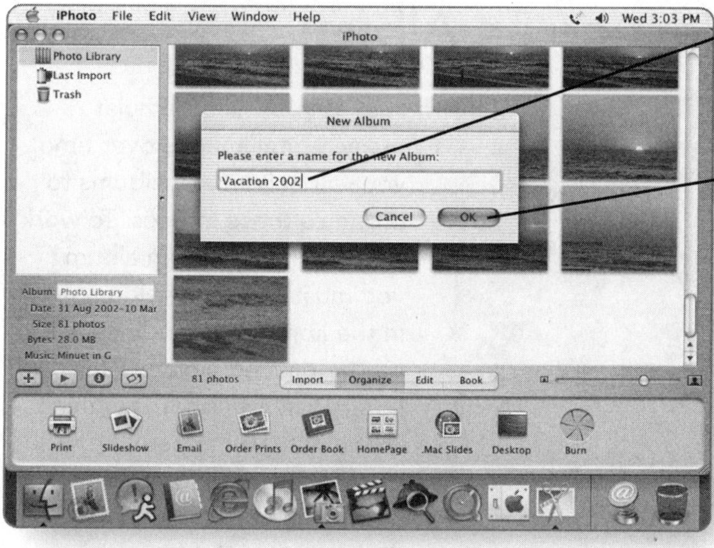


**2. Type** a **name** for the new album. It will appear in the New Album dialog box.

**3. Click** on **OK**. The New Album dialog box will close and the new album will appear in the list at the left side of the iPhoto window.

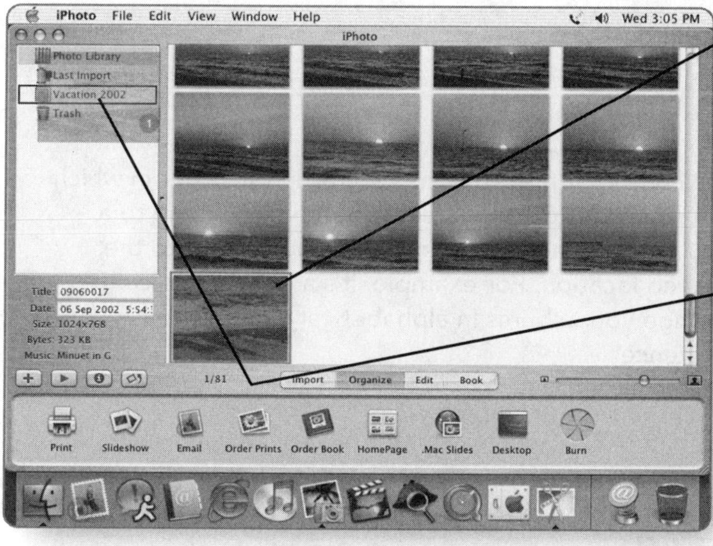


**4.** Leave Photo Library selected in the library list at the left, and **drag images from the library.** A gray box will appear behind the mouse pointer to represent the image as you drag it.

**5. Drop** the **image onto the new album**. Each time you release the mouse button, the photo(s) you dragged will be copied to the album.

## CAUTION

Make sure the black selection marquee appears around the name of the desired album, not the whole library list, before you release the mouse button. Otherwise, your photo won't copy to the album.

# Selecting an Album

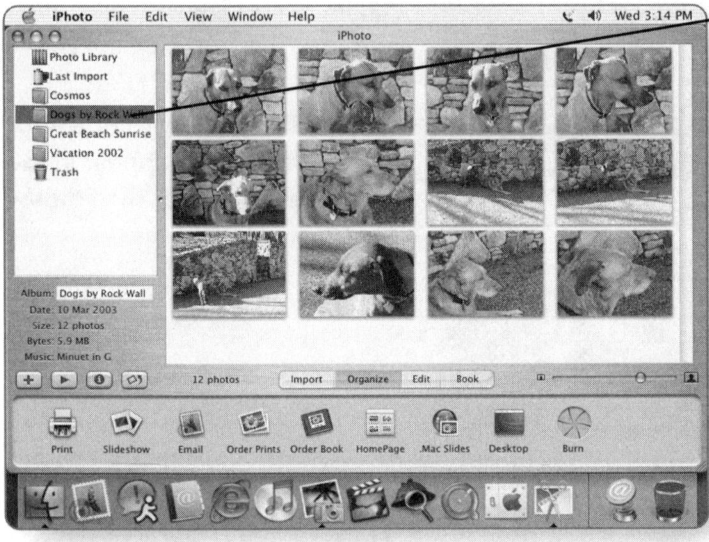


Just as you will accumulate many digital images over time, you will build many albums to organize those images. To work with the images in an album, you must select the album first in the library list. To do so, click on the desired album in the library list. The photos within that album will appear in the photo viewing area. To select multiple albums, you can use Shift+click or Control+click.

> **TIP**
>
> The library list presents the albums in the order in which you created them by default. To move an album to a new position in the list, drag the album name to the desired location. For example, it's a good practice to arrange your albums in alphabetical order, for easy reference.

# Rearranging Photos in an Album

If you plan to produce a book, Web home page, or slideshow from the images in an album, then you need to place the photos in the order that you wish for the finished product. You can sort photos automatically or arrange them manually, as required.

## Sorting Photos

You can choose one of three sort orders for the photos in an album:

- **by Film Roll.** Arranges the photos according to their film roll, from earliest roll to latest. (Remember, each film roll represents an import operation, so this sort order arranges photos according to the order in which they were imported into iPhoto.)
- **by Date.** Arranges photos according to the date you shot them.
- **by Title.** Arranges the photos by title. See "Working with Photo Titles" in Chapter 4 to learn how to replace the default titles—the alphanumeric file names assigned by your camera—with more descriptive titles.

To choose one of these sort orders for the images in the selected album, use the following steps.

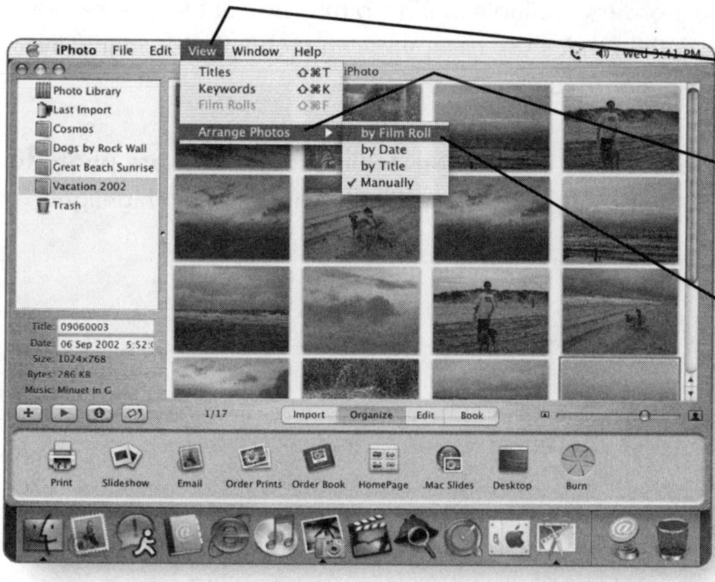


**1.** **Click** on **View**. The View menu will appear.

**2.** **Point** to **Arrange Photos**. The Arrange Photos submenu will appear.

**3.** **Click** on the **desired sort order**. The photos will appear in the new order.

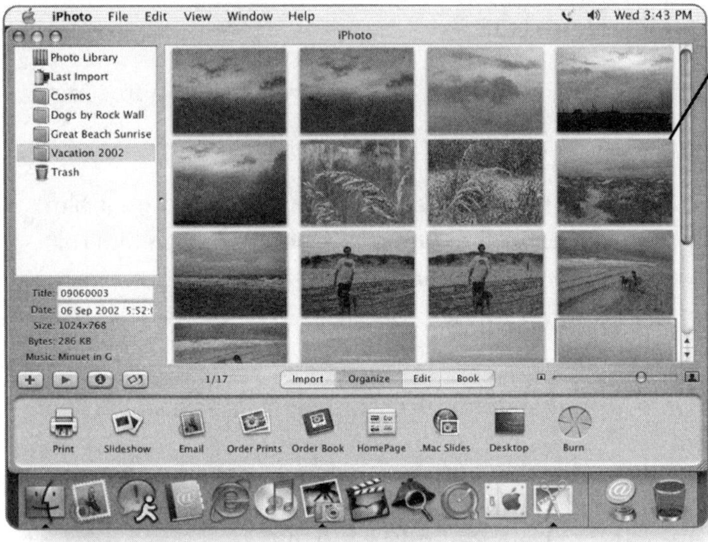


If you compare this illustration with the prior one, you can see that a new order has been applied.

## Moving Photos Manually

The sort orders available in iPhoto may not suit your creative needs. When that's the case, you can move photos manually within an album to change their order.

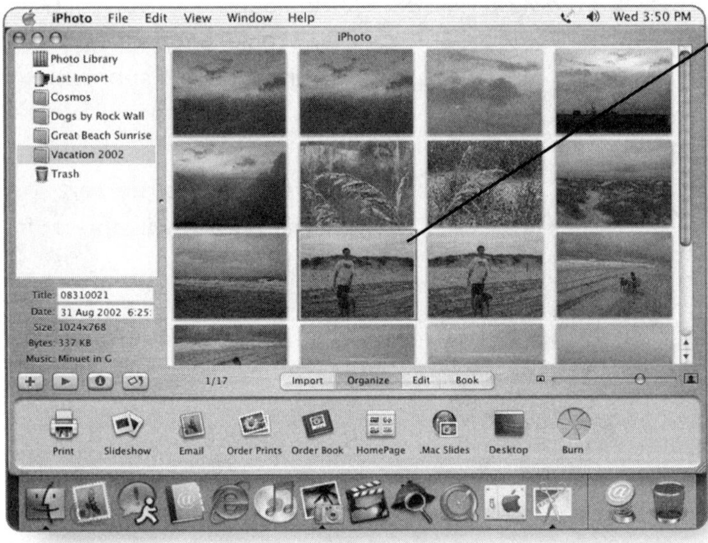


**1. Select one or more photo** to move. The selection highlight will appear.

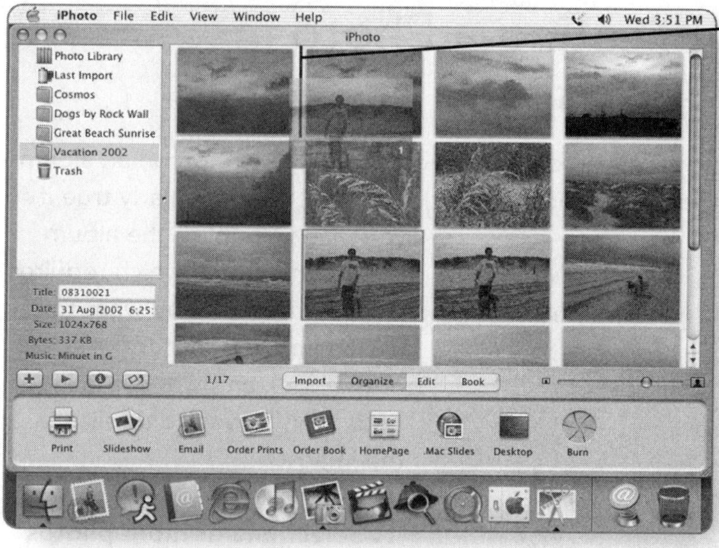


**2.** **Drag** the **selection** to the desired location. A black bar will appear to indicate the new photo location.

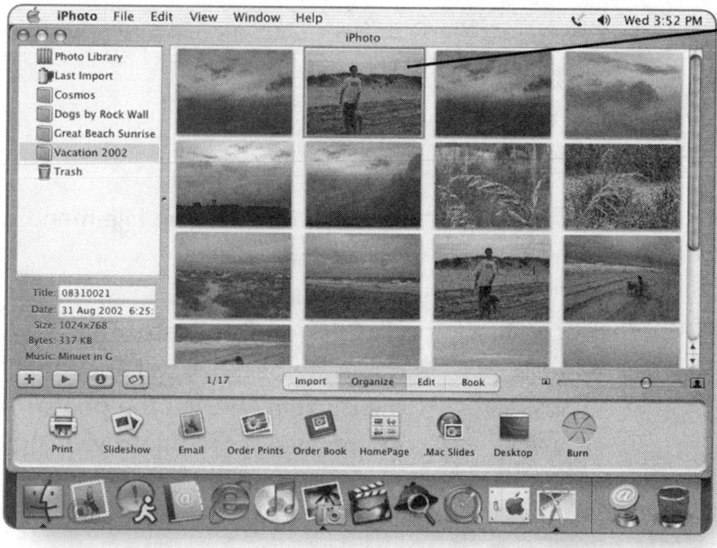


**3.** **Release** the **mouse button.** The selected photo(s) will appear in the location you specified in Step 2.

# Duplicating a Photo in an Album

You may want to create a second copy of a photo in an album (or even in the photo library). This may be particularly true if you plan to publish the album images in a book, which requires a cover image. If you want to use an image both for the cover of the book and within the book, you'll need to duplicate the image.

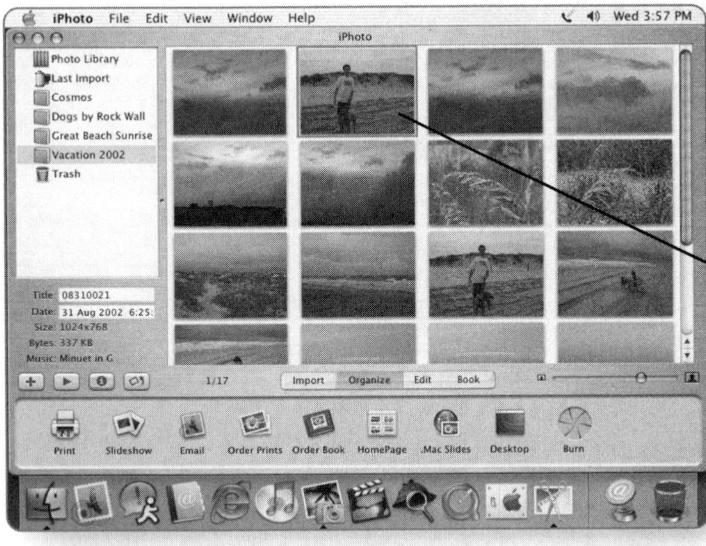


**1. Select one or more photos** to duplicate. The selection highlight will appear.

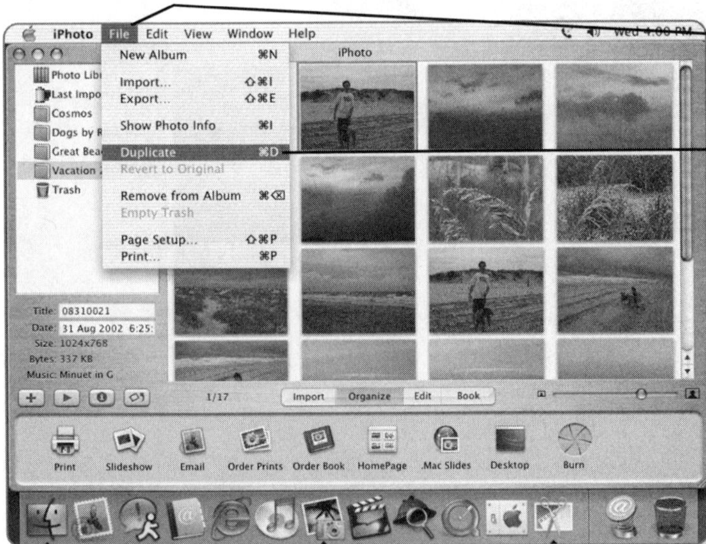


**2. Click** on **File**. The File menu will appear.

**3. Click** on **Duplicate**. The duplicate photo(s) will appear at the bottom (end) of the photo thumbnails in the photo viewing area.

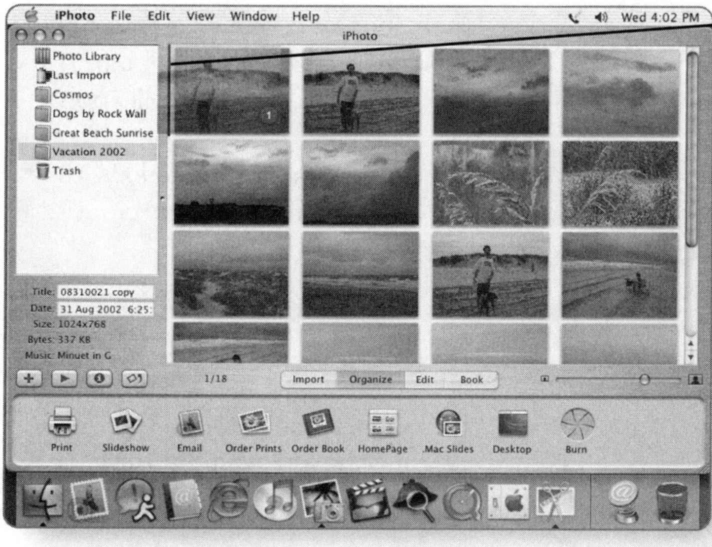


**4. Drag** the **duplicate(s)** to the desired location. The photo(s) will move to the new location.

# Deleting a Photo from an Album

If you decide that a particular image doesn't fit well with the other images you've included in an album, you can delete the photo from the album. Deleting a photo from the selected album removes that photo from the album only. The photo remains in the photo library so that you can use it in other albums as needed.

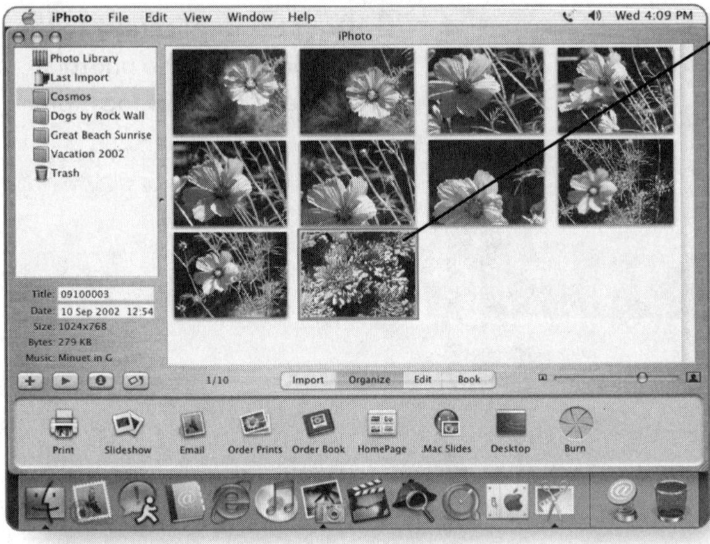


**1. Select one or more photos** to delete from the album. The selection highlight will appear.

**2. Press** the **Delete key**. The digital image will be removed from the album.

> **CAUTION**
>
> Deleting an image from an album does not place the image in the Trash.

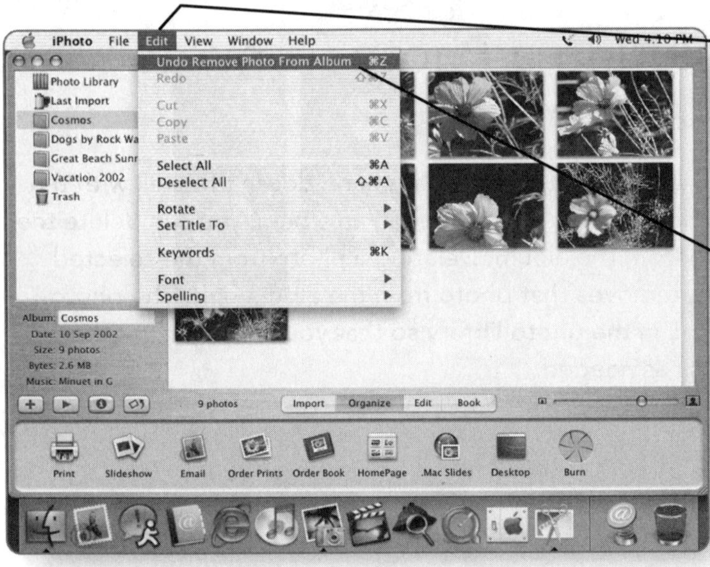


**3.** If you realize that you've mistakenly removed a photo from an album, immediately **click** on **Edit**. The Edit menu will appear.

**4. Click** on **Undo Remove Photo From Album**. The deleted photo(s) will reappear in the photo viewing area.

# Deleting an Album

You can delete an entire album if you've finished using it. For example, you may have made a copy of your iPhoto Library folder (Chapter 13 provides more details about working with photo libraries). You can then prune out the older albums within iPhoto, because you've stored those older albums elsewhere, in the copied folder.

As when you delete images from an album, deleting an entire album does not remove the images it contains from the photo library currently in use within iPhoto. Those photos remain available for inclusion in new or existing albums. The following steps review how to delete an album.

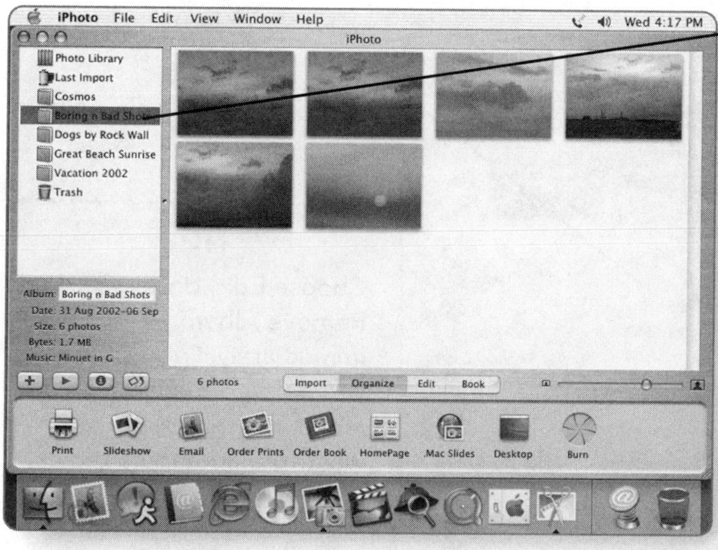


**1. Select** the **album** to delete. The album will be selected in the library list.

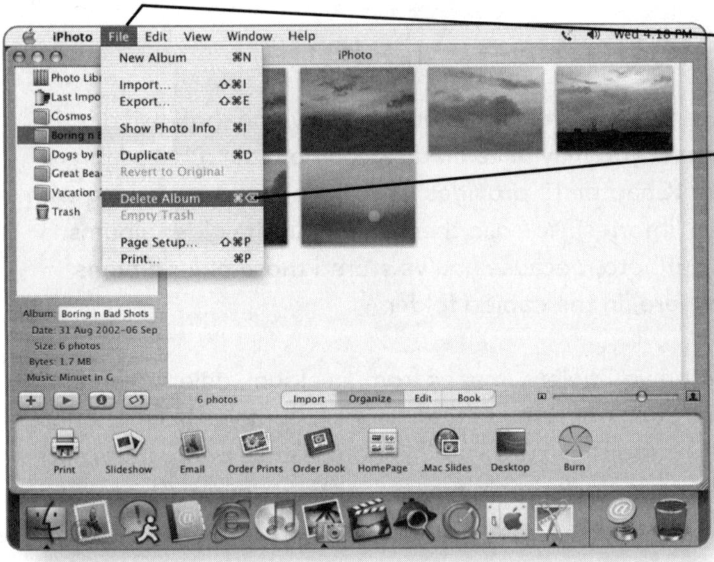

**2.** Click on **File**. The File menu will appear.

**3.** Click on **Delete Album**. A message box will open to prompt you to confirm the deletion.

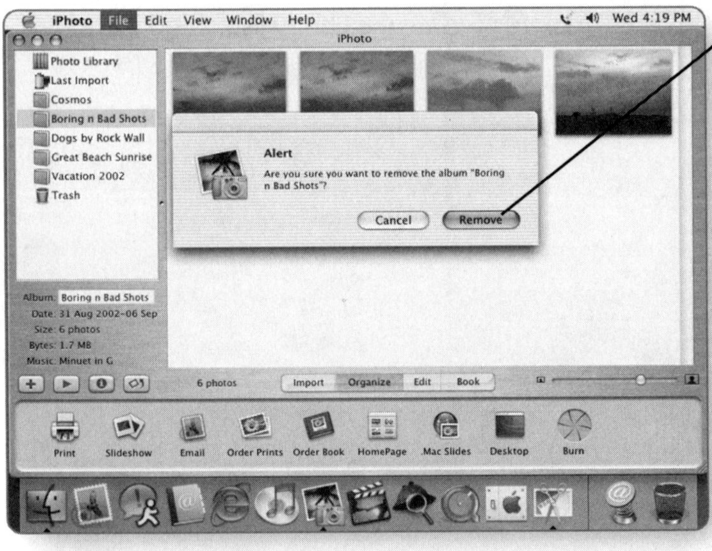

**4.** Click on **Remove**. The album will be deleted.

> **TIP**
>
> Choose Edit, Undo Remove Album immediately if you realize you deleted the wrong album or really didn't want to delete the album.

# Editing the Album Name

If you plan to create a book from the photos in an album, by default, iPhoto uses the album name on the cover page for the book. You can rename the album to use a snappier title, or to make a title more specific in some way, such as including a date. Use these steps when you want to rename an album.

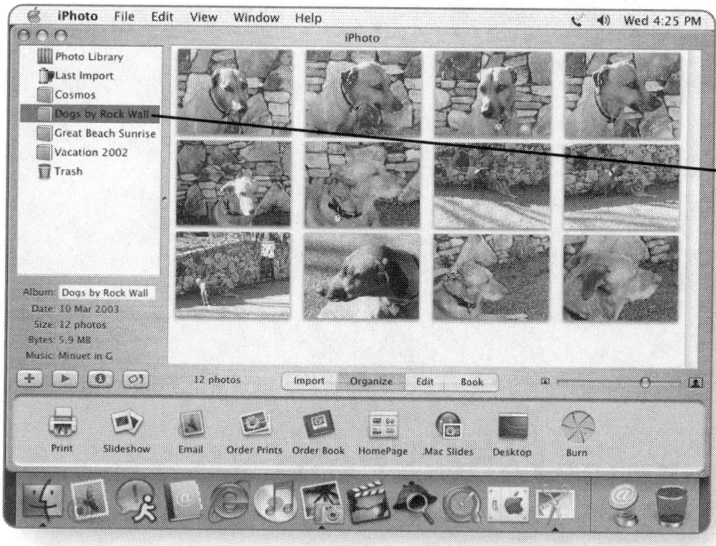


**1.** **Double-click a word** in the **album name**. An editing selector will appear around the album name, and the word will be highlighted.

> **TIP**
>
> You don't have to select the album name before double-clicking on it, but you can.

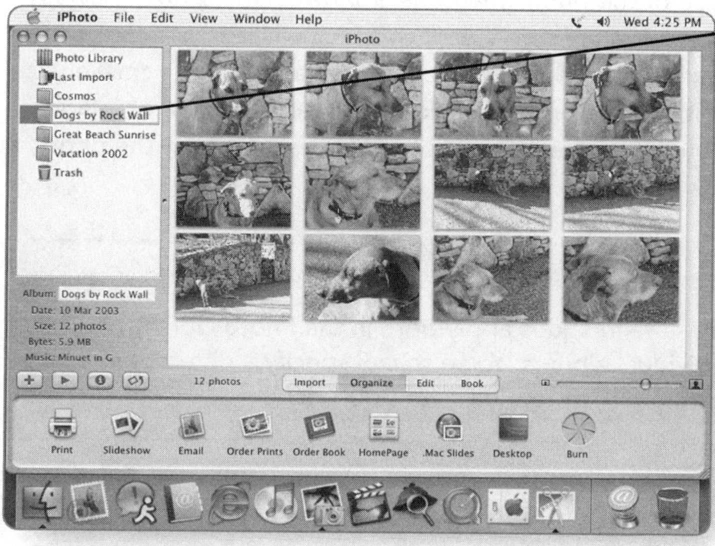


**2.** **Edit** the **album name** as desired. Your changes will appear within the editing selector.

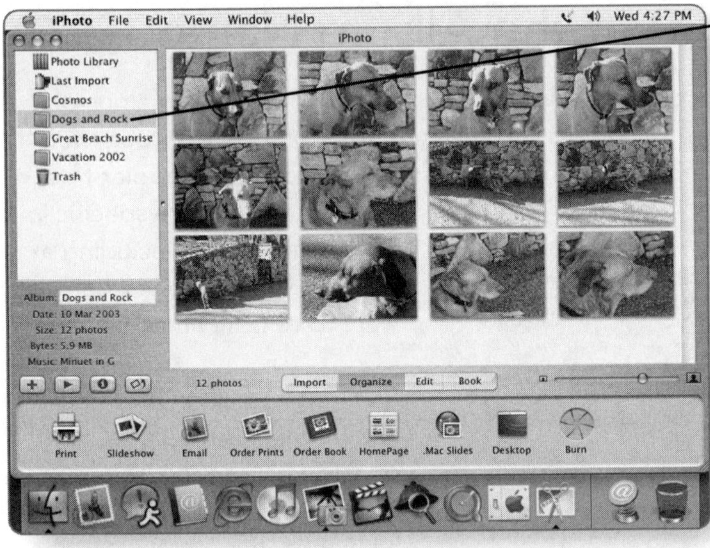

**3. Press Return**. The new album name will appear in the library list.

# Changing the Photo Display Size

Chapter 1 noted that you can use the size control found just below the right corner of the photo viewing area to change the size of the photo thumbnails shown in the photo viewing area. For example, you want to specify a larger size so you can examine individual photos more carefully, or a smaller size so that you can better check the overall sequence of images in an album. Use the following techniques to specify the photo display size.

> **TIP**
>
> These techniques apply both in the Photo Library and individual albums. You also can specify a different size for the Organize, Edit, and Book views.

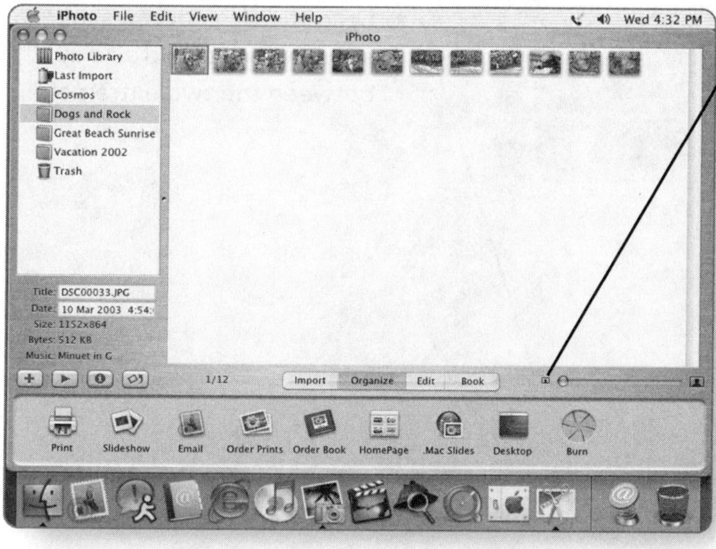


- Click on the icon at the left end of the size control to specify the smallest thumbnail size.

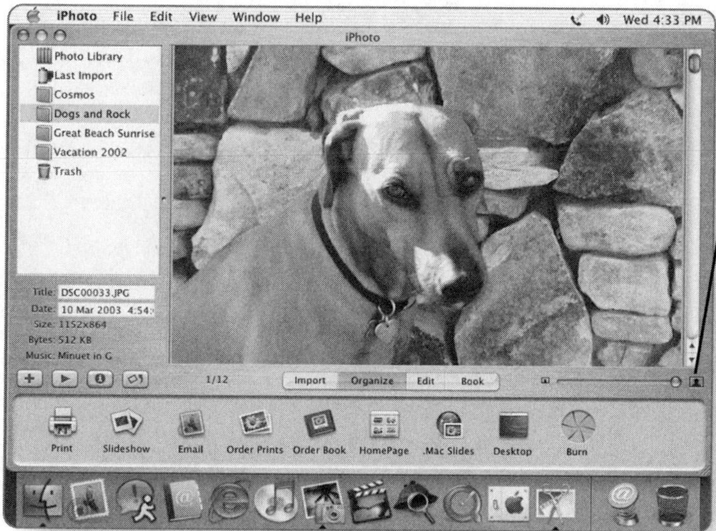


- Click on the icon at the right end of the size control to specify the largest thumbnail size.

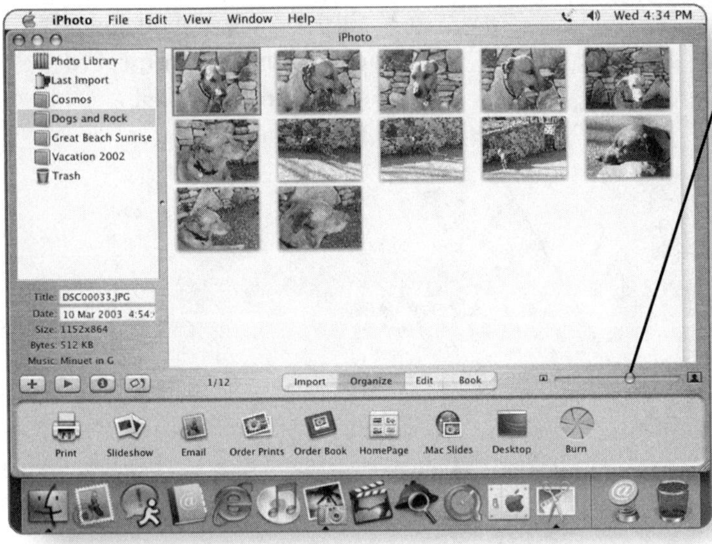


- Drag the size control slider to specify the desired size in between the two extremes.

## Part 1 Review Questions

1. How do I open the iPhoto 2 program? *See "Starting iPhoto" in Chapter 1.*
2. What are the features of the iPhoto window? *See "Navigating the iPhoto Window" in Chapter 1.*
3. How do I change views to work with images? *See "Taking a Look at the Views" in Chapter 1.*
4. How do I transfer images from my digital camera into iPhoto? *See "Importing Images from a Digital Camera" in Chapter 2.*
5. How do I transfer images from a digital media reader, CD-R, or hard disk folder into iPhoto? *See "Importing Images from a Digital Media Reader or Disk" in Chapter 2.*
6. How do I select one or more images in the photo library? *See "Selecting Images" in Chapter 2.*
7. How do I delete images from iPhoto? *See "Deleting Images from the Photo Library" in Chapter 2.*
8. How do I create an album and add photos into it? *See "Creating an Album and Adding Photos" in Chapter 3.*
9. How can I change the order of the photos in an album? *See "Rearranging Photos in an Album" in Chapter 3.*
10. Can I change the album's name? *See "Editing the Album Name" in Chapter 3.*

PART II

# Editing Your Photos

# 4

# Working with Photo Information

If you've ever spent a rainy Sunday using a felt-tip pen to write descriptive information on the back of a huge stack of photos, you know how time-consuming that activity can be. Nevertheless, you appreciate the effort in the future, when you want to figure out which distant relative is caught doing the Macarena at your wedding. In iPhoto 2, you electronically label your photos, and then use that information to sort and find the photos you want. In this chapter, you will learn how to:

- Change photo titles and add comments.
- Assign descriptive keywords to images.
- Create custom keywords.
- Delete unneeded keywords.
- Display photos in a particular keyword category.
- Search for a photo based on its title.
- Rename the film roll.

# Working with Photo Titles

By default, when you import an image into iPhoto, the program picks up the image file name and creation date (the date the photo was shot or scanned), using that information as the Title and Date. Because images shot with a digital camera or digitized by a photo lab typically use generic alphanumeric names, you may want to edit photo titles within iPhoto. In addition to editing the title and date for any photo, you can add an even more descriptive comment. When you create a book from your images, you can choose to include the Title and Comment for each photo.

**NOTE**

In the section called "Viewing Photo Titles and Info" in Chapter 2, you learned how to use the Information button to toggle the display of photo titles below the library list. Further, you learned that you can drag the bottom boundary of the library list up to better see that information.

iPhoto 2 offers two methods for working with photo titles and information, described next. You can work with photo titles and information from the photo library or any album. The changes you make will be applied to the image wherever it appears in iPhoto.

## Setting Titles

You can automatically change the titles for one or more photos that you've selected in the photo viewing area. While this approach enables you to work in "batches," it limits you to only a few title choices:

- **Empty.** Removes the title from the selected photos. You can use this choice when you don't want to include photo titles or when you want to remove previously-applied titles.
- **Roll Info.** Sets the title to the word Roll, followed by the roll number and shot number, both of which were assigned when the photo was imported. (See Chapter 2 for more about roll numbering.)
- **Filename.** Resets the name of each selected photo to its file name. Use this choice if you want to remove custom titles you've previously assigned.
- **Date/Time.** Enables you to assign the photo's creation date and time as the photo title. You also can specify the date format to be used.

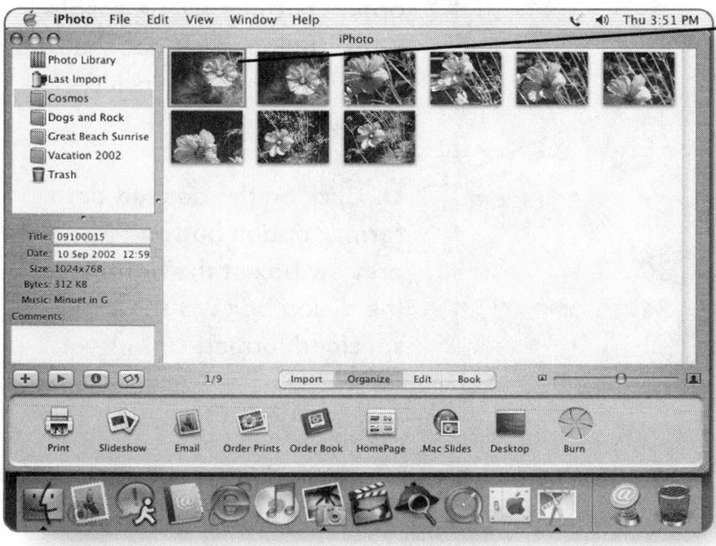


**1. Click** on the **photo(s)** to which you want to apply a new title. The selection highlight will appear around the photo(s).

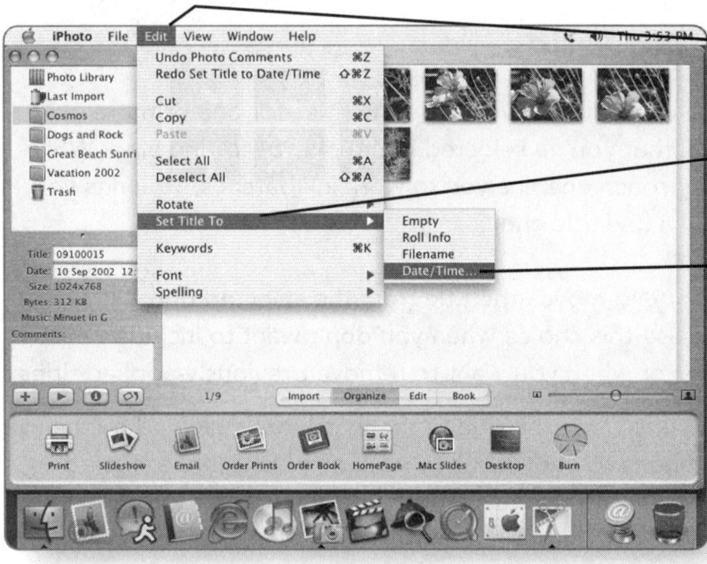


**2.** **Click** on **Edit**. The Edit menu will appear.

**3.** **Point** to **Set Title To**. The Set Title To submenu will appear.

**4.** **Click** on the **desired type of title**. The new title will appear, unless you chose Date/Time. If you chose Date/Time, the Set Title to Date/Time dialog box will open.

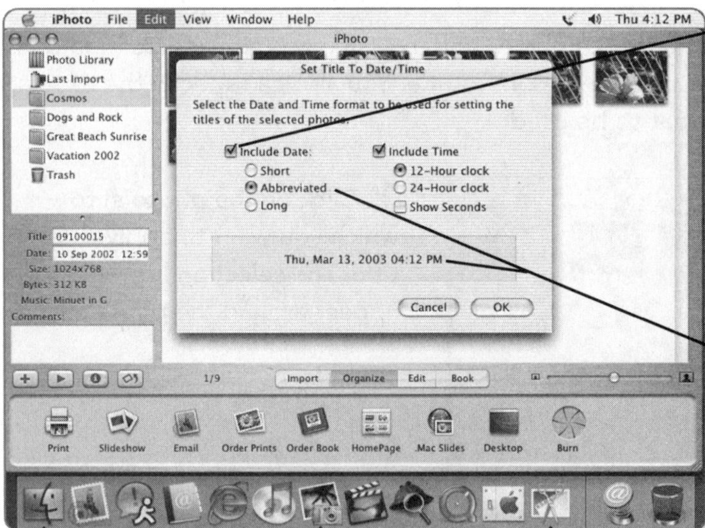


**5.** **Click** on **Include Date** as desired. When the option is checked, the date will be included in the title and the date option buttons will be enabled. When the option is not checked, the date will not be included in the title.

**6.** **Click** on the **desired date format** option button. The preview box at the bottom of the dialog box will show the specified format.

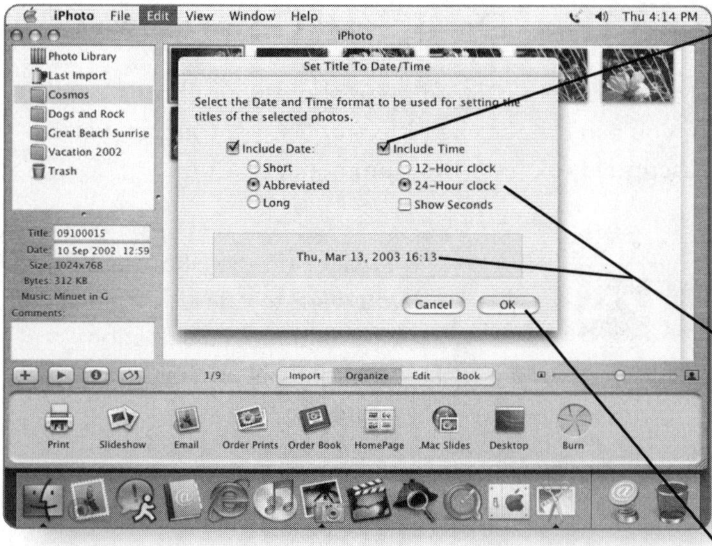


**7. Click** on **Include Time** as desired. When the option is checked, the time will be included in the title and the date option buttons will be enabled. When the option is not checked, the date will not be included in the title.

**8. Click** on the **desired time format** option button. The preview box at the bottom of the dialog box will show the specified format.

**9. Click** on **OK**. The Set Title to Date/Time dialog box will close and the Title text box will display the new title information.

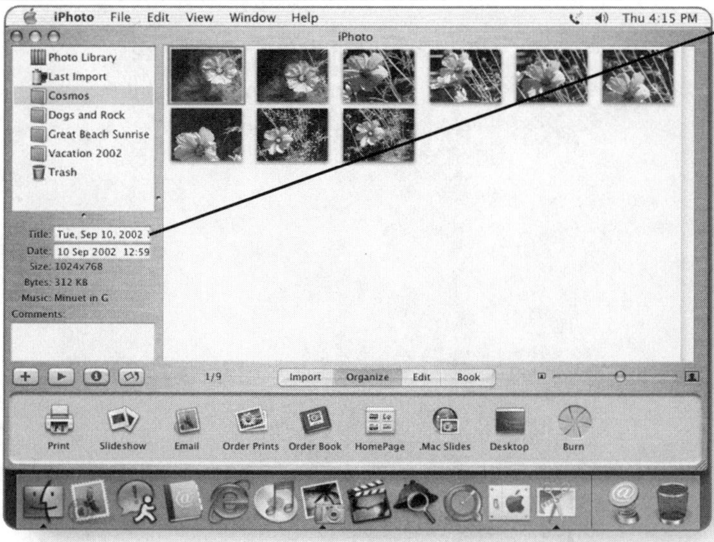


In this example, the title has been set to the photo creation date and time. You could drag the right border (near the dot) of the library list to make that pane wider so the file name could display completely.

## TIP

To undo the title change, press Command+Z or choose Edit, Undo Set Title to (Format).

## Editing Title, Date, and Comments

To store more specific information about your photos in iPhoto, you can change the Title and Date entries, as well as add descriptive text into the Comments text box.

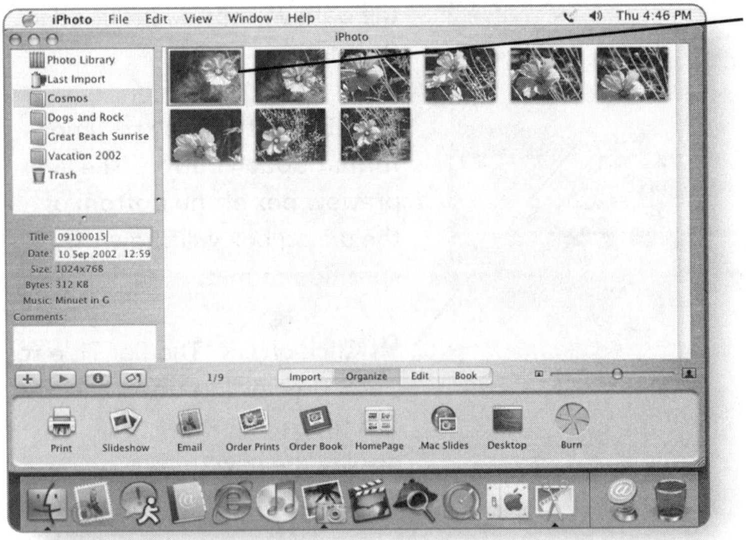

**1.** **Click** on the **photo** for which you want to edit title information. The selection highlight will appear around the photo(s).

> **CAUTION**
>
> You can only edit information about one photo at a time using this method.

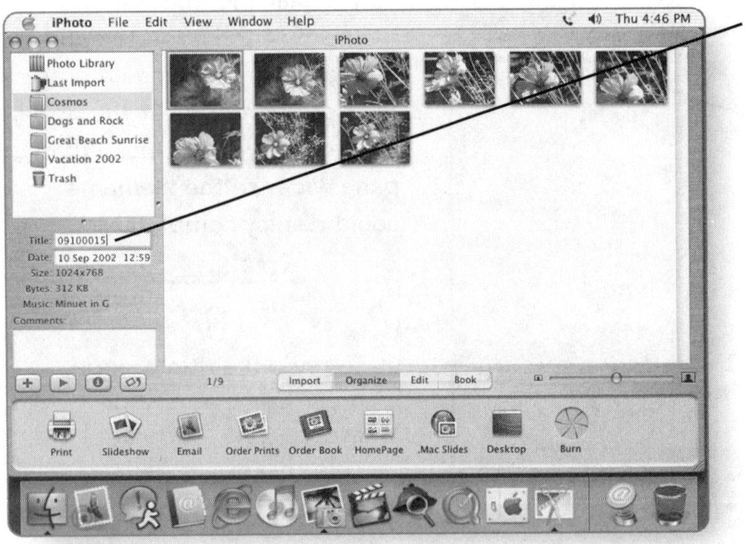

**2.** **Click** in the **Title text box.** The insertion point will appear in the text box.

> **TIP**
>
> Use the same editing techniques as in a word processing program. For example, press the Delete key to delete the character to the left of the insertion point. Or, drag over text to select it, then type new text to replace the selection.

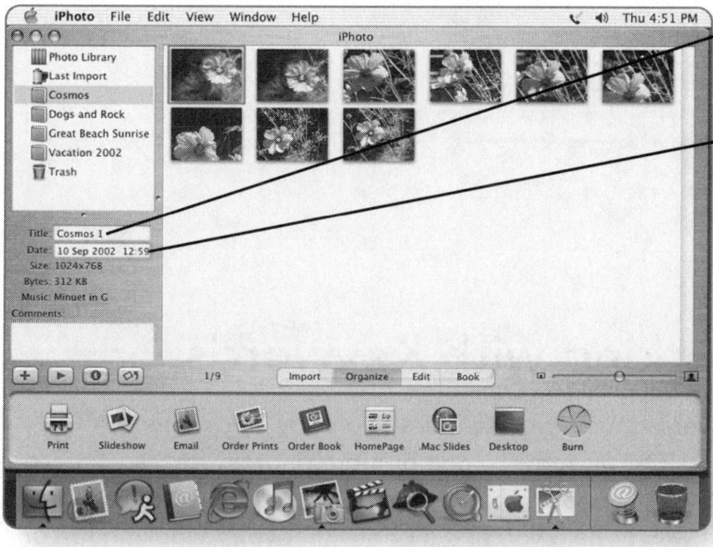


**3. Edit** the **title** as desired. The new title will appear.

**4. Click** in the **Date text box**. The insertion point will appear in the text box.

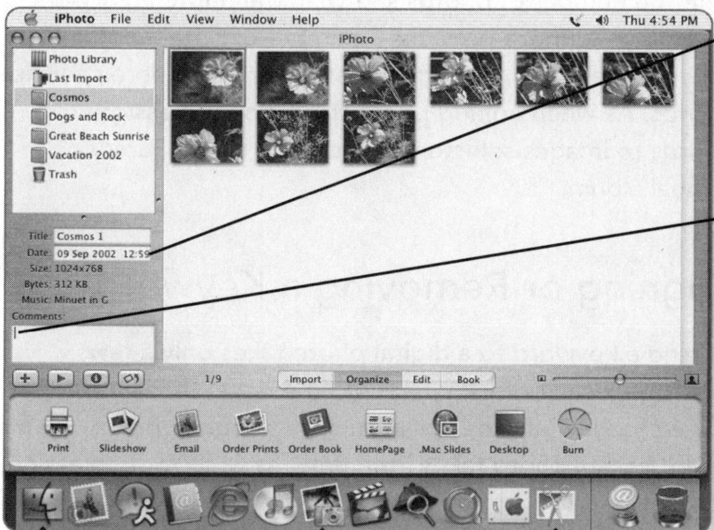


**5. Edit** the **date** as desired. The new date will appear in the date format used by the Date text box.

**6. Click** in the **Comments text box**. The insertion point will appear in the text box.

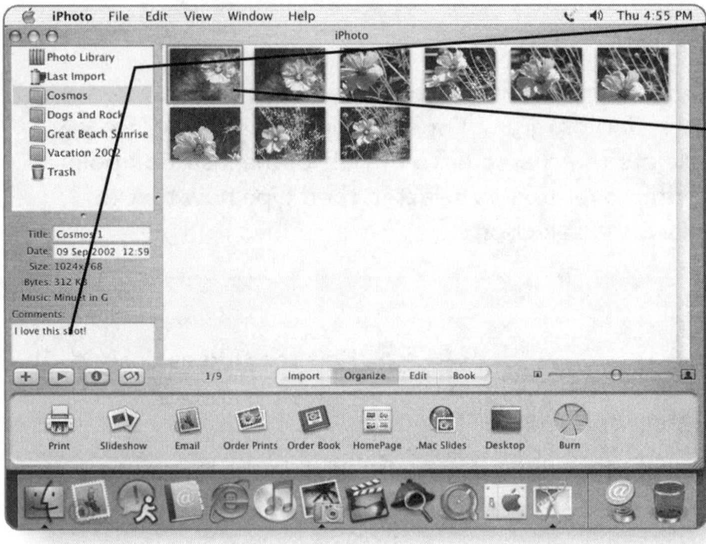


**7. Enter** the desired **comment text**. The comment will appear.

**8. Click** on the **selected photo**. This action will finish the entry in the Comments text box.

# Working with Keywords

*Keywords* enable you to identify photos by category. After you assign keywords to one or more photos, you can choose to view only photos that have a particular keyword. This is a great way to help you find a photo that you're looking for, or to limit the number of photos shown in the photo library or current album. iPhoto provides a number of predefined keywords. In addition, you can create your own, more specific keywords. As when editing photo titles, you can assign keywords to images selected either in the photo library or an individual album.

## Assigning or Removing a Keyword

Assigning a keyword to a digital photo takes only a few moments but can save you a lot of time down the line when you want to view photos in a particular category. Removing a keyword from a photo takes little time, as well. You can assign as many keywords as you wish to each photo, for additional descriptive power. Follow these steps to use the Keywords/Search window to add and remove keywords.

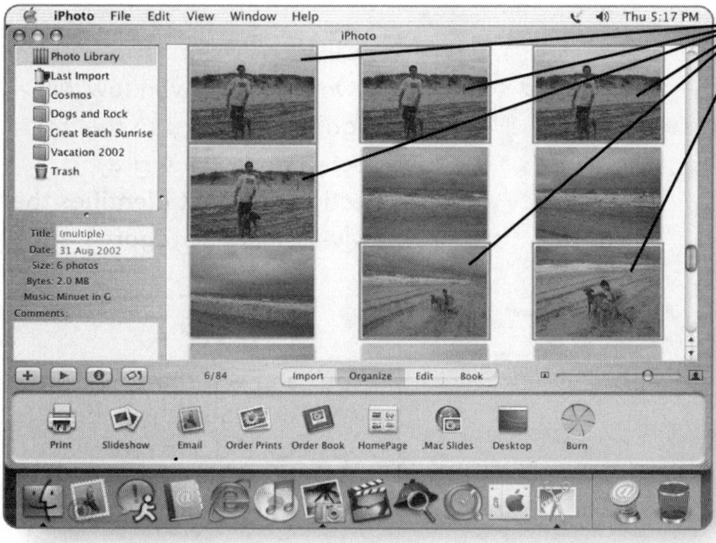


**1. Select** the **photo(s)** to which you want to assign keywords. The selection highlight will appear around the photo(s).

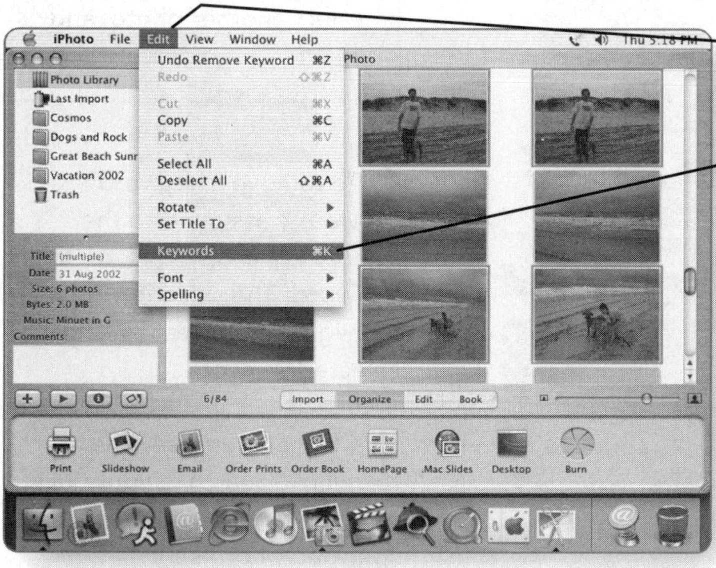


**2. Click** on **Edit**. The Edit menu will appear.

**3. Click** on **Keywords**. The Keywords/Search window will open.

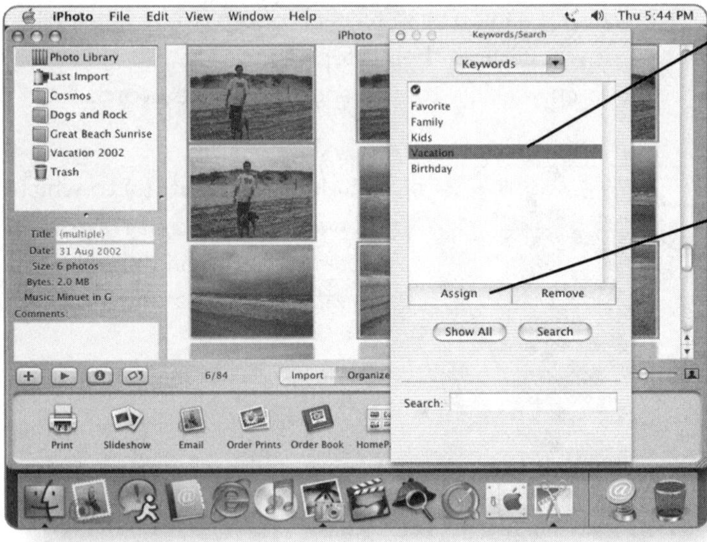

**4. Click** on the desired **keyword**. The selection highlight will appear for the selected keyword.

**5. Click** on **Assign**. The Keywords/Search window will assign the keyword to the selected photo(s). A gray selection highlight identifies the newly-assigned category.

### TIP

You can keep the Keywords/Search window open to add and remove keywords for numerous photos. Select a photo, assign a keyword to it, select another photo, and so on.

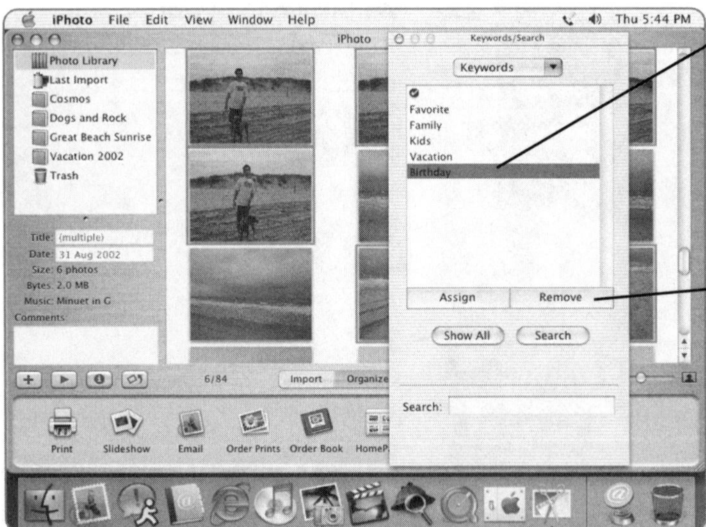

**6.** To remove a keyword previously assigned to the selected photo(s), **click** on the **keyword**. The selection highlight will appear for the selected keyword.

**7. Click** on **Remove**. The Keywords/Search window will remove the keyword from the specified photo(s).

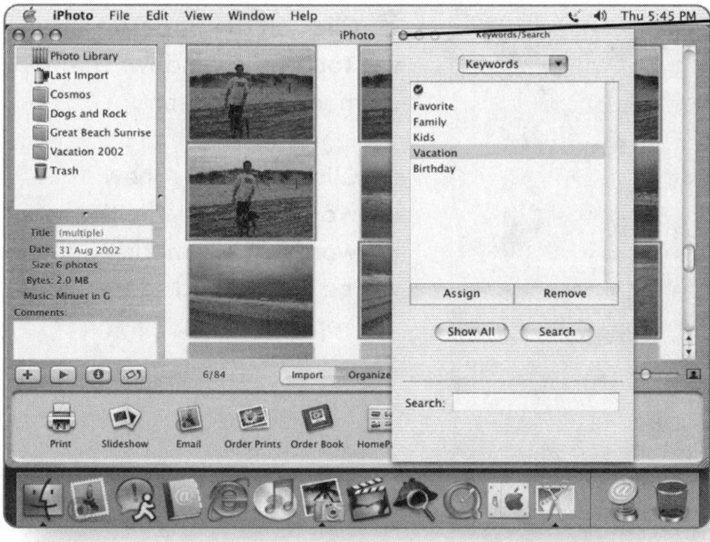


**8. Click** on the **window close button**. The Keywords/Search window will close.

# Creating a New Keyword

If the keywords supplied by iPhoto don't meet all your categorization needs, you can create additional keywords as needed in the Keywords/Search window. For example, if you've assigned the Vacation keyword to a number of photos, you might create and assign a separate keyword for each vacation location.

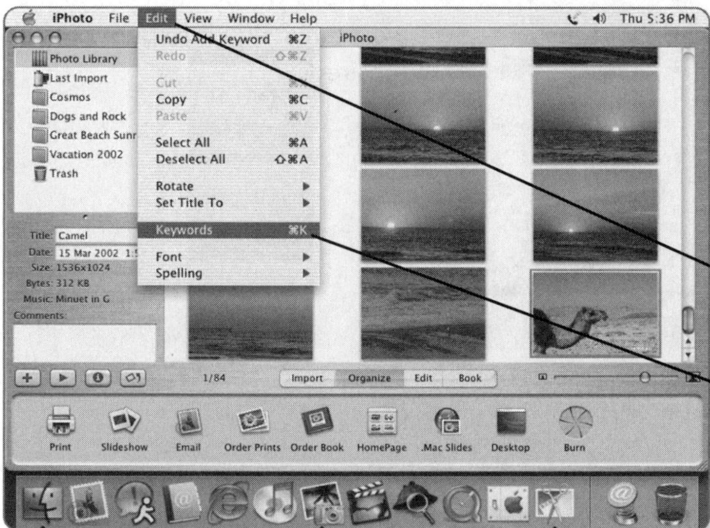


**1. Click** on **Edit**. The Edit menu will appear.

**2. Click** on **Keywords**. The Keywords/Search window will open.

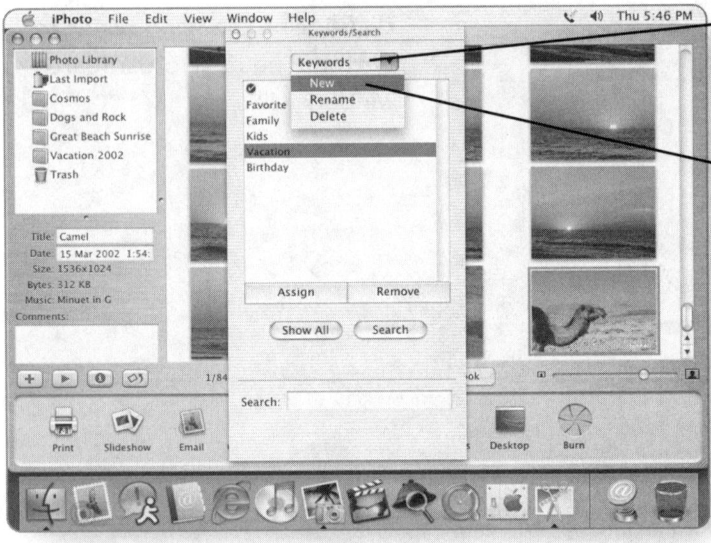


**3. Click** on the **pop-up menu** at the top of the window. The pop-up menu will appear.

**4. Click** on **New**. A new keyword will appear in the list of keywords. The temporary name will be highlighted so that you can replace it.

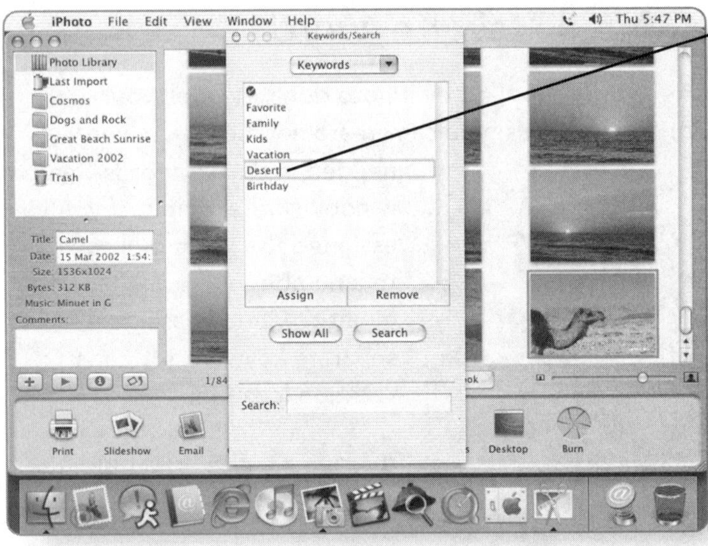


**5. Type** a **name** for the new keyword. The name will appear.

**6. Press Return**. The new keyword will be finished, so that you can assign it to photos as desired.

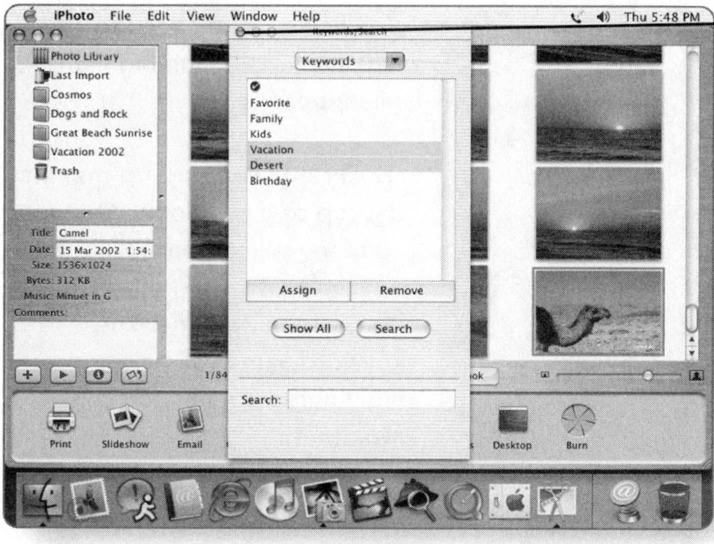


**7.** **Click** on the **window close button**. The Keywords/Search window will close.

## Renaming or Deleting a Keyword

When a keyword no longer suits your needs, you can either rename it or delete it. Renaming a keyword applies the new keyword name to all images to which you assigned the original keyword. Likewise, deleting a keyword removes that keyword from all digital images to which you've assigned it.

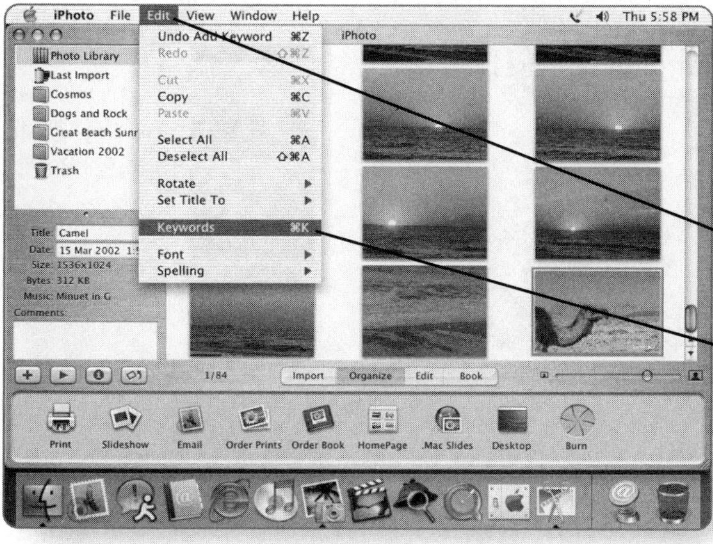


**1.** **Click** on **Edit**. The Edit menu will appear.

**2.** **Click** on **Keywords**. The Keywords/Search window will open.

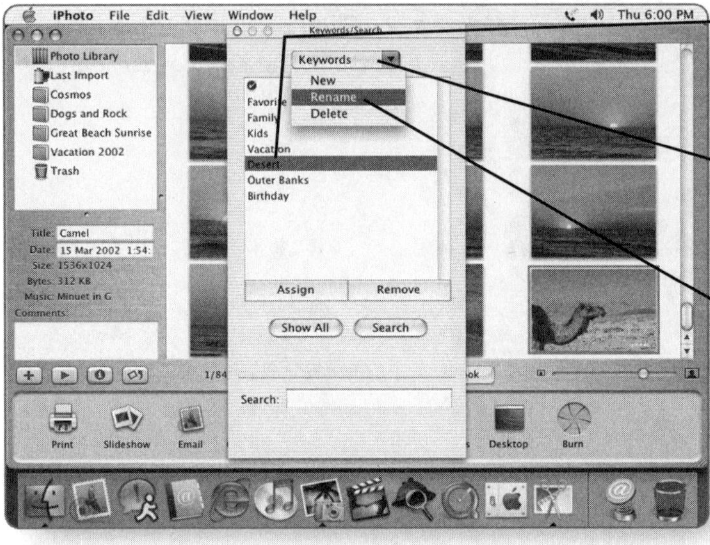


**3. Click** on a **keyword** to rename. A selection highlight will appear.

**4. Click** on the **pop-up menu** at the top of the window. The pop-up menu will appear.

**5. Click** on **Rename**. The keyword name will be highlighted so that you can replace it.

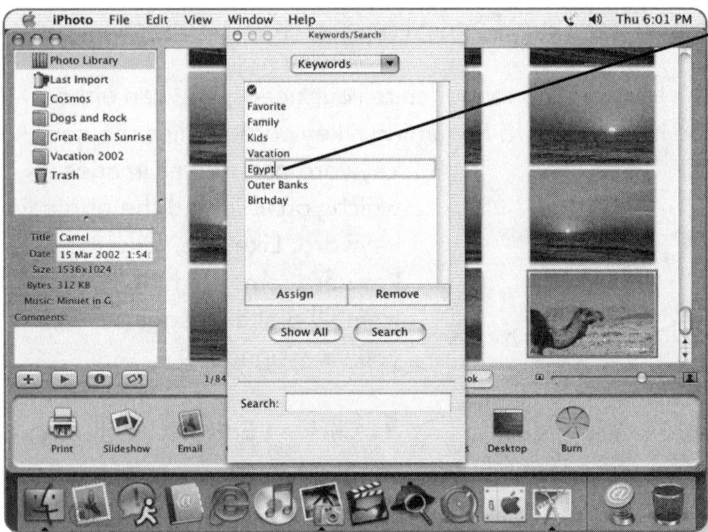


**6. Type** a **name** for the new keyword. The name will appear.

**7. Press Return**. The new keyword name will appear.

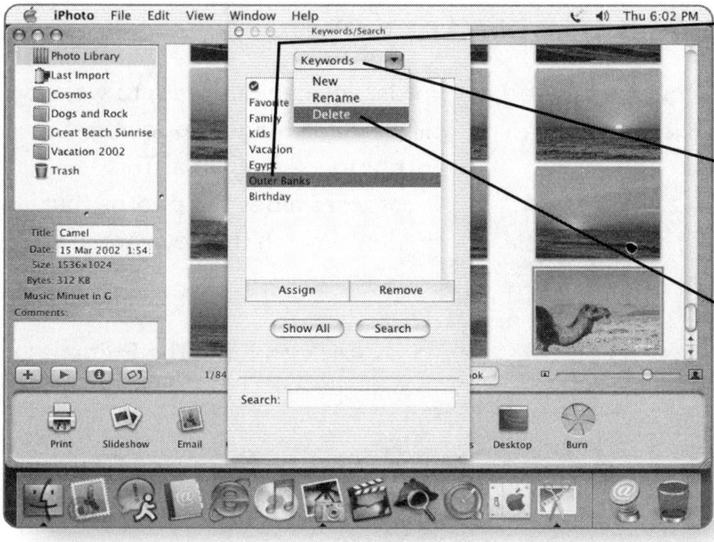


**8. Click** on a **keyword** to delete. A selection highlight will appear.

**9. Click** on the **pop-up menu** at the top of the window. The pop-up menu will appear.

**10. Click** on **Delete**. The keyword will be deleted and removed from all photos using it.

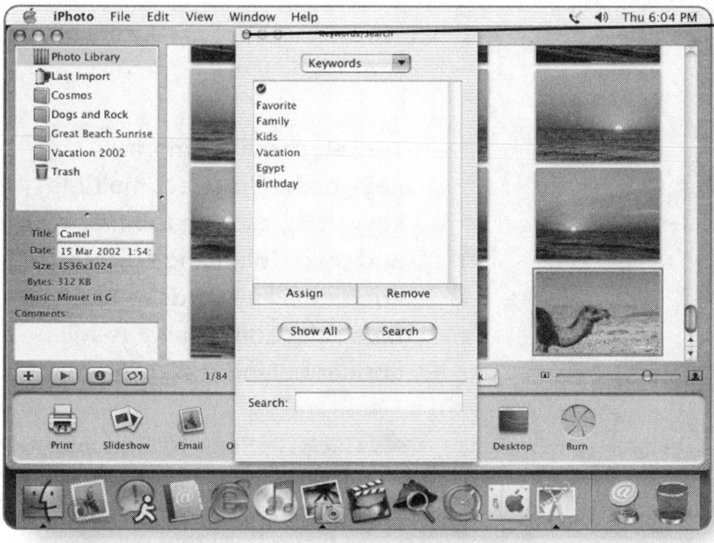


**11. Click** on the **window close button**. The Keywords/Search window will close.

## Viewing Photos by Keyword

Once you've assigned keywords, you can put them to work by using them to determine which digital images appear in the photo viewing area. This process hides the photos that don't match the keyword(s) you specify.

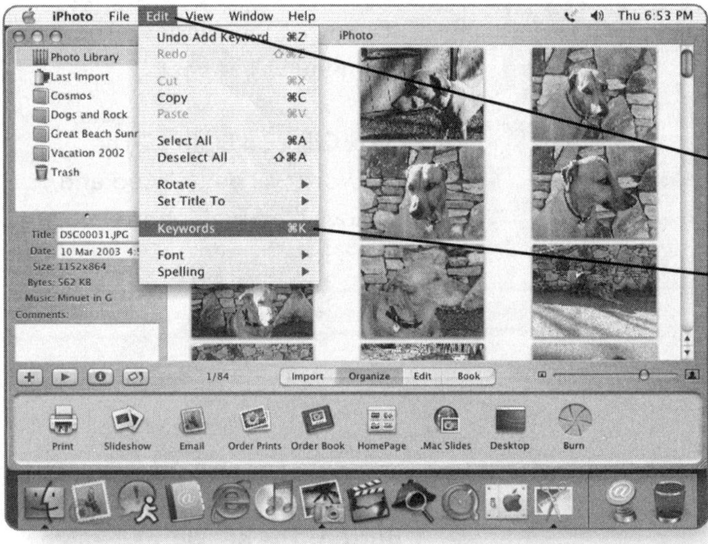


**1.** **Click** on **Edit**. The Edit menu will appear.

**2.** **Click** on **Keywords**. The Keywords/Search window will open.

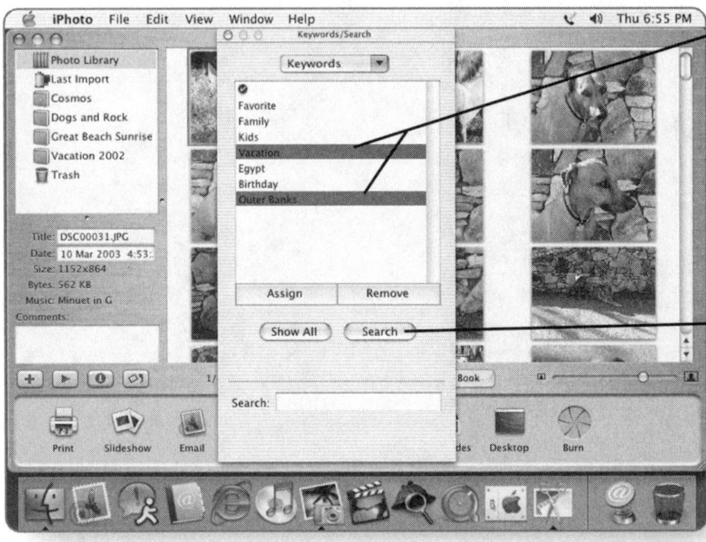


**3.** **Select** one or more **keywords**. (To select multiple keywords, click on the first one, and then Command+click on additional keywords as needed.) Blue selection highlights will appear behind the keywords.

**4.** **Click** on **Search**. Only photos to which you've assigned the specified keywords will appear in the photo viewing area.

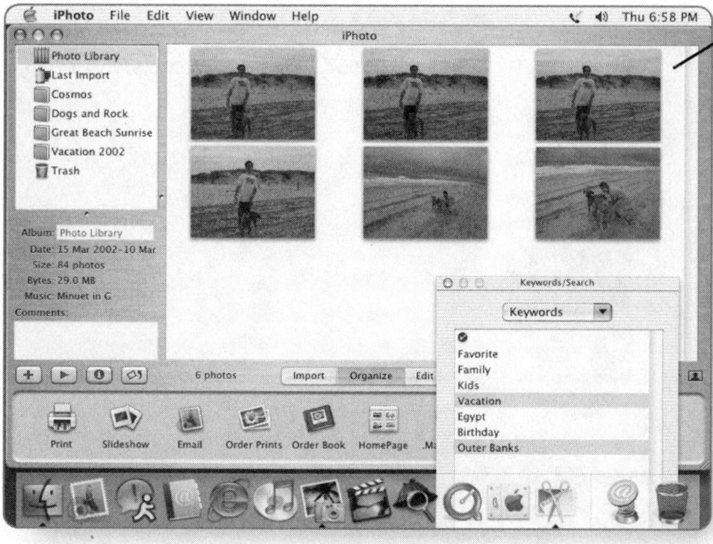

All other images will be hidden, as shown in this example.

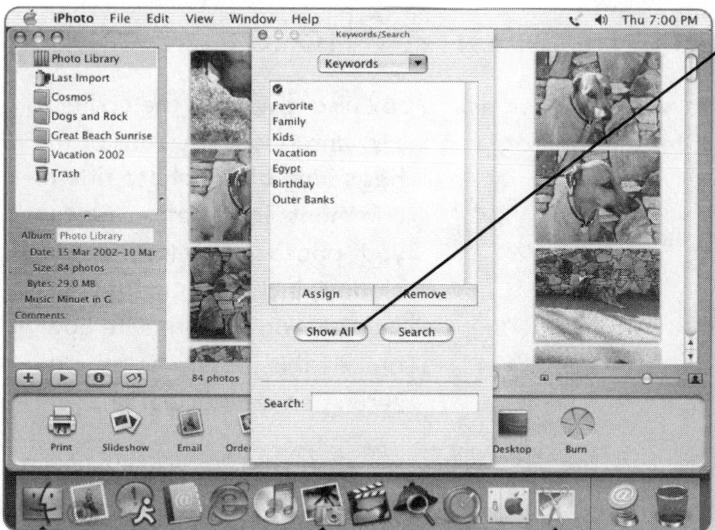

**5.** To redisplay all the images, **click** on **Show All**. The photo viewing area will redisplay the hidden digital images.

> **CAUTION**
>
> When you use the Keywords/Search window to find photos based on a keyword or a search term (as described next), closing the Keywords/Search window automatically redisplays all the digital photos.

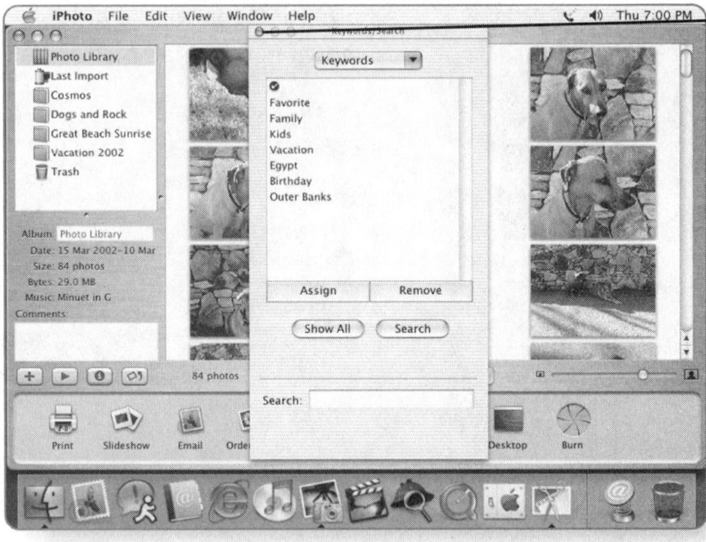


**6. Click** on the **window close button**. The Keywords/Search window will close.

# Searching for a Photo

The Keywords/Search dialog box also gives you the ability to search for one or more images by entering a keyword or the beginning of the photo title or comments information. Once your photo library (or individual albums) includes hundreds of photos, you'll appreciate how quickly this feature helps you zero in on a particular image!

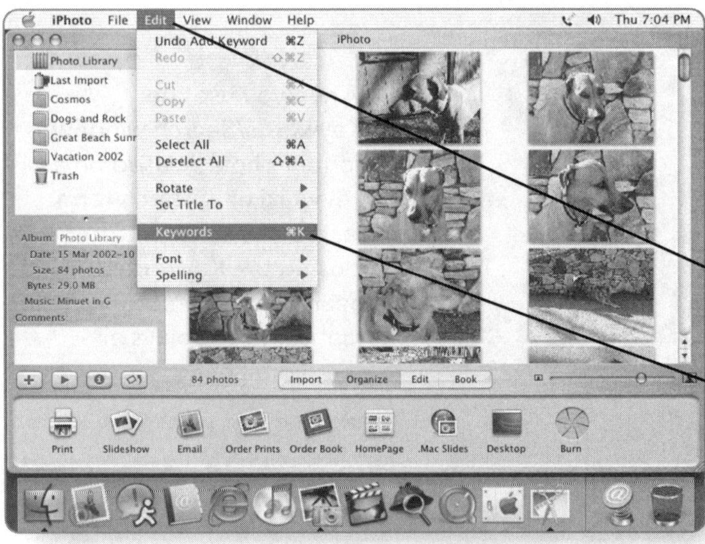


**1. Click** on **Edit**. The Edit menu will appear.

**2. Click** on **Keywords**. The Keywords/Search window will open.

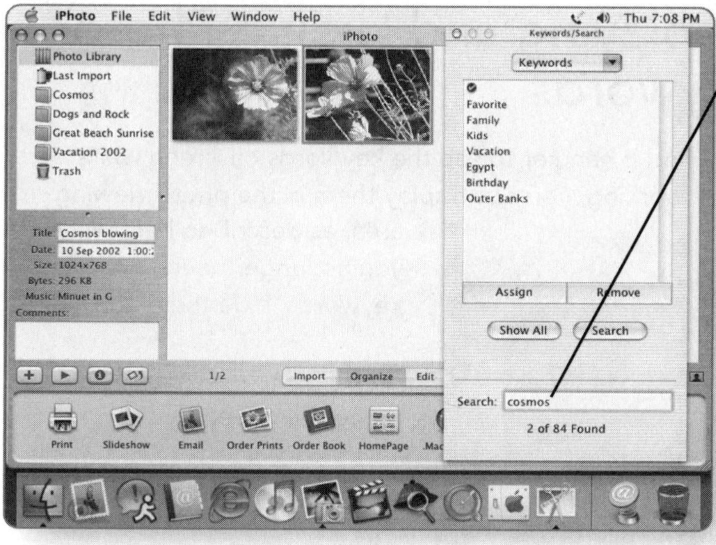

**3. Click** in the **Search text box**, and then **type** the **search information**. When you finish typing, the photo viewing area will show only matching images.

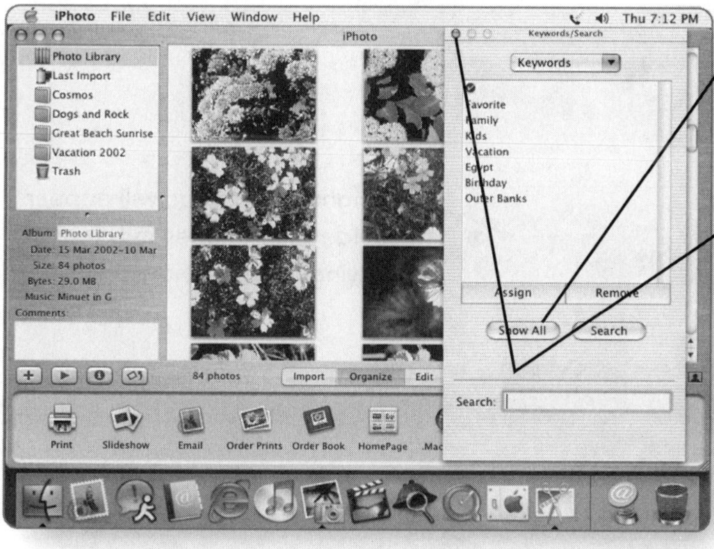

**4.** To redisplay all the images, **click** on **Show All**. The photo viewing area will redisplay the hidden digital images.

**5. Click** on the **window close button**. The Keywords/Search window will close.

# Displaying and Hiding Photo Keywords

If you find it handier to see the keywords onscreen while you're working, you can display them in the photo viewing area, as described here. When you no longer need to see the keywords, hide them again.

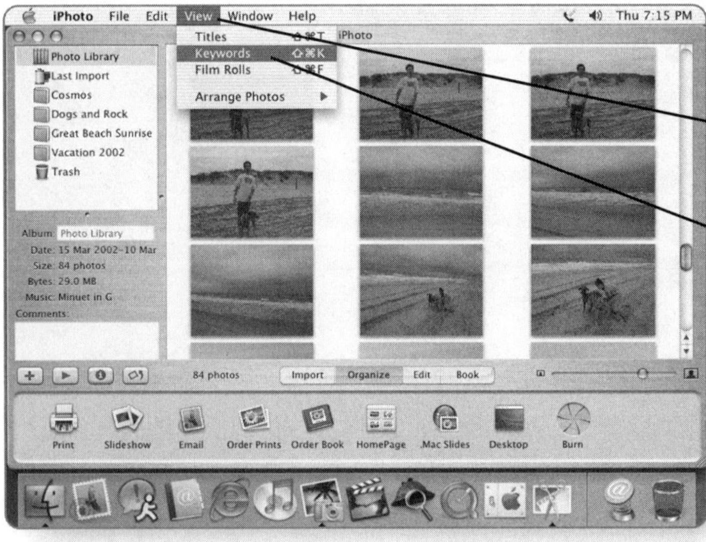

**1.** **Click** on **View**. The View menu will appear.

**2.** **Click** on **Keywords**.

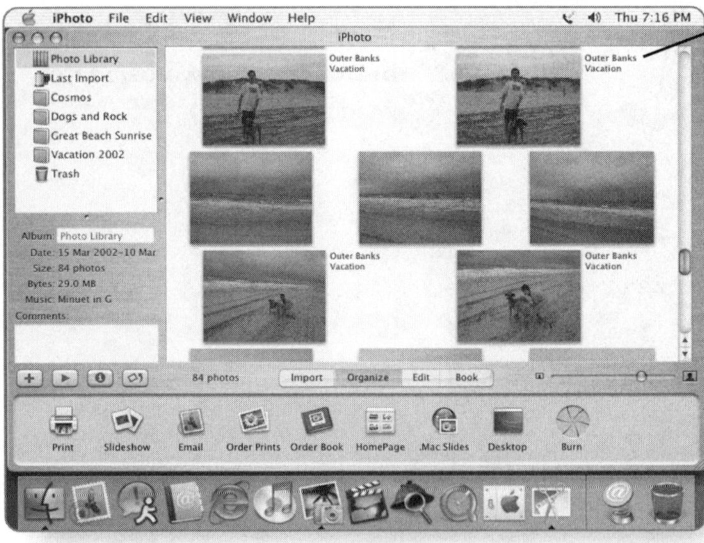

Assigned keywords will appear beside their images in the photo viewing area, as shown here.

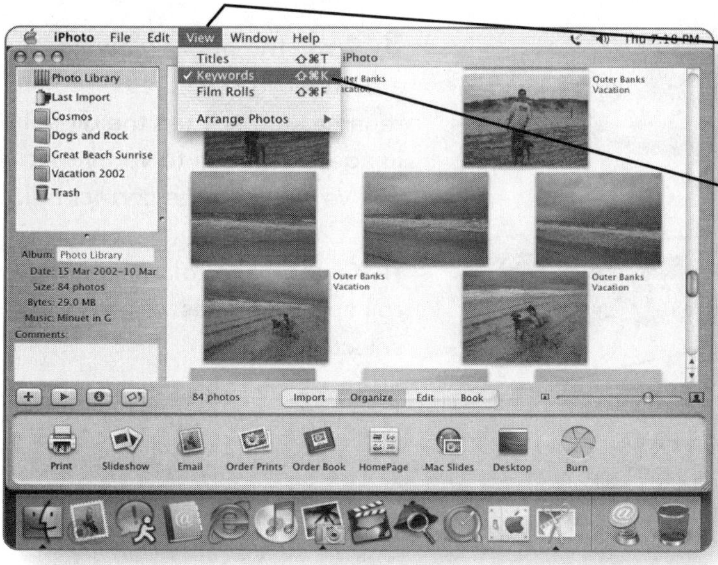


**3.** To turn off keyword display, **click** on **View**. The View menu will appear.

**4. Click** on **Keywords**. The keywords will no longer appear in the photo viewing area.

# Renaming the Film Roll

You also can revise the film roll name to replace the generic names assigned by iPhoto 2. Doing so will provide you additional clues for finding photos you want to view.

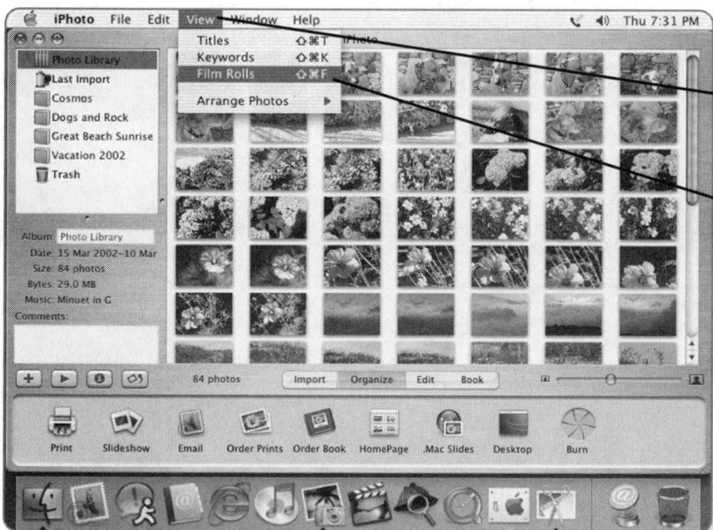


**1. Click** on **View**. The View menu will appear.

**2. Click** on **Film Rolls**. A film roll name and date will appear above each group of photos in the photo viewing area.

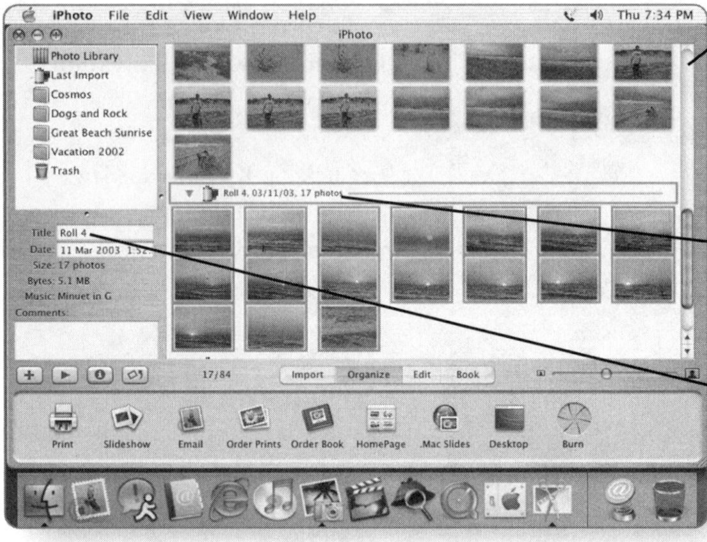

**3. Scroll** the **photo viewing area** until you see the film roll to rename. You will see the digital images in the roll to verify that you've selected the correct roll.

**4. Click** on the **roll name**. The roll and its images will be selected.

**5. Click** in the **Title text box**. The insertion point will appear in the text box.

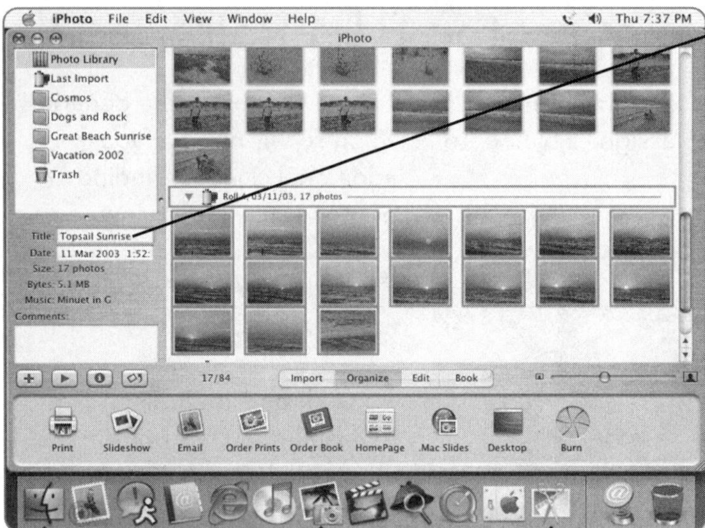

**6. Edit** the **title** as desired. The new roll title will appear.

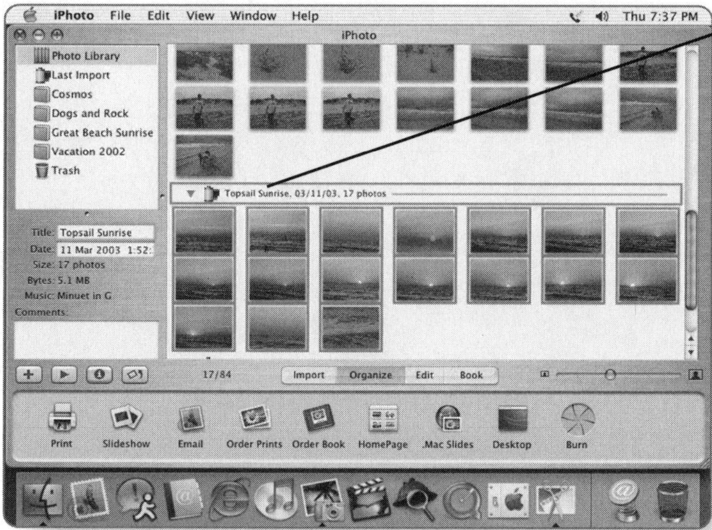

**7. Press Return**. The new roll title will appear in the photo viewing area. You can then hide the roll titles if needed.

# 5

# Making Basic Changes to Photos

Even great photographers don't take a perfect shot every time. In the past, pro photographers relied on their darkroom skills to improve so-so photos and make average photos great. Thankfully, you can use iPhoto 2 to improve photos digitally—a much faster process than working with equipment and chemicals in a darkroom. In this chapter, you will learn how to:

- Rotate a photo.
- Crop a photo to a new size.
- Improve the tone of a photo.
- Remove red eye.
- Convert a color photo to black and white.

# Rotating a Photo

When a photo's subject matter is tall rather than wide, you need to rotate the camera 90 degrees to shoot the picture in a tall orientation. When you then import such an image into iPhoto, the image subject will appear to be lying on its side. No problem. You can rotate any image as needed within iPhoto to specify the proper orientation. Whether you rotate a digital photo in the photo library or an individual album, the new rotation will be applied to the photo wherever it appears in iPhoto.

If you are rotating a GIF image that you imported, iPhoto will resave the rotated image in the JPEG format. The original image remains intact in a subfolder of the iPhoto Library folder in case you need to work with the GIF file again.

You can rotate photos in either the Organize view or the Edit view.

**NOTE**

By default, iPhoto's Rotate button rotates an image counter-clockwise. You can change this setting to clockwise if you (like me), are right-handed and tend to rotate the right end of your camera down, resulting in an image rotating in a clockwise direction. Choose iPhoto, Preferences, click on the desired Rotate option, and then click on the Preferences window Close button to make the change.

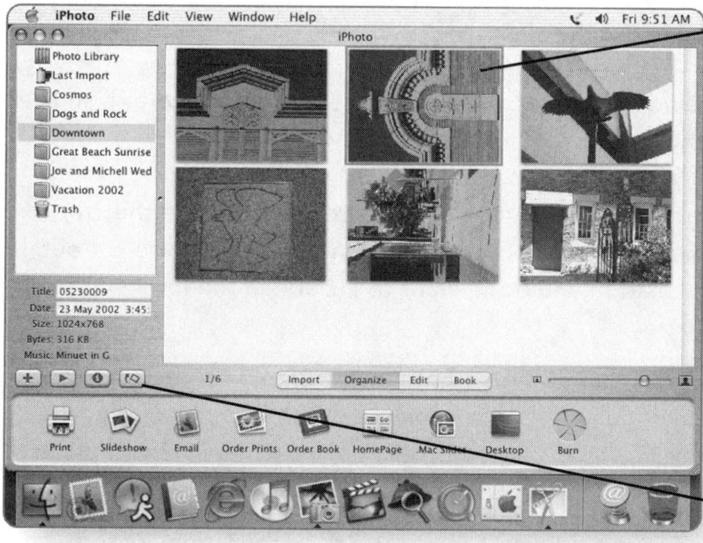

**1. Click** on the **photo** to rotate. The selection highlight will appear around the photo(s).

**TIP**

In the Edit view (pane), click on the Prev and Next buttons as needed to display (select) a photo to edit.

**2. Click** on the **Rotate button.** The photo will rotate 90 degrees.

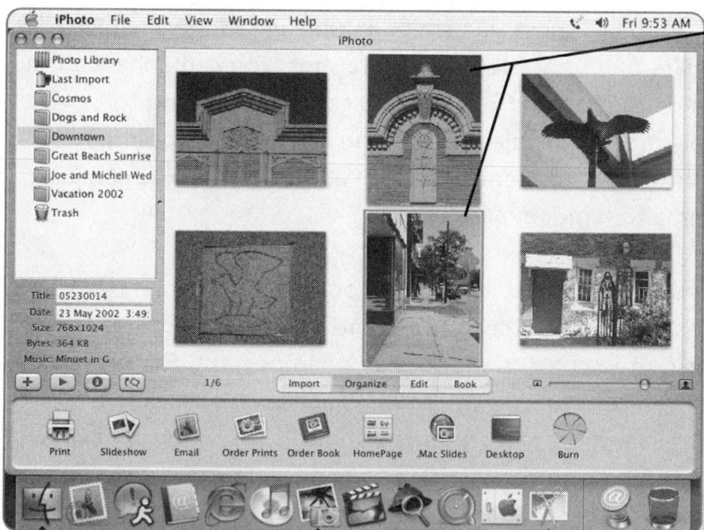

This example illustrates two photos that have been rotated 90 degrees clockwise.

**CAUTION**

Generally, the editing changes described in this chapter permanently alter your imported images. If you want to see how changes to an image might look but want to keep the original intact, duplicate the image and make your changes to the duplicate copy. The section called "Duplicating a Photo in an Album" in Chapter 3 explains how to create another copy of a digital image in iPhoto.

# Cropping a Photo

*Cropping* a photo enables you to resize the image to a smaller size and enhance it in a number of ways:

- Cropping eliminates the photo content outside the *crop zone* that you specify, so you can use cropping to cut out information you don't want to include in the finished picture.
- You can turn a single photo into multiple shots by copying the image and then cropping a different portion of each copy. For example, you could crop each individual's picture out of a larger group shot.
- With cropping, you can change the proportions of the image to prepare it for professional output, such as having prints made.
- By using cropping to specify an unusual shape such as a square or a very wide and short shot, you can enhance the drama of a photo. Further, you can use cropping to reposition the subject within the photo by cropping more information from one side than another. This also can lend drama to a mundane photo.

The cropping process includes choosing a *Constrain ratio* (if desired), selecting a crop zone, and then applying the crop. Choosing the constrain ratio may be important. For example, if you want to order photo prints, choose the proper Constrain size for the prints you want. If you want to have a photo book printed, you need to choose one of the 4 x 3 ratios for best results.

As when rotating, if you are cropping a GIF image that you imported, iPhoto will resave the cropped image in the JPEG format. The original image remains intact in a subfolder of the iPhoto Library folder in case you need to work with the GIF file again.

The following steps explain how to crop a photo, including how to choose the desired Constrain setting.

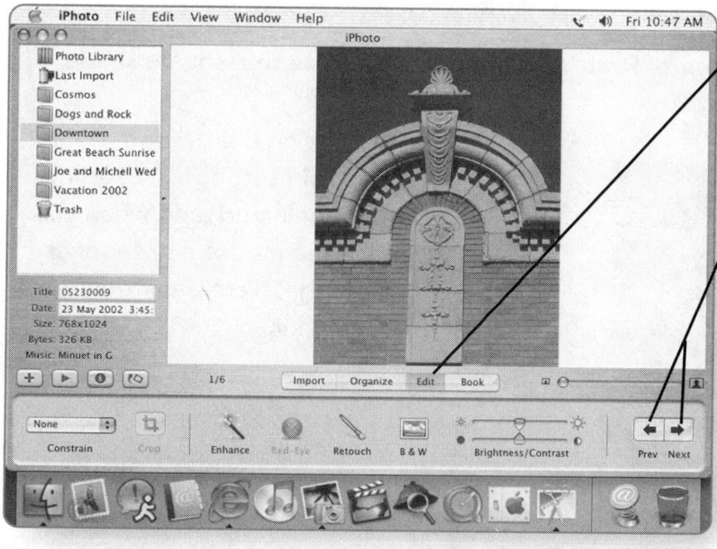


**1. Click** on the **Edit button.** The Edit view or pane will appear.

**2. Click** on the **Prev and Next buttons** as needed to display the photo to crop. The photo will appear in the photo viewing area.

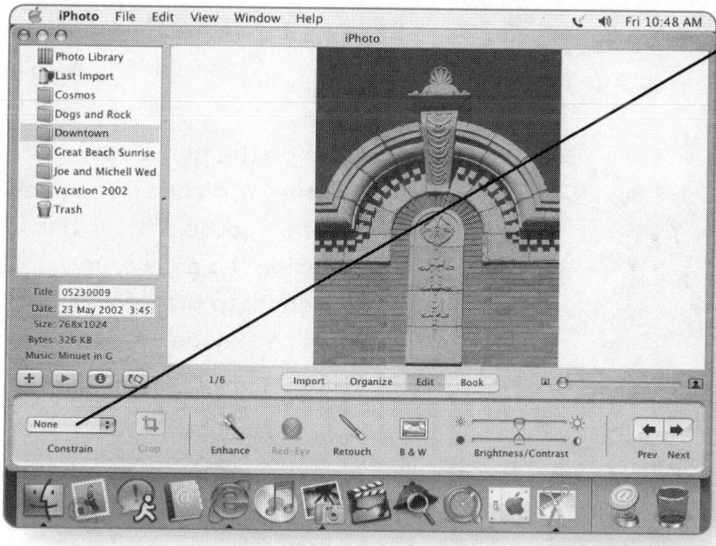


**3. Click** on the **Constrain pop-up menu.** The pop-up menu choices will appear. They include:

- **None.** Enables you to crop the image in any proportion you prefer.
- **800 x 600 (Display).** Restricts image crop size to 800 x 600 pixels, an optimum size for images to be used on the desktop or in slideshows.
- **4 x 3 (Book, DVD), 4 x 6 (Postcard), 5 x 7 (L, 2L), and 8 x 10.** Restricts image crop size to the specified photo print size, in a horizontal (wide) orientation.

- **4 x 3 Portrait (Book), 4 x 6 Portrait (Postcard), 5 x 7 Portrait (L, 2L), and 8 x 10 Portrait.** Restricts image crop size to the specified photo print size, in a vertical (tall) orientation.
- **Square.** Restricts the photo crop size to a square shape.

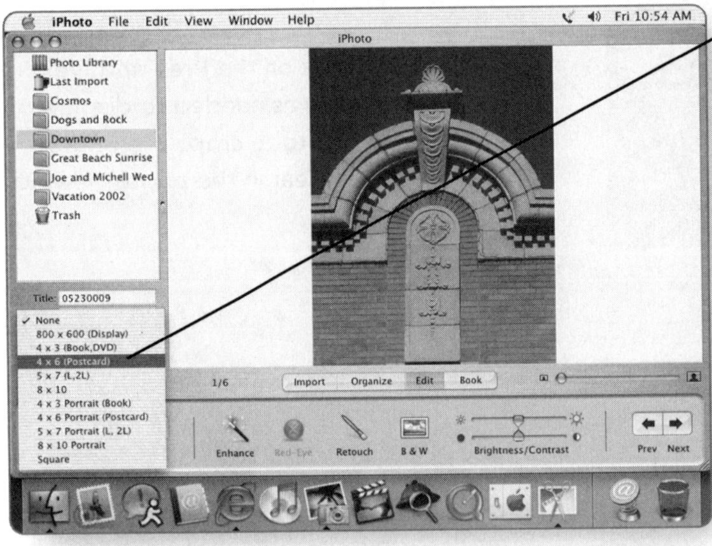


**4. Click** on the desired **Constrain** setting. The setting will be selected, and when you move the mouse pointer over the image, a crosshair pointer will appear.

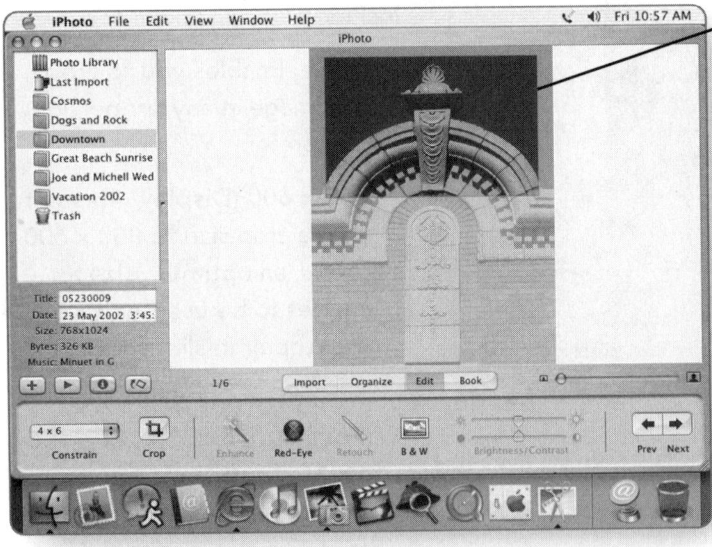


**5. Drag** on the **photo** to specify the crop zone. When you release the mouse button, the area outside the crop zone will be lightened, to graphically illustrate the image area to be cropped.

> **TIP**
>
> If you make a crop zone selection but don't like the selection, choose Edit, Deselect All to remove the selection.

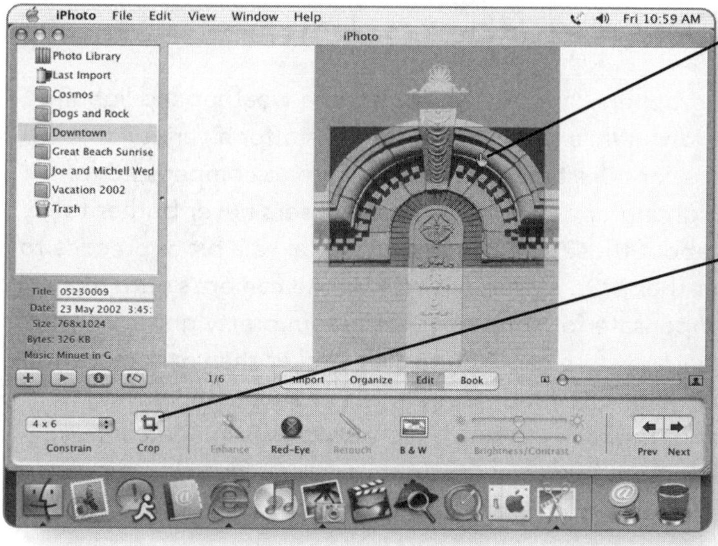


**6. Drag** the **selection** to reposition it, if needed. When you release the mouse button, the crop zone will appear in the new location.

**7. Click** on the **Crop button**. The image will be cropped as specified.

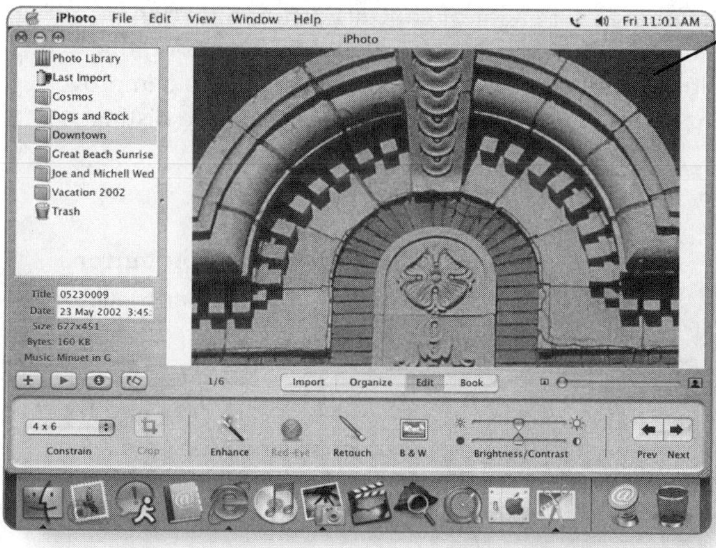


This example shows the newly-cropped image. As when you change photo titles or rotate a photo, iPhoto applies the new cropping to the image file in both the photo library and any albums including the photo.

# Adjusting Photo Tone

Photographers can't always control the weather and lighting conditions. While most digital cameras offer a variety of settings for adjusting a shot's exposure to compensate for poor lighting or a gloomy day, many users never bother to learn about those settings because it takes a bit of practice to master them. Or, a user may rely on the camera's auto mode to compensate for conditions that seem pretty good, only to find that a picture came out a little darker than expected. You can use iPhoto to fix the *brightness* of an image, making it lighter or darker as desired. You also can fix image *contrast*, the difference between the light and dark tones in an image. Make these changes in the Edit view.

> **TIP**
>
> I like photos with a lot of contrast just as a matter of personal preference. However, slightly increasing the contrast of even a well exposed image can help improve print quality by making color differences more distinct.

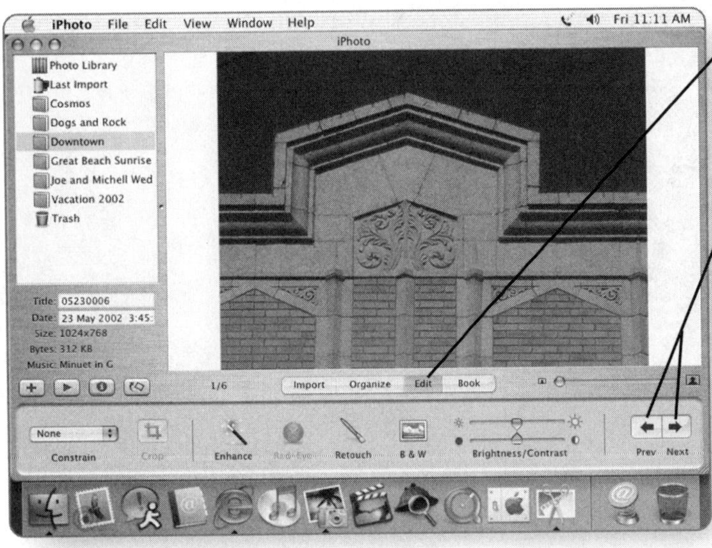


**1. Click** on the **Edit button**. The Edit view or pane will appear.

**2. Click** on the **Prev and Next buttons** as needed to display the photo to adjust. The photo will appear in the photo viewing area.

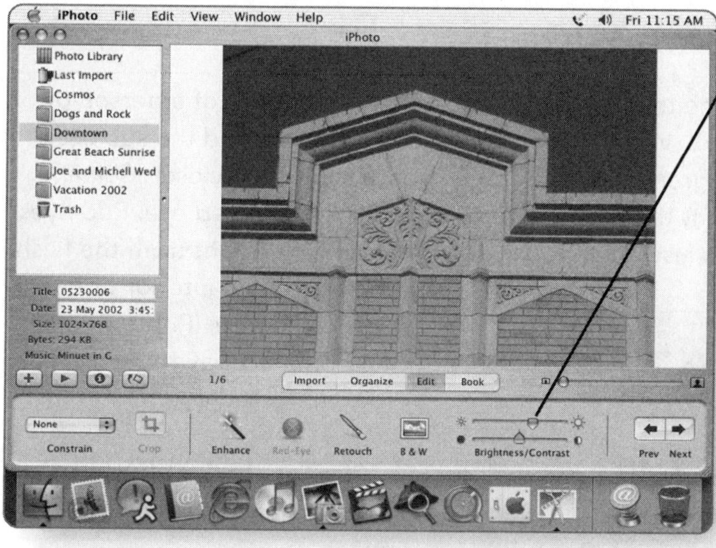


**3.** **Drag** the **brightness slider** as needed. (The brightness slider is the top slider above Brightness/Contrast.) The photo will preview the new settings in the photo viewing area.

> **TIP**
>
> If you try to make a brightness or contrast change and nothing happens, display another image, return to the desired image, and try again.

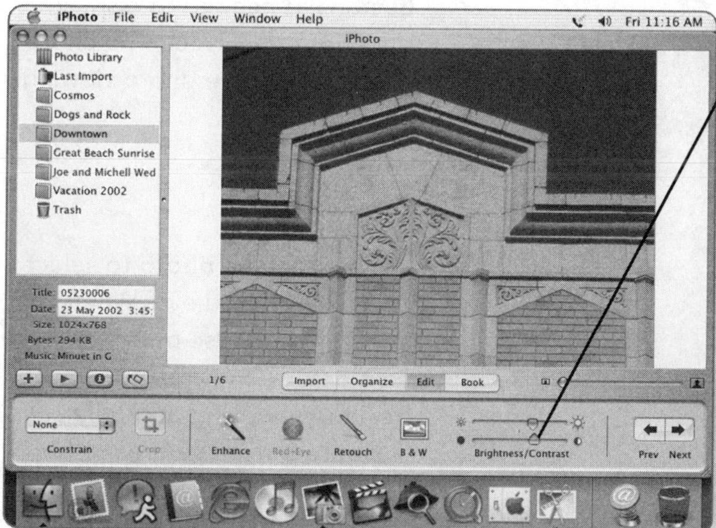


**4.** **Drag** the **contrast slider** as needed. (The brightness slider is the bottom slider above Brightness/Contrast.) The photo will preview the new settings in the photo viewing area.

> **TIP**
>
> Sometimes only mild brightness and contrast settings do the job. While the changes in the photo between Steps 1 and 4 may seem subtle in black and white, they're much more dramatic in color, and I'm pleased with the finished image appearance.

# Eliminating Red Eye

Imagine that you've taken a really neat photo of a person or pet. You've caught a spontaneous moment and the subject looks great. You're loving it—until you take a closer look and see that the subject's eyes are afflicted with *red eye*. Red eye (which also can appear green) results when light from the flash bounces off the interior of the eye. Fortunately, iPhoto 2 offers an automated way to edit the image to fix red eye.

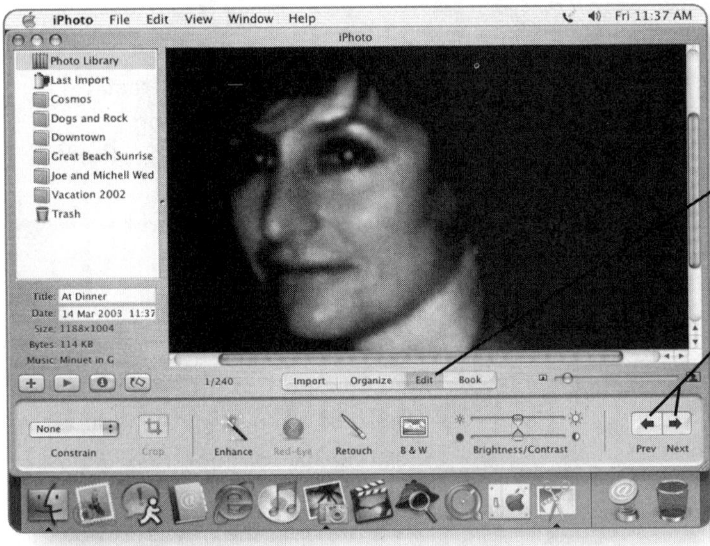


**1.** **Click** on the **Edit button**. The Edit view or pane will appear.

**2.** **Click** on the **Prev and Next buttons** as needed to display the photo to correct. The photo will appear in the photo viewing area.

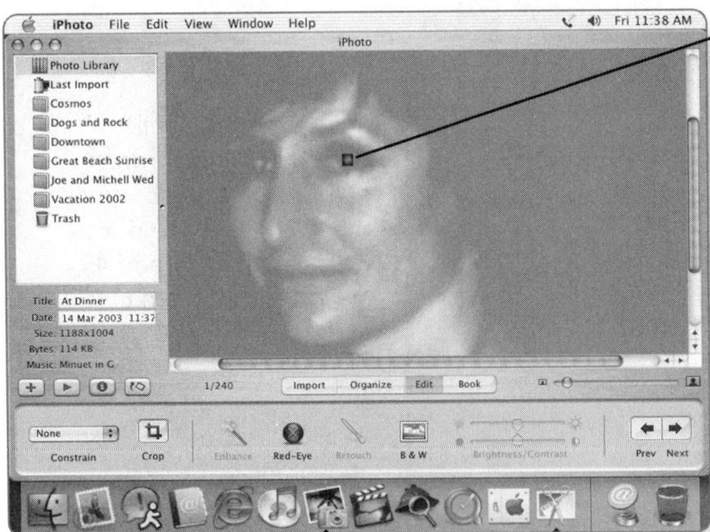


**3.** **Drag** on the **photo** to select the area with red eye. When you release the mouse button, the area outside the crop zone will be lightened, to graphically illustrate the image area to be corrected.

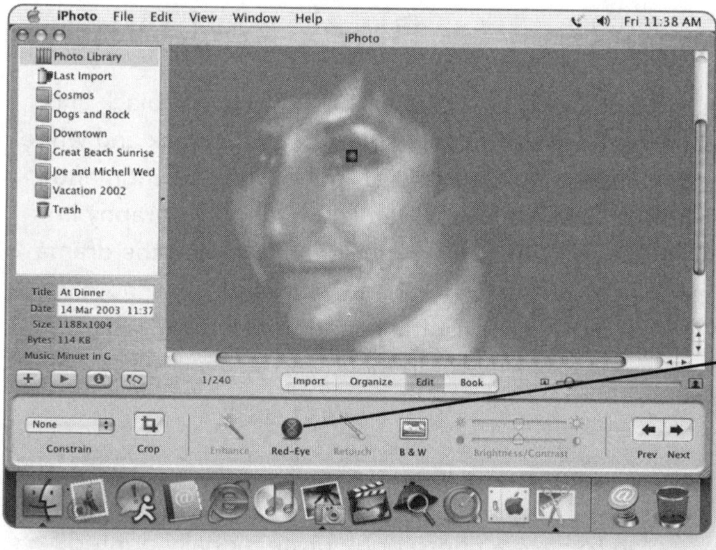


## TIP

If you make a selection to eliminate redeye but don't like the selection, choose Edit, Deselect All to remove the selection.

**4.** Click on the **Red-Eye button**. The red eye area will be corrected, and the area you selected in Step 3 will be deselected.

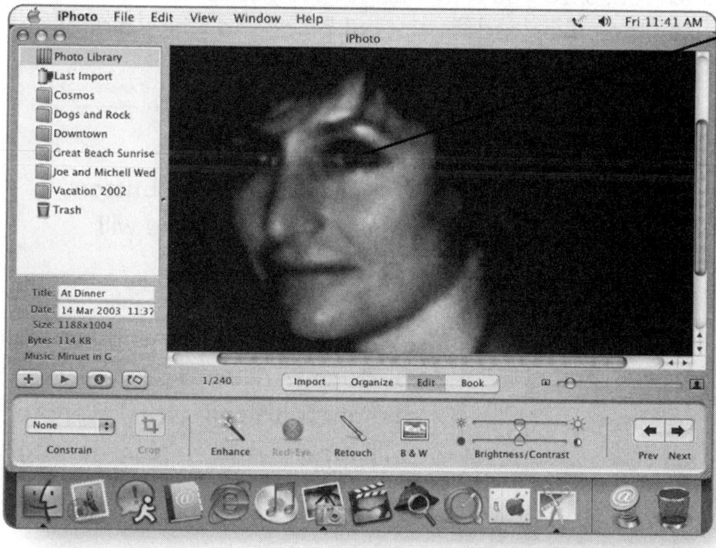


In this example, you can see that the red eye has been eliminated from the eye on the right of the image. The eye on the left still contains a red eye reflection.

## CAUTION

Be very precise in making your selection, because the red eye tool essentially fills red pixels in the selection with black. If you apply the red eye tool and are not satisfied with the results, immediately press Command+Z or choose Edit, Undo Reduce Red-Eye.

# Converting to Black and White

Just as I like photos with contrast, I'm a big fan of black and white photos. That's probably in part because black and white photos by nature present contrast, but probably sentimental reasons play a role, as well. When I studied photography in college, we used black and white film and studied the drama of shapes and patterns in black and white photos. iPhoto 2 enables you to convert a digital image to black and white, so you can see if it looks more dramatic and appealing without color.

> **CAUTION**
>
> If you plan to have a photo book professionally printed through iPhoto, do not include black and white photos. The Apple service uses a color printing process for bound books, so you may not get the desired results. You can, however, order prints of black and white digital images from the Apple service via iPhoto.

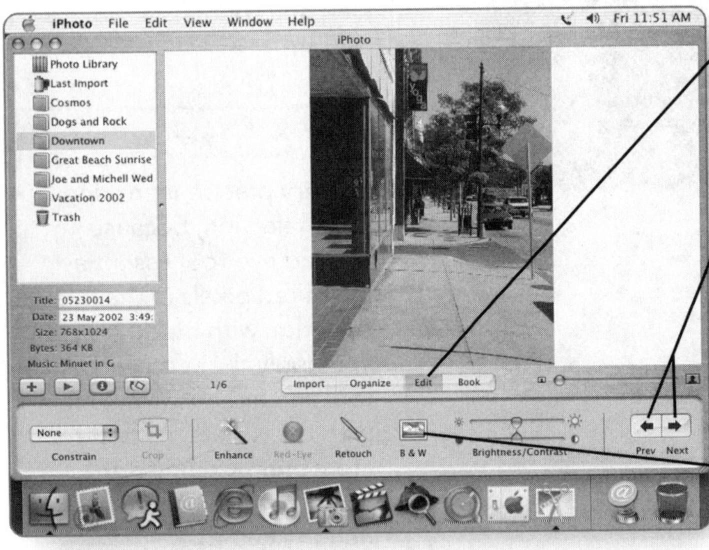


**1. Click** on the **Edit button**. The Edit view or pane will appear.

**2. Click** on the **Prev and Next buttons** as needed to display the photo to convert. The photo will appear in the photo viewing area.

**3. Click** on the **B & W button**.

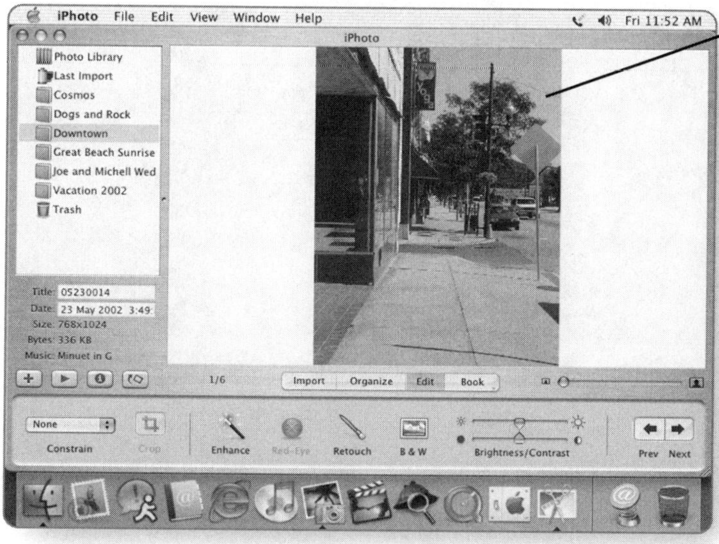


After a few moments, the converted image will appear.

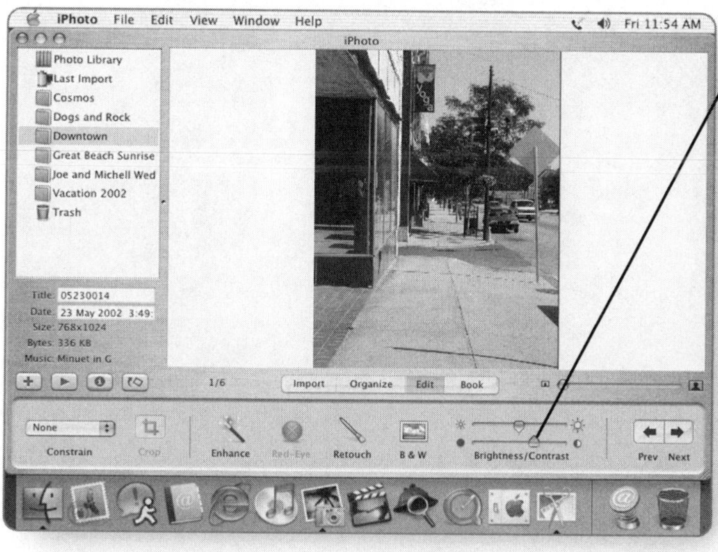


To really make the converted image pop, adjust its contrast and brightness settings.

> **TIP**
>
> You can use the Undo command multiple times in iPhoto to undo previous editing changes.

# 6

# Correcting and Enhancing Photos

I love to scan and reprint old family photos. The process rekindles my memories of important people in my life. Unfortunately, family photos sometimes take a beating over the years and can end up faded or become scratched or spotty. This chapter presents some new photo-correction tools included in iPhoto 2. In this chapter, you will learn how to:

- Correct a photo's colors.
- Remove scratches and spots.
- Revert a photo to its original appearance.

# Using the Enhance Feature

You learned in the last chapter how to adjust the brightness and contrast settings to improve the appearance of a digital image. Those changes deal with the light and darkness in an image. The new Enhance feature in iPhoto 2 automatically improves the colors in an image, making them more intense and attractive. In fact, for photos of colorful objects taken under dim lighting conditions, this may be the best tool to use to improve the image quality. You can use the *Enhance* feature either from the photo library or from a selected album.

> **CAUTION**
>
> As with the features covered in the last chapter, the editing changes described in this chapter permanently alter your imported images. If you want to see how changes to an image might look but want to keep the original intact, duplicate the image and make your changes to the duplicate copy. The section called "Duplicating a Photo in an Album" in Chapter 3 explains how to create another copy of a digital image in iPhoto.

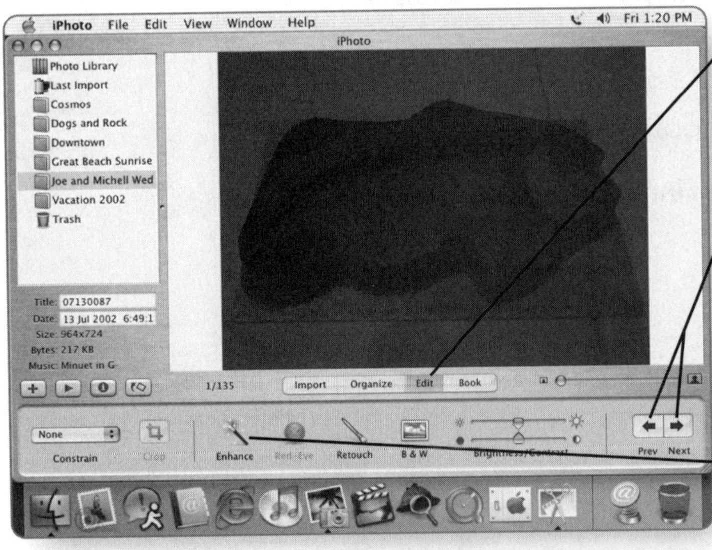


**1.** **Click** on the **Edit button.** The Edit view or pane will appear.

**2.** **Click** on the **Prev and Next buttons** as needed to display the photo to correct. The photo will appear in the photo viewing area.

**3.** **Click** on the **Enhance button.**

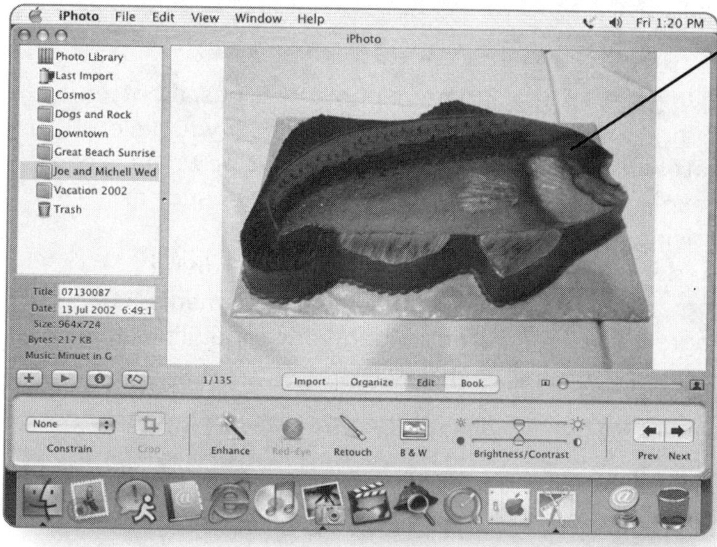

After a few moments, the corrected image will appear.

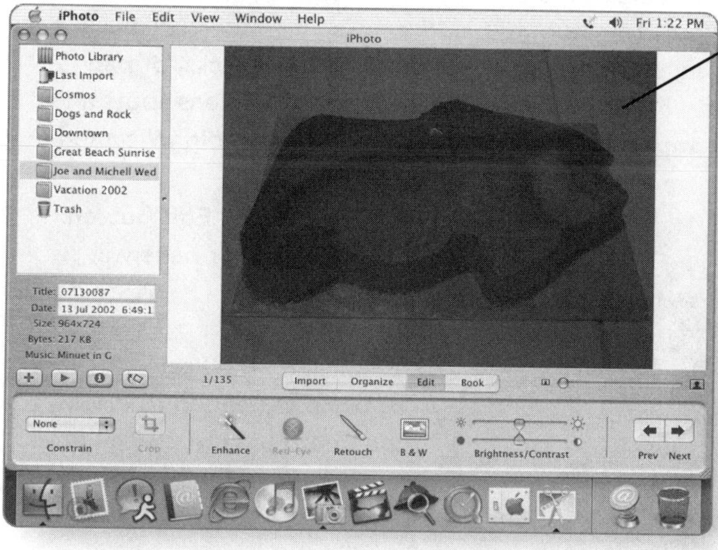

**4.** To compare the corrected image with the original, **press and hold** the **Control key** on your keyboard. When the Control key is depressed, iPhoto shows the photo in its original, uncorrected state.

**NOTE**

While great for making basic photo changes, iPhoto's editing tools don't offer much flexibility. If you have photos that need substantial corrections or would like to explore more photo editing possibilities such as applying fun filters to an image, you need to "graduate" to a more full-fledged photo editing program. For example, the Photoshop Elements 2.0 program from Adobe offers generous capabilities for a modest price—less than $100.

# Removing Scratches and Other Flaws

iPhoto 2 also offers a *Retouch* feature for the first time. Use the Retouch feature to blend away slight imperfections in scanned photos, such as spots, scratches, cracks, or pen marks. You also can use this tool to removes lens spots and other imperfections from images shot with a digital camera.

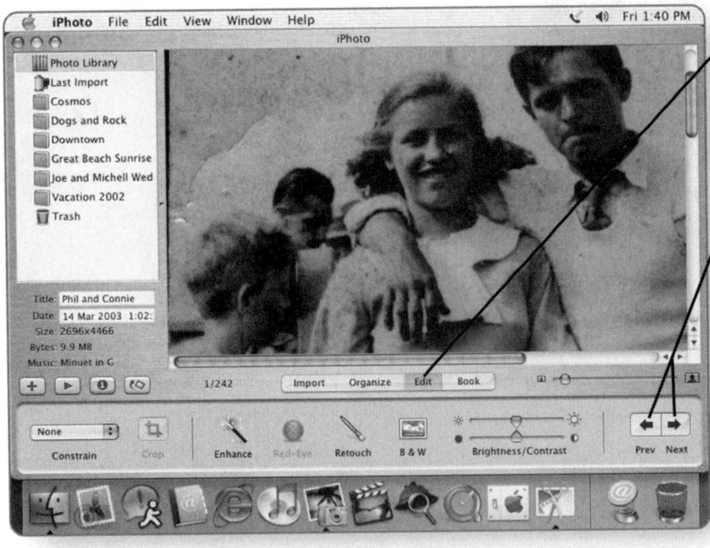


**1.** Click on the **Edit button**. The Edit view or pane will appear.

**2.** Click on the **Prev and Next buttons** as needed to display the photo to correct. The photo will appear in the photo viewing area.

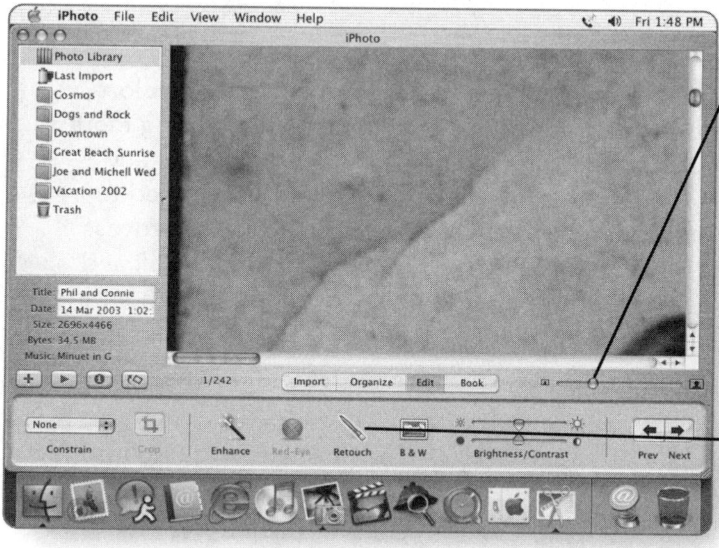


**3. Drag** the **Size Control** to set the desired zoom setting. Imperfections will be more visible, and you'll be able to see the area you're working with more clearly if you zoom in. This photo is quite spotty, which I'll have to live with to some degree, so I'll focus on fixing the cracked area at the left.

**4. Click** on the **Retouch button.** The Retouch feature will become active and when you move the mouse pointer over the image, a crosshair pointer will appear.

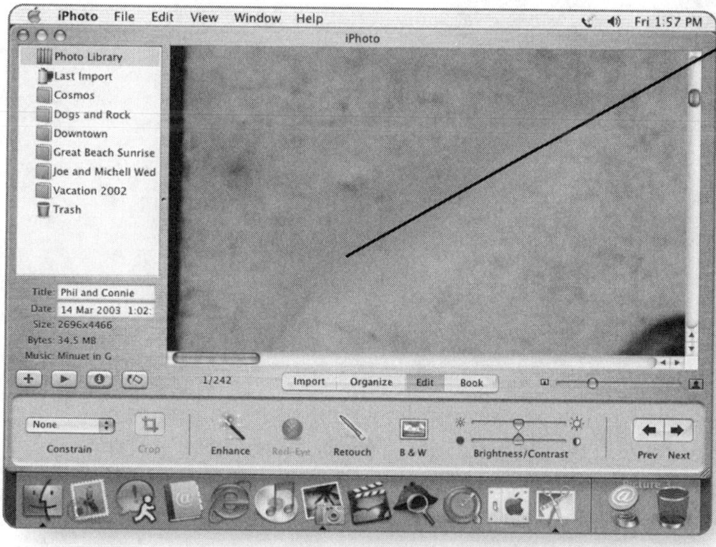


**5. Drag** with **short strokes** over the flaw to correct. The tool will subtly blend the imperfection away.

## NOTE

If the imperfection you're correcting is surrounded by mottled colors like the one shown here, drag in various directions to blend using more of the background colors. You can hold down the mouse button and "scrub" back and forth over the imperfection, but you'll be forced to pause every so often when the spiral appears for your Mac to process the changes. In fact, if you try to change the photo zoom or scroll and iPhoto won't work, pause a few more moments. Chances are, iPhoto is still processing changes.

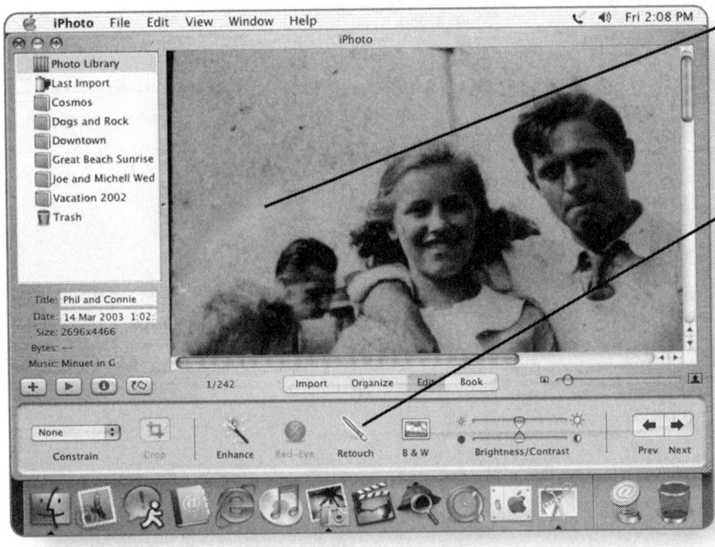


The finished image isn't perfect, but the great majority of the crack at the left has been blended away.

**6. Click** on the **Retouch button** again. The Retouch feature will be turned off.

## CAUTION

Using the Retouch feature also can dramatically increase an image's size. In this example, in which I started with a fairly large TIFF file, the size of the file nearly tripled. The size of the file can be a concern if you plan to have prints or a book made, because larger files take much longer to send, especially over a dial-up Internet connection. It also can become an issue in terms of displaying the photo in iPhoto. In some cases, iPhoto will be unable to redisplay an image file that's grown too large in Edit view.

# Reverting a Photo

Changes to an image file are permanent unless you undo them during the current work session. However, since the Undo feature works backwards from your most recent change, what do you do if you want to undo the changes you made earlier to an image, but not more recent changes you've made to a second image? And what can you do if you made changes to an image during a previous work session in iPhoto, and want to remove those changes the next time you use iPhoto? The answer in both cases is to *revert* the image. Reverting removes all changes you've previously made to the image, including cropping, color enhancements, and retouching. That is, you can't pick and choose which changes to remove. But, reverting can still get you out of a jam if you want to see the original image. Reverting works because iPhoto always keeps a copy of your original image in the iPhoto Library folder.

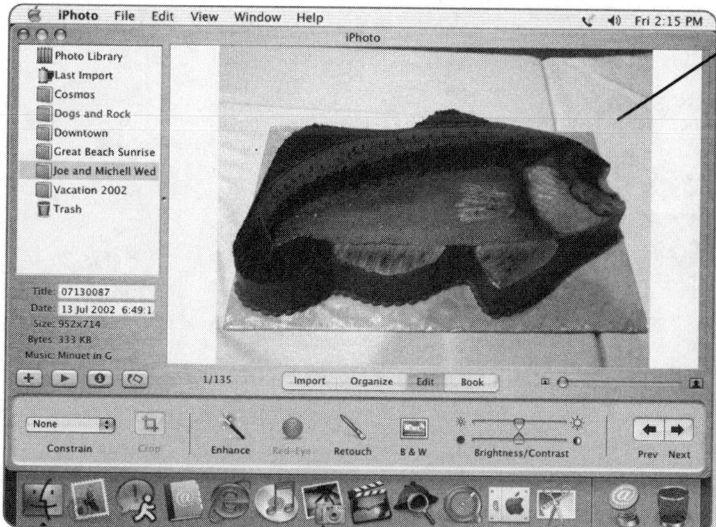


**1.** **Select or display** the **image to revert** in either Organize or Edit view. The edited image will appear.

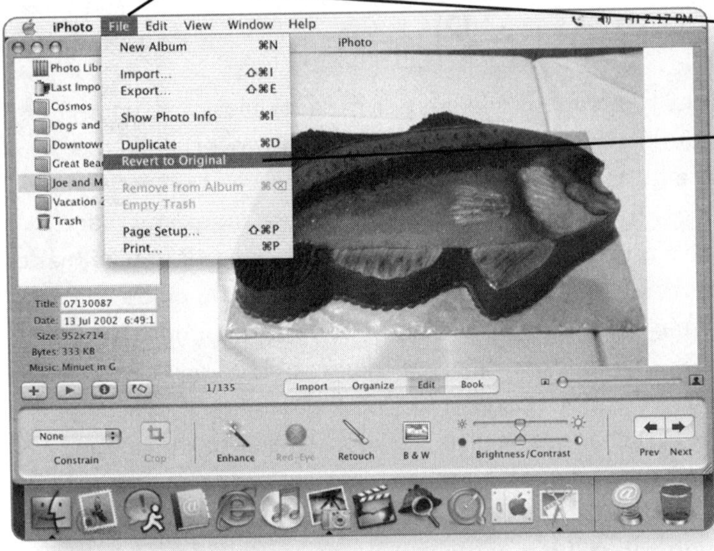


**2.** **Click** on **File**. The File menu will appear.

**3.** **Click** on **Revert to Original**. A message box will prompt you to confirm the revert operation.

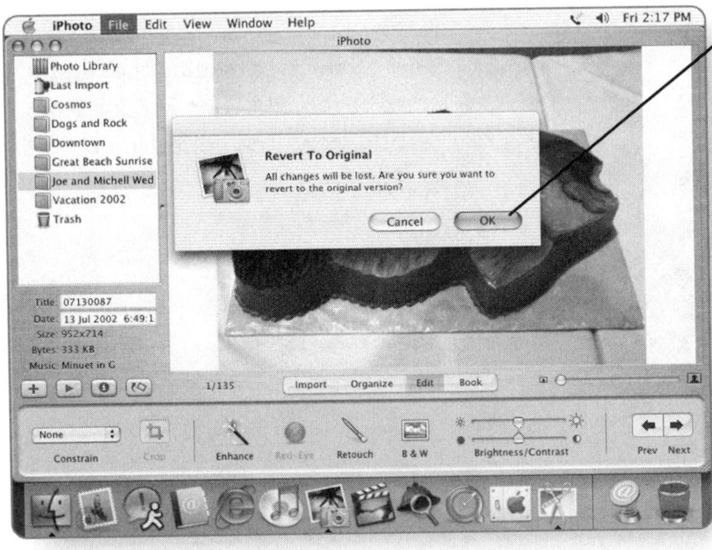


**4.** **Click** on **OK**. The changes will be removed from the image.

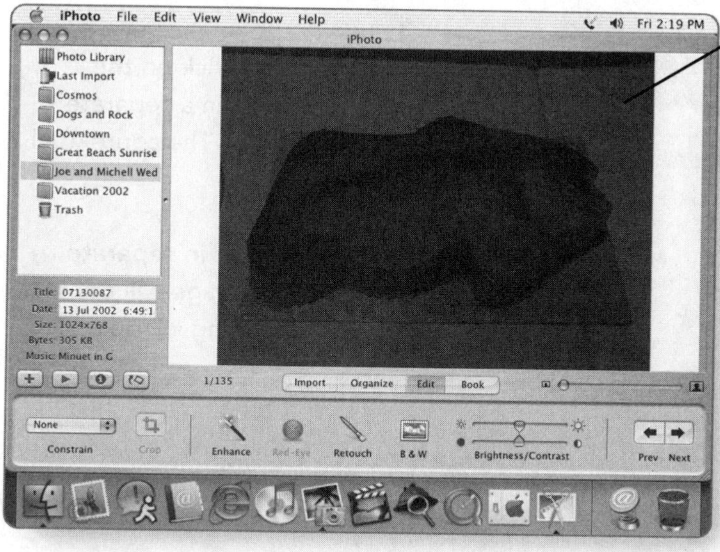


In this example, reverting removed cropping and color enhancement.

# Editing a Photo in a Separate Window

If you prefer, you can apply editing changes within a separate editing window in iPhoto. This approach offers you the advantage of being able to see the image changes in the editing window, while seeing the original image in the photo viewing area. Further, when you're working in the editing window, you can customize the toolbar at the top of the window to make your favorite editing tools more accessible.

> **NOTE**
>
> By default, when you double-click on an image in the Organize view, iPhoto displays that image in the Edit view. You can change iPhoto's preferences to have an image open in a separate editing window when you double-click on the image. For more, see Chapter 16, "Choosing iPhoto Preferences."

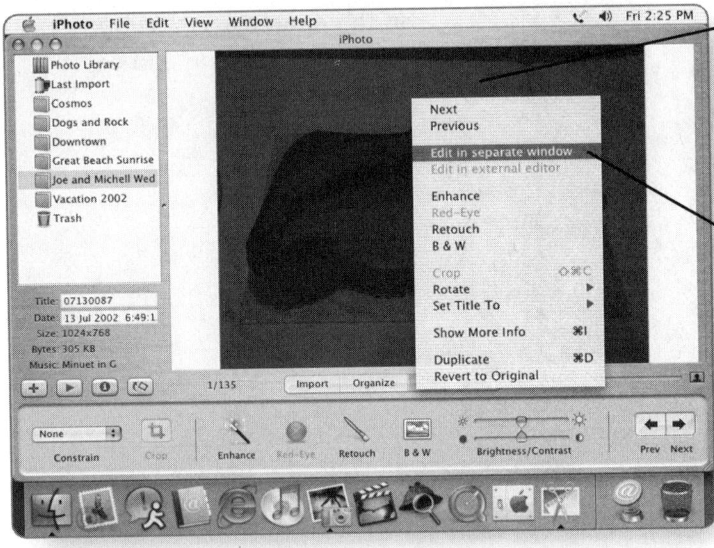


**1.** In either Organize or Edit view, **Control+click** on **the image to open** in a separate editing window. The contextual menu will appear.

**2.** Click on **Edit in separate window**. The image will open in a separate editing window.

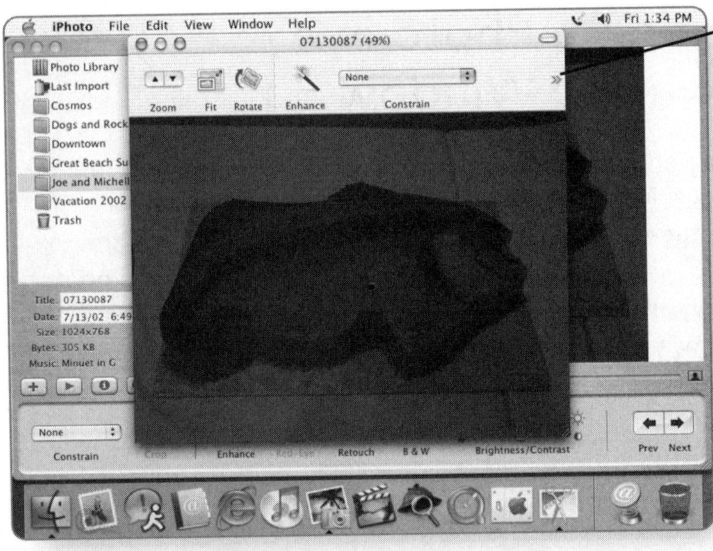


**3.** Click on the **double-arrow button** at the right end of the toolbar. A contextual menu will appear.

> **TIP**
>
> If you don't initially see the toolbar, click on the oval button at the far right end of the editing window title bar.

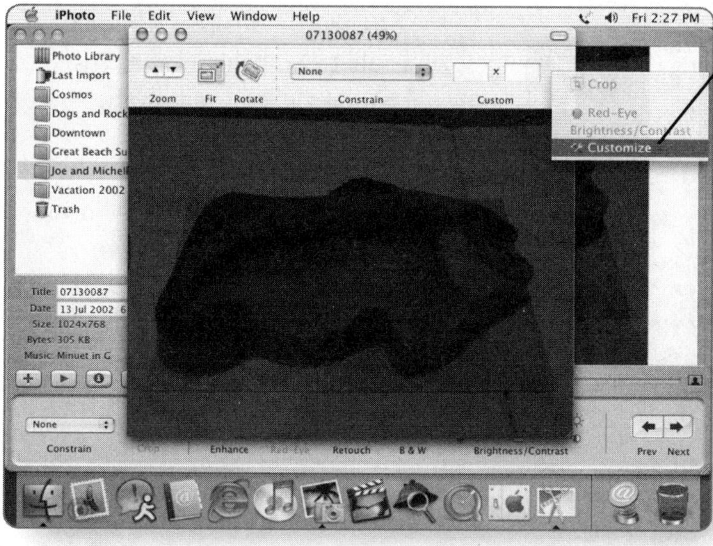


**4. Click** on **Customize**. A sheet with toolbar customization choices will appear.

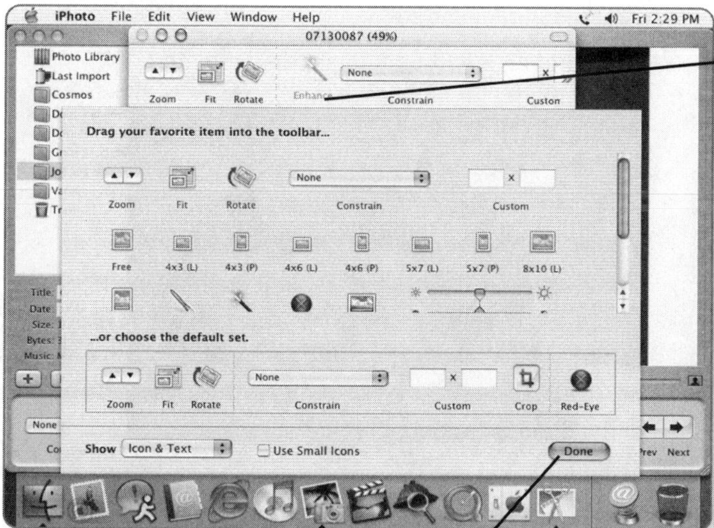


**5.** To add a toolbar button, **drag it** from **the sheet to the toolbar**. When you release the mouse button, the tool will appear in the specified toolbar location.

> **TIP**
>
> Conversely, drag an unneeded button off the toolbar to remove it. Or, click on the toolbar shown under "...or choose the default set" to revert the toolbar to its original choices.

**6. Click** on **Done**. The sheet will close and your toolbar changes will appear.

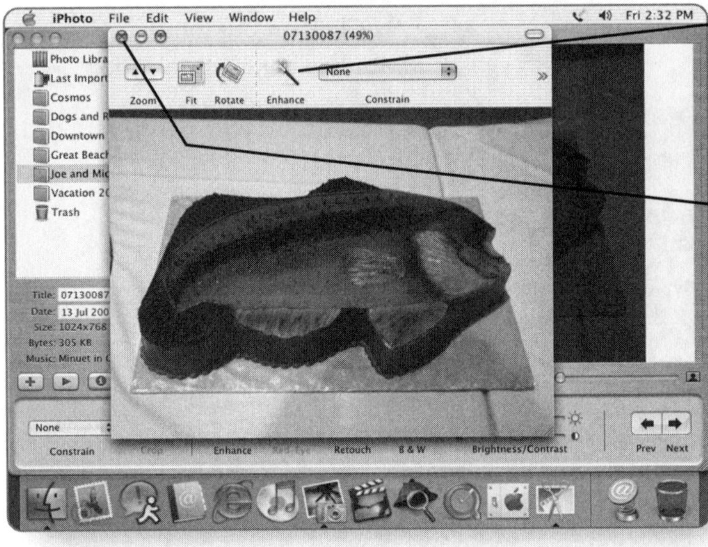


**7.** Use the **desired toolbar tools** to edit the image. The changes will appear in the editing window.

**8.** **Click** on the editing window **close button** when you've finished making changes. The window will close, and the changes will appear in the image in the Organize or Edit view.

## Part II Review Questions

1. How do I change a photo's title? *See "Working with Photo Titles" in Chapter 4.*
2. How do I add a comment to a photo? *See "Editing Title, Date, and Comment" in Chapter 4.*
3. What are keywords, and how do I use them with photos? *See "Working with Keywords" in Chapter 4.*
4. Is there a fast way to find a photo in the photo library? *See "Searching for a Photo" in Chapter 4.*
5. My photo's on its side. Can I fix it? *See "Rotating a Photo" in Chapter 5.*
6. I want to change a photo's proportions. Is there a tool for that? *See "Cropping a Photo" in Chapter 5.*
7. Help! My photo's too dark. *See "Adjusting Photo Tone" in Chapter 5.*
8. Oh, no. Red eye is ruining my photo! *See "Eliminating Red Eye" in Chapter 5.*
9. My photo looks drab. Can I fix it? *See "Using the Enhance Feature" in Chapter 6.*
10. Can I remove scratches or spots from an image? *See "Removing Scratches and Other Flaws" in Chapter 6.*

PART III

# Publishing Your Photos

# 7

# Setting Up a Photo Book

Even if you take the time to arrange your photo prints into nice albums, those albums can wear out over time. If you've ever picked up an album only to have some of the prints fall onto the floor in front of you, you know what I mean. iPhoto 2 provides a much more lasting and flexible way to arrange a group of photos. Once you set up the photos from an album into an electronic *book*, as described in this chapter, you can print the book yourself from your color inkjet printer or have a nice bound book printed. In this chapter, you will learn how to:

- Apply a theme to your book.
- Select a page design.
- Lock and unlock a page.
- Edit and format the text on a page.
- Spell check the page text.
- Preview the pages.

# Choosing a Theme and Page Contents

The *theme* you apply to a photo book determines how iPhoto positions the images and text on each page—except for the cover page, which always looks the same. iPhoto places the first image in the album on the cover, and then arranges each subsequent image based on the theme you select and the *page design* (number of images per page or type of page) you specify. You can choose one of the following themes for your picture book:

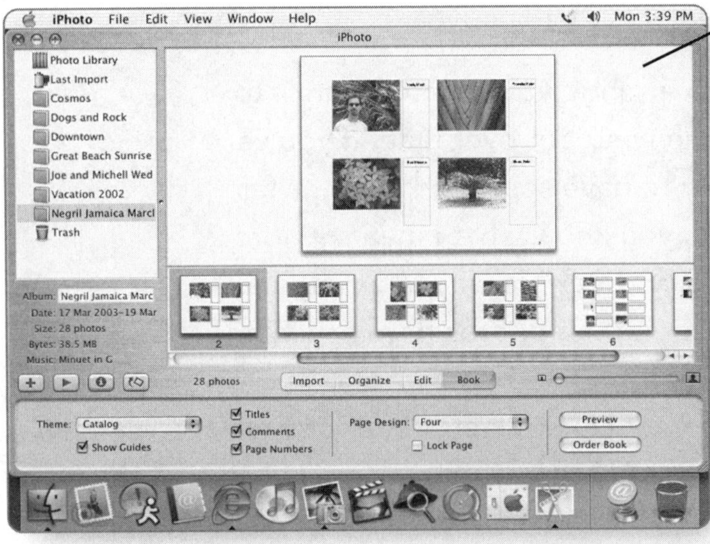


- **Catalog.** Enables you to place multiple images (up to eight) on each page, with the title and comments (description) to the right of each image.
- **Classic.** Enables you to place one to four images on each page, with the title and comments below each image. This theme leaves a white border around the images and text on each page.

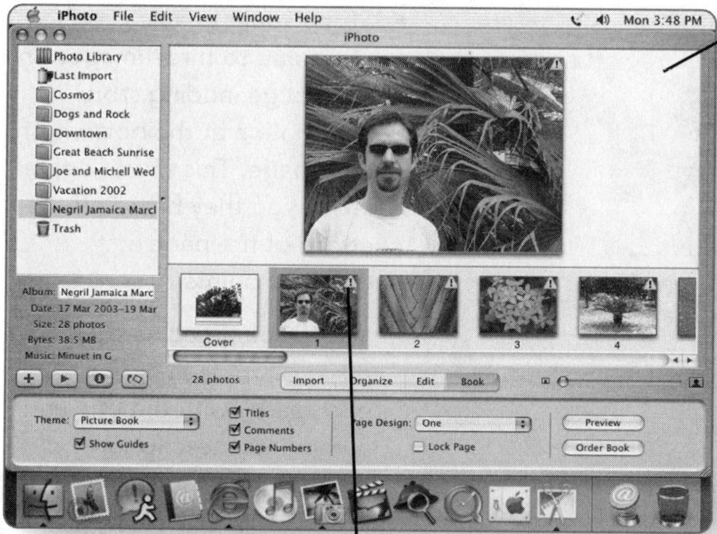


- **Picture Book.** Enables you to place one to four images on each page, with the title and comments below each image. For each page with one image, the image *bleeds* (prints without a margin) off the edges of the page. This is the default theme that iPhoto applies to the photos when you first display the Book pane.

## NOTE

A small exclamation mark indicator on a page thumbnail in the Book pane means that the image may not print as clearly at a large size, especially if you plan to have a bound book printed, due to the image size in pixels. You can choose a page design that includes more images per page to print the images at a smaller size. Alternatively, you can remove any cropping you previously applied to the image by reverting the image. Or, if you have access to image editing software like Adobe Photoshop Elements 2.0, you can increase the dimensions of the image files.

- **Portfolio.** Enables you to place multiple images (up to eight) on each page, with the title and comments (description) at the left side of the page. Images bleed off the right side of each page and the top and bottom if the page includes multiple pictures.

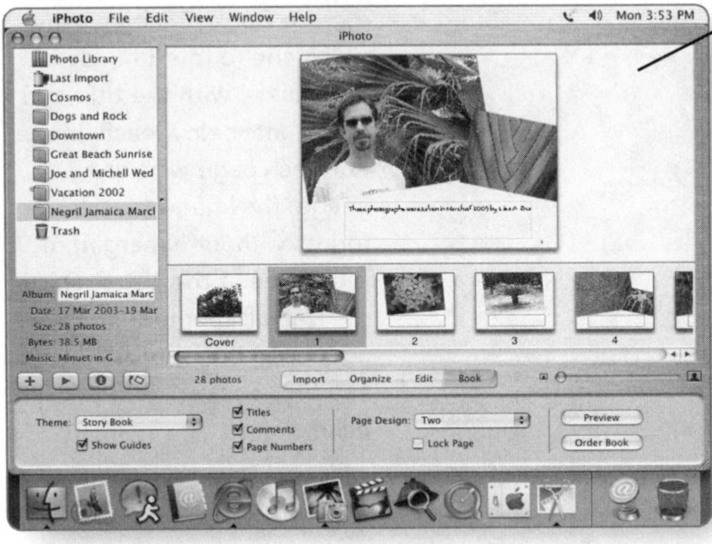


- **Story Book.** Enables you to place one to three images on each page, adding story information at the bottom of each page. This theme angles images so they bleed off the edges of the page at different points.
- **Year Book.** Enables you to place up to 32 images on each page, with the title and comments (description) below each image.

Follow these steps to choose a theme for your picture book and choose what information (image titles and comments, or a page number) prints on each page.

> **NOTE**
>
> You perform all the operations in this chapter in the Book pane (view) in iPhoto. Select the album that you want to share as a book, and then click on the Book button below the photo viewing area to display the Book pane or view.

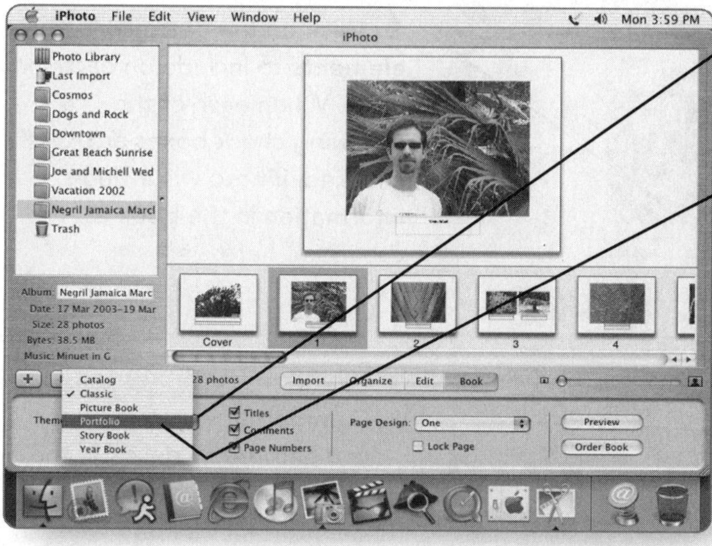


**1.** **Click** on the **Theme pop-up menu** in the Book pane. The available themes will appear.

**2.** **Click** on the **desired theme**. iPhoto will rearrange the photos and display the pages using the specified theme.

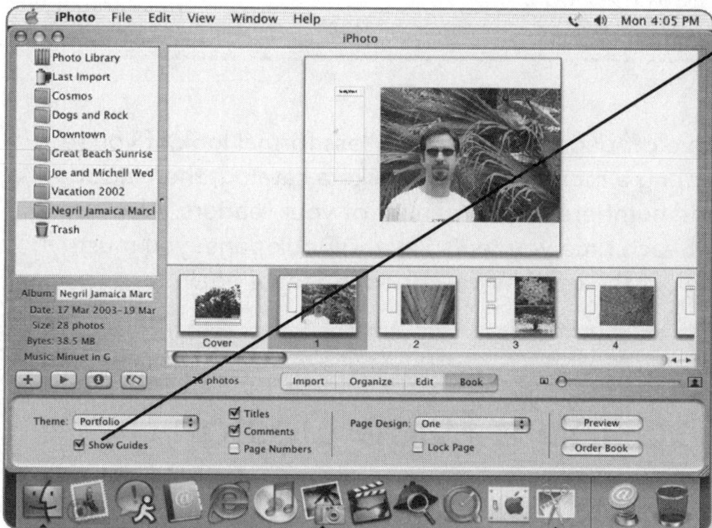


**3.** **Click** on **Show Guides** if desired. When you uncheck this option button, the blue guidelines defining the title and comment areas on each page will be hidden. (These guidelines do not print.)

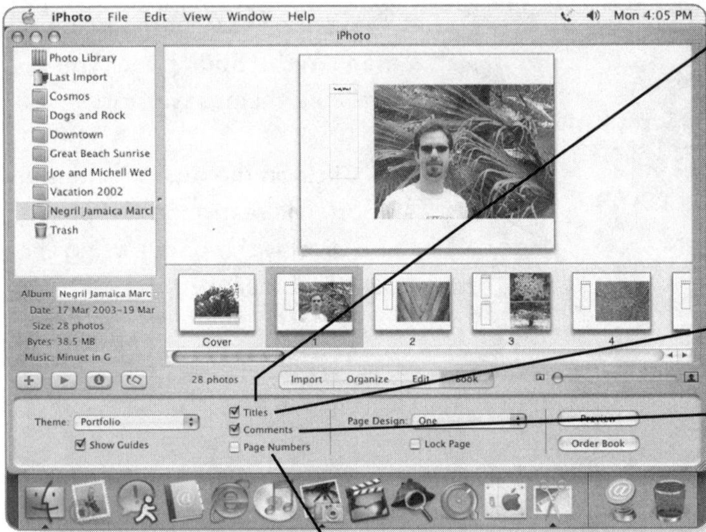

**4. Click** on the **desired elements** to include on each page. When each of the following check boxes are checked, iPhoto will include information in the book as described here:

- **Titles.** The photo title or name.
- **Comments.** Any comments you entered to describe the photo as described in Chapter 4, "Working with Photo Information."
- **Page Numbers.** The appropriate page number for each page in the book.

> **TIP**
>
> Leave off page numbers for a less formal look. If you're creating a more formal book like a catalog, then include page numbers for the benefit of your readers. Also note that each time you redisplay the Book pane, you must reselect the options described in Step 4 again.

# Choosing a Page Design

To make professionally printing-bound hard copies of your photo books cost effective, Apple's online service follows certain guidelines. For example, each bound book has a minimum of 10 pages. From there, you can increase the size of the book in increments of 10 pages, with 50 pages being the maximum. (The cover does not count as a book page.)

To help your book fit one of the page quantity increments, iPhoto may place multiple images on a particular page. You can override this "suggestion," and change the design of the page to hold a single image, instead. Conversely, you may want to increase the number of images on a page to reduce the number of pages in your book (thus avoiding blank or partially blank pages), or may want to choose a special layout for an introduction or end page.

> **CAUTION**
>
> You cannot change the page design for the cover page.

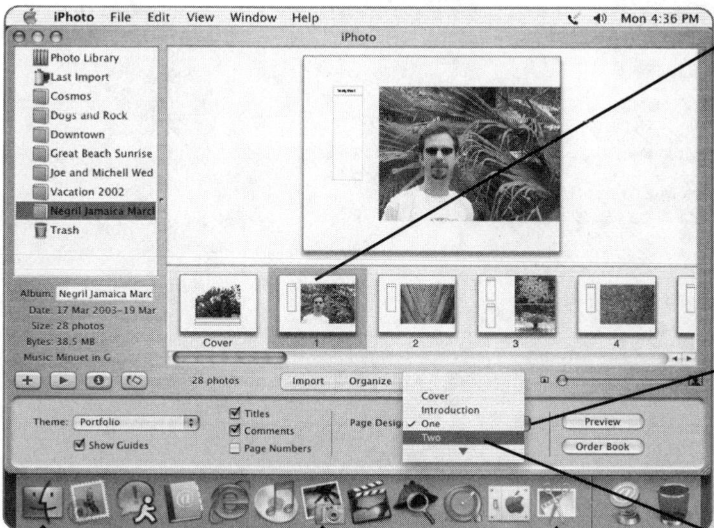


**1.** **Click** on the **page** to which you want to apply a new design in the strip of thumbnails at the bottom of the photo viewing area. The page will be selected, and its contents will appear above in the photo viewing area.

**2.** **Click** on the **Page Design pop-up menu**. The available page designs for the currently selected theme will appear.

**3.** **Click** on the **desired page design**.

> **TIP**
>
> If your book includes photos that are both horizontal and vertical in orientation, sometimes a three-image page design can help better fit images with mixed orientations on a single page. For example, iPhoto will place two horizontal images in a smaller size beside the vertical image on the page.

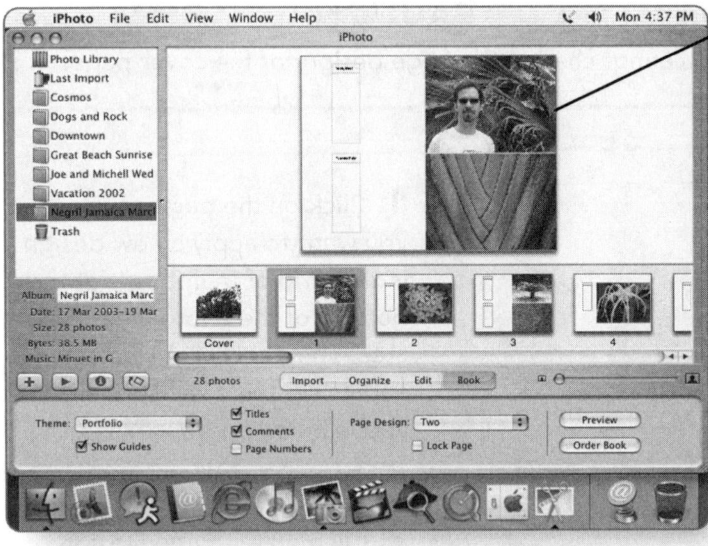


iPhoto will apply the new design to the page, and will rearrange the photos on subsequent pages as required.

> **NOTE**
>
> The Introduction and End page designs do not include images in some of the themes.

# Locking and Unlocking the Page Design

Once you've chosen the design you want for each page in the book, you can *lock* that page. Locking the page ensures that the page design you've selected will continue to be applied to the page any time you leave and return to the Book view. If you do not lock the page design, iPhoto returns to the page design choices it first "suggested" when you chose the book theme.

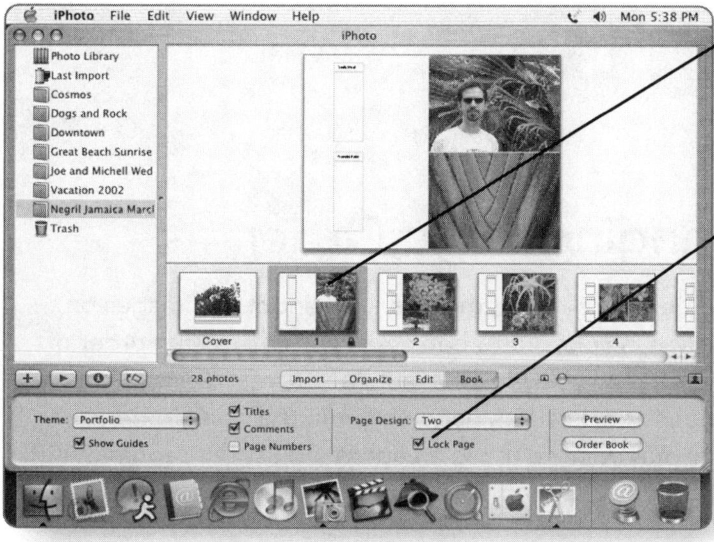


**1. Click** on the **page** to lock. The page will be selected, and its contents will appear above in the photo viewing area.

**2. Click** on the **Lock Page** check box. A check mark will appear, and the selected page will be locked.

> **TIP**
>
> A lock icon appears in the thumbnail for any locked page.

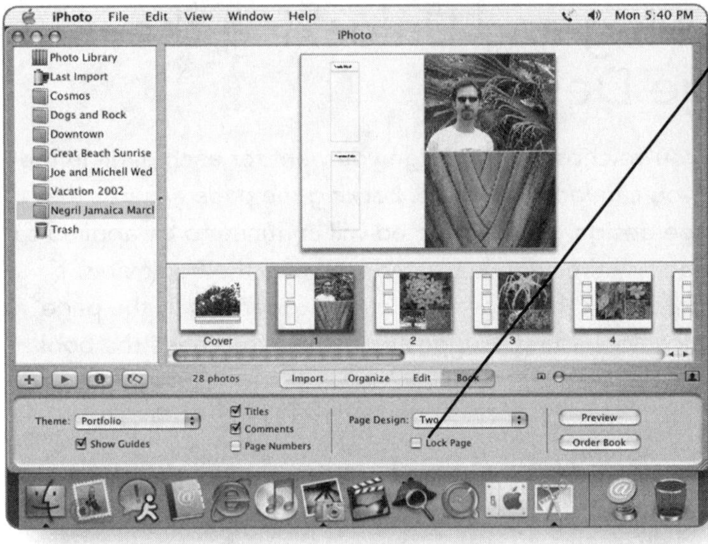


**3. Click** on the **Lock Page** check box again. The check mark will be removed, and the selected page will be unlocked.

# Changing Page Order

In addition to changing the arrangement of the images on each page in your photo book, you can change the order of the pages themselves. For example, you may want to move the images on a certain page earlier in the book for impact. Or, you may want to move a page to adjust the sequences of the page designs used by the pages in the book.

> **NOTE**
>
> This process also changes the order of the photos in the selected album, not just in the book. If you switch back to the Organize view, you'll see the new photo order.

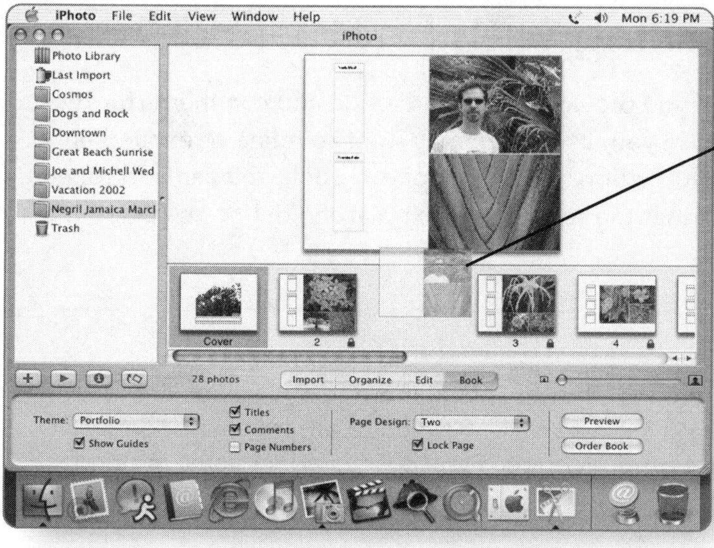


To move a page to a new position:

**1.** **Drag** the **page thumbnail** in the strip of page thumbnails at the bottom of the photo viewing area. A grayed-out version of the page will appear behind the mouse pointer.

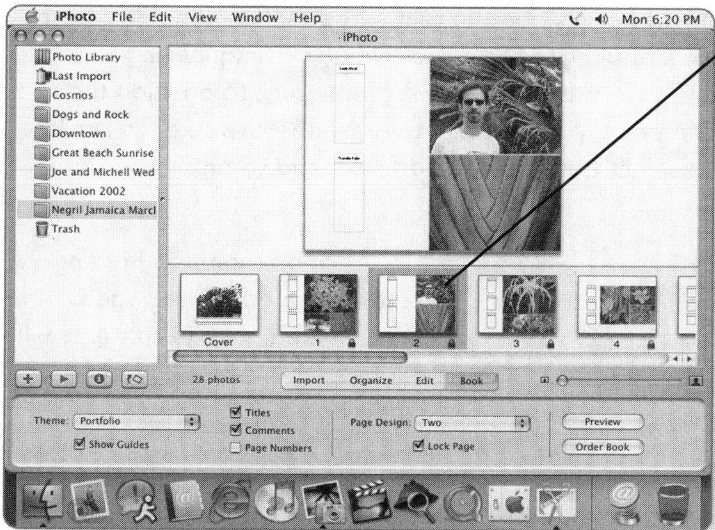


**2.** **Release** the **mouse button**. The page will appear in its new location. Page 2 in this example was previously Page 1.

# Working with Photo Text

Even if you previously entered a title and comments for the photos in your book, you may want to refine or expand on that information within your photo book. You can add to, edit, and format the text in any text placeholder on the page in a book.

> **NOTE**
>
> You cannot, however, add more text placeholders. iPhoto imposes this limitation to ensure your book will print properly, should you opt for professional printing.

## Editing Text

You can add or change the text in the text placeholder on any page of a book. Use the same editing techniques as you would in a word processing program: Click to position the insertion point, press Delete to erase the character to the left, drag to select text, type to add text, and so on.

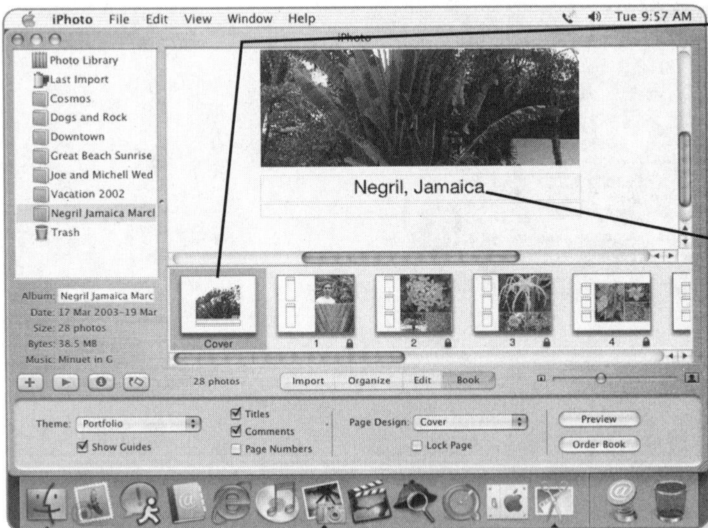


**1. Click** on the **page** holding the text to edit. The page will be selected, and its contents will appear above in the photo viewing area.

**2. Click** on the **placeholder** for the text to add or edit. The insertion point will appear, and the page will zoom to a larger size so that you can see your changes.

**TIP**

iPhoto may not zoom in as far as you prefer, so use the size control to zoom in further so that you can work more comfortably.

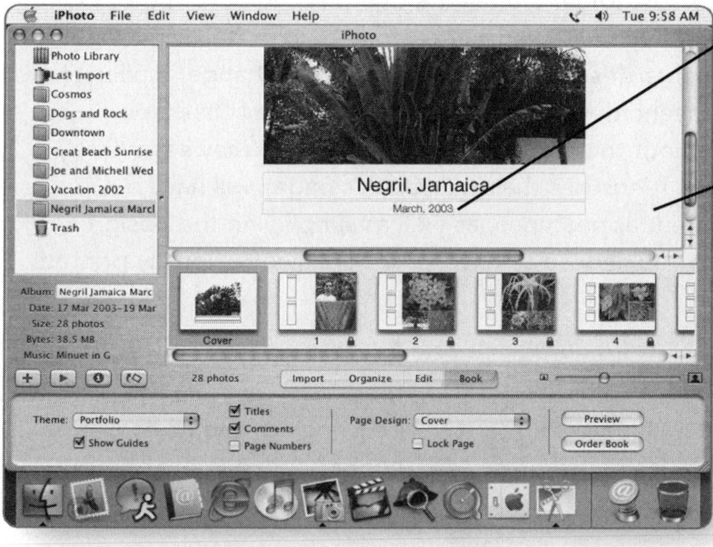

**3. Make** the desired **changes.** Your changes will appear in the placeholder.

**4. Click away from** the **placeholder** (or click another placeholder). iPhoto will display the new or edited text in the placeholder you selected in Step 2. Zoom the page as needed to see the results.

**CAUTION**

If you add text to a placeholder on an introduction or end page and then change the theme applied to the book, iPhoto will display a warning message telling you that the custom text will be reset. So, be sure to settle on the theme you prefer for the book before you add introduction, end, or story text.

## Applying Bold and Italics

You can apply bold and italics to any text placeholder on any page, or remove bold and italics as needed. The process works the same whether you are adding or removing these attributes. When you apply bold or italics to the text in a title placeholder, iPhoto 2 applies the same change to all the text in the placeholder and all the title placeholders in the book. Likewise, when you add or remove bold or italics to text in a comments/description placeholder, that change applies to all the placeholder text and all placeholders of that type throughout the book. While this approach may seem less flexible, it ensures that your book's pages will have a consistent appearance, as well as simplifying the design should you choose to have your book professionally printed.

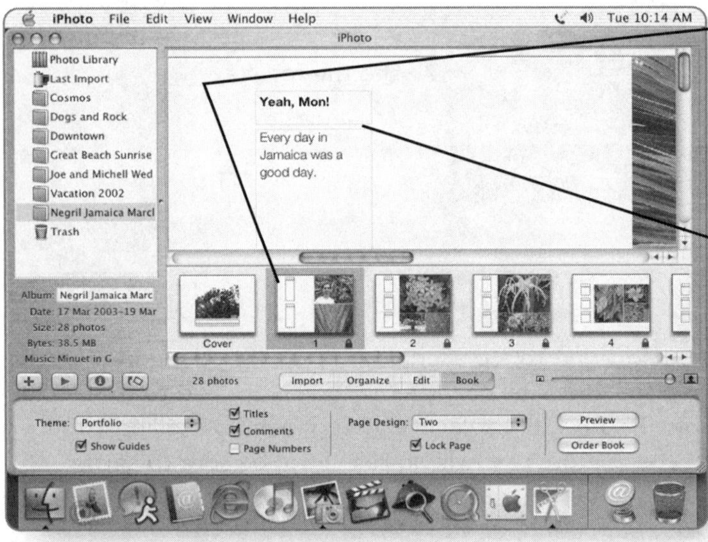

1. **Click** on the **page** holding the text to format. The page will be selected, and its contents will appear above in the photo viewing area.

2. **Click** on the **placeholder** for the text to format. The insertion point will appear. (Zoom in to see it better, if needed.) You need not drag over the text to select it.

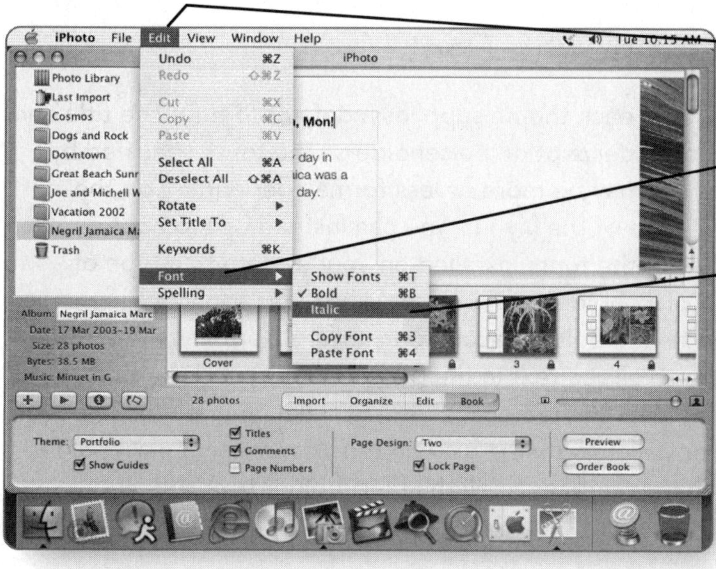


**3.** **Click** on **Edit**. The Edit menu will appear.

**4.** **Point** to **Font**. The Font submenu will appear.

**5.** **Click** on **Bold** or **Italic**. If your choice was previously unchecked, then bold or italics will be applied to the selected text. If your choice was previously checked, then bold or italics will be removed from the selected text.

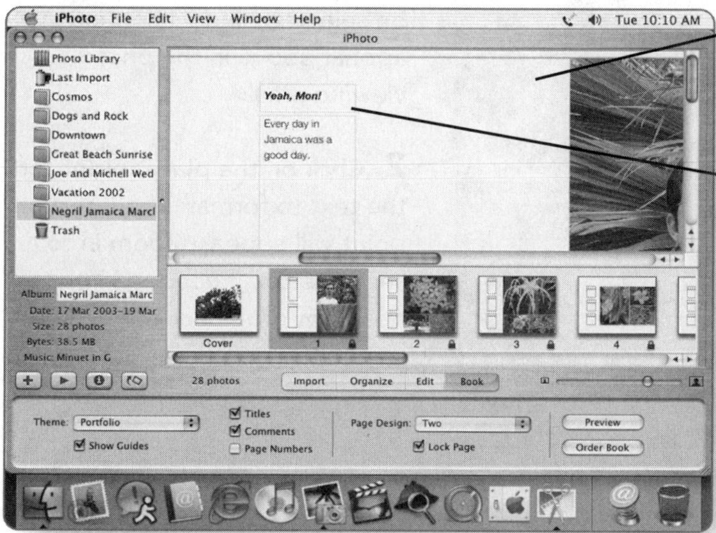


**6.** **Click away from** the **placeholder** (or click another placeholder).

iPhoto will display the new formatting for the text you selected in Step 2. Zoom the page as needed to see the results.

## Changing the Font

By default, each theme supplies a default *font* for the title and comments/description placeholders. The fonts specified by the layout may be more or less formal, depending on the overall tone of the layout. You can instead opt to apply another of the fonts installed on your system to a type of layout placeholder in the book. When you apply bold or italics to the text in a title placeholder, iPhoto 2 applies the same change to all the text in the placeholder and all the title placeholders in the book. Likewise, when you add or remove bold or italics to text in a comments/description placeholder, that change applies to all the placeholder text and all placeholders of that type throughout the book.

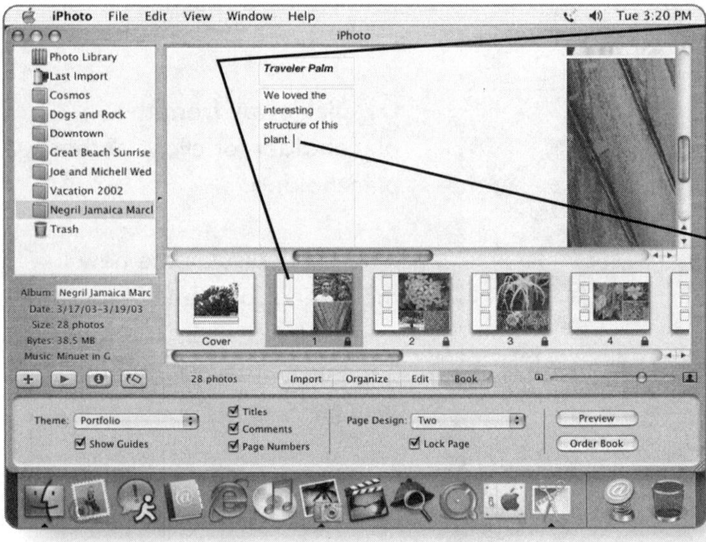


**1.** **Click** on the **page** holding the text to format. The page will be selected, and its contents will appear above in the photo viewing area.

**2.** **Click** on the **placeholder** for the text to format. The insertion point will appear. (Zoom in to see it better, if needed.) You need not drag over the text to select it.

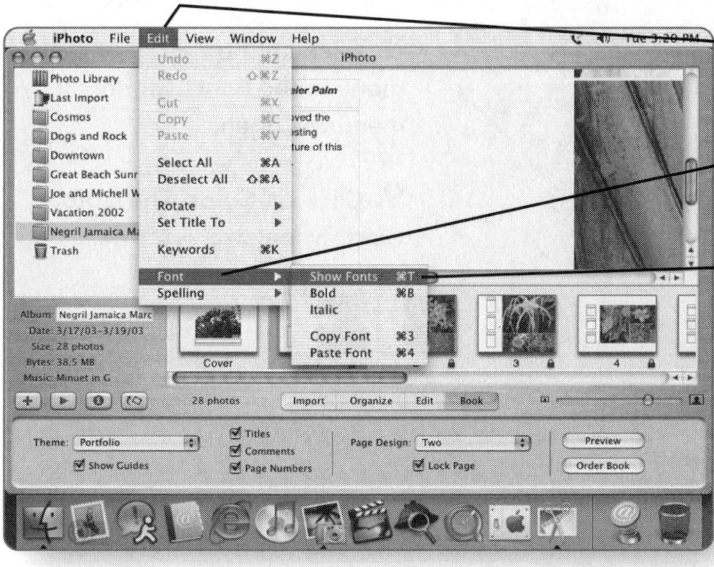


**3. Click** on **Edit**. The Edit menu will appear.

**4. Point** to **Font**. The Font submenu will appear.

**5. Click** on **Show Fonts**. The Fonts window (palette) will open.

## TIP

If you want to see a preview of the current font within the Fonts window, click on the Extras pop-up menu, and then click on Show Preview.

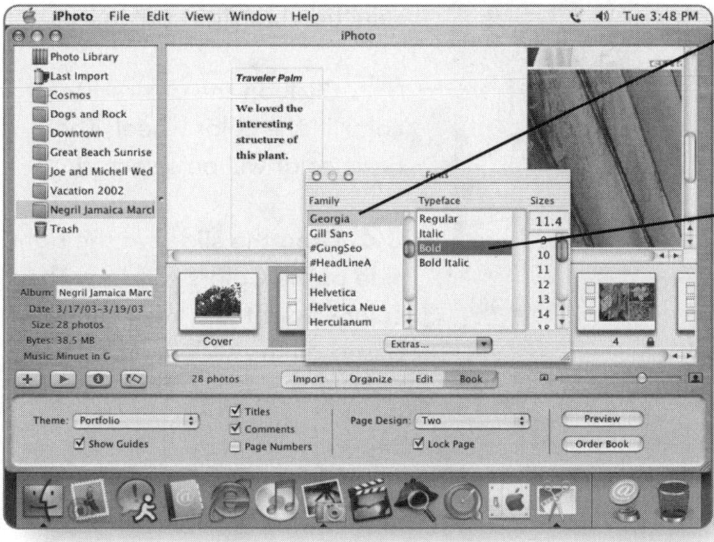


**6. Click** on the **desired font** in the Family list. iPhoto will apply the new font to the text in the placeholder.

**7. Click** on the **desired font style** in the Typeface list. iPhoto will apply the new typeface to the text.

## NOTE

iPhoto prevents you from changing the text size. The text size changes automatically when you zoom the page.

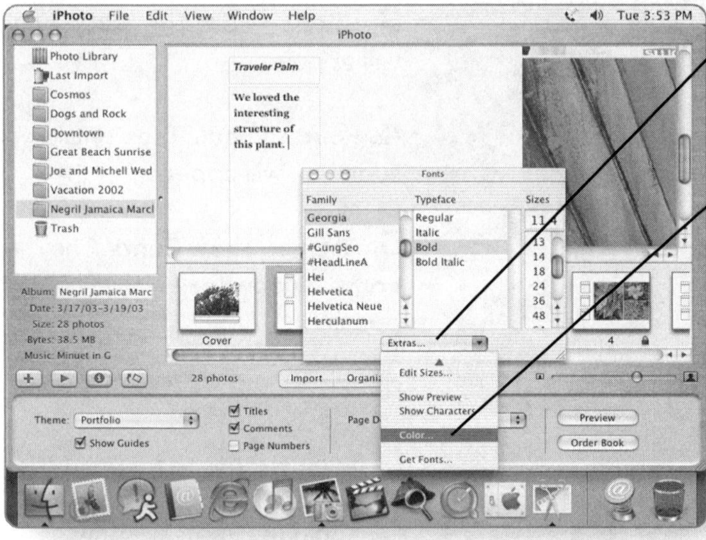


**8. Click** on the **Extras pop-up menu** in the Fonts window. The menu will open.

**9. Click** on **Color**. The Colors window (palette) will open.

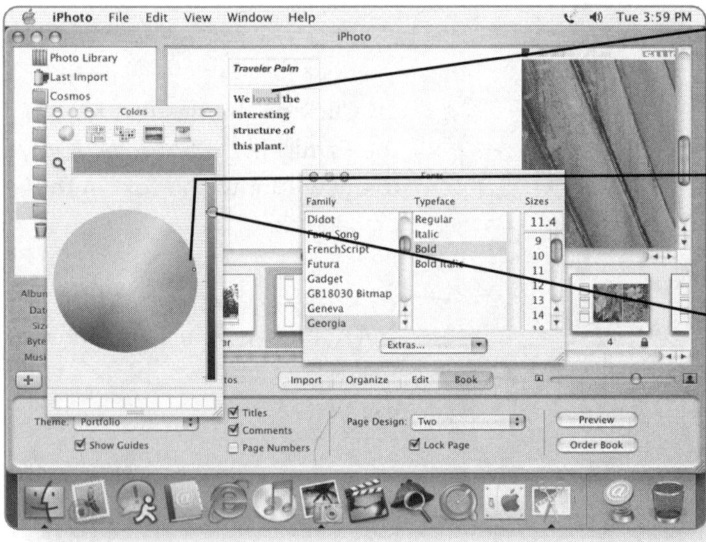


**10.** To change text color, **drag** over the **text to format**. A selection highlight will appear.

**11. Click** on the **desired text color** in the color wheel. The basic color will be selected.

**12. Drag** the **slider** at the right side of the Colors window. The color's brightness will change based on the slider setting you specify.

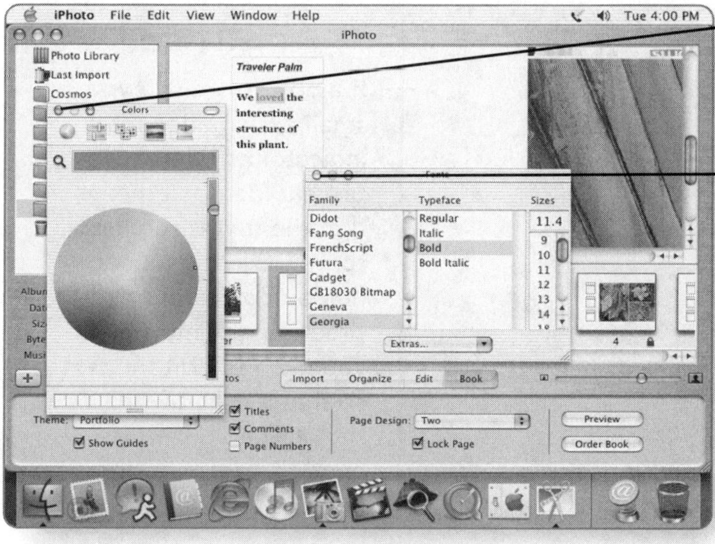

**13.** **Click** on the **close button** for the Colors window. The window will close.

**14.** **Click** on the **close button** for the Fonts window. The window will close.

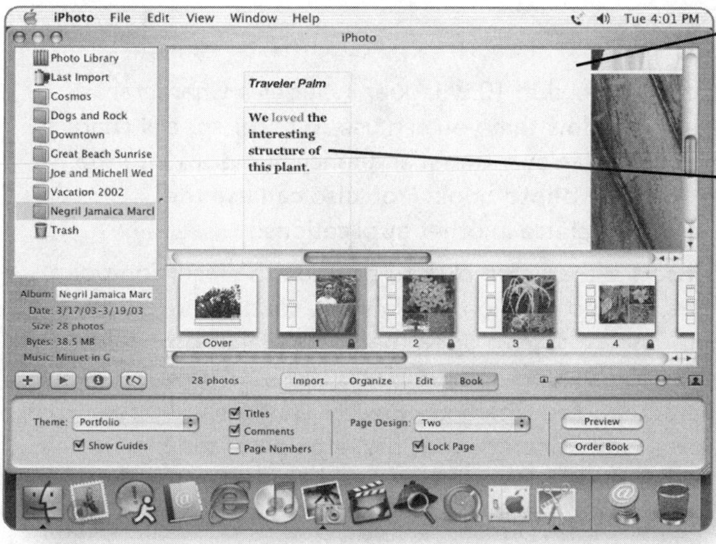

**15.** **Click away from** the **placeholder** (or click another placeholder).

iPhoto will display the new formatting for the text. Zoom the page as needed to see the results.

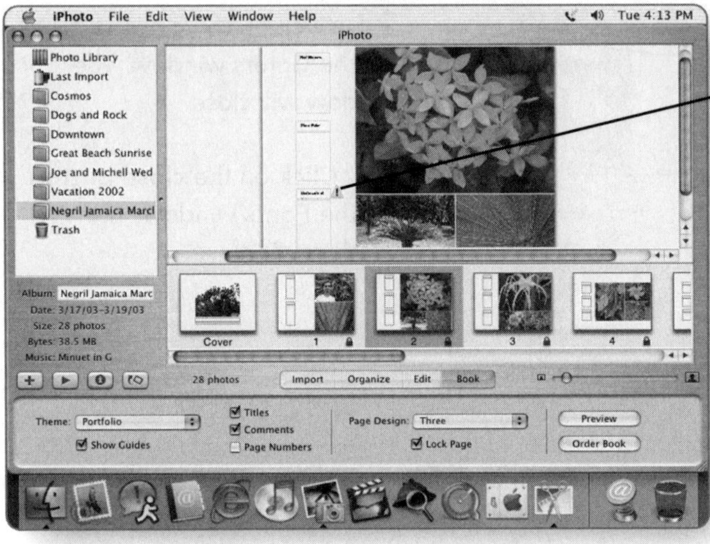


## CAUTION

If a book page shows a small exclamation mark indicator beside a text placeholder, that means that the text is too long to fit within the placeholder. Before printing or ordering a printed book, you need to edit the text so that it will fit within the placeholder, or try another, more condensed (narrow) font.

## ENTERING SPECIAL CHARACTERS

Mac OS X Version 10.2 Jaguar includes a Character Palette window that you can use to enter special characters such as arrows, stars, and fancy numerals into the text on your photo book. (You also can use the Character Palette in other applications!)

To insert a character, click to position the insertion point in the desired location within some text. Choose Edit, Font, Show Fonts to open the Fonts dialog box. Click on the Extras pop-up menu, and click on Show Characters. The Character Palette window will open. Click a symbol category at the left side of the by Category tab, click on the desired symbol at the right, and then click on Insert.

Here you see some symbols inserted into a title placeholder.

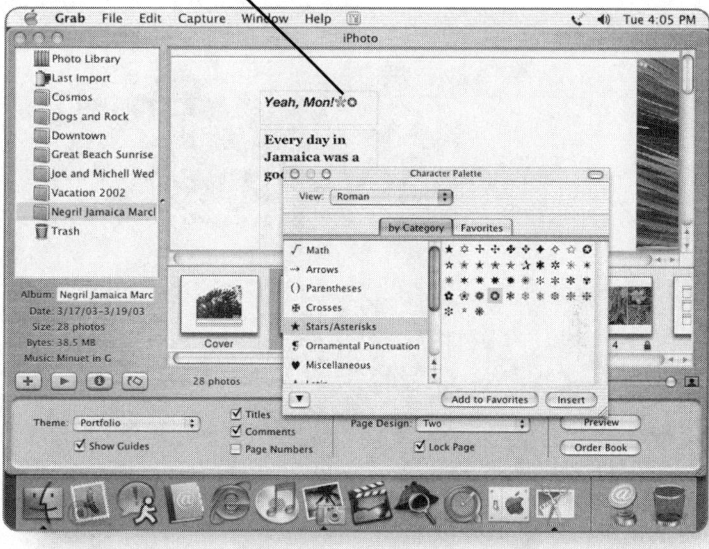


To close the character palette, click its window close button. To remove the character palette's icon from the menu bar (in Finder and other applications), click on its icon in the menu bar, and then click on Customize Menu. In the International panel of System Preferences, click on the Input Menu tab. Clear the check box beside the Character Palette choice at the top of the list. Finally, choose System Preferences, Quit System Preferences to close the System Preferences application.

## Copying a Font

As you've seen, applying a font with the Fonts window changes all of the text in a placeholder. If you want to copy the formatting from one placeholder to the text in another placeholder, you can do so.

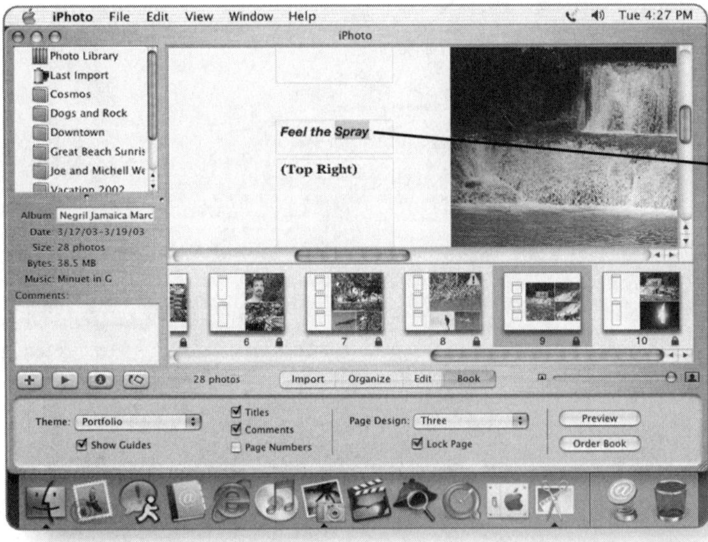


**1. Drag** over the **text** with the formatting to copy. A selection highlight will appear.

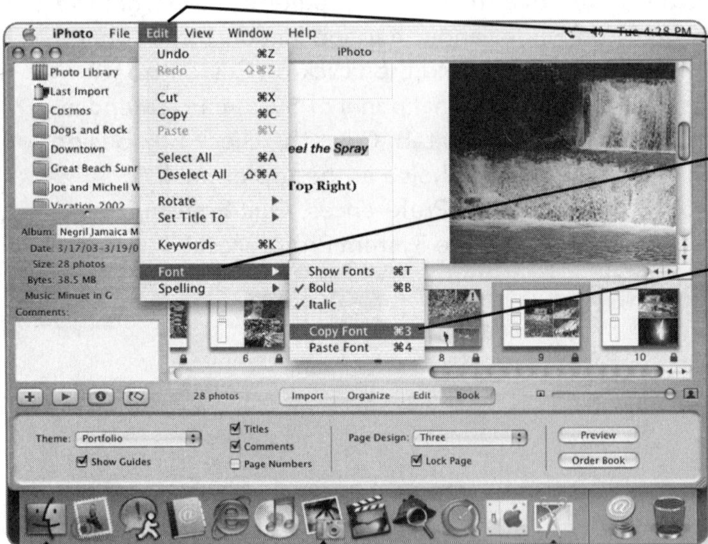


**2. Click** on **Edit**. The Edit menu will appear.

**3. Point** to **Font**. The Font submenu will appear.

**4. Click** on **Copy Font**. iPhoto will copy the font information from the selected text.

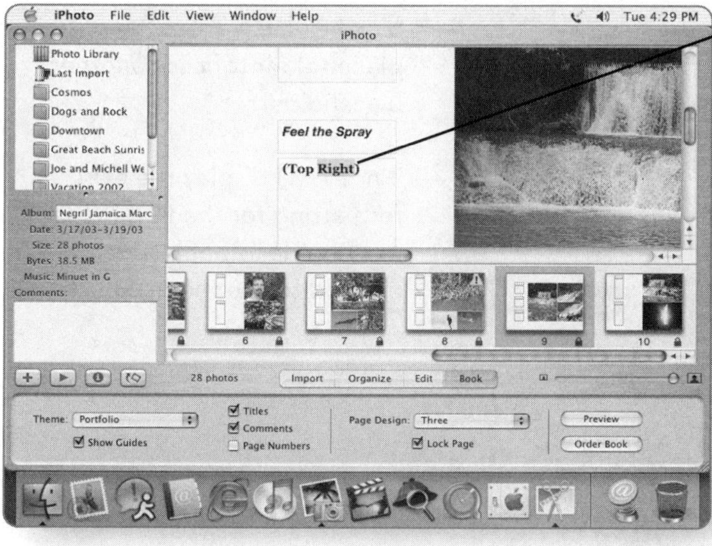

**5. Drag** over **text** in the placeholder to which you want to apply the copied formatting. A selection highlight will appear.

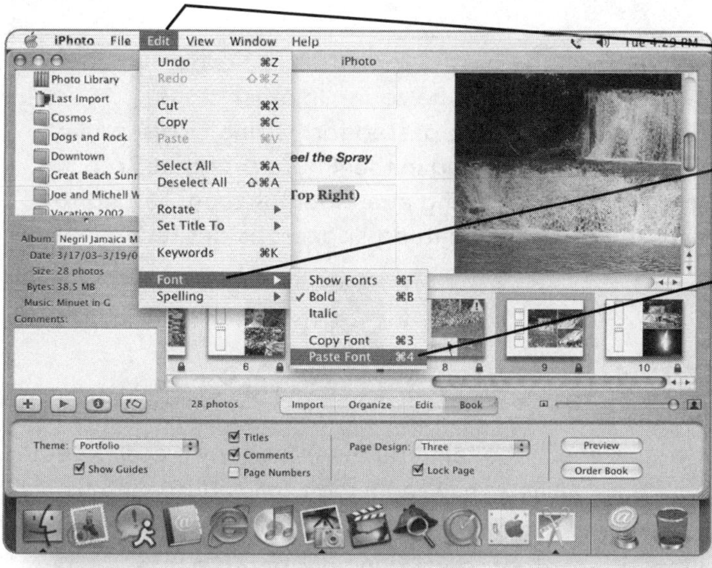

**6. Click** on **Edit**. The Edit menu will appear.

**7. Point** to **Font**. The Font submenu will appear.

**8. Click** on **Paste Font**. iPhoto will copy the font information from the selected text.

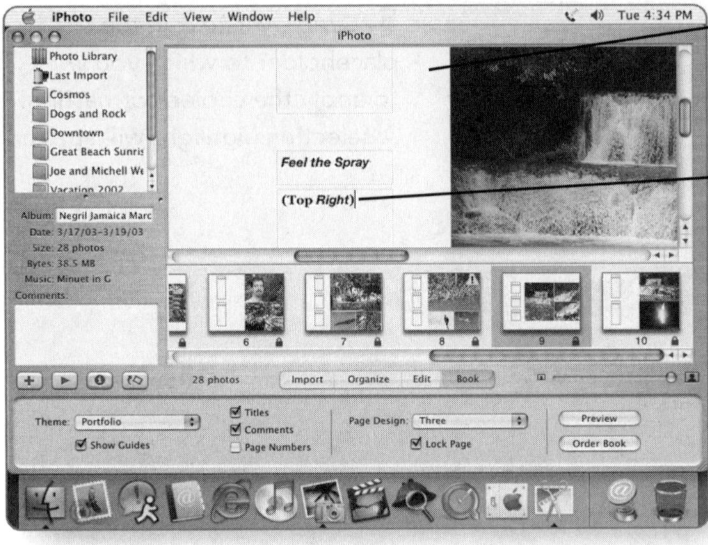

**9. Click away from** the **placeholder** (or click another placeholder).

iPhoto will display the new formatting for the text in the placeholder. Zoom the page as needed to see the results.

### CAUTION

In some cases, the pasted formatting does not appear until you change the page zoom. In other cases, zooming may cause the pasted formatting to disappear, which seems to be a bug in the iPhoto program. Try reapplying the formatting at a different zoom setting to ensure the pasted formatting appears as desired.

# Spell Checking the Text

You can spell check the text you enter into any placeholder in a photo book. While it may seem a bit time consuming to check every placeholder, performing the check will ensure that you put your best foot forward in your photo books—especially if you plan to share copies with friends or colleagues.

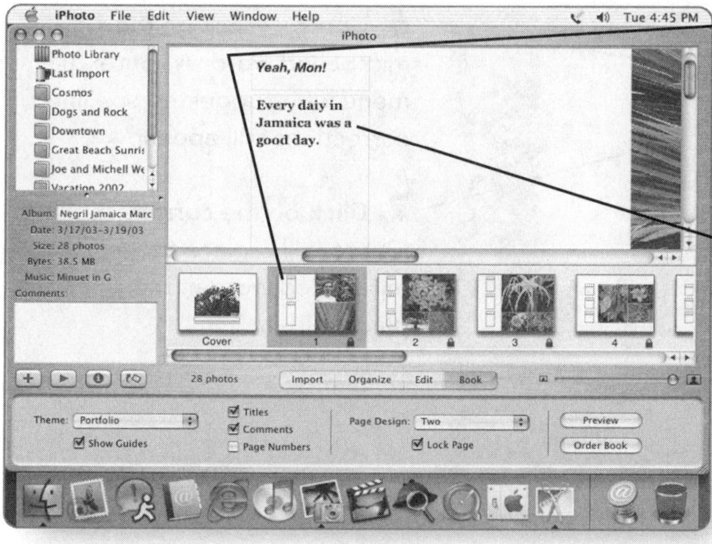


1. **Click** on the **page** holding the text to format. The page will be selected, and its contents will appear above in the photo viewing area.

2. **Click** on the **placeholder** for the text to spell check. The insertion point will appear. (Zoom in to see it better, if needed.)

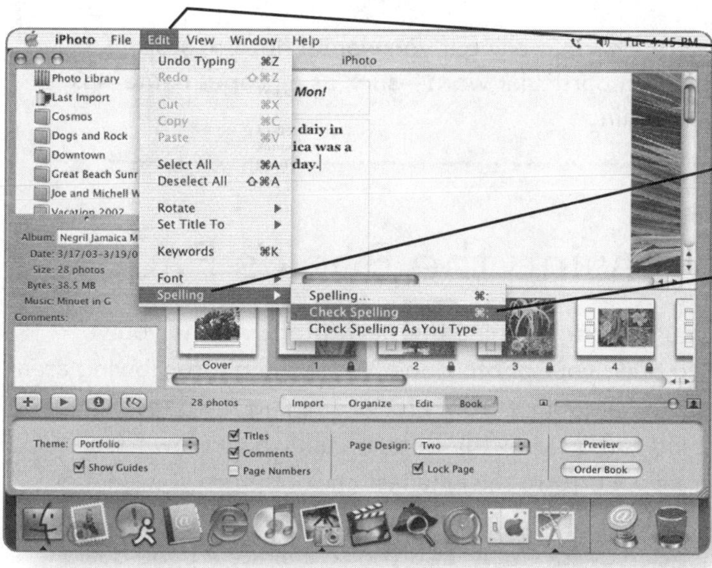


3. **Click** on **Edit**. The Edit menu will appear.

4. **Point** to **Spelling.** The Spelling submenu will appear.

5. **Click** on **Check Spelling**. iPhoto will display a selection highlight and red dotted underline for any word that it suspects is misspelled.

> **TIP**
>
> iPhoto simply beeps when there are no misspelled words.

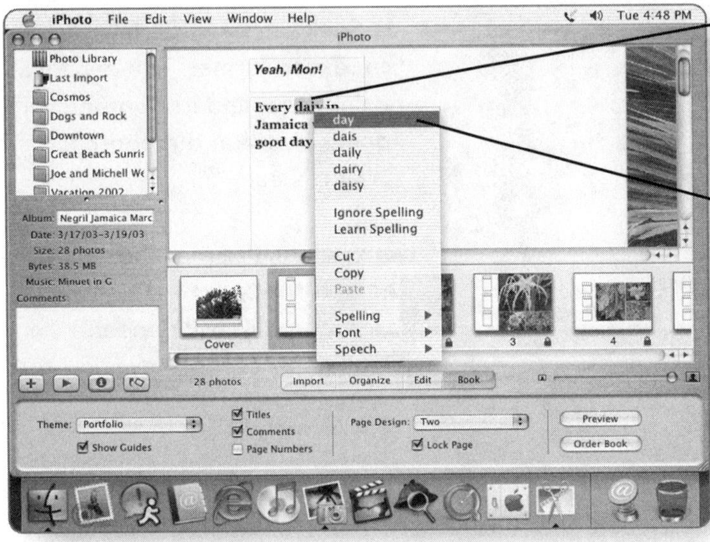


**6. Control+click** on the misspelled word. A contextual menu with suggested spelling corrections will appear.

**7. Click** on the **correct spelling.** iPhoto will replace the misspelled word in the placeholder.

> **TIP**
>
> Click on Learn Spelling if you want iPhoto to stop flagging a particular word—such as a proper name—as a misspelling.

# Previewing the Book's Pages

Now you can begin to see the payoff for the time you've taken to build your photo book. While the photo viewing area allows a fair amount of room for examining the pages in your book, you can preview the book in its own window for a better view. Perform this one last check before you print a book or order a printed copy. Sometimes, seeing the pages in another perspective may lead you to change a page design, the font you've specified for text, or some other key design element.

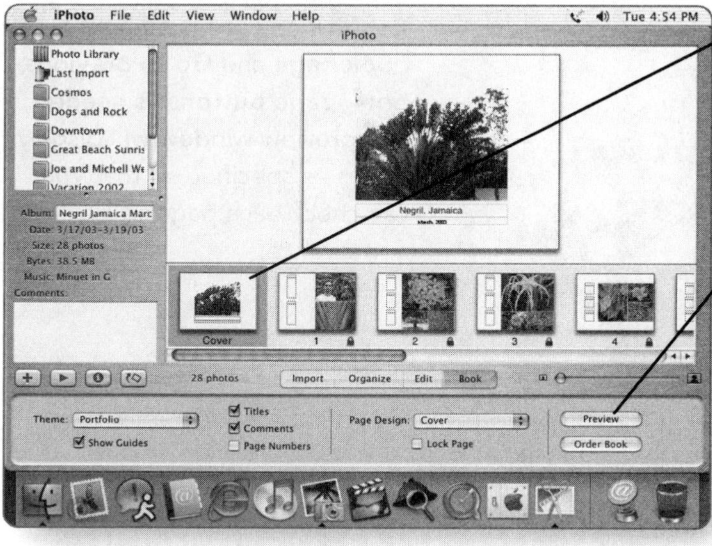


**1.** **Click** on the **Cover thumbnail**. The cover will be selected, so that you can start previewing the book from the beginning.

**2.** **Click** on **Preview** at the bottom of the Book pane. The preview will appear in its own window.

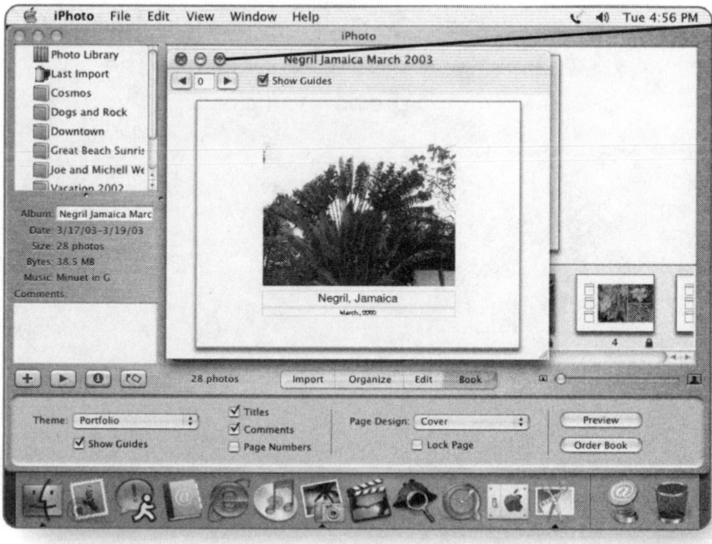


**3.** **Click** on the window **zoom button**. The preview window will increase in size so that you can see your book more clearly.

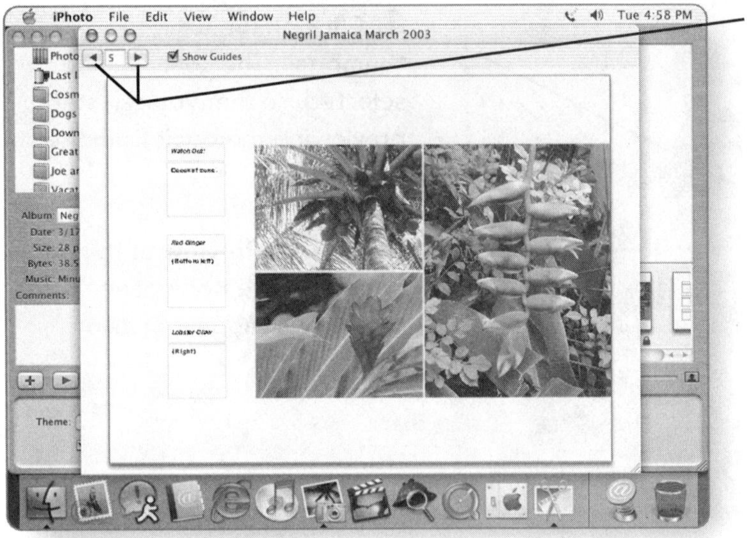

**4. Click** on the **Go to next book page** and **Go to previous book page buttons** as needed. The preview window will display pages as specified so that you can check each page's appearance.

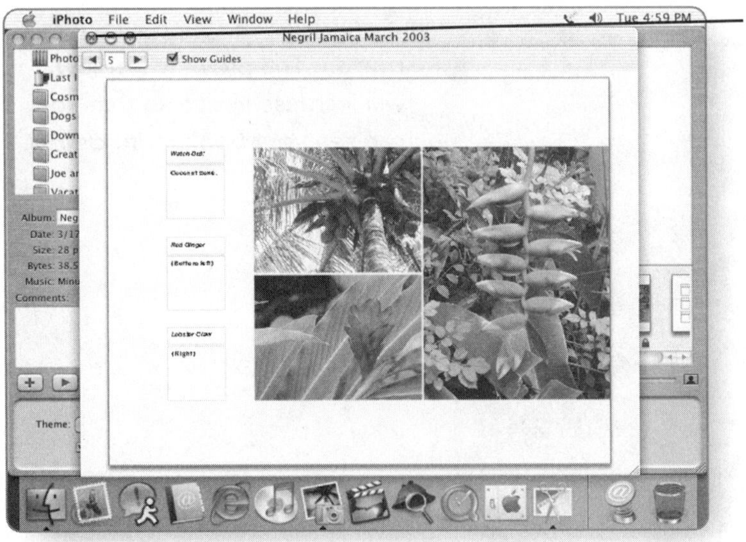

**5. Click** on the **close button** for the preview window. The preview will close.

# 8

# Printing Your Book Yourself

In some applications, printing can be as easy as clicking on a toolbar icon. While printing an iPhoto book doesn't require an engineering degree, you'll benefit from perusing this chapter. It reviews the variety of print settings that may come into play when you print a photo book, so that you can end up with a quality result. In this chapter, you will learn how to:

- Work with page setup choices.
- Choose a number of different print settings, such as the selected printer or number of copies.
- Preview and print the photo book.
- Save printing presets.
- Save a photo book as a .PDF file for printing and sharing.

# Changing the Page Setup

In the last chapter, you learned how to organize the photos in an album into an attractive book. At the conclusion of the chapter, you previewed the book onscreen. Once you're satisfied with that preview, you can prepare to print your photo book. The Mac OS X operating system offers a variety of settings that you can use to fine tune each print job. While you may be in a hurry to hold the final printout, keep in mind that quality printing supplies—such as inkjet paper and ink cartridges—can be costly, so you want to take your time and set up the print job correctly.

To start, use the Print Setup dialog box. There, you can change the orientation, choose a paper size, and scale the printout.

> **NOTE**
>
> Again, perform all of the operations in this chapter in the Book pane (view) in iPhoto because you are printing a full book. Select the album that you want to print as a book, and then click on the Book button below the photo viewing area to display the Book pane or view. Chapter 10, "Making and Ordering Prints and More," explains how to print single photos in a variety of formats.

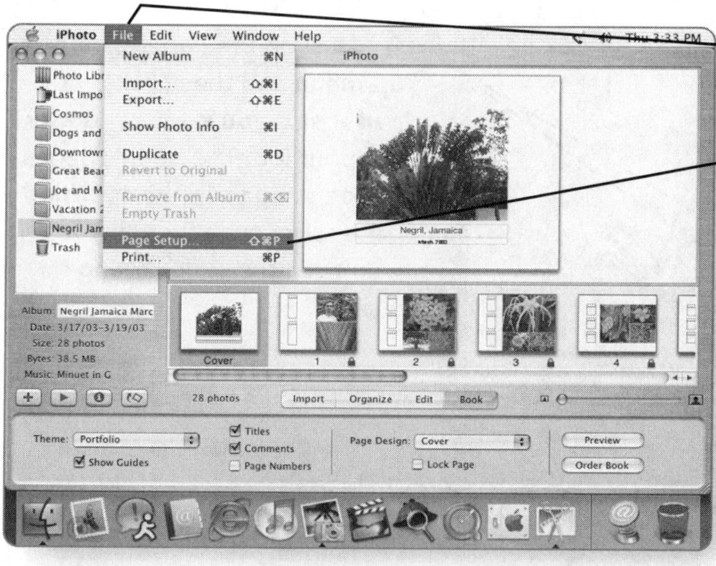


**1.** **Click** on **File**. The File menu will appear.

**2.** **Click** on **Page Setup**. The Page Setup dialog box will open.

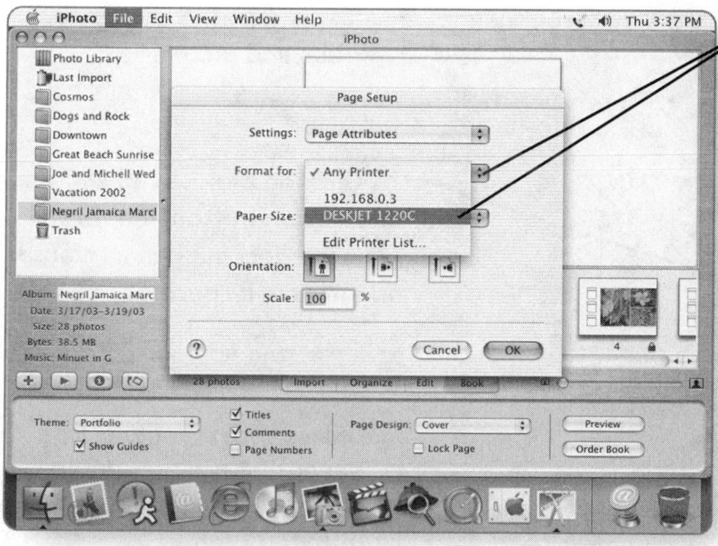


**3.** **Click** on the **Format for pop-up menu** and then **click** on the **printer you want** to use for the print job. The Page Setup dialog box will display your choice.

> **TIP**
>
> If you do not see the desired printer in the Format for pop-up menu, you may not have the printer installed. To install a printer, click on the Edit Printer List choice in the Format for pop-up menu. (Connect the printer and turn it on to install it.)

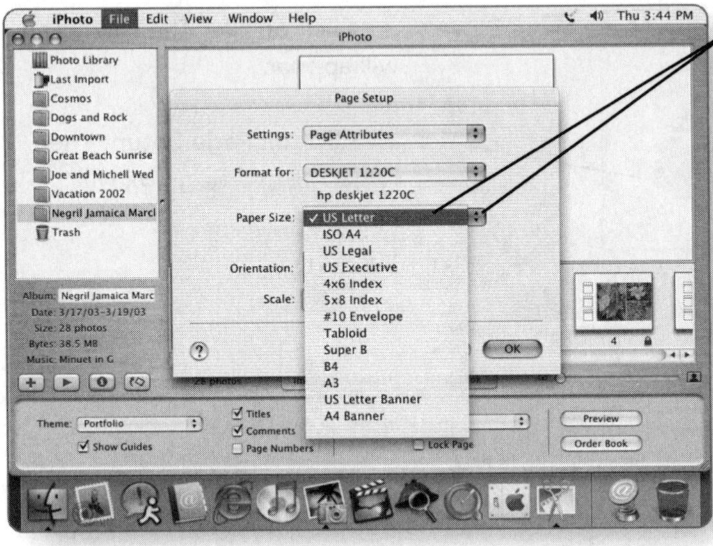


**4. Click** on the **Paper Size pop-up menu** and then **click** on the **paper size you want** to use for the print job. The book's pages will be sized to fit the specified paper size, even though you won't see the scale setting change.

## CAUTION

The 4 × 6 Index and 5 × 8 Index sizes are not for printing individual images. Making your own photo prints requires a different process, as described in Chapter 10, "Making and Ordering Prints and More."

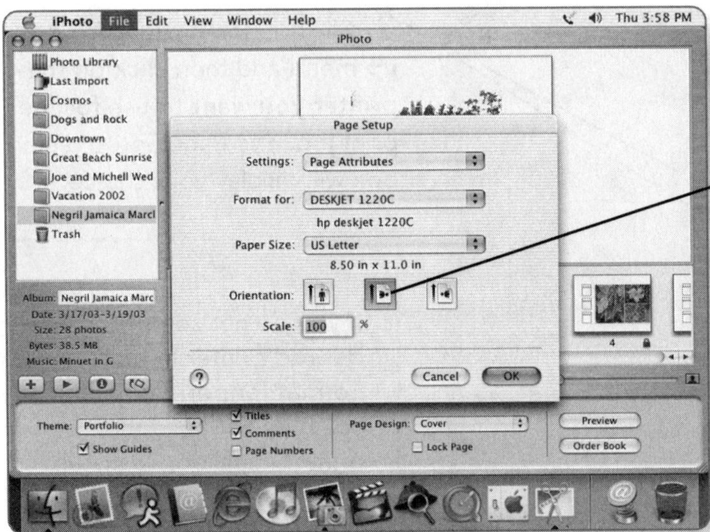


**5. Click** on the desired **orientation button**. iPhoto will print the document in a rotated orientation, if specified.

## TIP

Unless you're printing on paper that has preprinted elements (like letterhead) or perforations, you typically do not need to change the print orientation for a photo book.

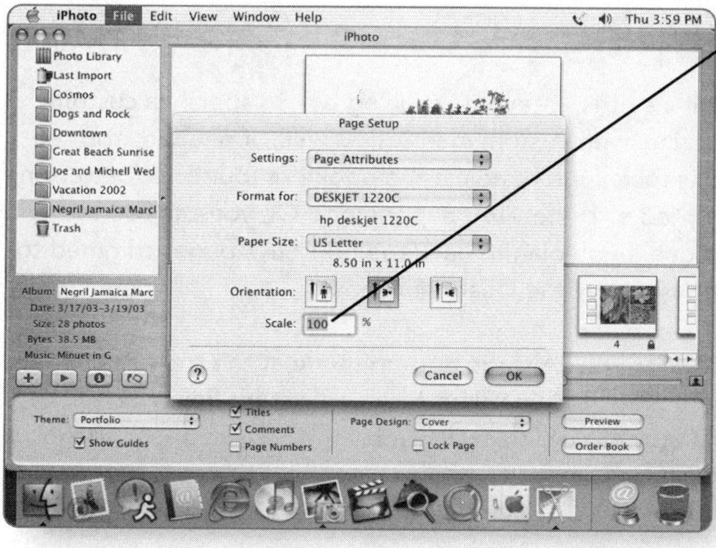


**6. Edit** the **Scale setting,** if necessary. iPhoto will print the document with the specified scaling.

## TIP

Reducing the Scale setting allows for more white space around the images on the page. However, don't reduce the Scale setting if you want the images to bleed off the edge of the page, assuming your printer supports bleeds.

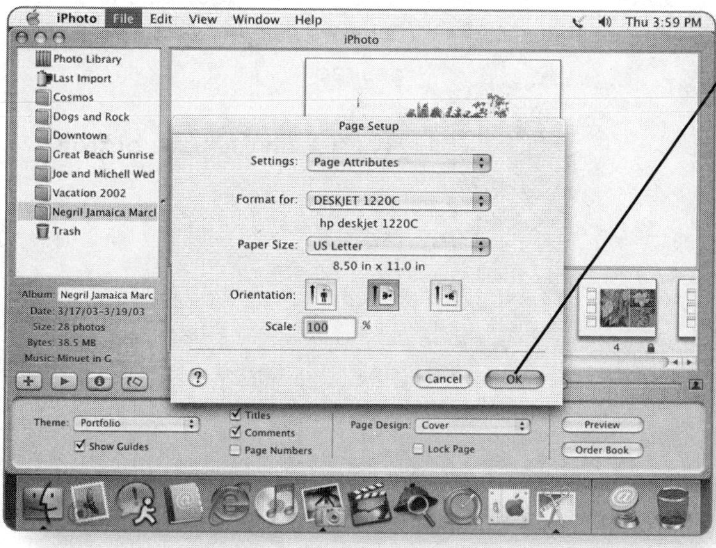


**7. Click** on **OK**. Your Page Setup choices will be applied to the document.

# Creating a Custom Paper Size

You can use the Page Setup dialog box to specify a custom paper size (with custom margins, as well), if needed. You can use this technique to adjust the book printout to fit better on preprinted or perforated paper stock. Or, you can use this technique if you plan to have the printout's pages trimmed to a special size by the local print shop.

**1. Click** on the **Settings pop-up menu** at the top of the Page Setup dialog box, and then **click** on **Custom Paper Size**. The Page Setup dialog box will display the custom paper size choices.

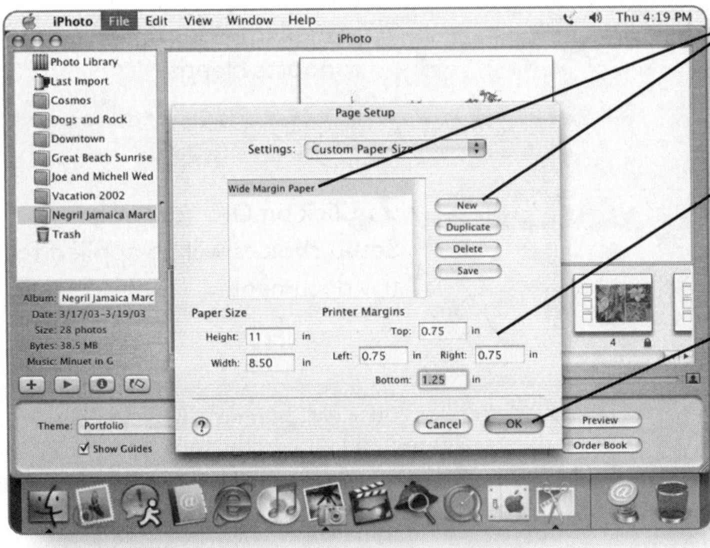


**2. Click** on the **New button, type** a **name** for the paper size, and then **press Return**.

**3. Edit** the **Paper Size** and **Printer Margins settings** as desired.

**4. Click** on the **Save button**.

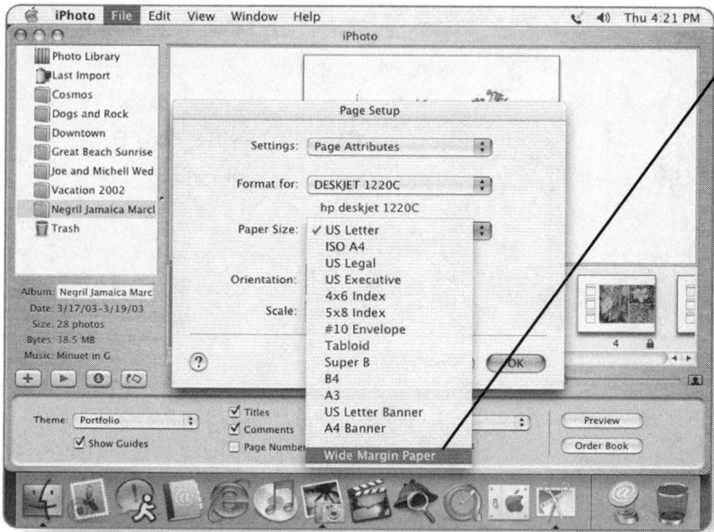


**5. Click** on the **Settings pop-up menu** at the top of the Page Setup dialog box, and then **click** on **Page Attributes**. You can then choose your custom paper size from the Paper Size pop-up menu.

# Changing Print Settings

In addition to choosing the page settings found in the Page Setup dialog box, you can also change a variety of print settings in the Print dialog box before you send the job to the printer. Follow these steps to open the Print dialog box, choose a printer, and display additional print options. The remainder of this section details the settings available in each of the print settings categories. The available categories of advanced printing options will vary depending on the capabilities of your printer.

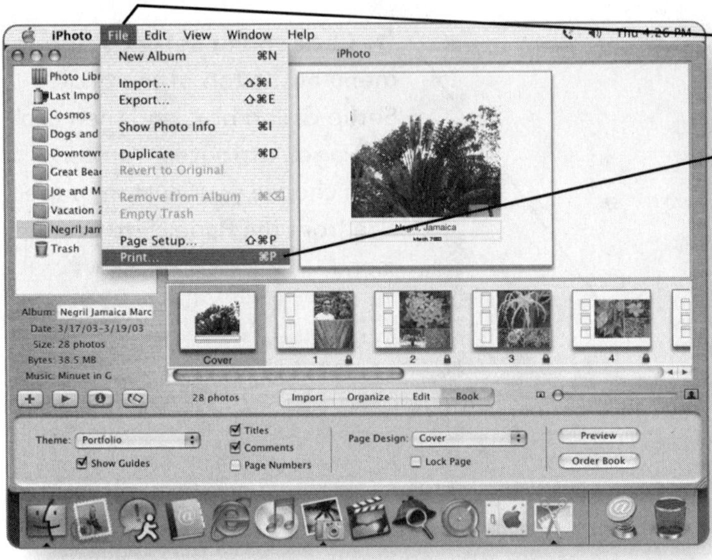

**1. Click** on **File**. The File menu will appear.

**2. Click** on **Print**. The Print dialog box will open.

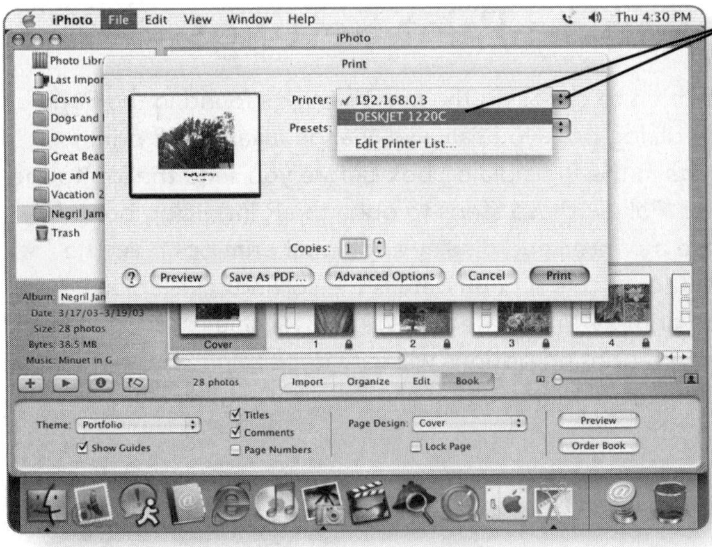

**3. Click** on the **Printer pop-up menu** and then **click** on the **printer** to use for the print job. (This should be the same printer that you chose in the Page Setup dialog box.) The Print dialog box will display your choice.

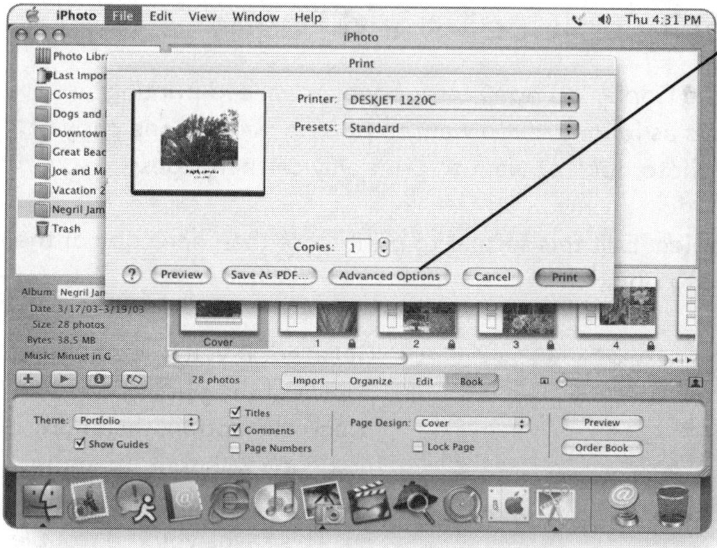

**4.** **Click** on **Advanced Options**. The Print dialog box will adjust to include the advanced printing options.

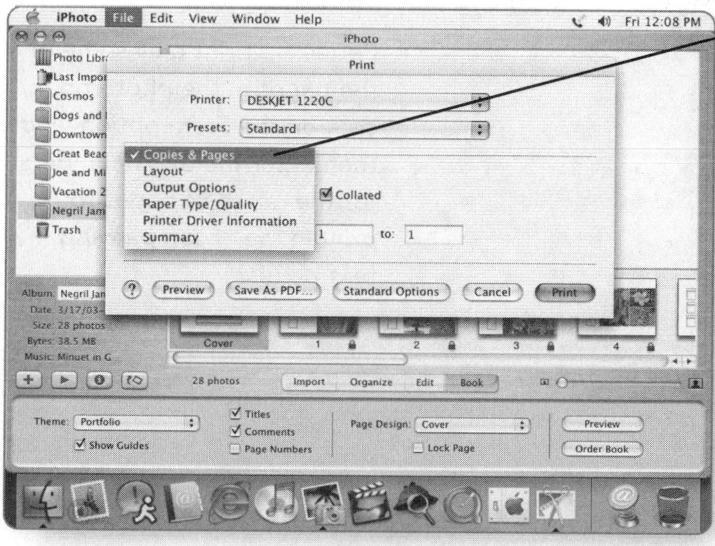

**5.** **Click** on the **category pop-up menu** at the center left of the dialog box, and then **click** on the **desired category**. The available advanced printing option categories for your printer will appear.

## Specifying Copies and Pages

Use the Copies & Pages category of advanced printing options as follows if you want to print more than one copy of your photo book or want to print only certain pages:

- **Copies.** Edit this setting to print more than one copy of the photo book.

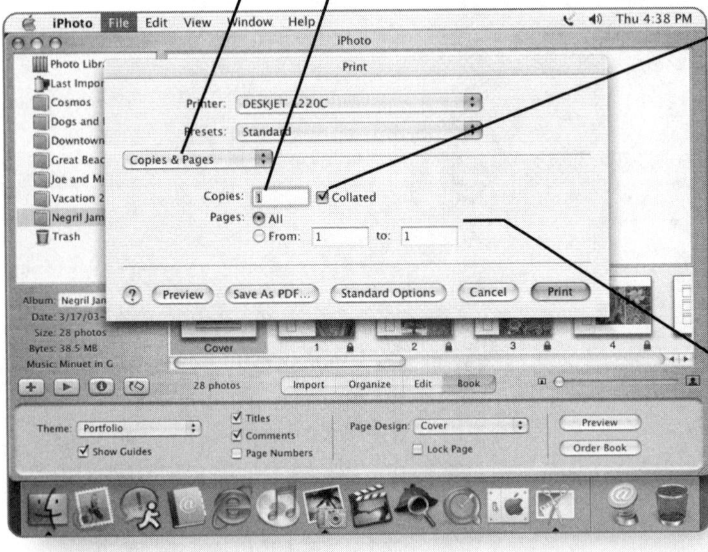


- **Collated.** If you print multiple copies of the photo book and check this option, the entire first copy will print, then the entire second copy, and so on. This saves you the trouble of having to separate the pages for each copy after printing.
- **Pages.** To print only some of the pages in the photo book, click on the From option, and then enter the page numbers for the range of pages to print in the accompanying text boxes.

## Adjusting the Layout

If your printer supports special capabilities such as printing multiple document pages on each piece of paper, use the Layout category of advanced printing options to choose the desired settings for your print job:

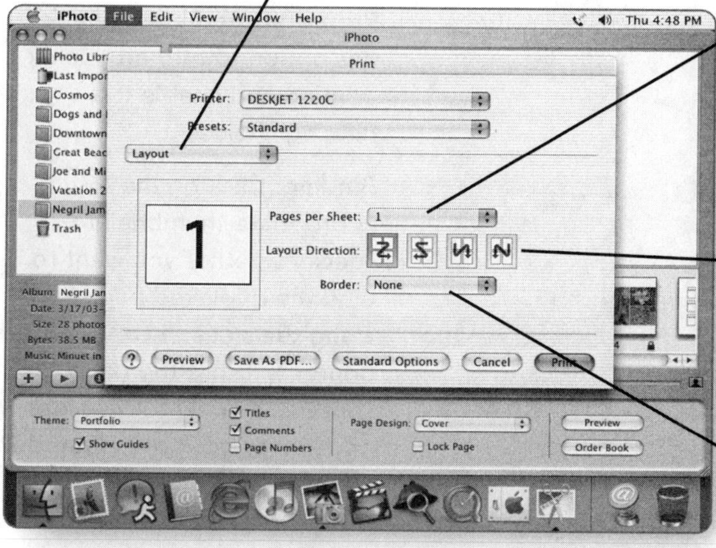


- **Pages per Sheet.** Open this pop-up menu and click on the number of book pages to print on each sheet of paper: 1, 2, 4, 6, 9, or 16 pages per sheet.
- **Layout Direction.** Click on one of the thumbnails here to control the order in which the printer prints multiple pages on each sheet of paper.
- **Border.** If you want to include a border around each book page, whether or not you're printing multiple pages per sheet, choose the desired border style from this pop-up menu.

## Printing Duplex Pages

Some printers support *duplex printing*—printing on both sides of each sheet. If the printer you've selected supports duplex printing, use the following advanced printing options to enable and control duplex printing:

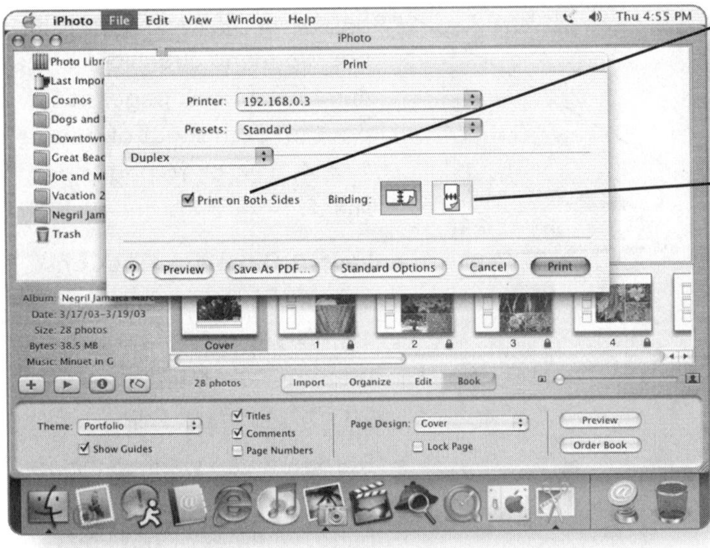


- **Print on Both Sides.** Check this option to turn on duplex printing and enable the Binding choices.
- **Binding.** Click on the appropriate thumbnail to specify whether you want to bind the duplexed pages along the sides or top. Your printer will shift the page contents slightly to the sides or down to accommodate the selected binding style.

> **NOTE**
>
> Unless your printer has a special duplex tray or feeder, you will have to print one side of the pages, turn them over, and then print the other side when prompted. This can be tricky, because it requires that you rotate the pages in a certain way for the second print pass. Consult the printer's documentation for more help on using it for duplex printing.

## Specifying Print Quality, Paper Feed, and More

The category of settings that controls the quality of a print job, specified paper tray, and so on will use a different name, depending on the selected printer. For example, for my laser (black and white) printer, this category is called Image Quality. When I select my color inkjet printer to print a book, the category becomes Paper Type/Quality. In addition, the settings in the category vary dramatically depending on the selected printer. The following examples enable you to review some of the settings that may be available for your printer.

> **NOTE**
>
> The available settings also depend somewhat on how well Mac OS X supports your printer. Check the Apple Web site and the Web site for your printer manufacturer to ensure you have the latest drivers for running your printer under Mac OS X. This ensures that the best control possible will be available to you when you use the printer under Mac OS X.

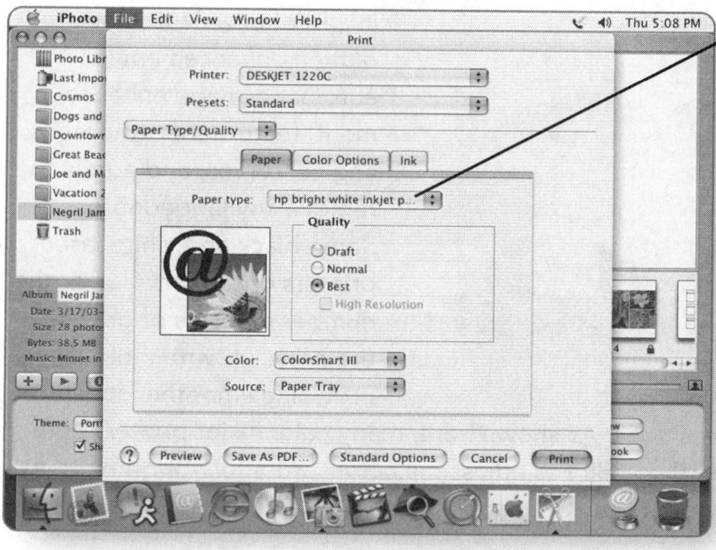


- **Paper type.** If your printer offers a pop-up menu for choosing a paper type, be sure to make the appropriate choice. Inkjet printers will automatically adjust the amount of ink applied to best saturate the selected paper type.

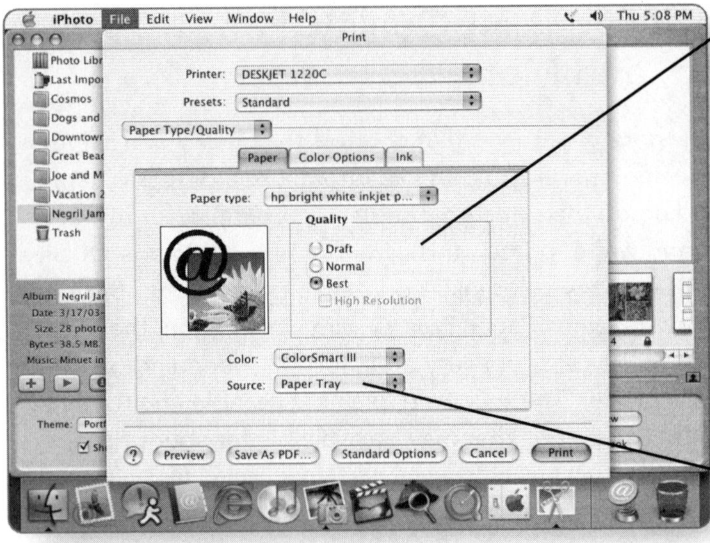


- **Quality or resolution.** Choose the desired print quality setting from among the choices presented. If your printer instead presents a *resolution* choice, note that a higher resolution setting (with a larger *dpi* number) results in a higher-quality printout. Keep in mind that a better quality printout also requires longer to print.
- **Paper source or tray.** If you've placed the paper for the print job in a particular tray or feeder, be sure to choose the appropriate location.

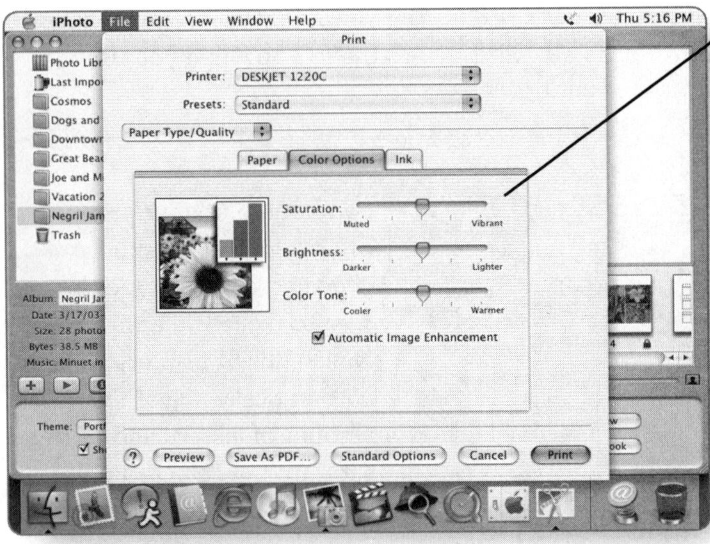


- **Color or tone options.** Some printers offer settings for fine-tuning image appearance during printing. For example, many printers (both laser and inkjet) offer an *automatic resolution enhancement* (or automatic image enhancement) feature that smoothes angles, curves, and edges to remove any jaggedness. Some black and white laser printers offer control over the number of levels of gray in the printout, with more levels providing smoother tonal transitions. As shown here, many color inkjet printers give you the ability to adjust the color saturation, brightness, or tone (warm versus cool) of the printed images.

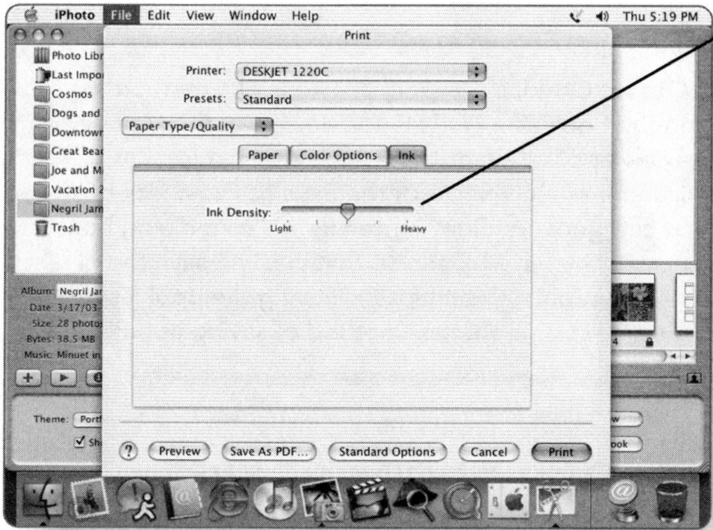


- **Ink or toner coverage.** For most printers, you can adjust the amount of ink or toner used for the printout. For example, my laser printer offers an automated feature for conserving toner. Note that uncoated (non-glossy or non-photo) papers typically have a more porous surface, and require more inkjet ink for satisfactory results.

> **TIP**
>
> If you have any doubts about the printing settings you've chosen, print a single page of the photo book as a test. Because photo book printouts can take several minutes, a faster test will save you time and supplies.

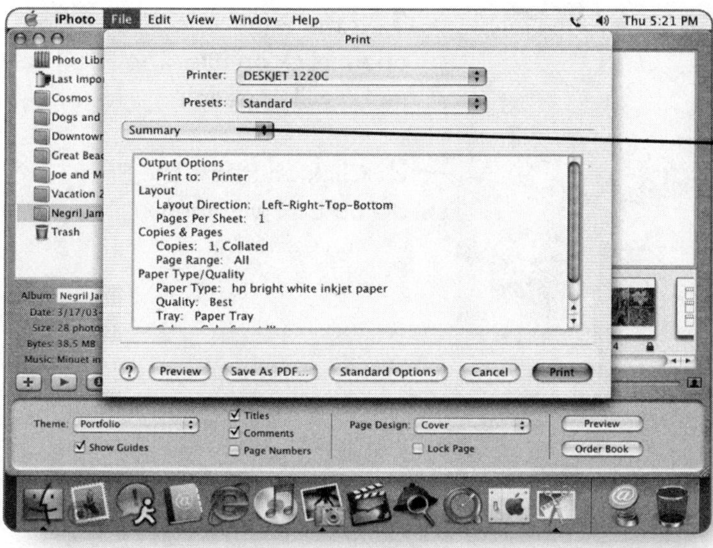


## Viewing Summary Information

Rather than reviewing each category of advanced printing settings, you can check the Summary category to check your choices one last time before you send the job to the printer.

> **NOTE**
>
> The Output Options category provides one method for saving the book as a *PDF* file for viewing in the Mac OS X Preview application or the Adobe Acrobat Reader application. When you check the Save as File check box in that category, the Print button in the Print dialog box changes to the Save button so that you can save the file. The final section in this chapter, "Saving the Book as a PDF File," explains another method of saving as a PDF.

# Printing the Book at Last

No need to hold back any longer. It's time to print your photo book.

> **TIP**
>
> Don't forget to verify the checked options at the bottom of the Book pane to make sure you've checked Titles, Comments, and/or Page Numbers as needed.

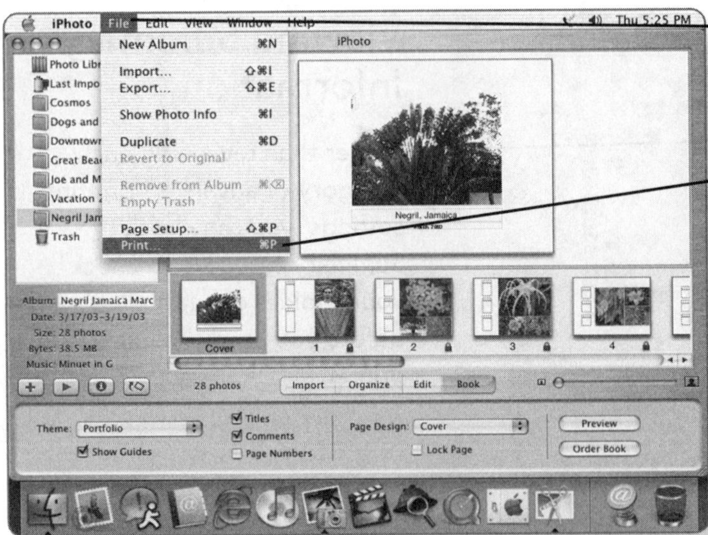


**1.** If the Print dialog box is not open, **click** on **File**. The File menu will appear.

**2. Click** on **Print**. The Print dialog box will open.

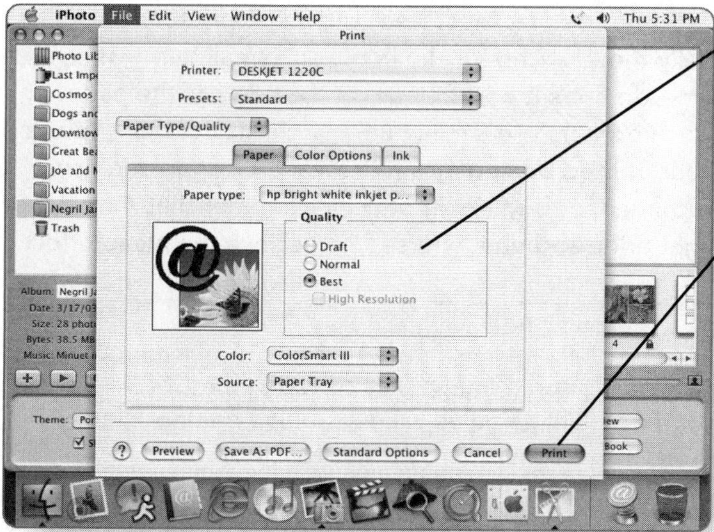


**3. Choose print settings** as described in the previous section. The settings will be used for the print job.

**4. Click** on **Print**. The Print dialog box will close, and the Mac OS X Print Manager will send the book to the specified printer.

Processing a print job, sending it to the printer, and the actual printing may take several minutes, depending on the number of pages and images in the book, the amount of memory in your system, the print settings you chose, and your printer's speed. Grab a cup of coffee while you wait for the results. Don't worry about the caffeine. The real jolt will come from how great your book looks!

> **NOTE**
>
> The Preview button in the Print dialog box opens the book in the Mac OS X Preview application so that you can review the pages, or print from that application, instead. The Preview application does not preview unusual print settings, such as printing multiple book pages per sheet of paper, so a print job like that may require a little trial and error.

One last item to note. Most laser and inkjet printers—especially those priced for the home and small business markets—do not support bleeds off the edge of the page. Most such printers use a minimum margin size of .25". You can take your printed book pages to a local print shop and have them trimmed, or buy a craft or paper trimmer that runs along a straight edge and do it yourself, to achieve the bleed effect.

**CAUTION**

iPhoto cannot print image files stored in the *CMYK color* mode. So, if you've used an image editing application to convert image files to CMYK color for professional printing, you'll need to convert them back to RGB color before importing them into iPhoto.

## Saving and Choosing Printing Presets

If you use certain advanced printing options frequently, you can save those choices as a printing *preset*. Then, rather than having to choose the desired group of print settings for a print job, you can simply select the preset. For example, if you like to print your books with two pages per sheet, with a single line border around each page, and with certain color settings, you can save that collection of settings as a preset called "Two Up." Here's how to save and choose a printing preset.

**NOTE**

The print drivers for some printers may include printing presets that will appear in the Presets pop-up menu of the Print dialog box.

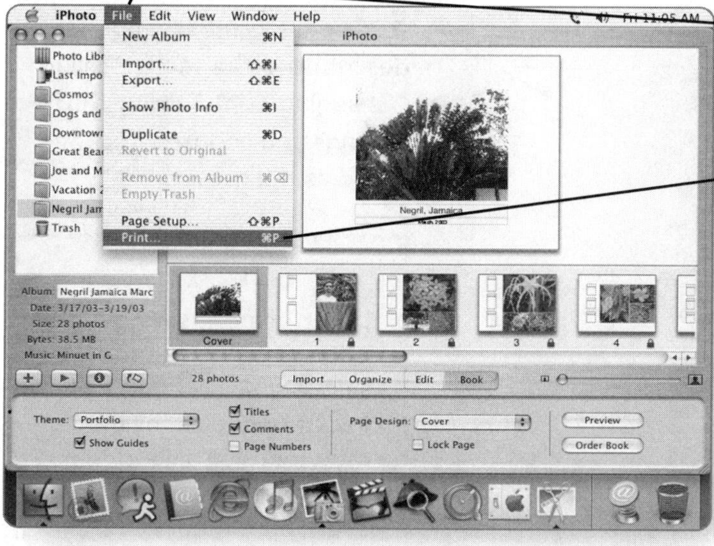

**1.** If the Print dialog box is not open, **click** on **File**. The File menu will appear.

**2. Click** on **Print**. The Print dialog box will open.

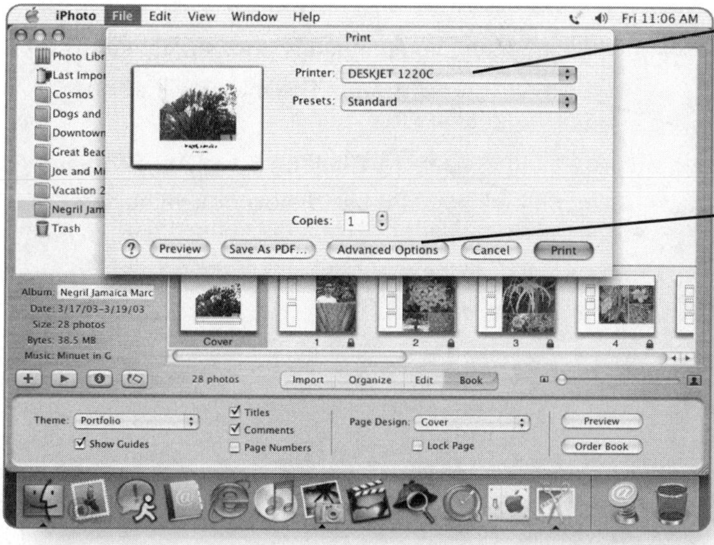

**3. Choose** the **desired printer** from the Printer pop-up menu. The printer will become the selected printer.

**4. Click** on **Advanced Options**. The Print dialog box will adjust to include the advanced printing options for the selected printer.

**NOTE**

Step 3 is necessary to ensure all the desired advanced printing options will be available. As is indicated later, you need to select both the desired printer and preset for each print job using a preset.

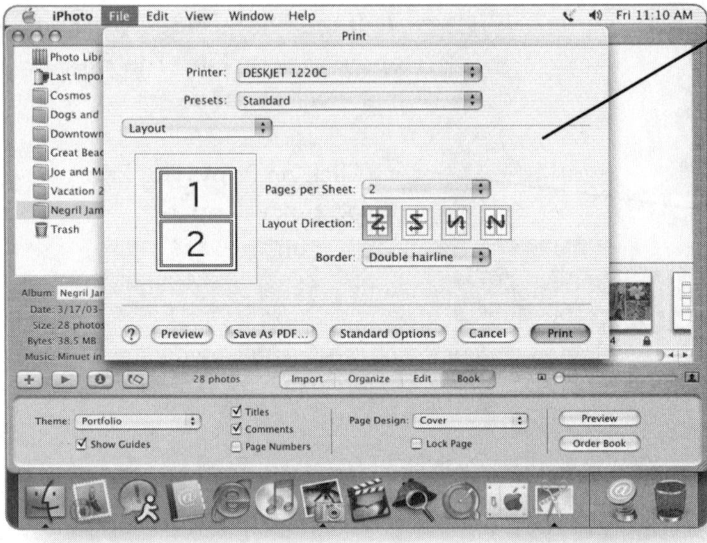


**5. Choose print settings** as described in the section called "Changing Print Settings." The settings you choose will be saved as the preset.

> **NOTE**
>
> Unfortunately, saving printing presets does not save a specified range of pages or copies for the print job. You'll need to choose those settings for every print job, even if you apply a preset.

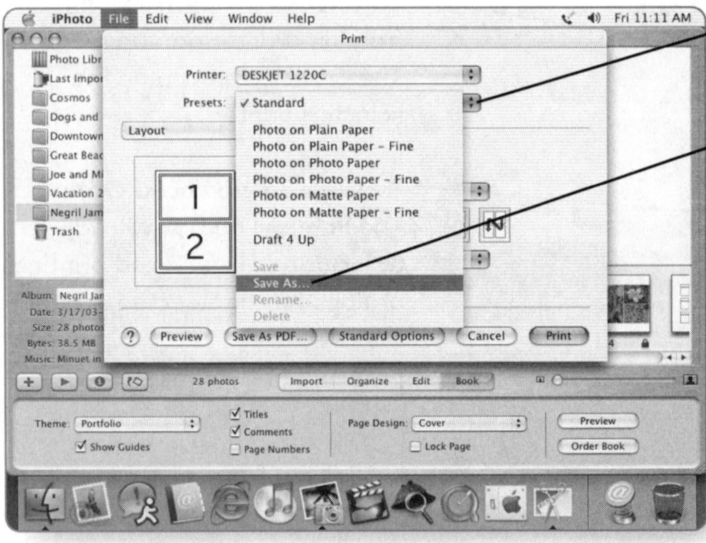


**6. Click** on the **Presets pop-up menu.** The menu will appear.

**7. Click** on **Save As.** The Save Preset dialog box will open.

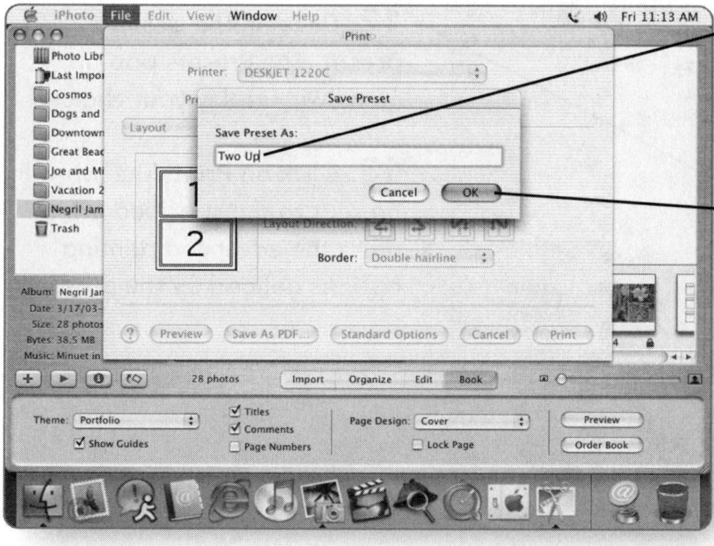


**8. Type** a **name for the preset** in the Save Preset As text box. The name will replace the suggested text.

**9. Click** on **OK**. The Save Preset dialog box will close, and the new preset will be added to the Presets pop-up menu in the Print dialog box. The preset will be selected for the current print job.

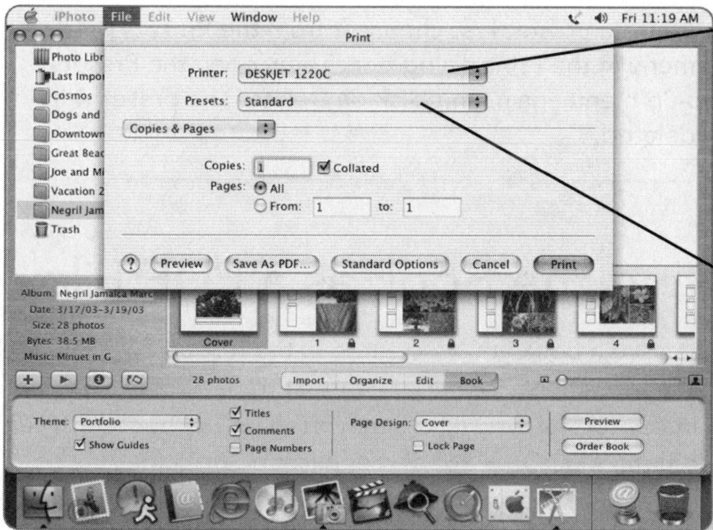


**10.** To select a preset for the current print job, first **choose** the **desired printer** from the Printer pop-up menu. The printer will become the selected printer.

**11. Click** on the **Presets pop-up menu** in the Print dialog box. The menu will appear.

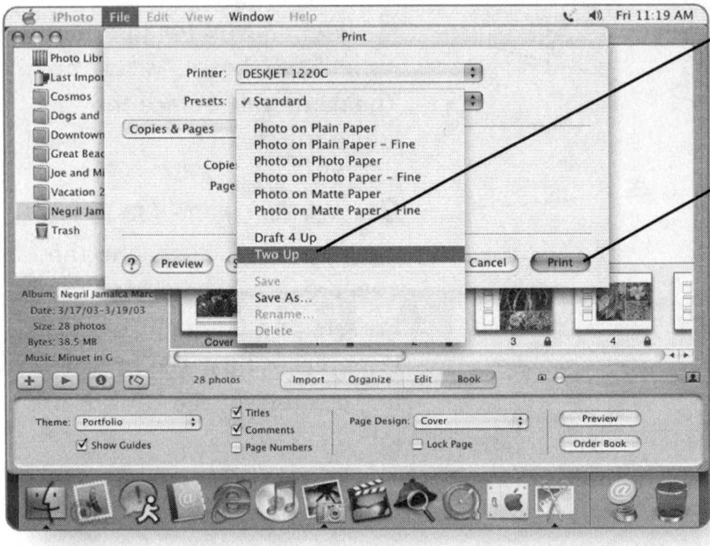


**12. Click** on the **desired preset**. The Presets pop-up menu will display your choice.

**13. Click** on **Print**. The job will be sent to the specified printer using the advanced printing options defined by the preset.

> **NOTE**
>
> To delete a preset, first choose it from the Presets pop-up menu in the Print dialog box. Then, open the Presets pop-up menu again, and click on Delete. The preset will be deleted.

# Saving the Book as a PDF File

You can save a book you've created in the Adobe PDF (Portable Document Format) file format. When you save the book in this format, you or others you share the book with can view it in the Mac OS X Preview application or in the Adobe Acrobat Reader application. So, you can burn the book PDF file to a CD-R or other removable media to share the book with other users. (The PDF files will typically be dozens of megabytes in size and therefore not practical to e-mail.)

## TIP

Windows users don't have Preview, but they can download the Acrobat Reader software for free from http://www.adobe.com/products/acrobat/readstep2.html.

You also can burn the book PDF file to a CD-R or other removable media if you want a color printout of the book but don't have a color printer. Most print shops—both instant print places and larger operations—can make color printouts of PDF files for a reasonable fee.

Once you've set up your photo book, use the steps that follow to save it as a PDF file.

## NOTE

Any advanced printing options you select, such as placing multiple book pages per sheet, will not apply in the PDF file.

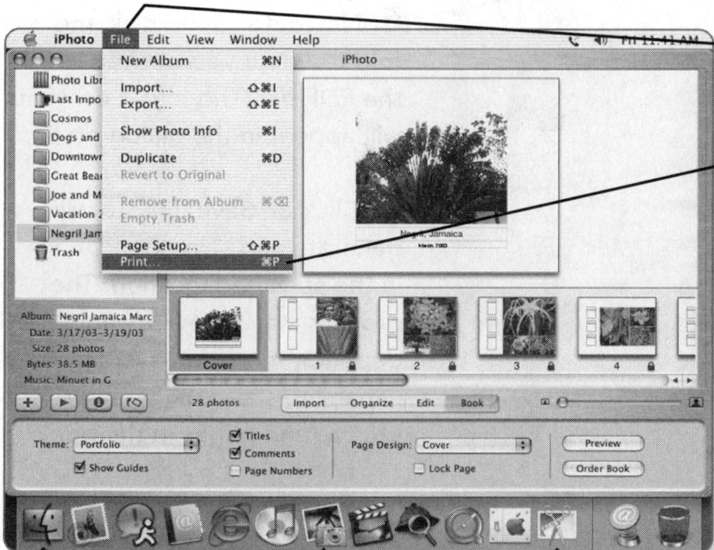


1. **Click** on **File**. The File menu will appear.

2. **Click** on **Print**. The Print dialog box will open.

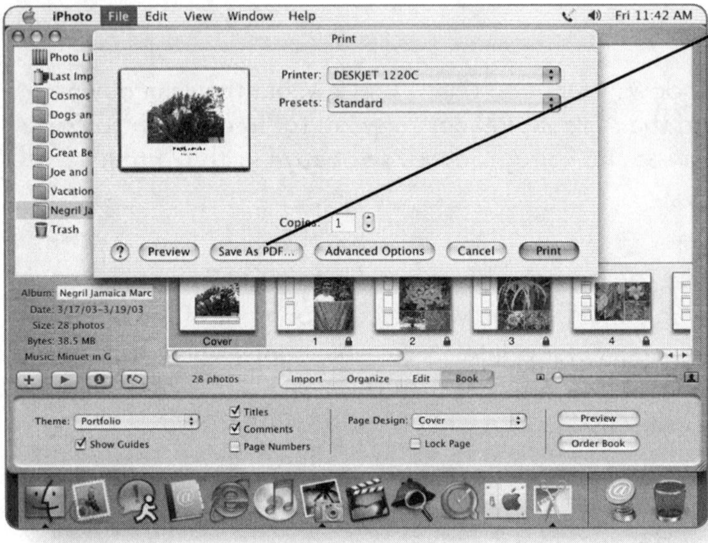

**3. Click** on **Save As PDF**. The Save to File dialog box will open.

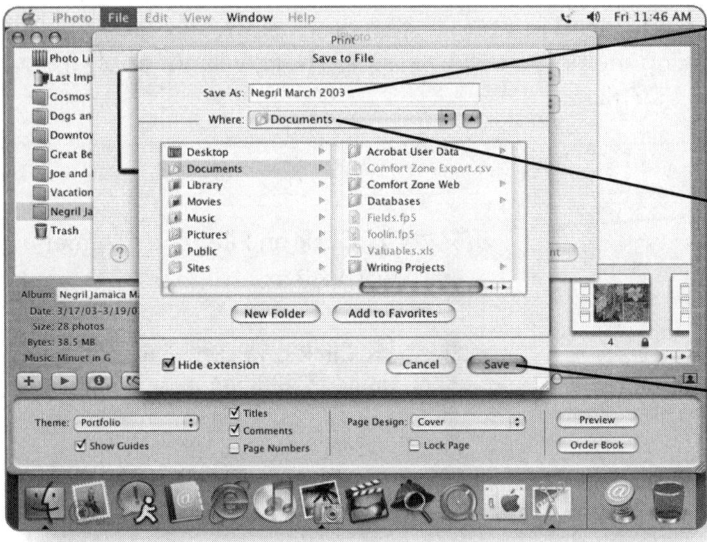

**4. Type** a **file name** for the PDF file in the Save As text box. The name will replace the original entry, **Untitled**.

**5. Navigate** to the **disk and folder** where you want to save the PDF file. The folder contents will appear in the dialog box.

**6. Click** on **Save**. iPhoto will generate and save the PDF file in the specified location. The process may take a few minutes, depending on your system's capabilities and the number of photos and pages in the book.

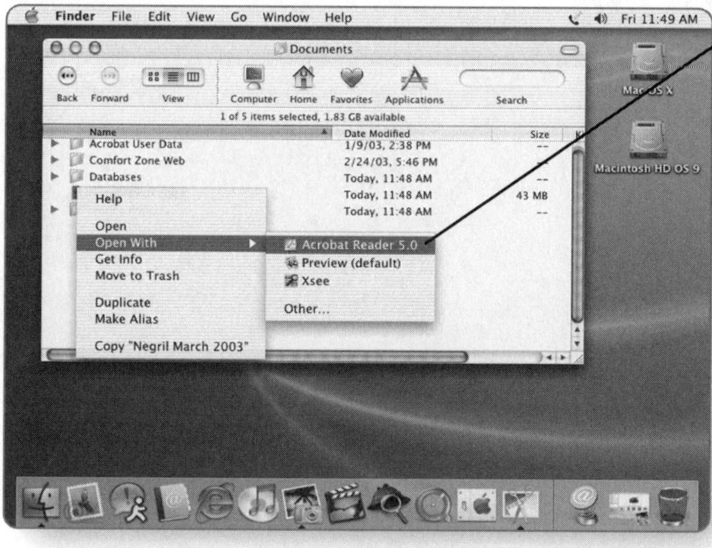


To view the PDF file, you can navigate to the Finder window holding the file, and then double-click on the file icon. Or, you can Control+click on the file icon, point to Open With, and choose another application in which to view the file.

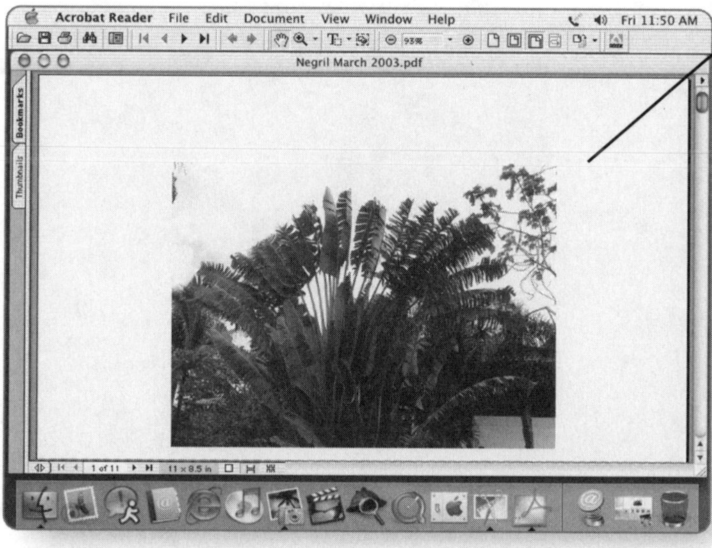


My example book appears here in the Adobe Acrobat Reader program for the Mac OS X platform.

# 9

# Sharing Your Photos Online

In the old days of photo film and prints, it took a week or more to get your first look at your magnificent photos of your vacation, pets, kids, or new home. If you wanted to share your masterpieces with friends or relatives, those folks had to wait another week or so to receive a set of prints from you in the mail—assuming you remembered to mail them in the first place. With iPhoto 2 and an Internet connection, you can share your photos with others almost as soon as you import them. In this chapter, you will learn how to:

- Send photos via e-mail.
- Sign up for a .Mac subscription for an online HomePage and more.
- Publish photos to your .Mac HomePage.
- View your HomePage.
- Update and protect your HomePage.

# E-Mailing Your Photos

E-mail offers the fastest way to share your photos with other e-mail users. Work in the Organize pane to select the photos to send, click on a button, and iPhoto automatically inserts the copies of the selected photos into a new e-mail message for you.

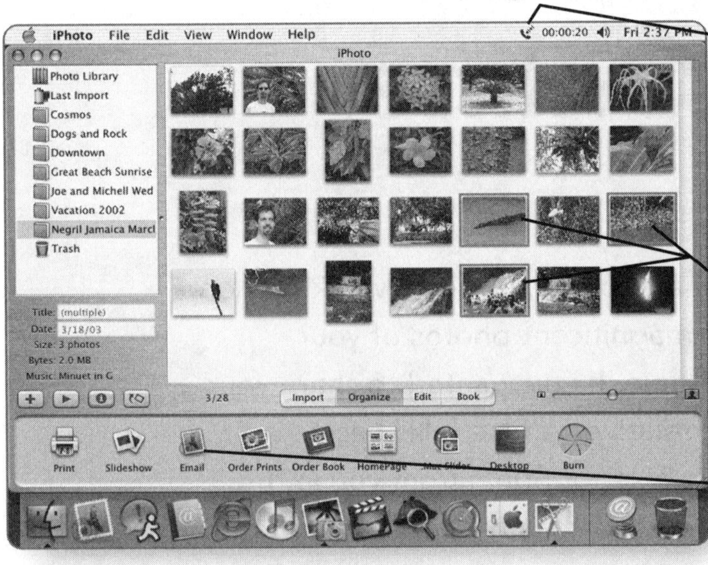

1. **Connect** to the **Internet**, if your system doesn't have an always-on connection. See Appendix C, "Dialing the Internet If Needed," to learn how.

2. In the Organize pane, **select** the **photo(s) to e-mail**. A blue selection highlight will appear around each selected photo.

3. **Click** on **Email**. The Mail Photo dialog box will open.

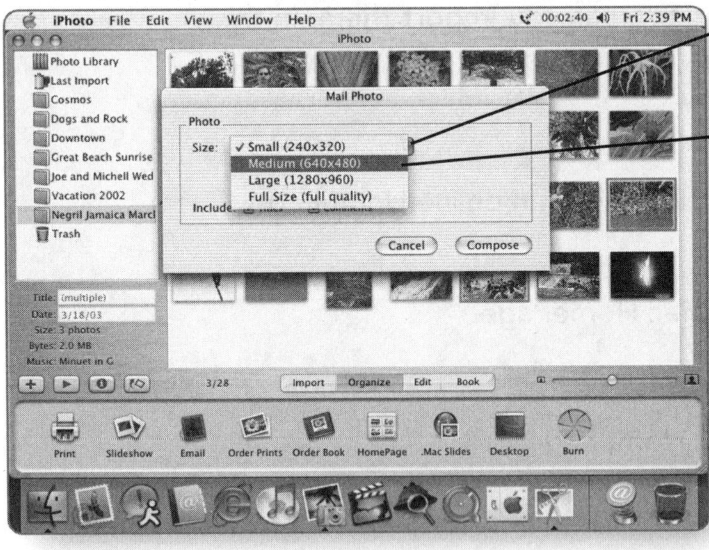

4. **Click** on the **Size pop-up menu**. The menu will open.

5. **Click** on the **desired size** for the sent photos. The photo copies will be sized as specified.

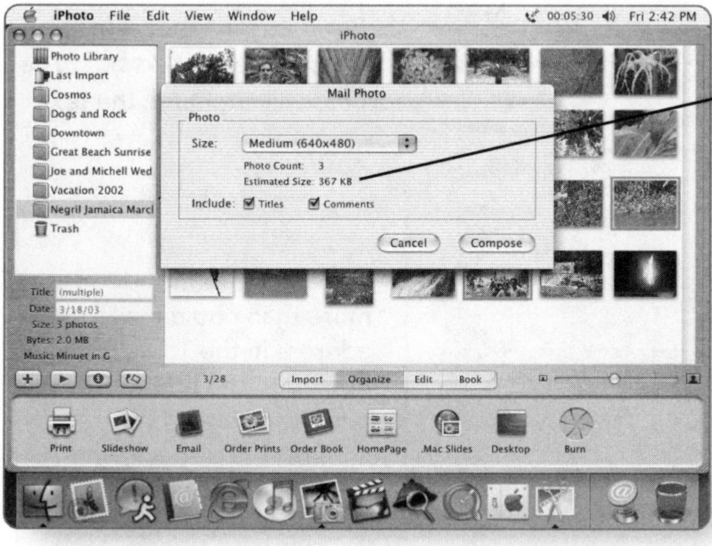


## TIP

Virtually all ISPs limit the total size of attachments you can make to any e-mail message. So, after you choose the photos to send and make a choice from the Size pop-up menu, check the Estimated Size calculation to make sure the photo attachments will not exceed your ISP's limitations.

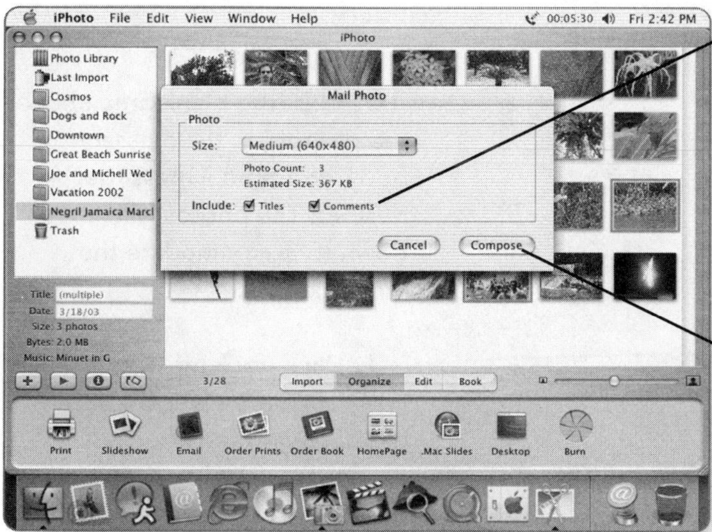


**6. Click** on the **Include check boxes** as needed. When one of these check boxes is checked, the designated information (Titles or Comments you've entered for the selected photos) will be inserted below the photos in the e-mail message.

**7. Click** on **Compose**. iPhoto will launch your e-mail program, compose a new message, and insert the selected photos into the message.

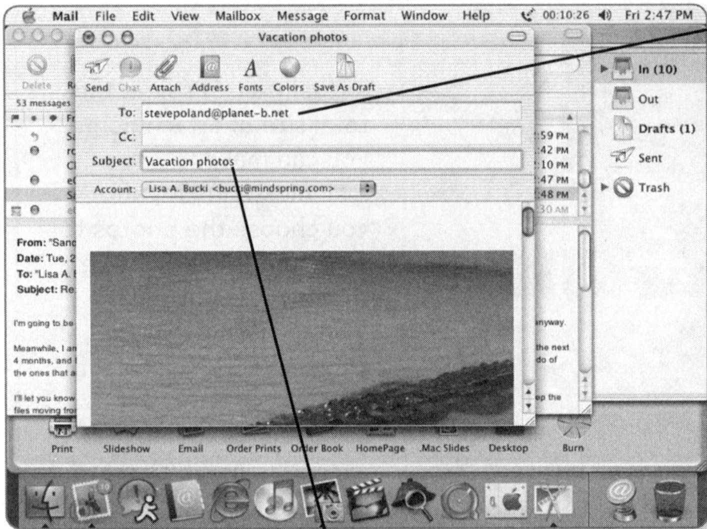


**8. Enter** a recipient's **e-mail address** in the To: text box. The address will appear in the text box.

> **TIP**
>
> If you want to include more than one e-mail address in the To: text box, type the first address followed by a comma and a space, and then type the next one.

**9. Edit** the **Subject information** as desired. The new subject will appear.

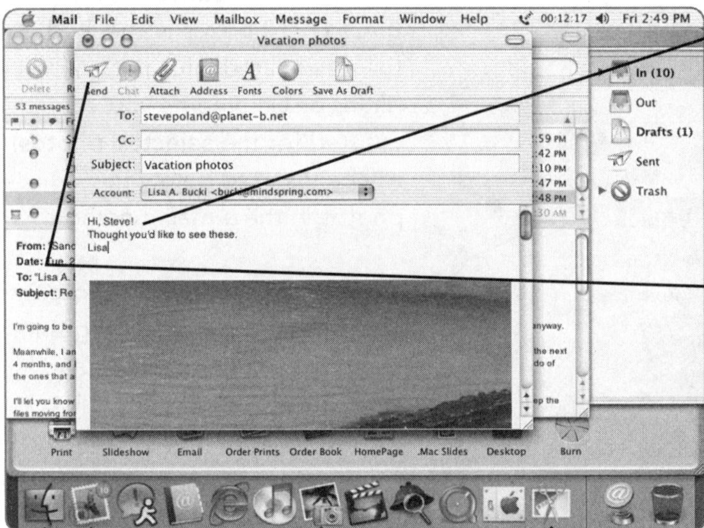


**10. Click** the **blank area** above the photo(s) in the message body, and **type** a **message**, if desired. The photos will move down to accommodate the message text.

**11. Click** on **Send**. Your mail program will deliver the message and the attached photos via your Internet account.

**NOTE**

By default, iPhoto sends selected photos to a new e-mail message in the Mail application in Mac OS X. If you want to use an alternate e-mail program like AOL, Eudora, or Entourage, you can choose the desired e-mail program in the iPhoto Preferences window. See Chapter 16, "Choosing iPhoto Preferences," to learn how to set iPhoto preferences.

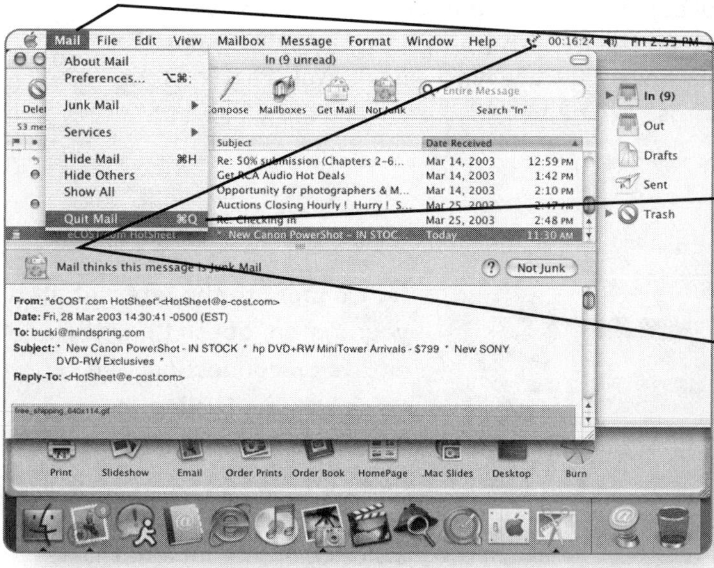


**12.** **Click** on **Mail,** or the name of your e-mail program. The Mail (program) menu will open.

**13.** **Click** on **Quit Mail** or Quit (program). Your mail program will close.

**14.** **Disconnect** from the **Internet**, if needed. Your Mac will hang up the Internet connection. Appendix C, "Dialing the Internet If Needed," also describes this process.

# Obtaining a .Mac Subscription

Apple offers an online service called *.Mac*. With .Mac, you get a .Mac e-mail address, the ability to publish a .Mac HomePage Web site, 100M of online iDisk storage space, and more for $99.95 per year. When you have a .Mac subscription, iPhoto 2 can publish an album or group of selected photos as your

.Mac HomePage. Signing up for .Mac takes just a few minutes (and requires a credit card). After you sign up, you need to be sure that your .Mac membership information has been entered into System Preferences, a process the following steps also describe.

> **NOTE**
>
> If you are not a .Mac member and are not interested in membership because you already have Web space available through your Internet Service Provider (ISP), you can still publish your photos as a Web page. To learn how, see "Creating a Basic Web Page of Your Photos" in Chapter 12.

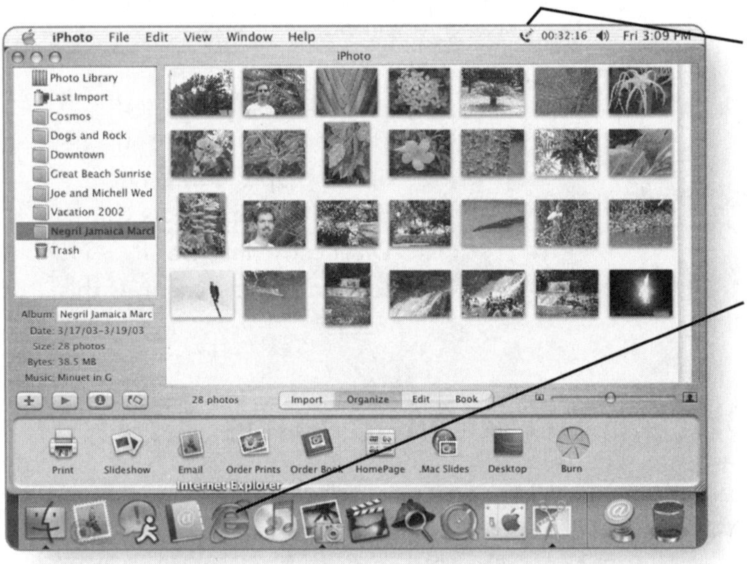


**1. Connect** to the **Internet**, if your system doesn't have an always-on connection. See Appendix C, "Dialing the Internet If Needed," to learn how.

**2. Click** on the **Internet Explorer icon** on the Dock. Internet Explorer will launch and display the start page that you've specified. (Of course, if you've installed an alternate Web browser such as Safari on your system, launch it, instead.)

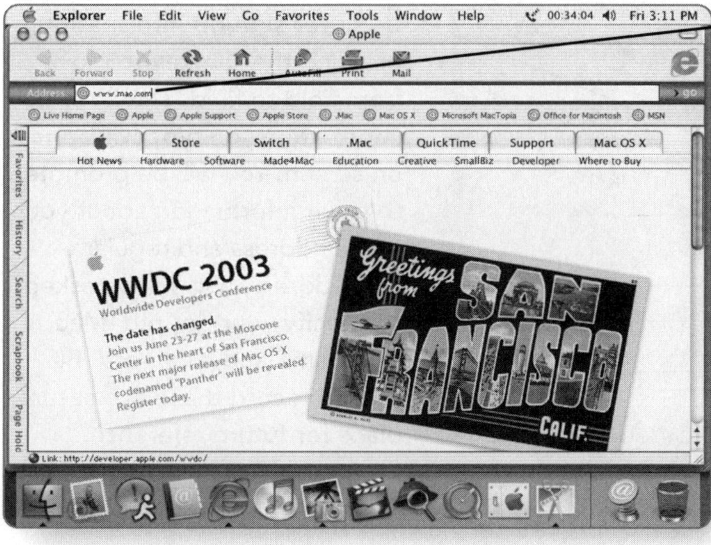

**3. Enter www.mac.com** in the Address text box, and **press Return**. The main .Mac Web page will load.

> **NOTE**
>
> If the main Apple page loads as your start page, you can click the .Mac tab on that page instead of using Step 3.

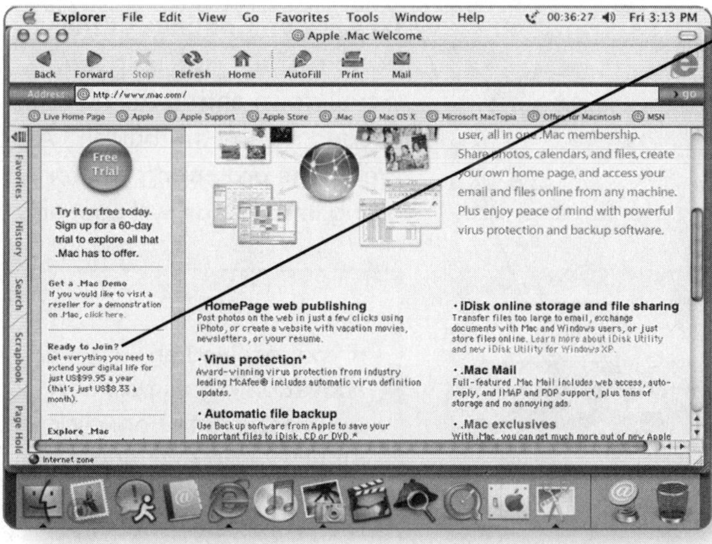

**4. Scroll down**, and then **click** on the **Ready to Join? link**. The .Mac Signup page will load.

> **NOTE**
>
> If a Security Notice message box appears at any point, click on OK to continue the sign-up process.

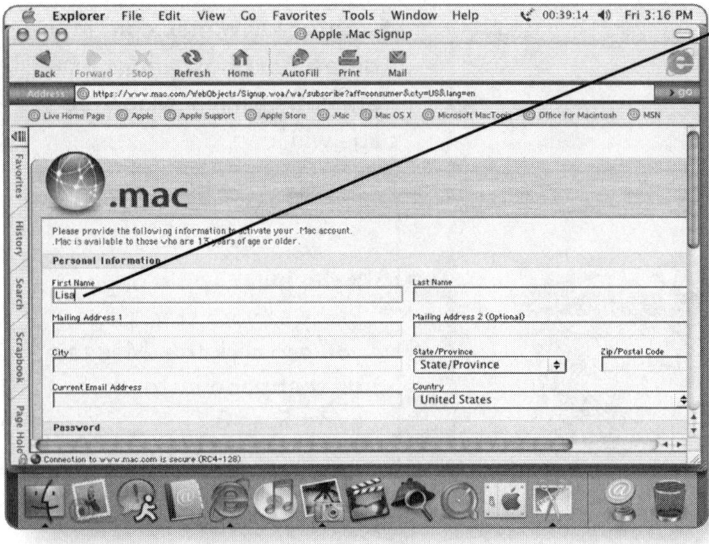


**5. Enter sign-up information**, pressing the Tab key to move from field to field. The information you type will appear on-screen. You will be prompted to enter information about your home address and regular e-mail address, and will be asked to specify your desired .Mac user name and password. Be sure to record those in a secure place for future reference.

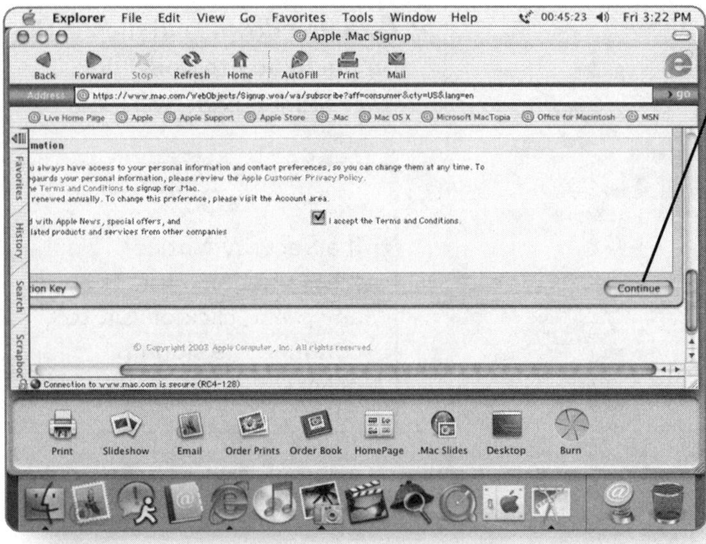


**6. Click** on **Continue** at the bottom of the sign-up page. (Scroll down and to the right, if needed, to see this button.) A Web page prompting you for billing information will appear.

> **NOTE**
>
> If you received an activation key as part of a purchase promotion, click on I Have An Activation Key, instead, and follow the prompts to enter the key and finish the sign-up process.

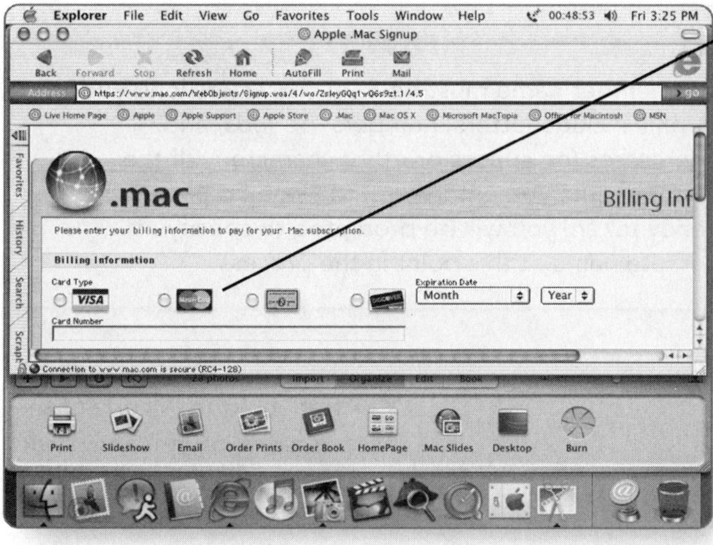

**7. Enter billing information,** pressing Tab to move from field to field. The information you specify will appear on-screen. You will be prompted to enter billing and credit card information.

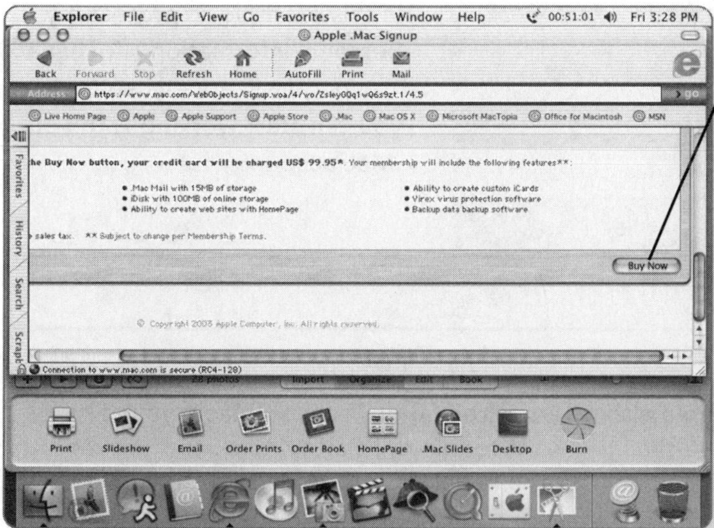

**8. Click** on **Buy Now** at the bottom of the billing information page. (Scroll down and to the right, if needed, to see this button.) After .Mac processes your order, a page with your member name, e-mail address, password, and billing information will appear.

## NOTE

Your member name must be 3-20 characters long and can only include letters, numbers, periods, and underscores (no spaces or other characters). If the member name you entered on the sign-up page is already taken, you will be prompted to specify an alternate name at this point in the process.

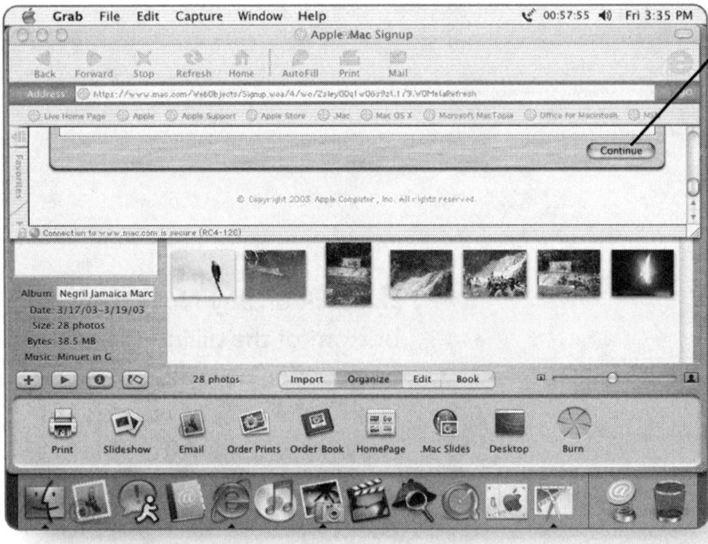


**9.** After you print a copy of the .Mac account information, **click** on **Continue** at the bottom of the page. (Scroll down and to the right, if needed, to see this button. I've made the Internet Explorer window much smaller in this example to protect my personal information.) A Thank You page will appear, so that you can start working with your .Mac account.

## TIP

Apple also offers a free 60-day trial of .Mac if you're not sure that you want to join right away. Click on the Free Trial button on the initial .Mac Web page to sign up.

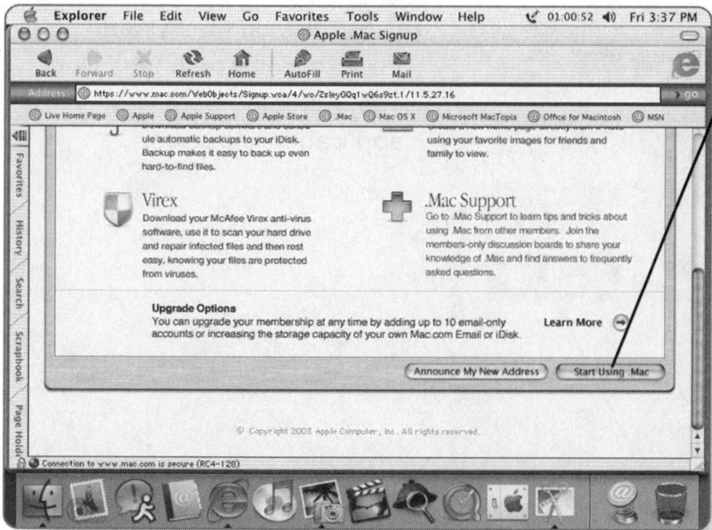


**10.** Click on **Start Using .Mac** at the bottom of the page. (Scroll down and to the right, if needed, to see this button.) The initial .Mac page will reappear, so that you can use the Log in link to log in to your account.

Or, if you're finished working, you can close Internet Explorer and disconnect from the Internet.

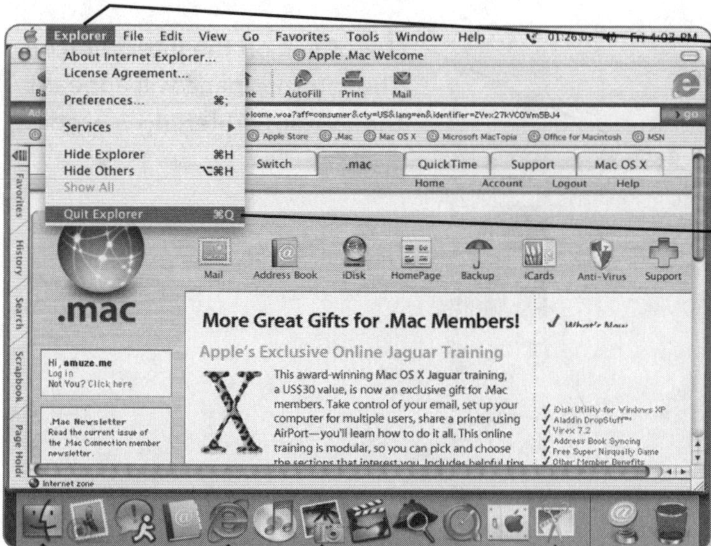


**11.** Click on **Explorer**, or the name of your browser program. The Explorer (program) menu will open.

**12.** Click on **Quit Explorer** or Quit (program). Your browser program will close. You also can disconnect from the Internet, if needed.

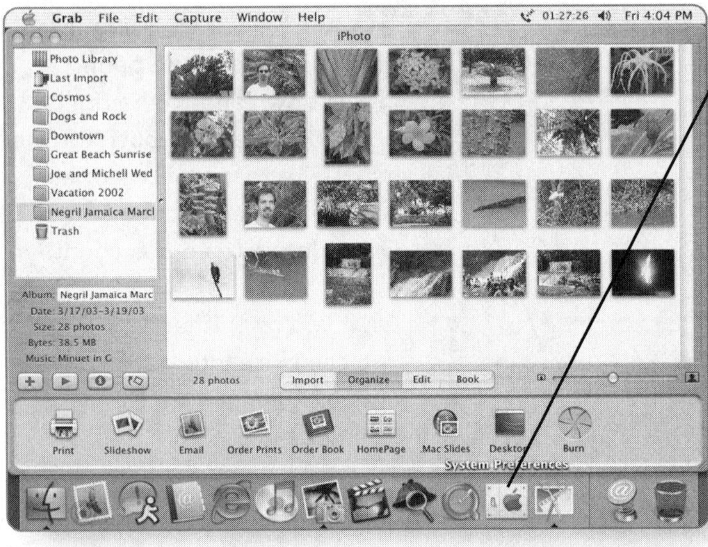


**13. Click** on the **System Preferences icon** on the Dock. The System Preferences application will open.

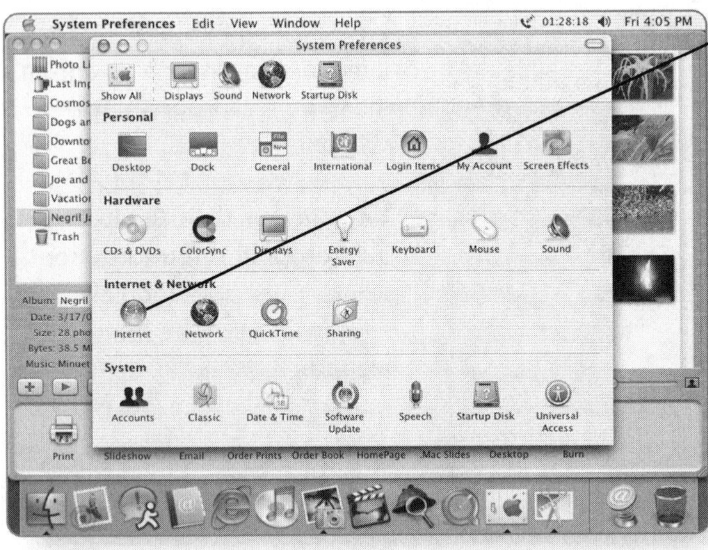


**14. Click** on the **Internet icon**. The Internet pane will appear in the System Preferences window.

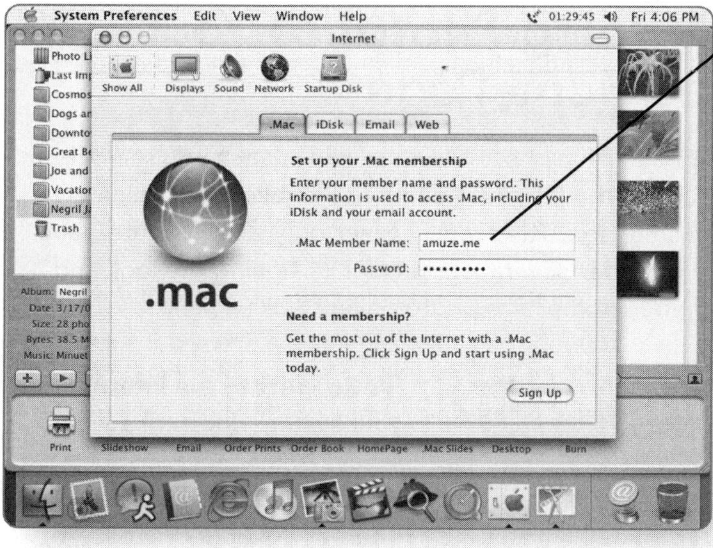


**15. Enter** your **.Mac Member Name** and **Password.** The name will appear, along with an asterisk for each character in the password.

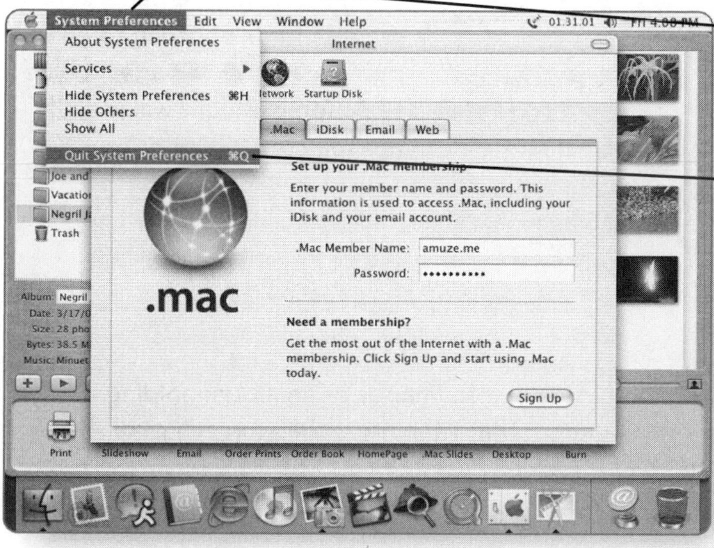


**16. Click** on **System Preferences.** The System Preferences menu will open.

**17. Click** on **Quit System Preferences.** The System Preferences application will close and accept your new .Mac membership information, so that Mac OS X can access .Mac services automatically.

# Publishing Photos to Your .Mac HomePage

You can publish a photo album or any images you select from an album (in the Organize pane) and publish them as your .Mac HomePage. The process takes only a few minutes, and iPhoto provides several options for designing the look and feel of your HomePage photo gallery.

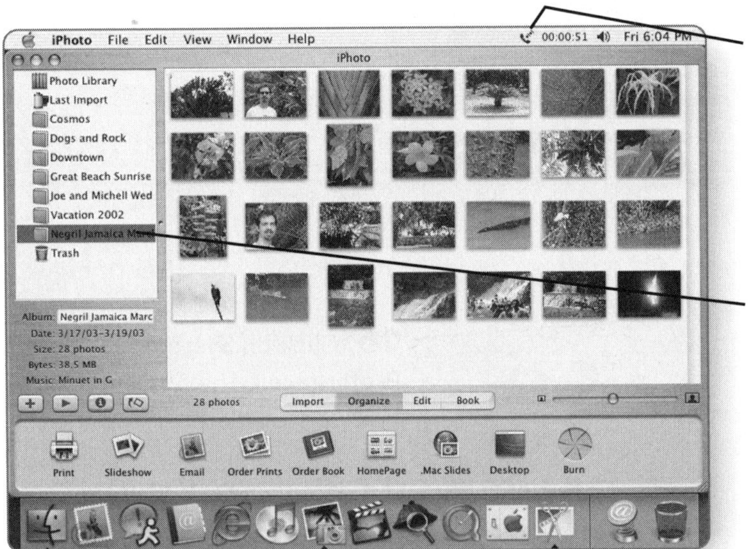


**1. Connect** to the **Internet**, if your system doesn't have an always-on connection. See Appendix C, "Dialing the Internet If Needed," to learn how.

**2.** In the Organize pane, **select** the **album or photo(s) to publish as a Web page.** A blue selection highlight will identify the selected album or photos.

> **CAUTION**
>
> Select no more than 48 images or an album holding 48 or fewer images. That's the most that you can publish as your HomePage.

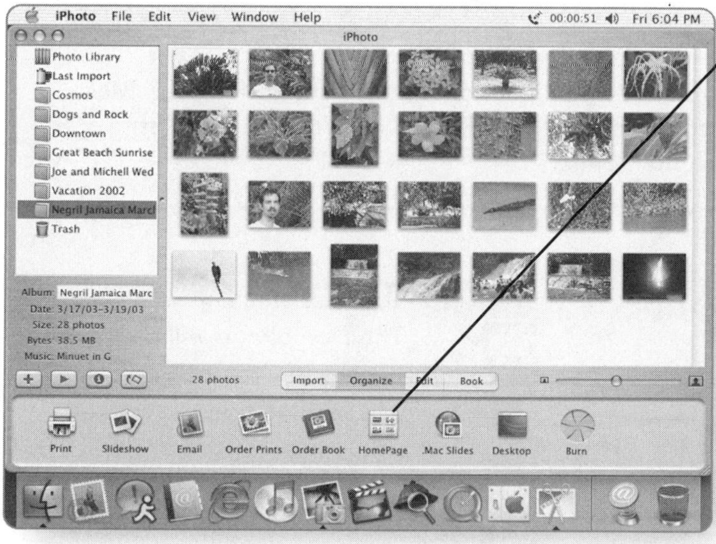


**3. Click** on **HomePage**. The Publish HomePage window will open.

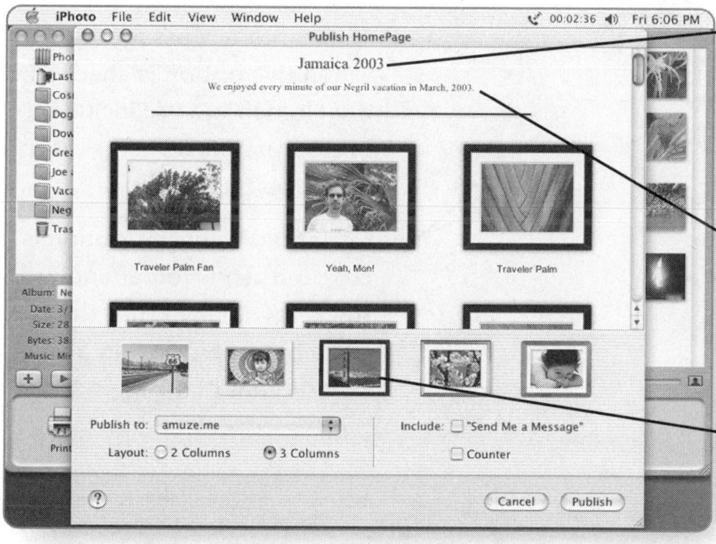


**4. Type** a **HomePage title**. Your new title will replace the text that previously appeared in the text box at the top of the window.

**5.** Select the text below the title, and **enter** a **new description**. Your text will replace the placeholder text.

**6. Click** on the desired **design theme** thumbnail. The specified theme will be applied to the thumbnails in the window.

## NOTE

If you have multiple home pages set up for your .Mac account, choose the desired one from the Publish to pop-up menu.

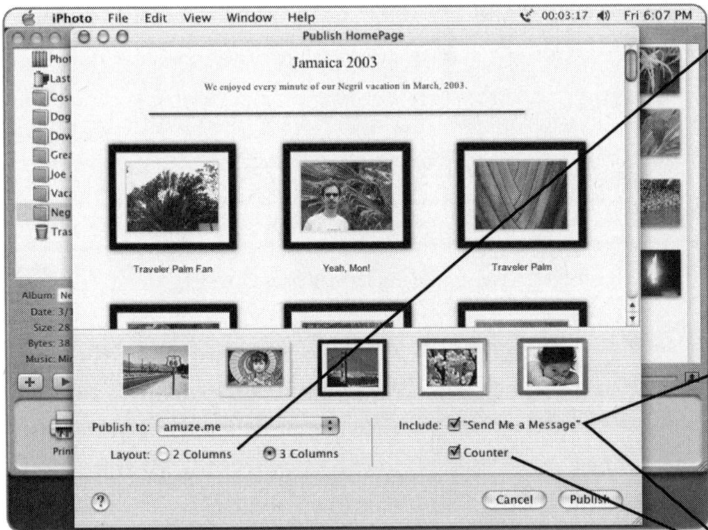


**7. Click** on a **Layout option**. The HomePage will display the photos in two or three columns, as specified by the selected option.

**8. Click** on **Include** options as desired:

- **"Send Me a Message."** When this option is checked, the HomePage will include a button that users can click to send you an *iCard*.
- **Counter.** When this option is checked, The HomePage will track how many times the page has been viewed and include that number on the page.

## TIP

You can drag photos in the Publish HomePage window to change their order in the finished HomePage.

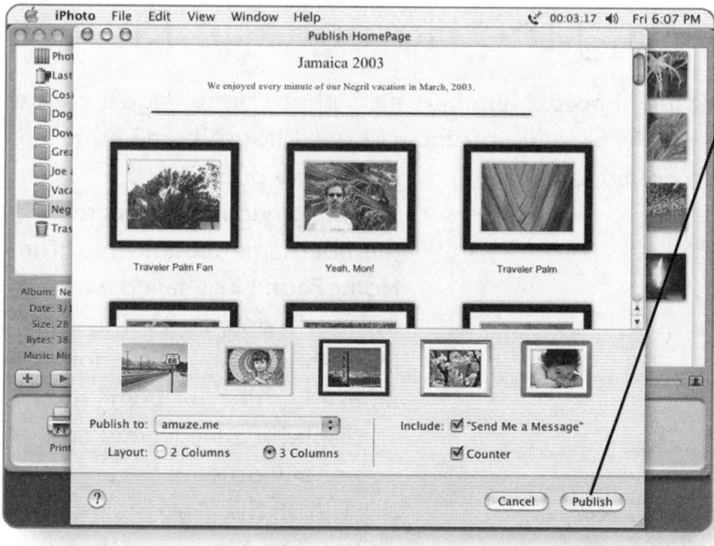


**9. Click** on **Publish**. iPhoto will connect to your .Mac account, transfer the pictures, and set up your HomePage. Keep in mind that even though the pictures included on your HomePage will be resized to a smaller size than the original, the transfer can take some time over a slower Internet connection. When the transfer finishes, a message alerting you of the Web address (URL) for the new HomePage will appear.

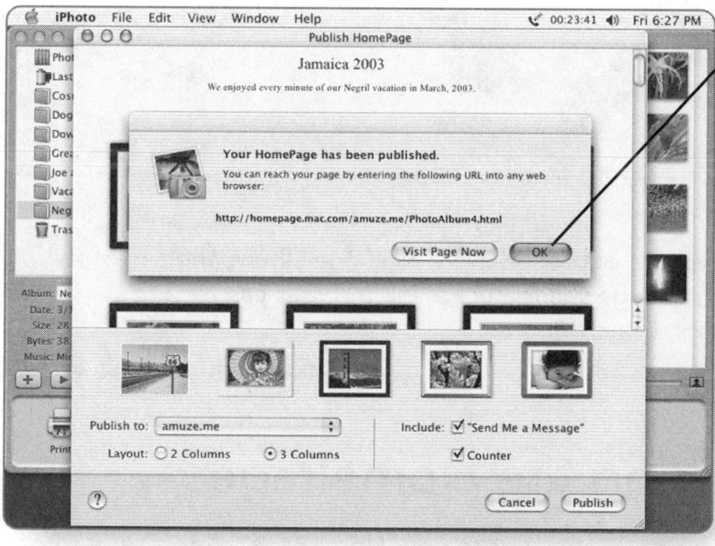


**10.** After you make a note of the URL for your HomePage, **click** on **OK**. iPhoto will close the message and the Publish HomePage window. You can then disconnect from the Internet if you want.

> **NOTE**
>
> Of course, you could click on Visit Page Now in Step 9 instead, to go directly to your new HomePage.

## Viewing the HomePage Photos

By default, iPhoto 2 numbers each photo HomePage it creates sequentially, as in PhotoAlbum1.html, PhotoAlbum2.html, and so on. So, the full URL for any home page is http://homepage.mac.com/membername/albumname. The HomePage I just saved was my fourth one, so its URL is http://homepage.mac.com/amuze.me/PhotoAlbum4.html. To display a .Mac HomePage, you or any other user can enter the URL in the Web browser's Address text box, and then press Return. The photo HomePage will load.

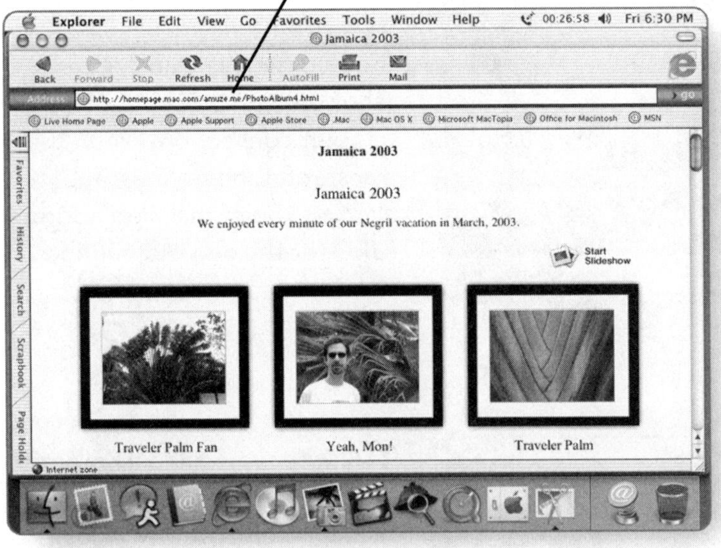


> **NOTE**
>
> If you've published more than one album, the top of the HomePage will feature a link the user can click to display each album.

## Editing the HomePage

You can make changes to your HomePage, even after it's been posted to your .Mac account space online. iPhoto need not be running for you to make these changes.

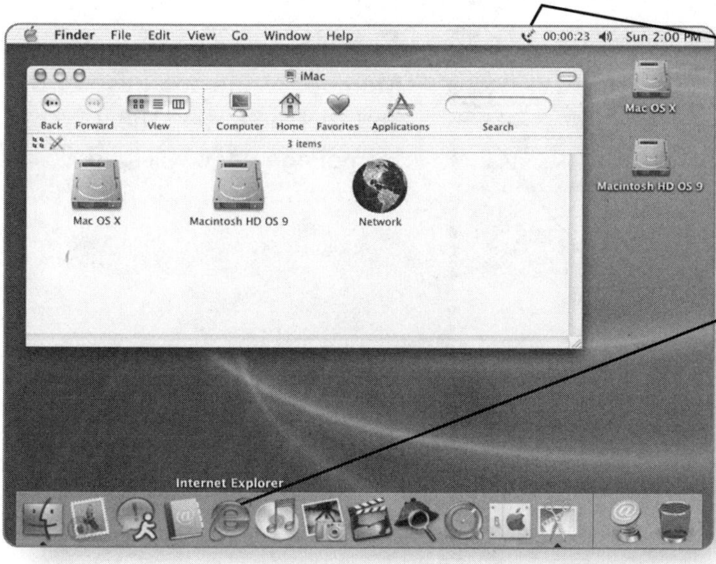


**1. Connect** to the **Internet,** if your system doesn't have an always-on connection. See Appendix C, "Dialing the Internet If Needed," to learn how.

**2. Click** on the **Internet Explorer icon** on the Dock. Internet Explorer will launch and display the start page that you've specified. (Of course, if you've installed an alternate Web browser on your system, launch it, instead.)

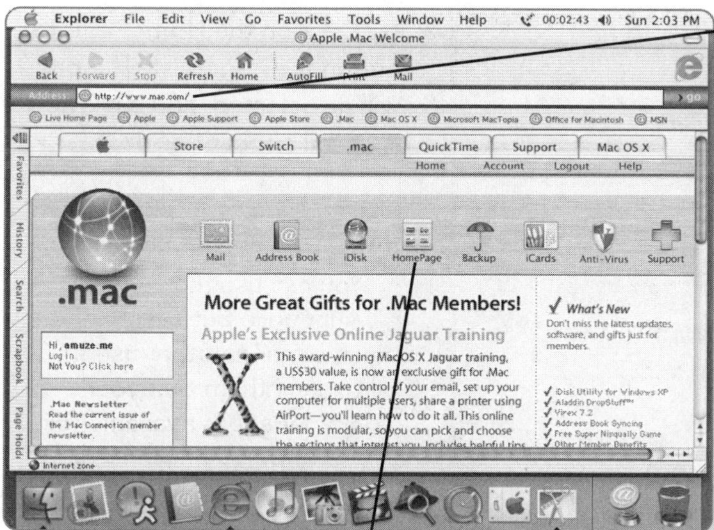


**3. Enter www.mac.com** in the Address text box, and **press Return**. The main .Mac Web page will load.

> **TIP**
>
> You don't have to enter http:// in the URL. Your Web browser will add that information automatically after you press Return.

**4. Click** on **HomePage**. A page will prompt you to enter your password to log in so that you can make changes to your HomePage.

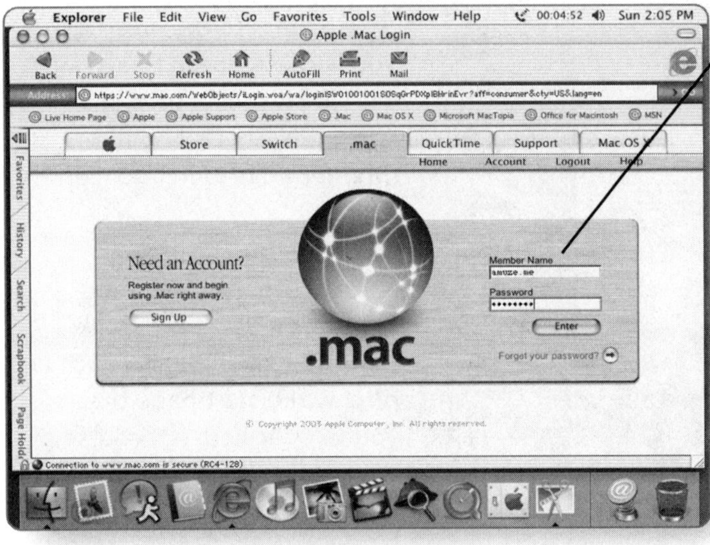


**5.** If prompted, **enter your Member Name** and **Password,** and **click** on **Enter**. The .Mac HomePage page will load.

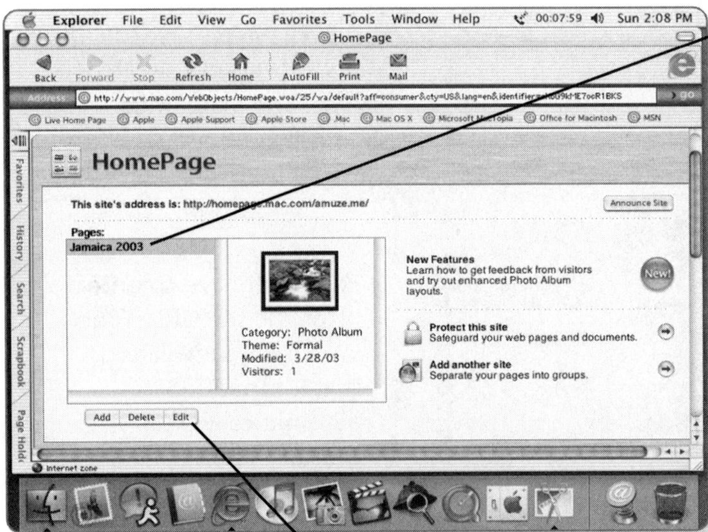


**6. Click** on the **HomePage to edit** in the Pages list. The page will be selected, and a preview icon will appear beside it.

> **NOTE**
>
> You can use the Announce button to send an e-mail to other users to alert them that your HomePage is available for viewing.

**7. Click** on **Edit** below the Pages list. The Edit your page page will appear. It will include a thumbnail of each of the images included in your HomePage.

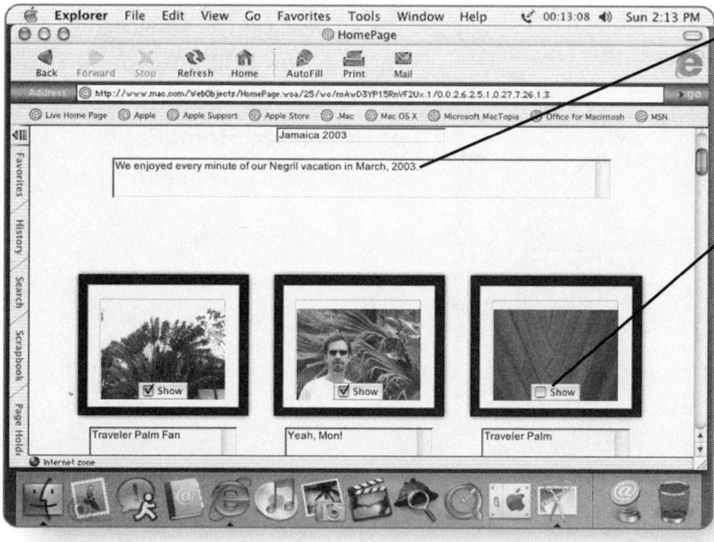


**8. Edit text** as desired. You can edit page titles or the comment for any photo. Your changes will appear on-screen.

**9.** To hide a photo, **click** on its **Show** check box. The check mark will be cleared and the image will be masked (hidden) from the online album.

## TIP

You can drag photos on the Edit your page page to change their order in the finished HomePage.

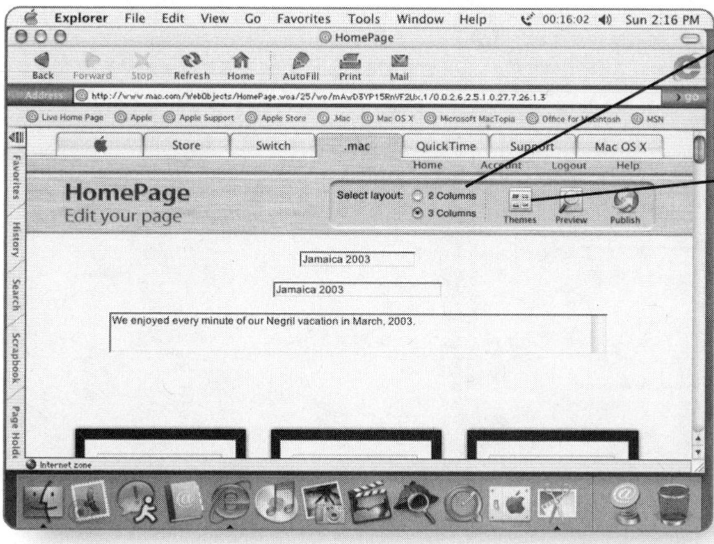


**10. Choose another layout** if desired. The preview will adjust to show your changes.

**11. Click** on **Themes**. The Change your theme page will appear.

## TIP

You can drag photos on the Edit your page page to change their order in the finished HomePage.

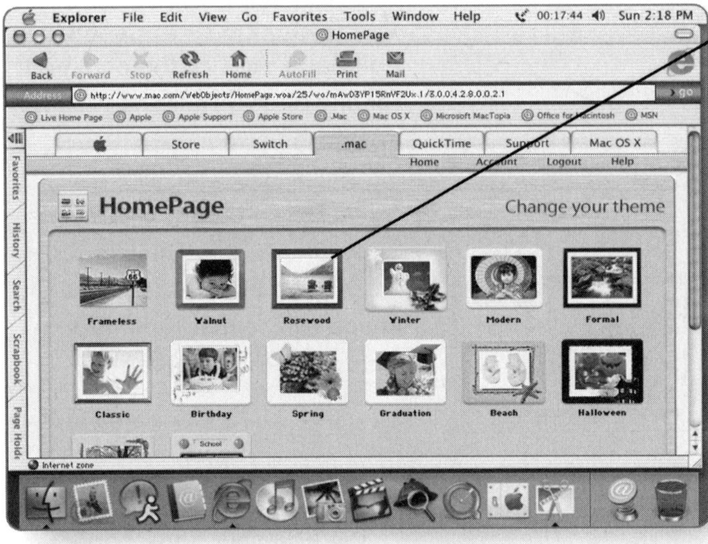


**12. Click** on the desired **theme**. The Edit your page page will reappear, showing a preview of the edited HomePage.

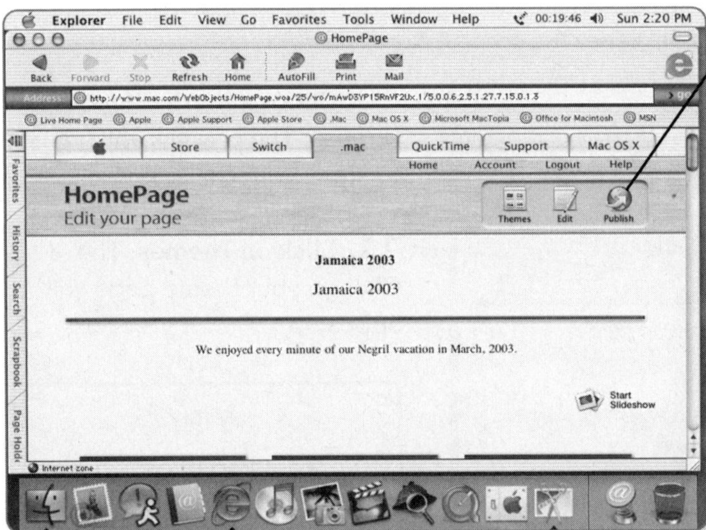


**13. Click** on **Publish**.

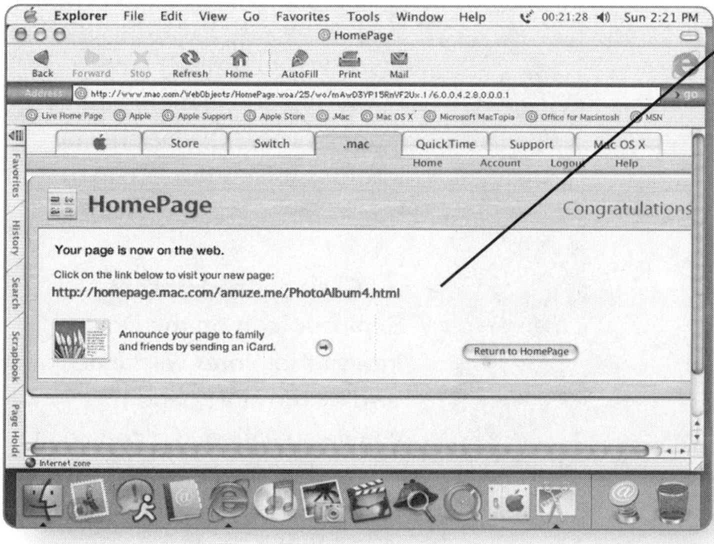


The HomePage will be republished, and you will have the option of sending an iCard to announce the page or returning to the HomePage.

# Protecting the HomePage

You can assign a password to your site to protect it. Users will have to enter the correct password in order to view your site. This adds one greater level of security to the photos you've posted online, in case they display confidential subject matter, such as a photo of a product prototype.

> **NOTE**
>
> .Mac applies the password protection to all of the pages you've posted to your .Mac HomePage area.

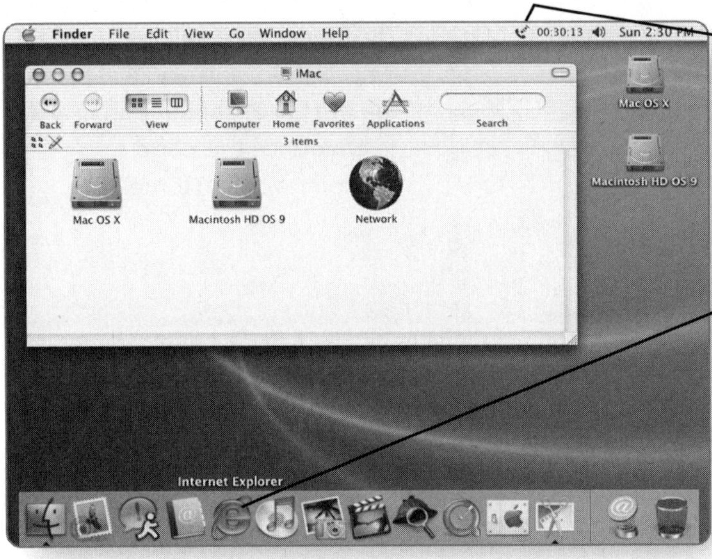


**1.** **Connect** to the **Internet**, if your system doesn't have an always-on connection. See Appendix C, "Dialing the Internet If Needed," to learn how.

**2.** **Click** on the **Internet Explorer icon** on the Dock. Internet Explorer will launch and display the start page that you've specified. (Of course, if you've installed an alternate Web browser on your system, launch it, instead.)

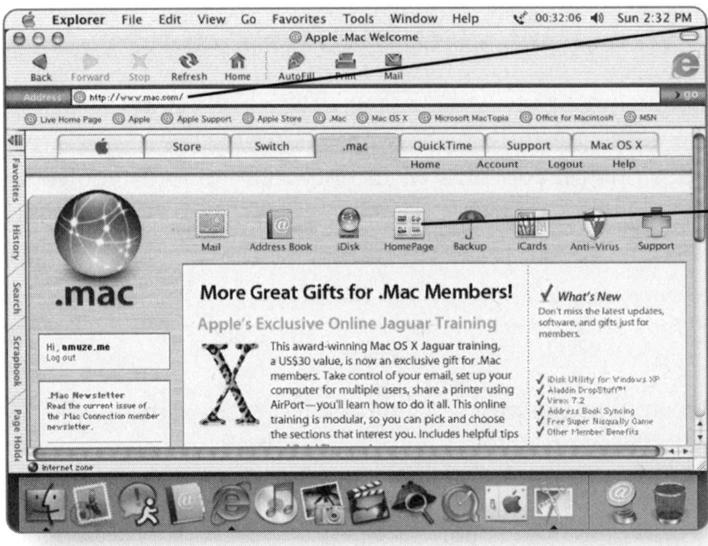


**3.** **Enter www.mac.com** in the Address text box, and **press Return**. The main .Mac Web page will load.

**4.** **Click** on **HomePage**. A page will prompt you to enter your password to log in so that you can make changes to your HomePage.

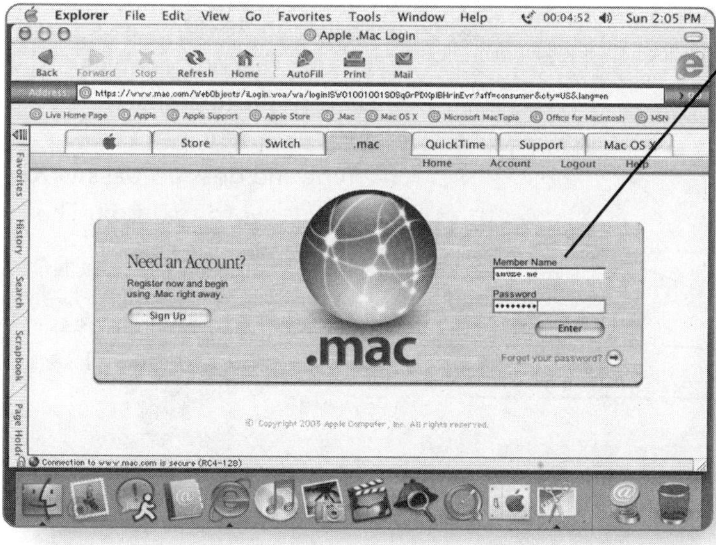


**5. Enter your Member Name** and **Password,** and **click** on **Enter**. The .Mac HomePage page will load.

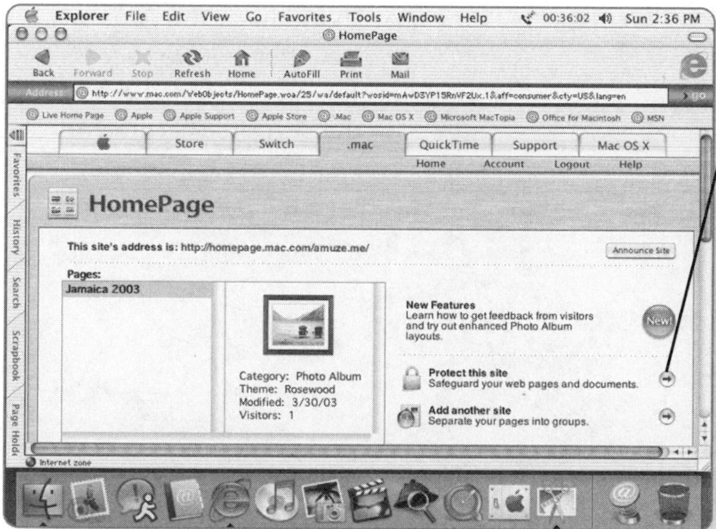


**6. Click** on the **Protect this site arrow button**. The Edit your site page will appear, this time showing the choices for password-protecting the site.

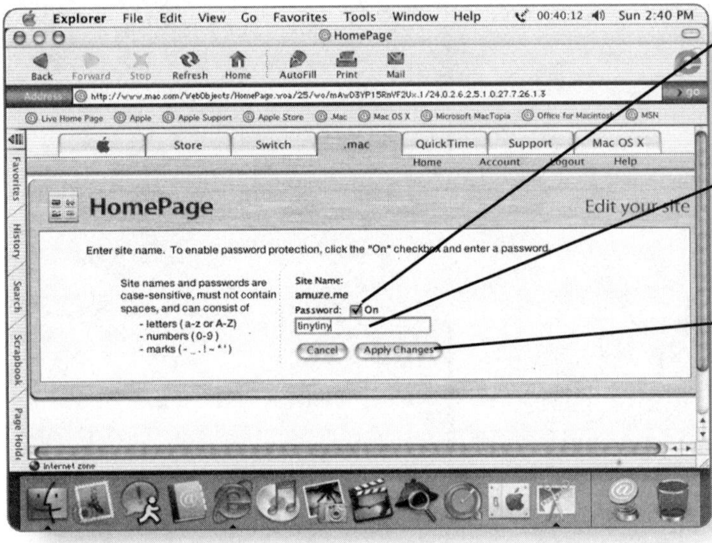


**7. Click** on the **On check box.** Checking this box enables password protection.

**8. Type** the **desired password** in the Password text box. The password will appear.

**9. Click** on **Apply Changes.** Your HomePage page will reappear.

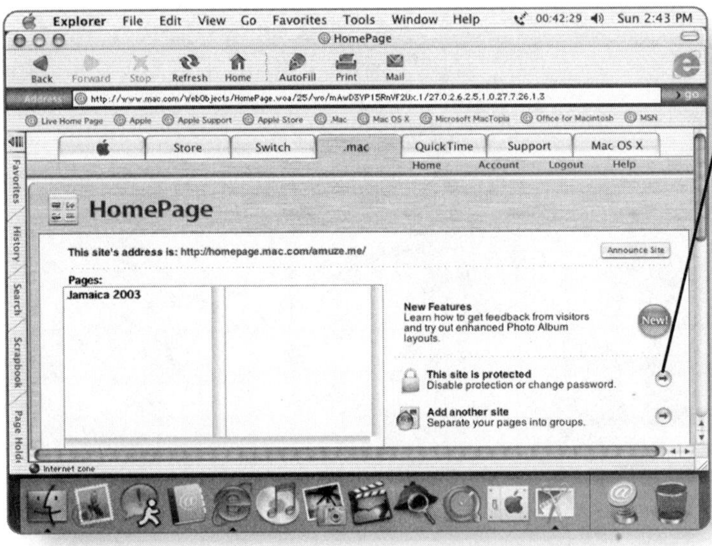


As shown here, the page will indicate that you've successfully protected the HomePage. Click on the This site is protected arrow button to change or remove the password in the future.

# 10

# Making and Ordering Prints and More

If you've invested in a color inkjet printer—or even better, received one as a bonus when you purchased your Mac—you can make your own photo prints and photo cards. If you don't have a printer that can handle the job, don't worry. You can order photo prints or a nicely bound photo book from Apple. In this chapter, you will learn how to:

- Print your photos on photo paper.
- Use a photo as a greeting card.
- Set up an Apple ID and 1-click ordering.
- Order prints or a photo book.
- Disable and enable 1-click ordering.

# Printing on Photo Paper

You enjoy the greatest immediacy and flexibility if you can make your own photo prints on a color printer at home or in the office. A package of 20 4″ × 6″ sheets of photo paper costs about $8.95, however, so printing your own photos won't save you much over having professional prints made. A package of 8.5″ × 11″ photo paper starts at about $13, but can cost much more if you choose higher quality finishes. You can even get canvas cloth stock to make prints that resemble paintings!

Before you use iPhoto to make your first photo print, however, take the time to review your printer's features, particularly how to position the photo paper. You don't want to discover that you've printed on the wrong side of an expensive piece of paper.

The steps that follow show various examples of how to make a print. The steps include constraining the print to match the paper size you'll be using. This important part of the process helps you to avoid printing a photo that appears cut off along two sides. You also have to choose the precise size of the photo paper that you're printing to, as well as the finish of the paper (glossy versus matte, for example).

**CAUTION**

Remember once again that iPhoto cannot print image files stored in the *CMYK color* mode. So, if you've used an image editing application to convert image files to CMYK color for professional printing, you'll need to convert them back to RGB color before importing them into iPhoto.

## Printing a 4 × 6 Photo

If you've purchased 4 × 6 photo stock, you must choose the proper paper size, as well as other settings, to have the print job work correctly. Because the process is a bit counter-intuitive, take a moment to review it here.

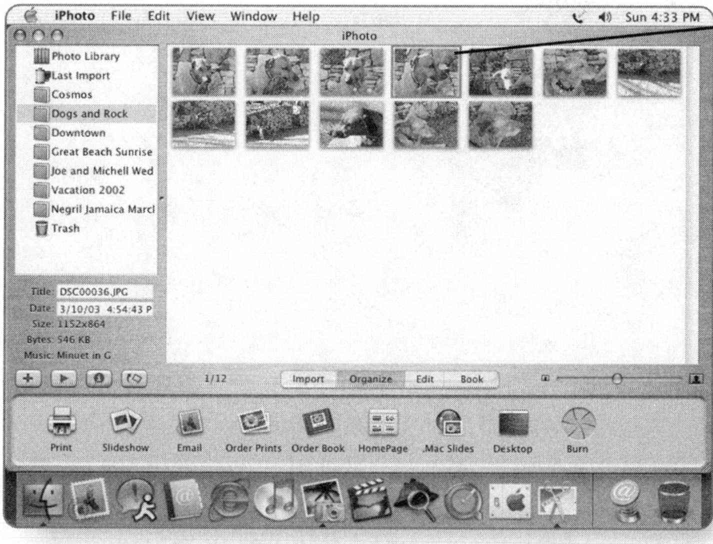


**1.** Working in the Organize pane, **double-click** on the **photo to print** in either the photo library or the current album. The photo will appear in the Edit pane.

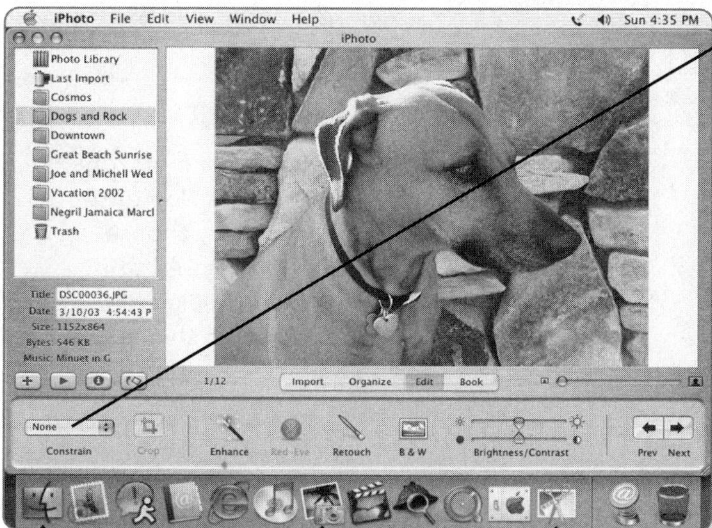


**2. Click** on the **Constrain pop-up menu**. The pop-up menu choices will appear.

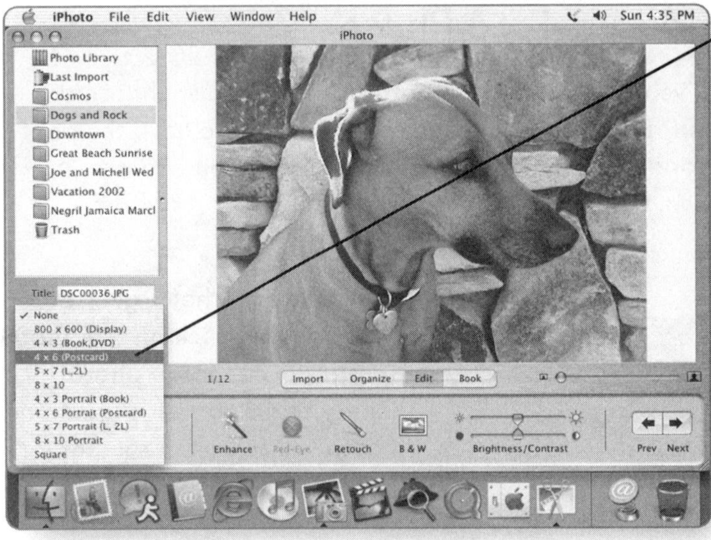


**3. Click** on the desired **Constrain** setting. The setting will be selected, and when you move the mouse pointer over the image, a crosshair pointer will appear. To make a 4″ × 6″ print, for example, choose one of the 4 × 6 Constrain choices as shown here.

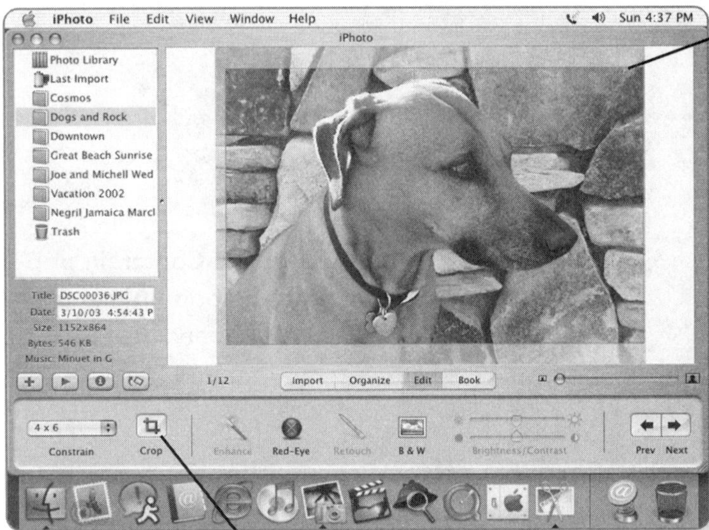


**4. Drag** on the **photo** to specify the crop zone. When you release the mouse button, the area outside the crop zone will be lightened, to graphically illustrate the image area to be cropped.

> **TIP**
>
> If you make a crop zone selection but don't like the selection, choose Edit, Deselect All to remove the selection. Or, you can drag the crop zone to reposition it.

**5. Click** on the **Crop button**. The image will be cropped as specified.

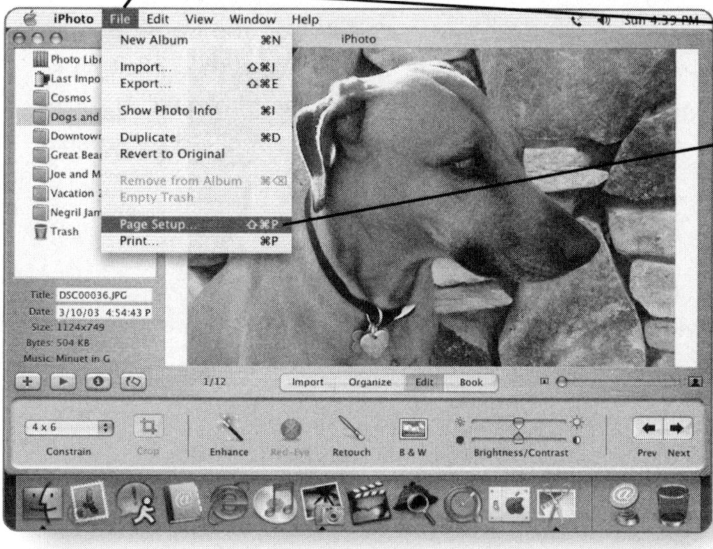


**6.** **Click** on **File**. The File menu will appear.

**7.** **Click** on **Page Setup**. The Page Setup dialog box will open.

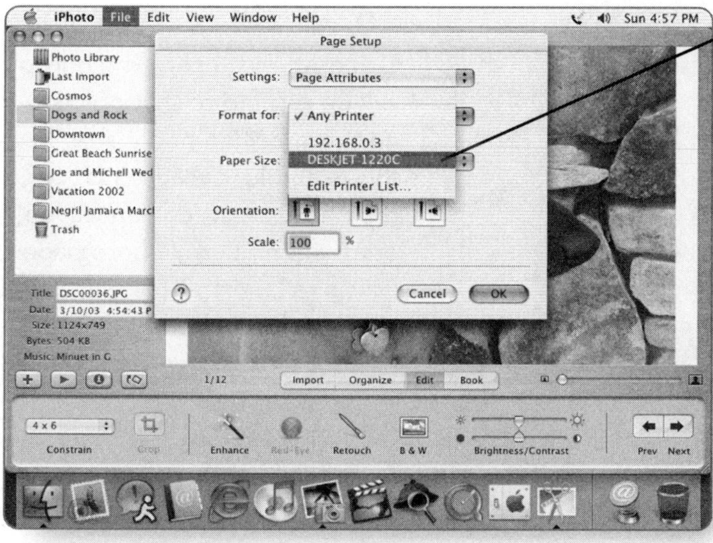


**8.** **Click** on the **Format for pop-up menu** and then **click** on the **printer you want** to use for the print job. The Page Setup dialog box will display your choice.

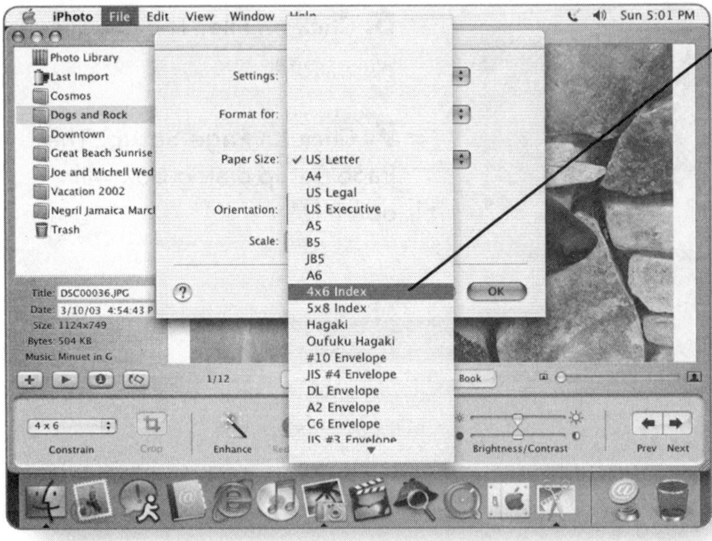

**9. Click** on the **Paper Size pop-up menu** and then **click** on **4 × 6 Index**. The photo will be sized to fit the specified paper size.

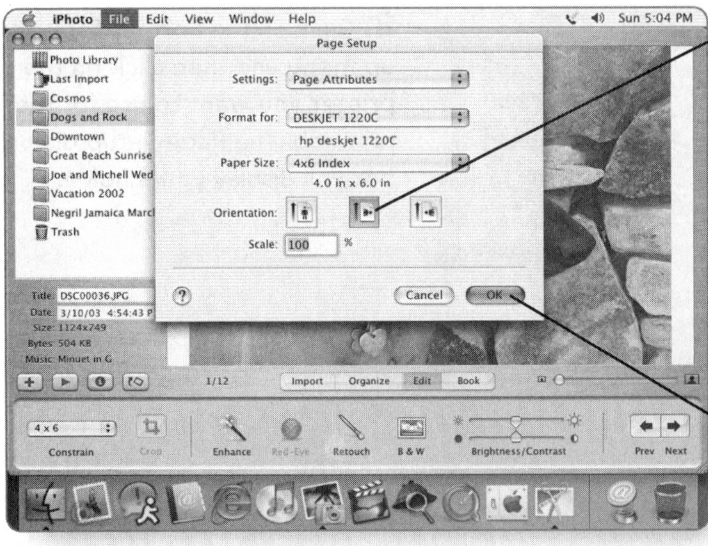

**10. Click** on the proper **Orientation button**. The photo will be rotated to that position on the specified paper size. In this example, because I cropped the photo in a wide (landscape) orientation but my photo paper uses a tall (portrait) orientation, I have to click either the middle or right Orientation choice.

**11. Click** on **OK**. The Page Setup dialog box will close.

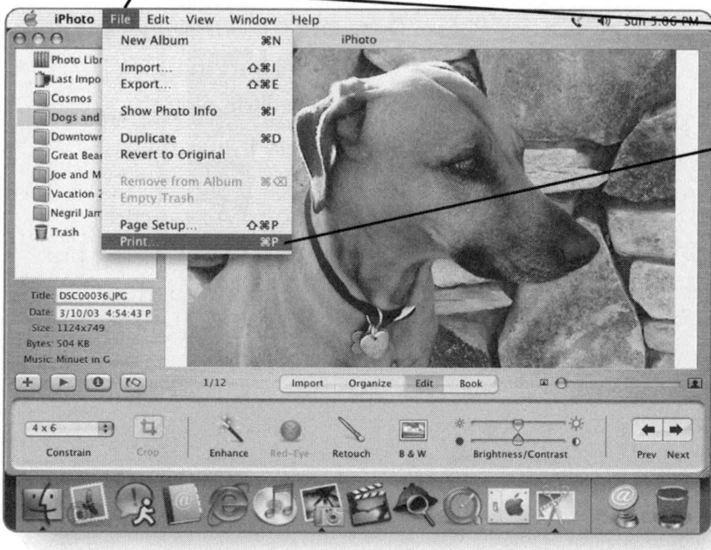

**12. Click** on **File**. The File menu will appear.

**13. Click** on **Print**. The Print dialog box will open.

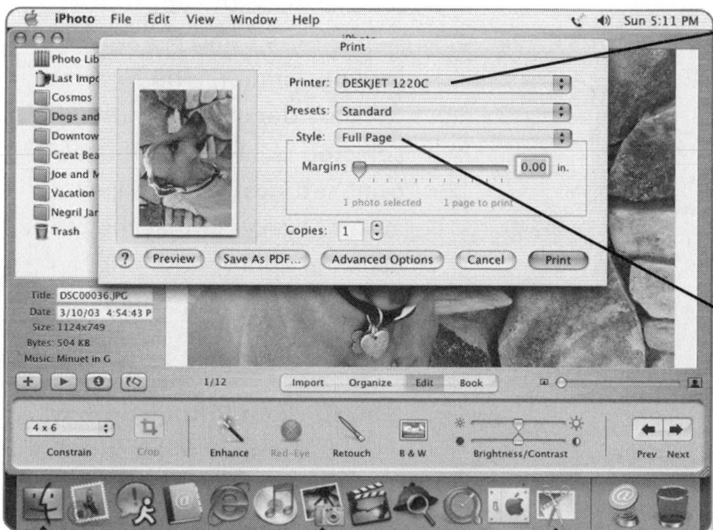

**14. Choose** the **printer to use** from the **Printer pop-up menu**. (This should be the same printer that you chose in the Page Setup dialog box.) The Print dialog box will display your choice.

**15. Choose** the **Full Page** from the **Style pop-up menu**. The Print dialog box will display your choice.

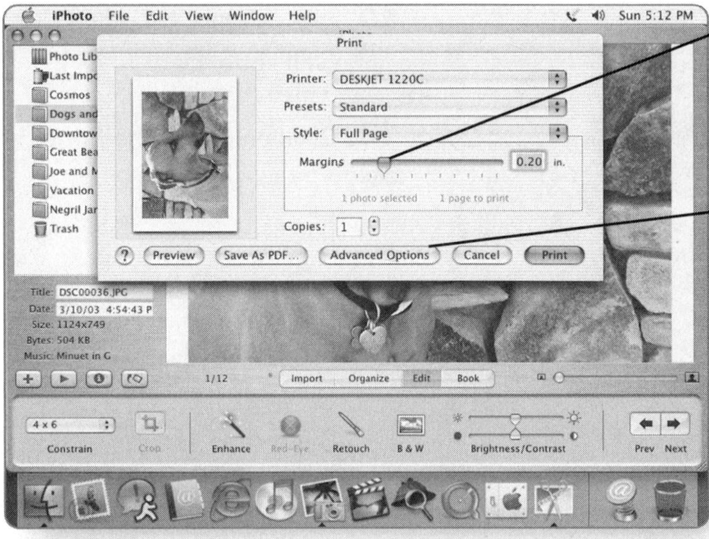


**16. Drag** the **Margins slider** to set the desired margin size. The preview will display the specified margins.

**17. Click** on **Advanced Options.** The Print dialog box will adjust to include the advanced printing options.

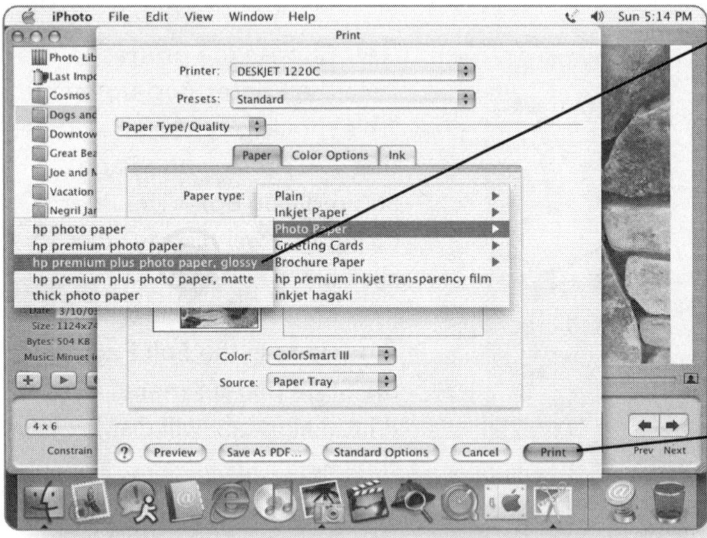


**18. Choose** the **appropriate paper type** using the settings for your printer. (The settings will vary depending on the selected printer.) Additional print settings will be adjusted automatically, so that the printer uses the appropriate print quality and ink saturation for the selected printer.

**19. Click** on **Print.** iPhoto will send the photo to the specified printer.

### TIP

Don't forget that you can choose File, Revert to Original to remove cropping after you make prints.

## SOLUTIONS WHEN MAKING PRINTS

Even with the frequent updates released for Mac OS X, the operating system may not support every capability for every printer. For example, Mac OS X may not let you print borderless prints (prints that bleed off the edge of the photo paper) through iPhoto, even if your printer supports full bleeds. Or, you might encounter an update problem. For example, after I installed the Mac OS X 10.2.4 update, my iMac could no longer print to my HP DeskJet.

If you encounter such a problem in iPhoto, first go to the driver downloads area on the Web site for your printer manufacturer and check for a new Mac OS X printer driver. Following are the Web sites for leading inkjet printer manufacturers:

http://www.canon.com

http://www.epson.com

http://www.hp.com

http://www.lexmark.com

You also can use an open source driver solution to help resolve printing problems. (Software developers collaborate to create free open source software.) Go to http://gimp-print.sourceforge.net/MacOSX.php3. There, you can download the Gimp-Print drivers for printing under Mac OS X. Review the documentation carefully for installation instructions.

Some problems simply require a manual work around. If you can't get your printer to print a full bleed on particular photo paper, print to a larger paper size and trim each printed page to achieve the desired print size.

## Printing an 8 × 10 Photo

Printing an 8 × 10 photo works the same, except you choose the 8 × 10 constrain size and print to 8 1/2" × 11" paper, as follows.

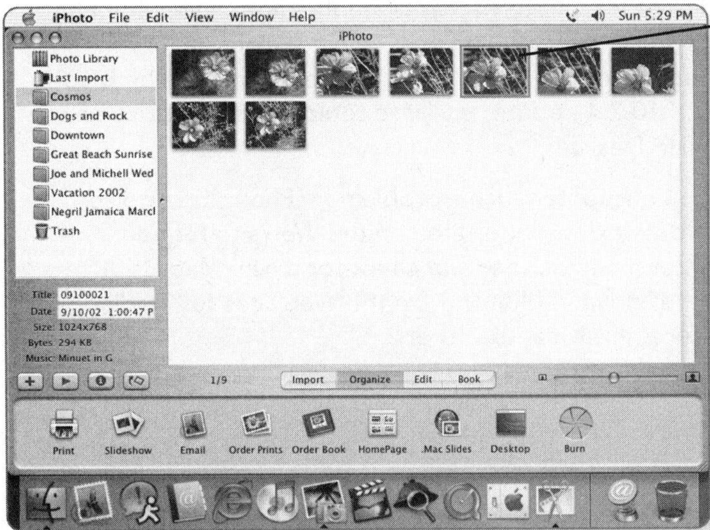

**1.** Working in the Organize pane, **double-click** on the **photo to print** in either the photo library or the current album. The photo will appear in the Edit pane.

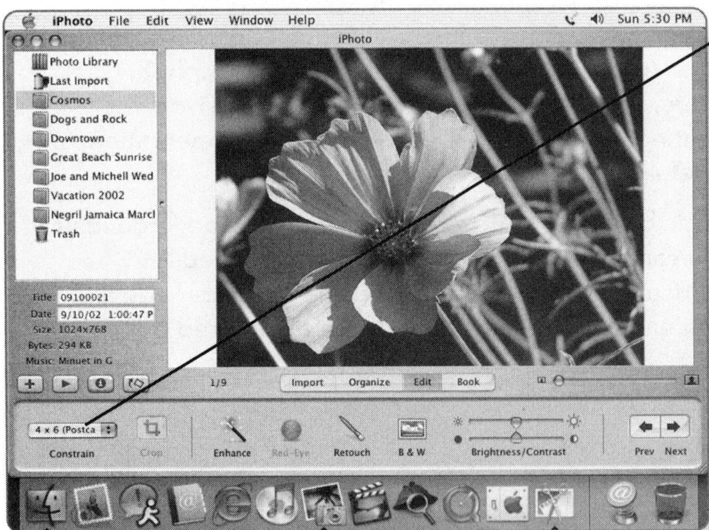

**2. Click** on the **Constrain pop-up menu**. The pop-up menu choices will appear.

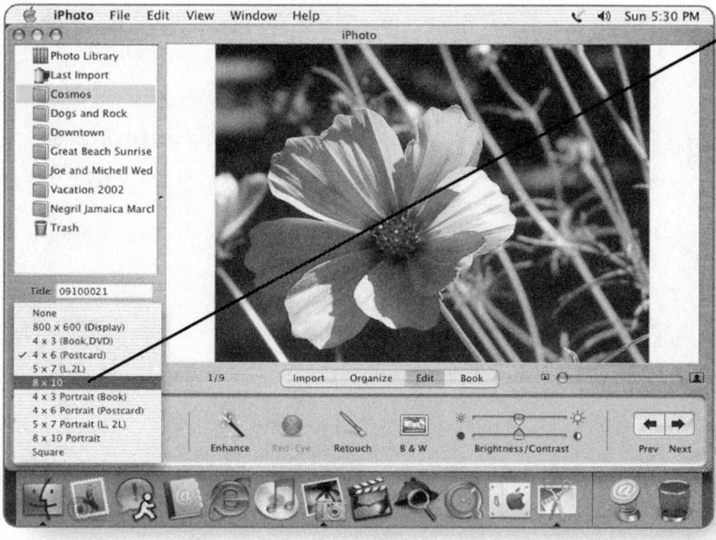

**3. Click** on the desired **Constrain** setting. The setting will be selected, and when you move the mouse pointer over the image, a crosshair pointer will appear. To make an 8″ × 10″ print, for example, choose one of the 8 × 10 Constrain choices as shown here.

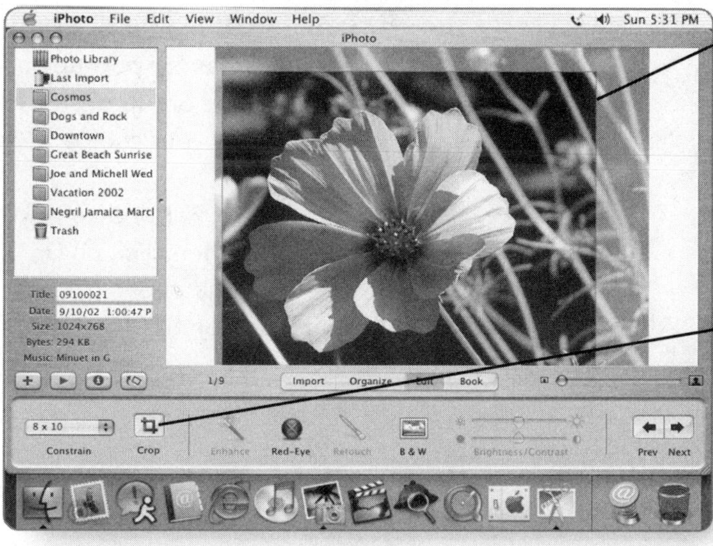

**4. Drag** on the **photo** to specify the crop zone. When you release the mouse button, the area outside the crop zone will be lightened, to graphically illustrate the image area to be cropped.

**5. Click** on the **Crop button**. The image will be cropped as specified.

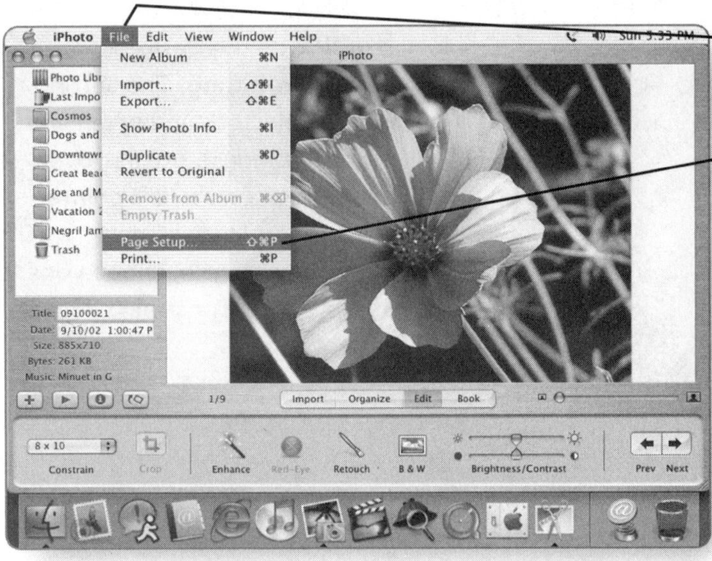


**6. Click** on **File**. The File menu will appear.

**7. Click** on **Page Setup**. The Page Setup dialog box will open.

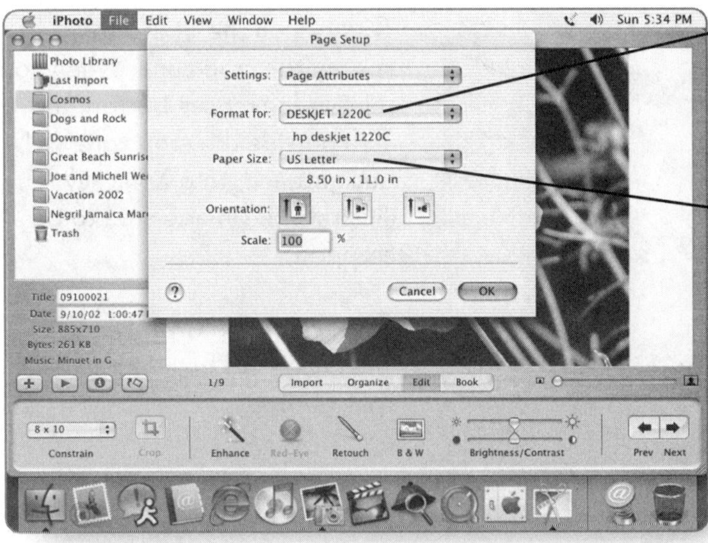


**8. Choose** the **printer to use** from the **Format for pop-up menu**. The Page Setup dialog box will display your choice.

**9. Click** on the **Paper Size pop-up menu** and then **click** on **US Letter**. The large paper size will accommodate an 8 × 10 photo.

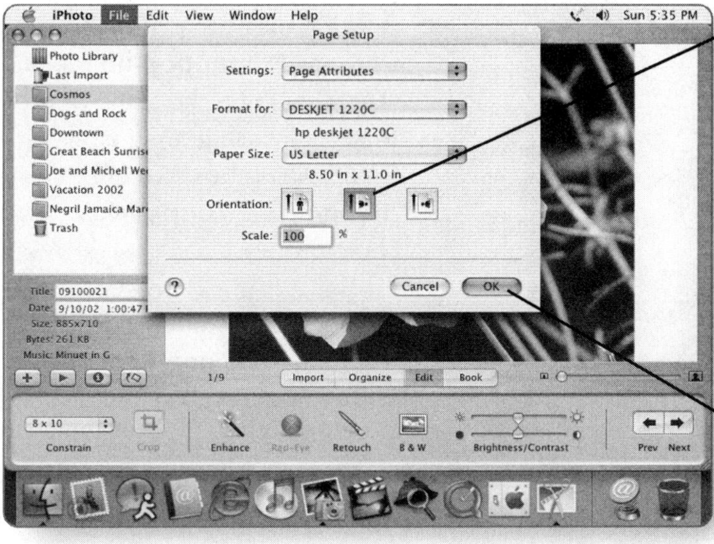

**10. Click** on the proper **Orientation button**. The photo will be rotated to that position on the specified paper size. In this example, because I cropped the photo in a wide (landscape) orientation but my photo paper uses a tall (portrait) orientation, I have to click either the middle or right Orientation choice.

**11. Click** on **OK**. The Page Setup dialog box will close.

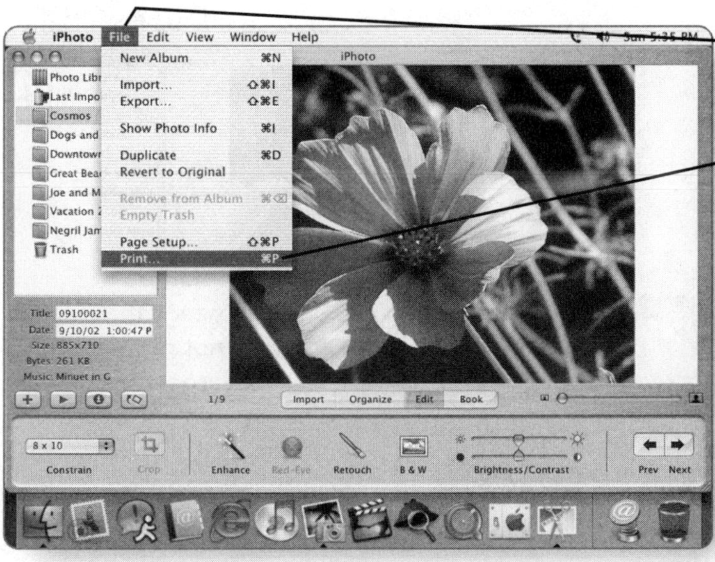

**12. Click** on **File**. The File menu will appear.

**13. Click** on **Print**. The Print dialog box will open.

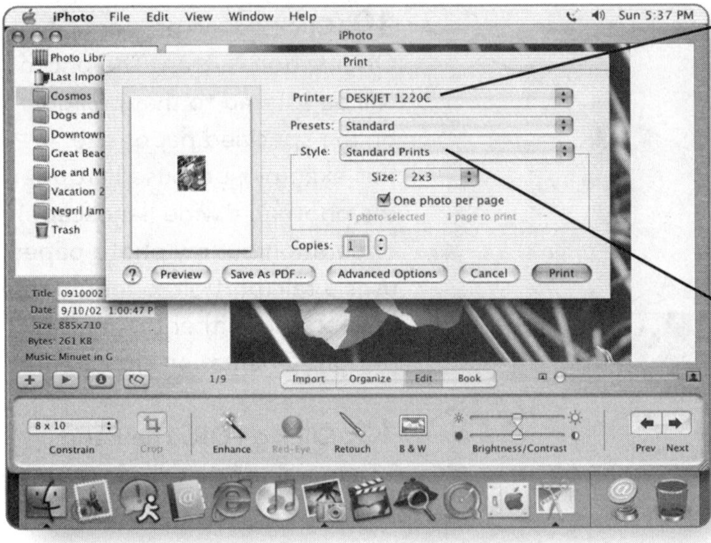


**14. Choose** the **printer to use** from the **Printer pop-up menu**. (This should be the same printer that you chose in the Page Setup dialog box.) The Print dialog box will display your choice.

**15. Choose Standard Prints** from the **Style pop-up menu**. The Print dialog box will display your choice.

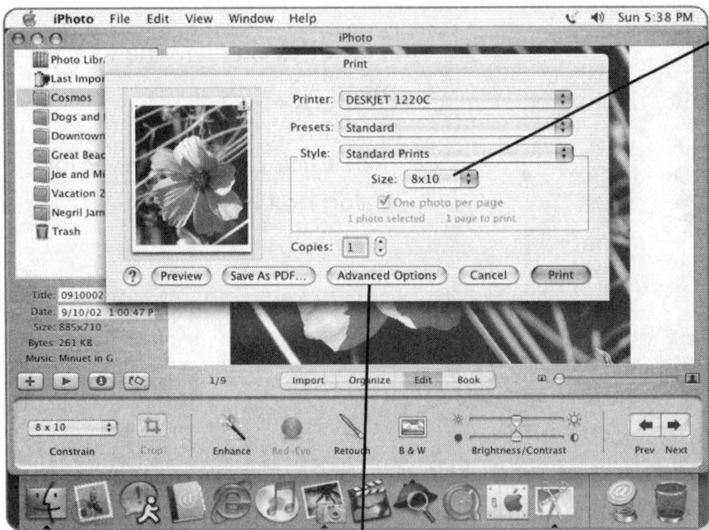


**16. Choose 8 × 10** from the **Size pop-up menu**. The preview area will show the photo in the specified size.

### TIP

The exclamation point icon again means that the photo may not print as well at the larger size. If you're worried about the print quality, try removing the cropping applied earlier and printing the image as is.

**17. Click** on **Advanced Options**. The Print dialog box will adjust to include the advanced printing options.

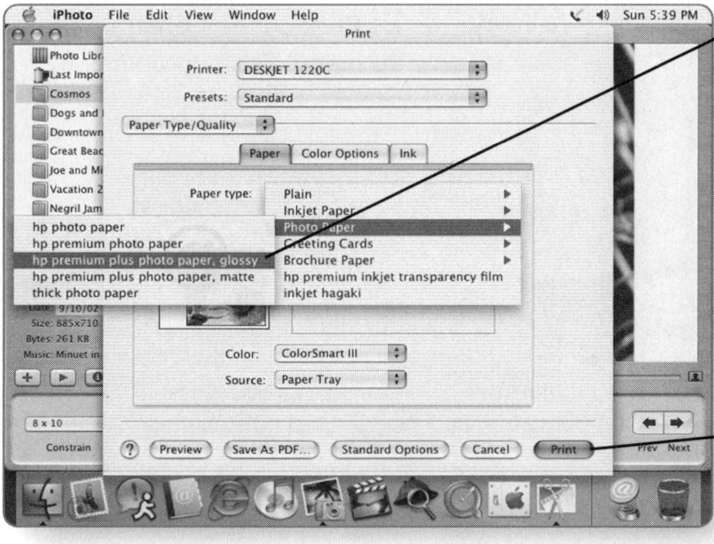

**18. Choose** the **appropriate paper type** using the settings for your printer. (The settings will vary depending on the selected printer.) Additional print settings will be adjusted automatically, so that the printer uses the appropriate print quality and ink saturation for the selected printer.

**19. Click on Print.** iPhoto will send the photo to the specified printer.

## Printing Multiple Photos per Page

If you want multiple prints of a particular image, you can print them on a larger paper size and then trim them yourself. I use this feature often, because even though my printer can print on 4 × 6 paper, it often has trouble with feeding that smaller size. The following example shows how you can print multiple 5 × 7 prints on a single letter-sized page.

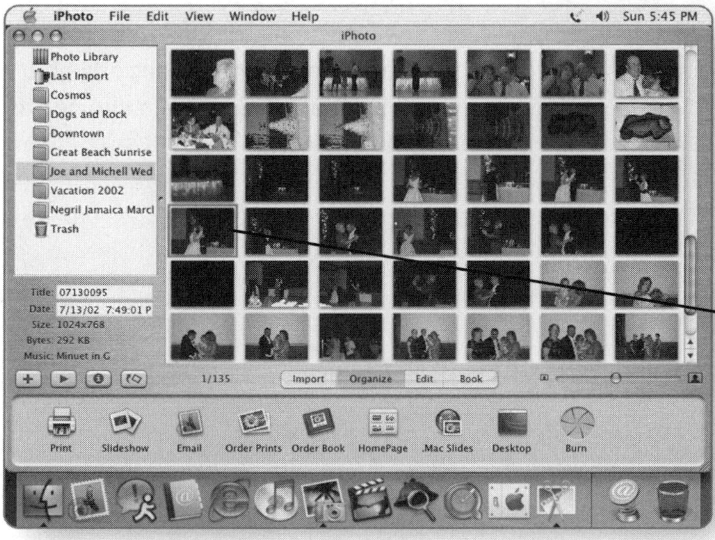

**1.** Working in the Organize pane, **double-click** on the **photo to print** in either the photo library or the current album. The photo will appear in the Edit pane.

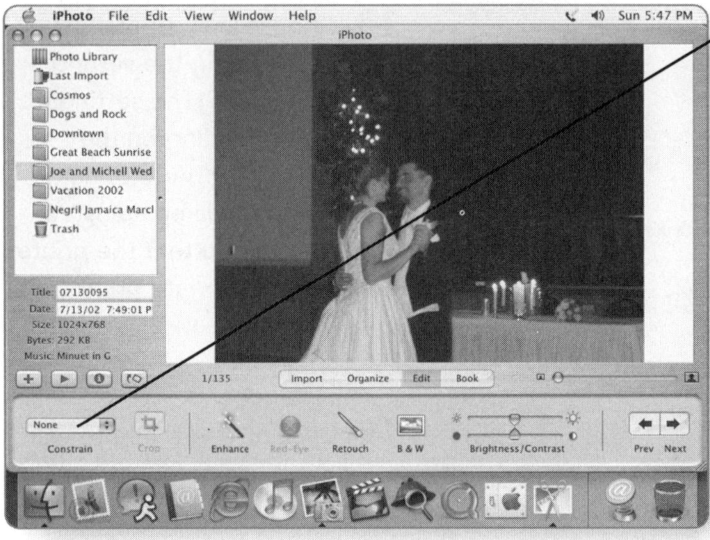


**2. Click** on the **Constrain pop-up menu**. The pop-up menu choices will appear.

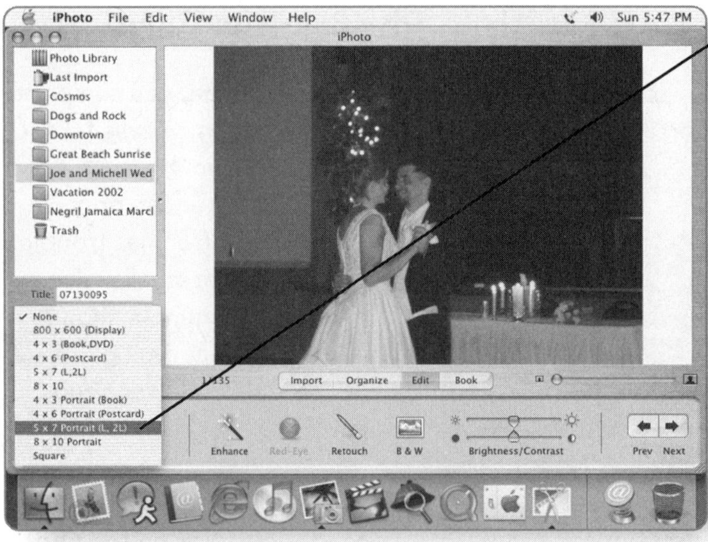


**3. Click** on the desired **Constrain** setting. The setting will be selected, and when you move the mouse pointer over the image, a crosshair pointer will appear. To make a 5″ × 7″ print, for example, choose one of the 5 × 7 Constrain choices as shown here.

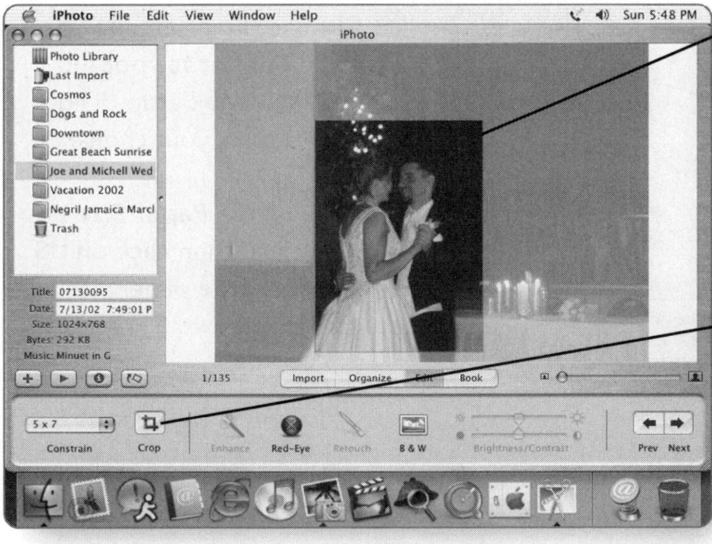


**4. Drag** on the **photo** to specify the crop zone. When you release the mouse button, the area outside the crop zone will be lightened, to graphically illustrate the image area to be cropped.

**5. Click** on the **Crop button**. The image will be cropped as specified.

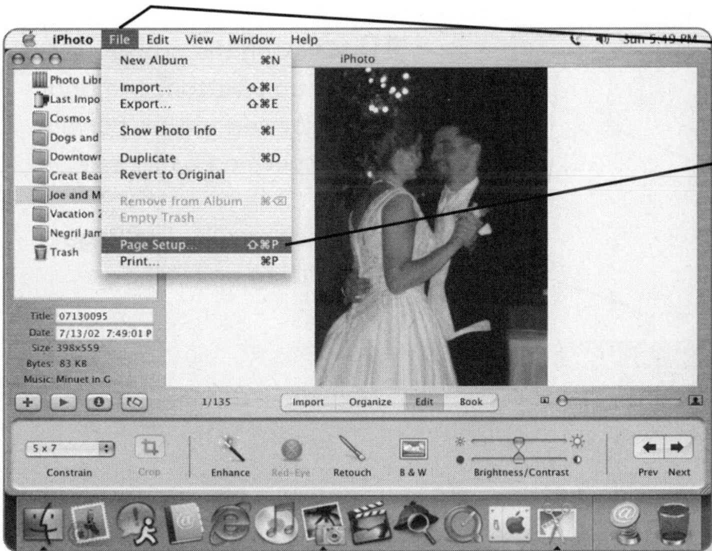


**6. Click** on **File**. The File menu will appear.

**7. Click** on **Page Setup**. The Page Setup dialog box will open.

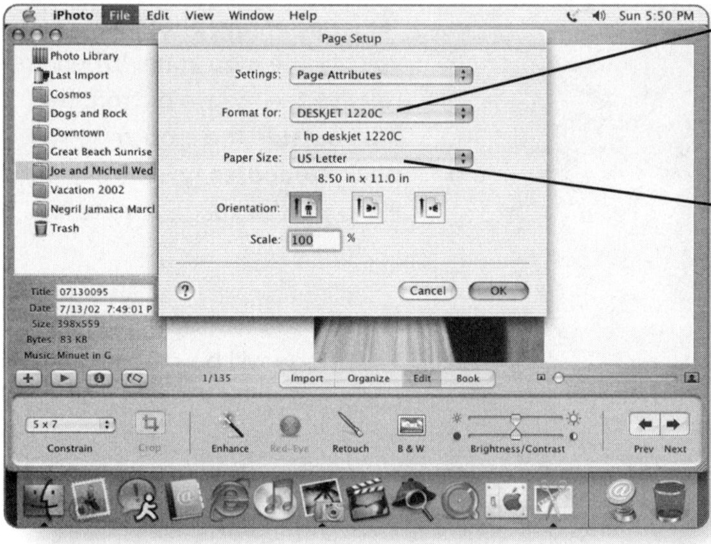


**8. Choose** the **printer to use** from the **Format for pop-up menu**. The Page Setup dialog box will display your choice.

**9. Click** on the **Paper Size pop-up menu** and then **click** on **US Letter**. The large paper size will accommodate two 5 × 7 photos.

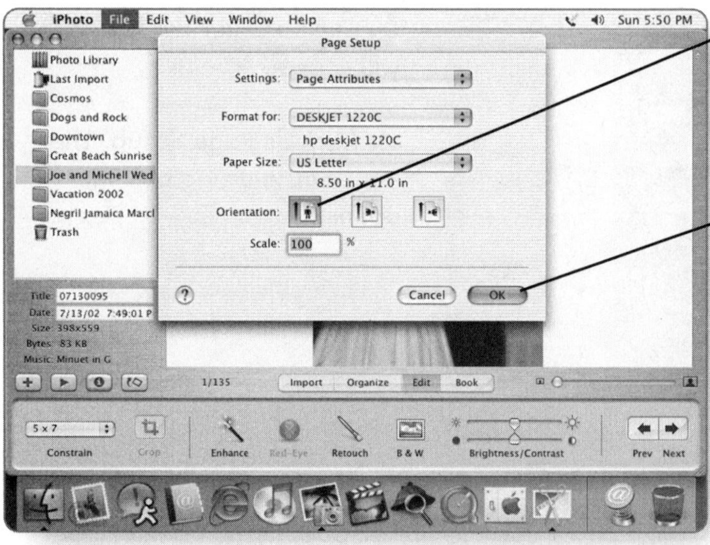


**10. Click** on the proper **Orientation button**. The photo will be rotated to that position on the specified paper size.

**11. Click** on **OK**. The Page Setup dialog box will close.

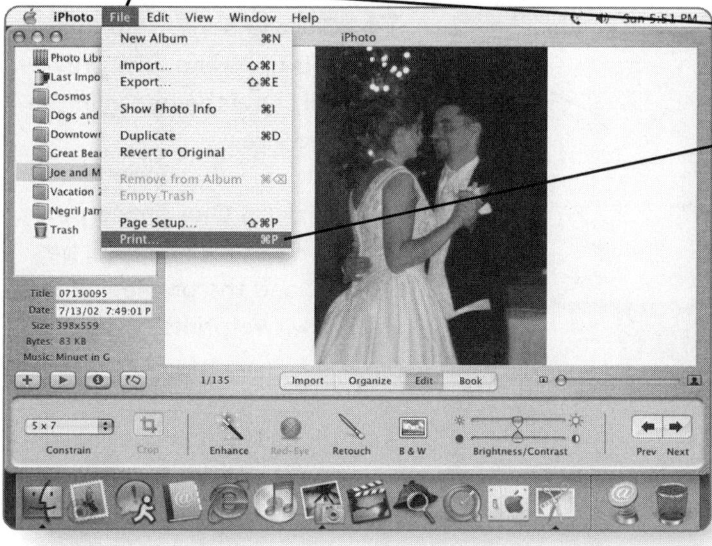

**12.** **Click** on **File**. The File menu will appear.

**13.** **Click** on **Print**. The Print dialog box will open.

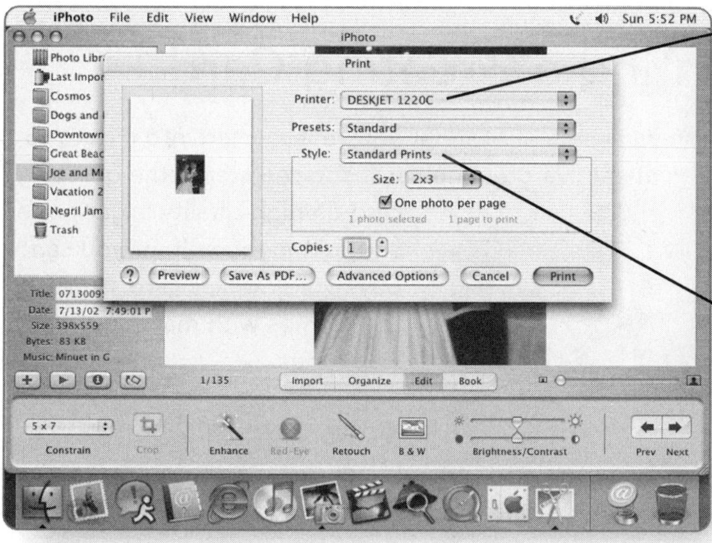

**14.** **Choose** the **printer to use** from the **Printer pop-up menu**. (This should be the same printer that you chose in the Page Setup dialog box.) The Print dialog box will display your choice.

**15.** **Choose Standard Prints** from the **Style pop-up menu**. The Print dialog box will display your choice.

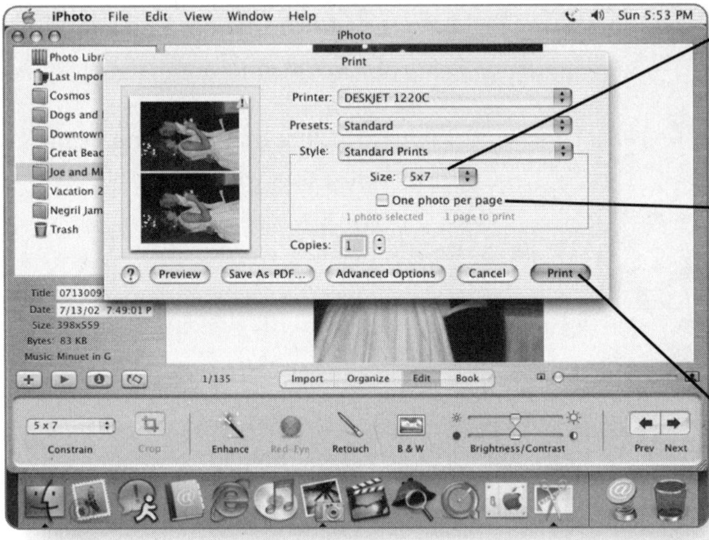


**16.** **Choose 5 × 7** from the **Size pop-up menu**. The preview area will show the photo in the specified size.

**17.** **Click** on **One photo per page**. The check mark will be cleared, and the preview area will show two prints on the page.

**18.** If needed, choose the appropriate paper type as described in the preceding steps. Then, **click** on **Print.** iPhoto will send the photo to the specified printer.

# Printing a Greeting Card

You also can use a photo that you've imported into iPhoto to make an attractive greeting card. You can create the greeting card on high-quality inkjet paper and fold it yourself, or you can buy nice greeting card stock that comes with matching envelopes.

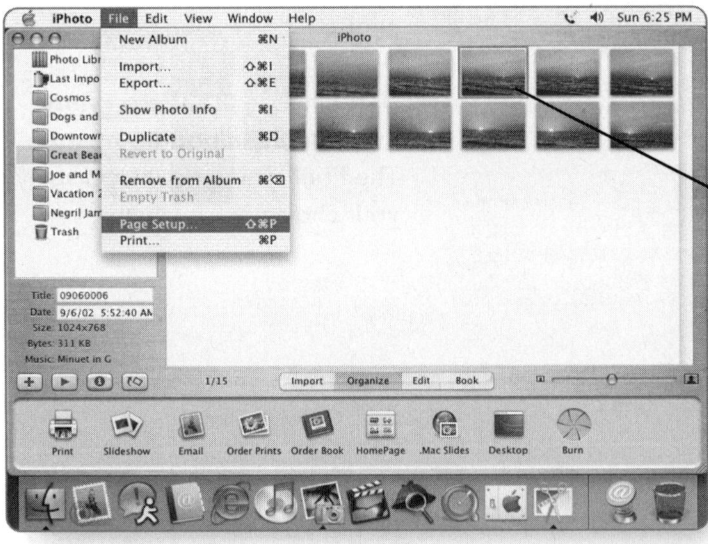


**1.** Working in the Organize pane, **click** on the **photo to print** in either the photo library or the current album. The photo will be selected.

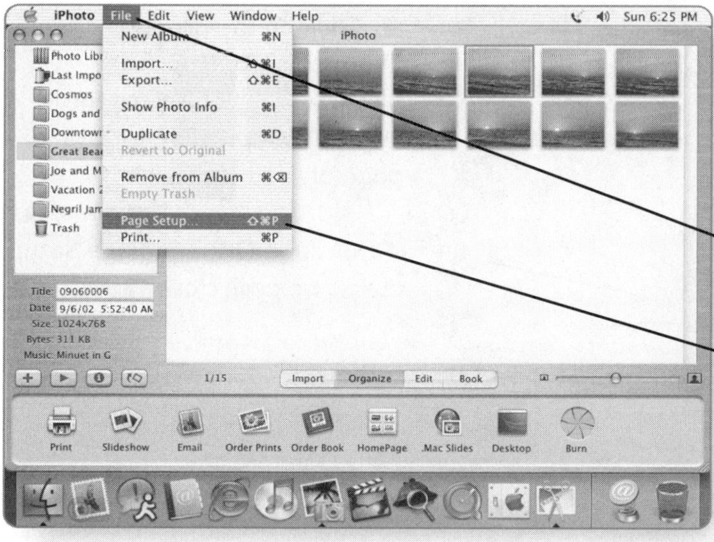


**TIP**

At this point, you can crop the image if desired.

**2. Click** on **File**. The File menu will appear.

**3. Click** on **Page Setup**. The Page Setup dialog box will open.

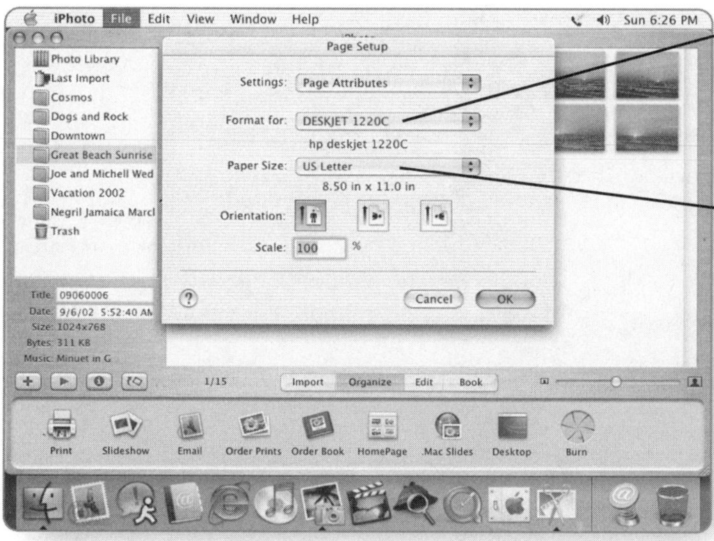


**4. Choose** the **printer to use** from the **Format for pop-up menu.** The Page Setup dialog box will display your choice.

**5. Click** on the **Paper Size pop-up menu** and then **click** on the **appropriate page size.** (Check the packaging if you're using greeting card stock.) The selected paper size will appear.

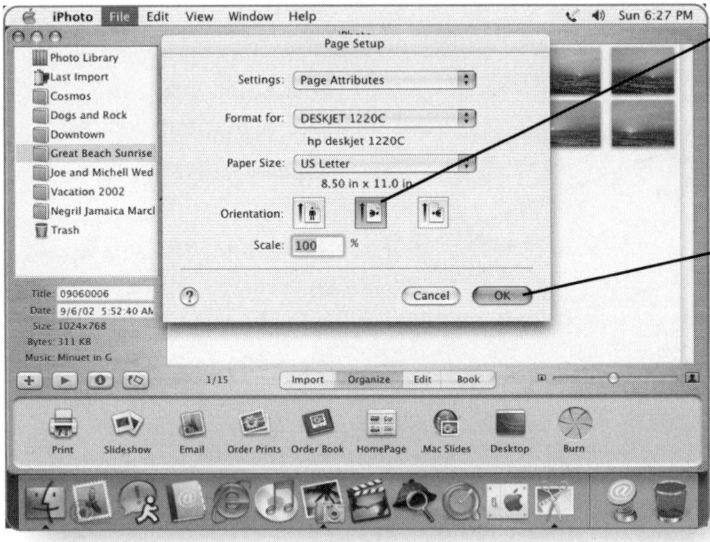

**6. Click** on the proper **Orientation button**. The photo will be rotated to the appropriate position for the page or card stock.

**7. Click** on **OK**. The Page Setup dialog box will close.

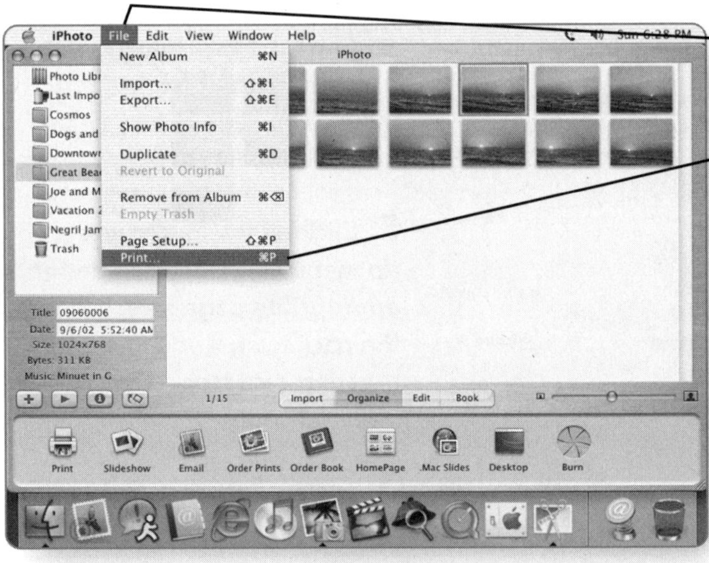

**8. Click** on **File**. The File menu will appear.

**9. Click** on **Print**. The Print dialog box will open.

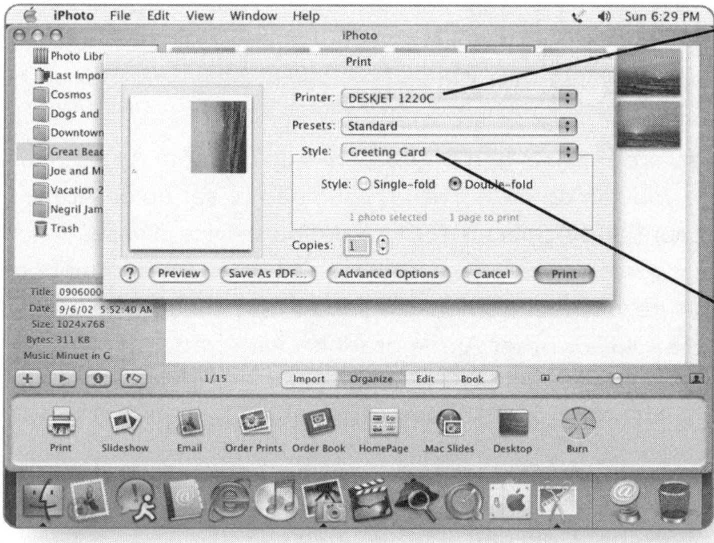

**10.** **Choose** the **printer to use** from the **Printer pop-up menu.** (This should be the same printer that you chose in the Page Setup dialog box.) The Print dialog box will display your choice.

**11.** **Choose Greeting Card** from the **Style pop-up menu.** The Print dialog box will display your choice.

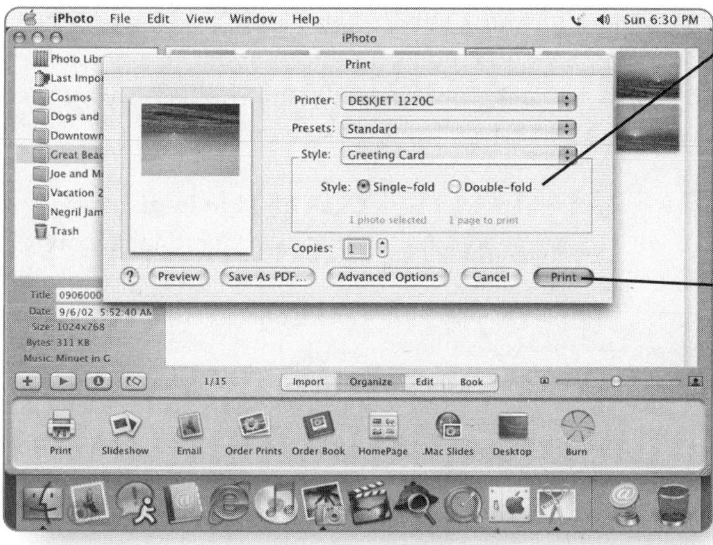

**12.** **Click** the **Single-fold** or **Double-fold Style** as needed. The preview area will show the photo in the appropriate size and position depending on your choice.

**13.** If needed, choose the appropriate paper type as described in the preceding steps. Then, **click** on **Print.** iPhoto will send the photo to the specified printer.

# Signing Up for an Apple ID and 1-Click Ordering

You can order prints and photo books online from Apple. Before you can do so, however, you need to set up an *Apple ID* account and Apple's *1-Click Ordering* service. These services not only store your contact and payment information in a secure way, but also enable you to save time if you order prints, books, or other Apple products with frequency.

> **CAUTION**
>
> You must sign up for 1-Click ordering to order prints or a photo book online.

You can sign up for these services via Apple's Web site. You'll need your contact and credit card information. To sign up for both of these services, connect to the Internet, start your Web browser, and go to http://store.apple.com.

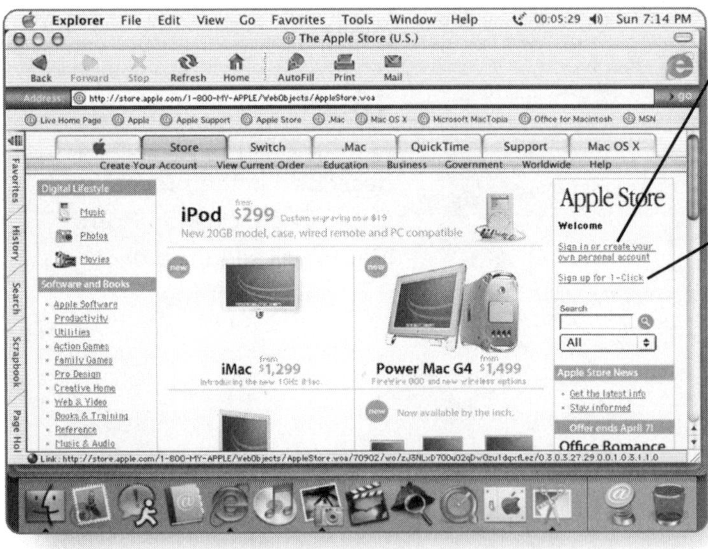


- **Click** on **Sign in or create your own personal account,** and then follow the on-screen directions to create your Apple ID.
- **Click** on **Sign up for 1-Click,** and then follow the on-screen directions to sign up for 1-Click ordering.

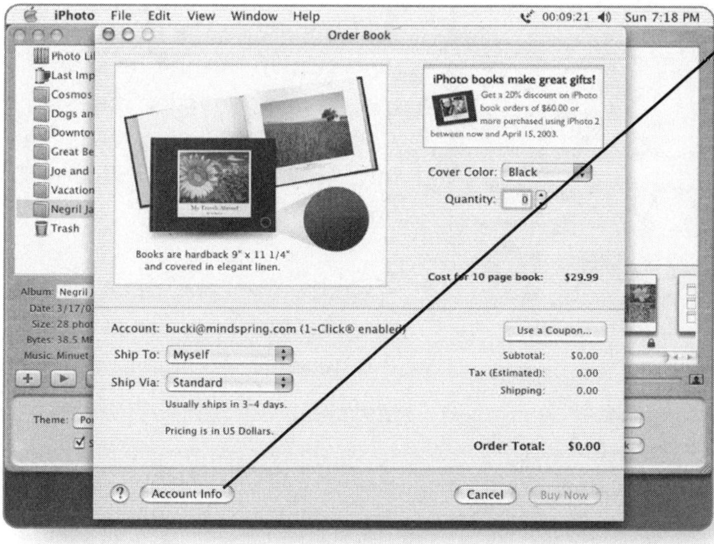

- Alternately, if you've already started the process of ordering prints or a book as described next, you can **click** on the **Account Info** button in the Order window, and then click on the Create Account button in the Account Info window that appears.

Be sure to record your Apple ID and 1-Click ordering information so that you can supply it to iPhoto if prompted.

# Ordering Prints

iPhoto 2 enables you to order prints from Apple online. Your prints will be printed via the Kodak Print Service on Kodak paper. If this is your preferred method of obtaining photo prints, use the following steps to place your order. Note that no photo title or comment information will appear on your prints.

> **CAUTION**
>
> You should crop photos in the Edit pane using a Constrain setting that's consistent with the size of the prints you want to order. Otherwise, your prints might have portions cut off. For example, if you crop a photo to a square size but order a 4″ × 6″ print, the sides of the image will likely be cut off in the finished print.

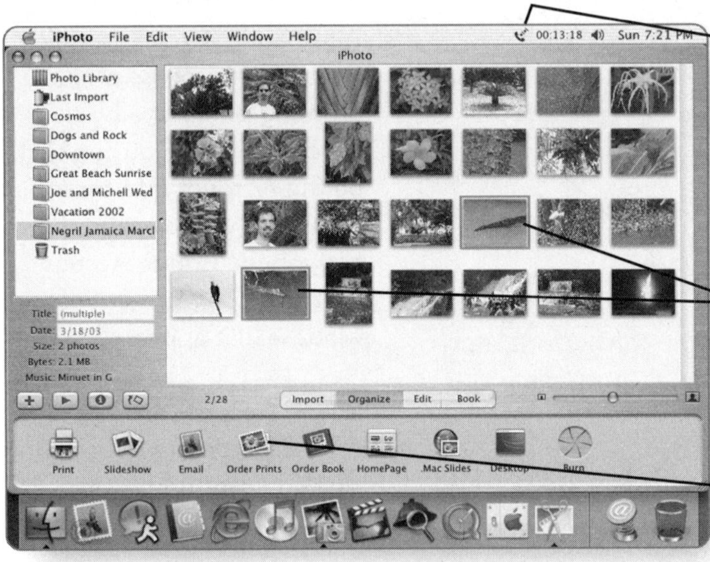


**1. Connect** to the **Internet**, if your system doesn't have an always-on connection. See Appendix C, "Dialing the Internet If Needed," to learn how.

**2.** In the Organize pane, **select** the **photo(s) to order as prints.** A blue selection highlight will identify the selected photo(s).

**3. Click** on **Order Prints.** iPhoto will connect to the online ordering service. The Order Prints window will open.

## CAUTION

If one of the selected photos has a question mark (?) in its file name, the Apple service will not be able to make prints from it. Rename the original photo file to remove the question mark, re-import the photo into iPhoto, and then select it and order the prints.

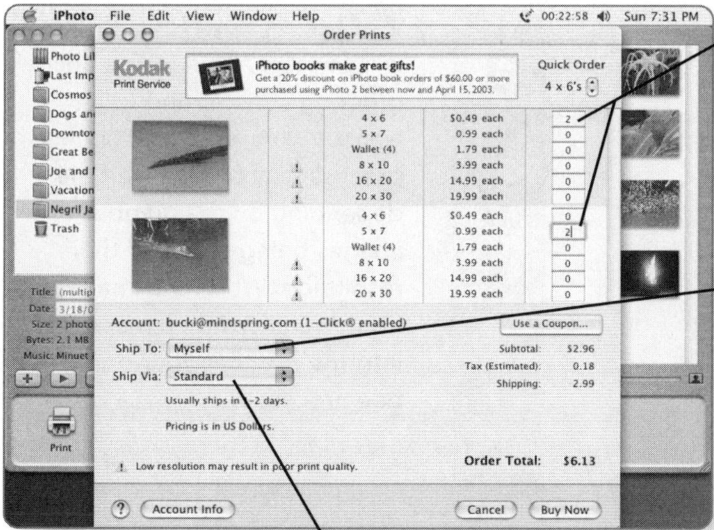


**4.** **Enter** the **desired number** of prints in the **text box** for the **desired size** beside each photo. The calculated Order Total will update to reflect the number of prints requested.

**5.** If you want to ship to someone other than yourself, **click** on the **Ship To pop-up menu**, click on **Add New Address**, and then **follow** the **on-screen instructions** to set up a new address. The address will be selected.

**6.** **Choose** a **shipping method** from the **Ship Via pop-up menu**. The calculated Shipping Amount and Order Total will update to reflect your choice.

> **NOTE**
>
> If you are not prompted for account information the first time you order, see the later section called "Updating Account Information" to learn how to ensure that iPhoto is using the correct Apple ID, shipping, and 1-Click information.

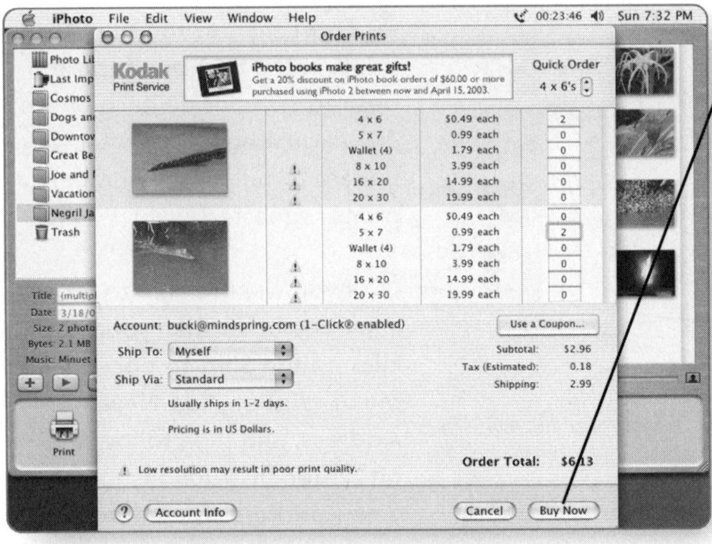

**7. Click** on **Buy Now**. iPhoto will connect again to the online ordering service, and will transfer your images. This process may take some time, depending on the number of images being sent and their resolution. When the images finish transferring, a message informs you that your order has been received.

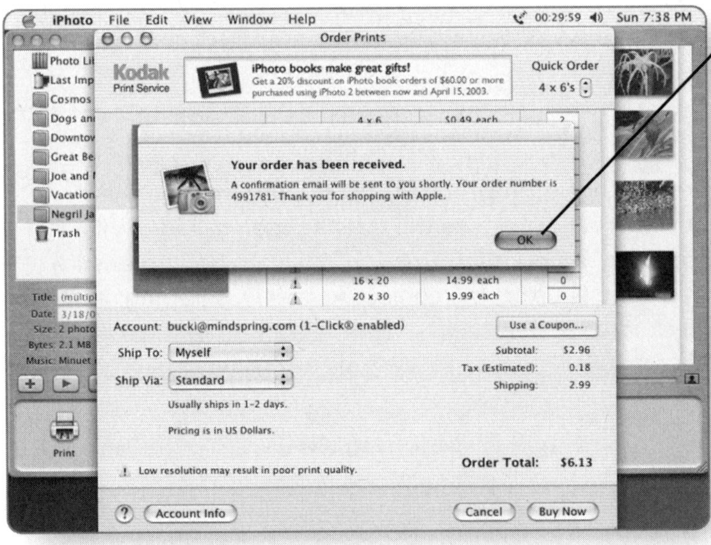

**8. Record your order number**, and then **click** on **OK.** iPhoto will close the message box and the Order Prints window. You can then disconnect from the Internet, if desired.

# Ordering a Photo Book

Only recently has it become cost effective to order a professionally-printed photo book. Use this first-class method to preserve memories of an important event or trip. Thrill your friends and relatives by creating a thoughtful keepsake of a child's early days, a favorite pet, or a 40th birthday party. iPhoto 2 makes it easy to order one or more books based on a photo book that you've set up within the program.

> **TIP**
>
> If you've previously set up an album as a book, you can select the book and then click on Order Book at the bottom of the Organize pane, and then skip to Step 4.

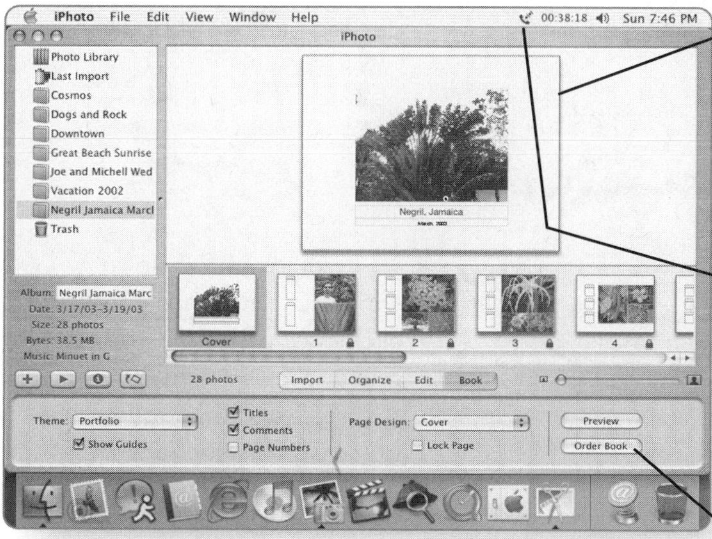


**1. Create** a **photo book** in the Book pane as described in Chapter 7, "Setting Up a Photo Book." The book will be set up using the theme and other choices that you've made.

**2. Connect** to the **Internet**, if your system doesn't have an always-on connection. See Appendix C, "Dialing the Internet If Needed," to learn how.

**3. Click** on **Order Book**. iPhoto will connect to the online ordering service. The Order Book window will open.

> **TIP**
>
> If a photo has a low resolution, iPhoto will display a warning. You can either click on Stop to correct the problem, or Continue. Similarly, if text is too large to fit in a placeholder, a warning will appear. Warnings about text are of greater concern than warnings about images, as a fuzzy image is (slightly) easier to live with than cut off (and therefore unreadable) text.

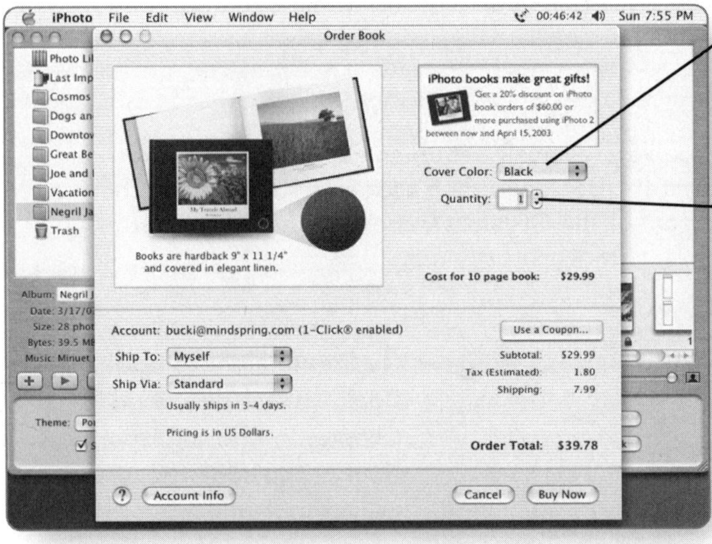


**4. Choose** the **desired color** from the **Cover Color pop-up menu**. The preview will display the specified cover color.

**5. Enter** the **desired number** of book copies in the **Quantity text box.** The calculated Order Total will update to reflect the desired number of books.

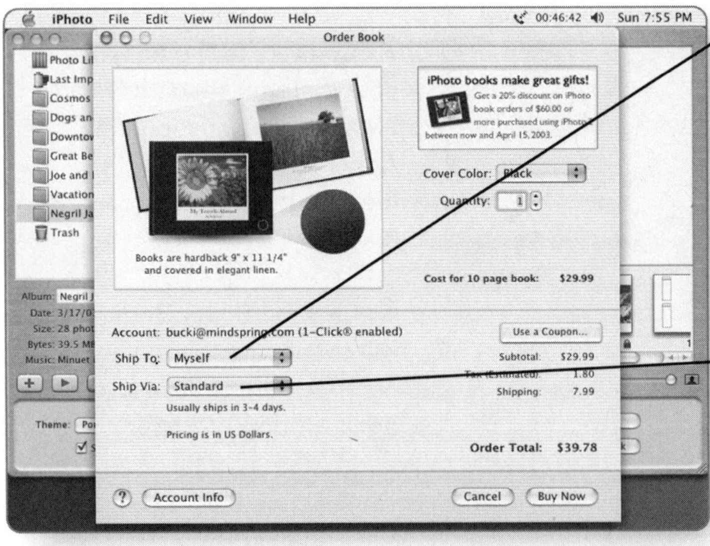


**6.** If you want to ship to someone other than yourself, **click** on the **Ship To pop-up menu, click** on **Add New Address**, and then **follow** the **on-screen instructions** to set up a new address. The address will be selected.

**7. Choose** a **shipping method** from the **Ship Via pop-up menu**. The calculated Shipping Amount and Order Total will update to reflect your choice.

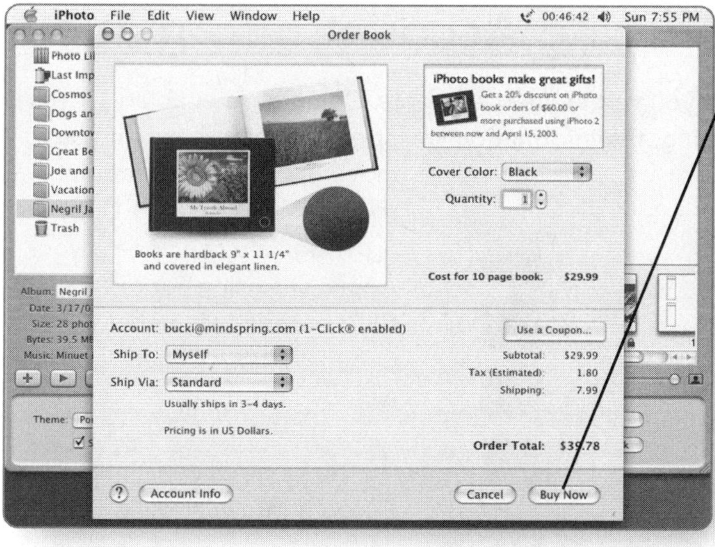


**8. Click** on **Buy Now.** iPhoto will connect again to the online ordering service, and will transfer your images. This process will again take some time (an hour or two on a slow dial-up connection), depending on the number of images being sent and the number of pages in the book. When the book finishes transferring, a message informs you that your order has been received.

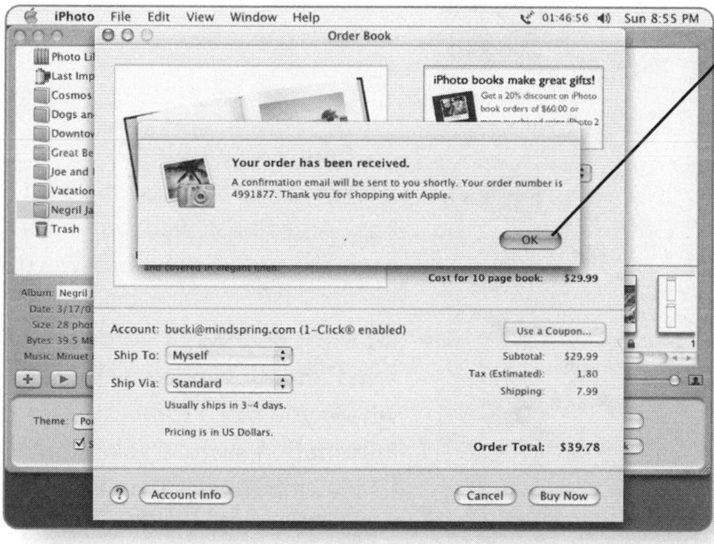


**9. Record your order number**, and then **click** on **OK.** iPhoto will close the message box and the Order Book window. You can then disconnect from the Internet, if desired.

# Updating Account Information

After you've obtained an Apple ID and have enabled 1-Click ordering, the information you specified may change if you move or no longer need (for some reason) to use 1-Click ordering. You can update your Apple ID settings or disable 1-Click ordering via either the Order Prints or Order Book window.

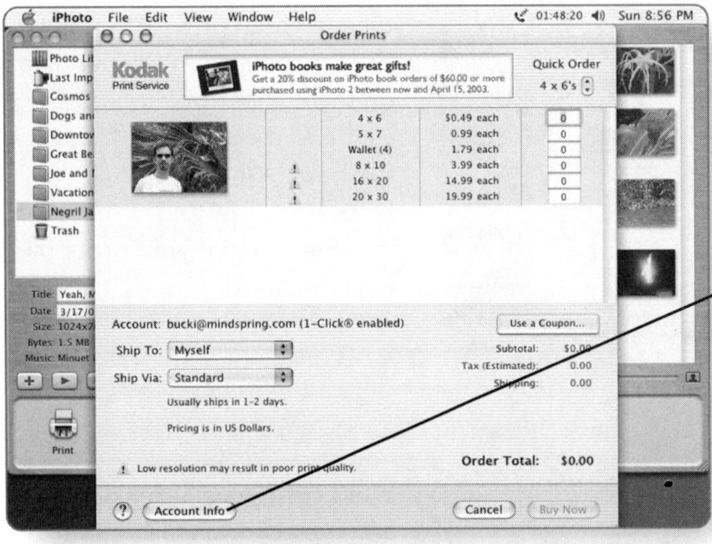


1. **Click** on **Account Info**. The Account Info window will open.

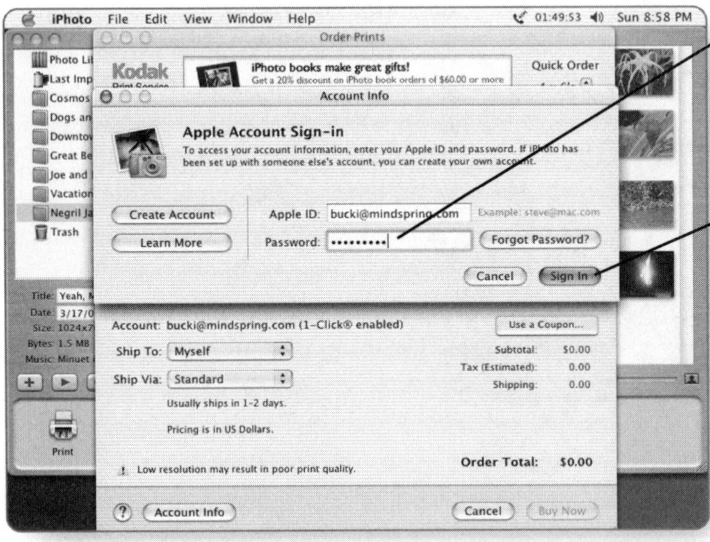


2. **Type** your **Apple ID Password** in the Password text box. An asterisk will appear for each character in the password.

3. **Click** on **Sign In**. Another Account Info window will open, where you can update information such as your Apple ID information (click on Edit Apple ID), or your billing (Edit Billing) or shipping (Edit Shipping) information. You also can click on the Enable 1-Click Purchasing check box. When you clear this check box, 1-Click Ordering will be turned off.

# 11

# Viewing Your Photos on Your Mac

For a few chapters now, you've looked at things you can do to share your photos with others. iPhoto 2 also enables you to use your photos for your own enjoyment on your Mac. In this chapter, you will learn how to:

- Set up a slideshow with custom timing and music.
- Play an album slideshow.
- Use a photo as your desktop background.
- Use the photos in an album as your screen saver.

# Viewing a Slideshow on the Desktop

When you display an iPhoto album as an on-screen slideshow, iPhoto displays each image at full-screen size (no application window) for a designated amount of time, and plays the background music that you specify. You can set up a slideshow for pleasure, but you also can use slideshows for other purposes. For example, if you're taking your iBook or PowerBook along with you for a sales presentation, you could set up a slideshow that shows photos of your key products in use or shows customers benefiting from using your products. Whether you create it for pleasure or business, a slideshow shows off your photos for maximum impact.

## Setting Slideshow Preferences for an Album

While you can display a slideshow at any time, you may want to take the time to set up slideshow preferences first. You can specify how long each image appears on-screen, choose a random display order, repeat the slideshow, and assign music you've added to your *iTunes library*.

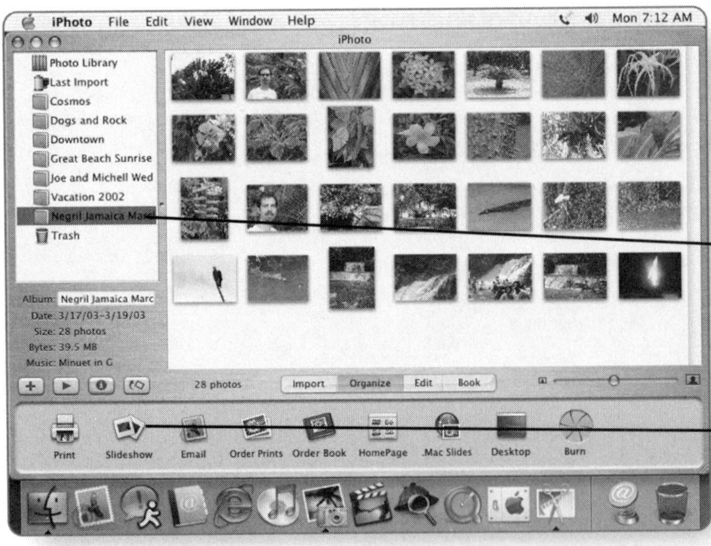


1. **Select** the **album** to view as a slideshow in the library list. The album's photos will appear in the photo viewing area.

2. **Click** on **Slideshow**. The Slideshow Settings window will open.

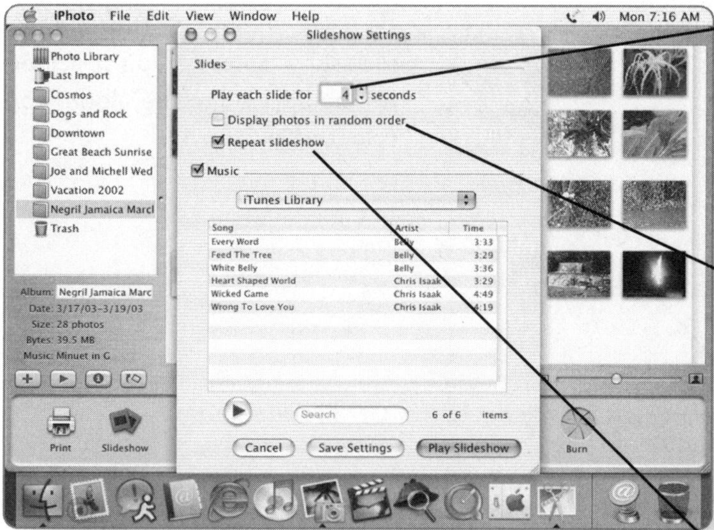


**3. Edit** the **Place each slide for (X) seconds** setting as desired. Your entry here will determine how many seconds each photo appears on-screen when you run the slideshow.

**4. Click** on **Display photos in random order** if desired. When you check this option, iPhoto will display the photos randomly, rather than in the order in which they appear in the album.

**5. Click** on **Repeat slideshow** if desired. When you uncheck this option, iPhoto will play the slideshow only once after you start playback.

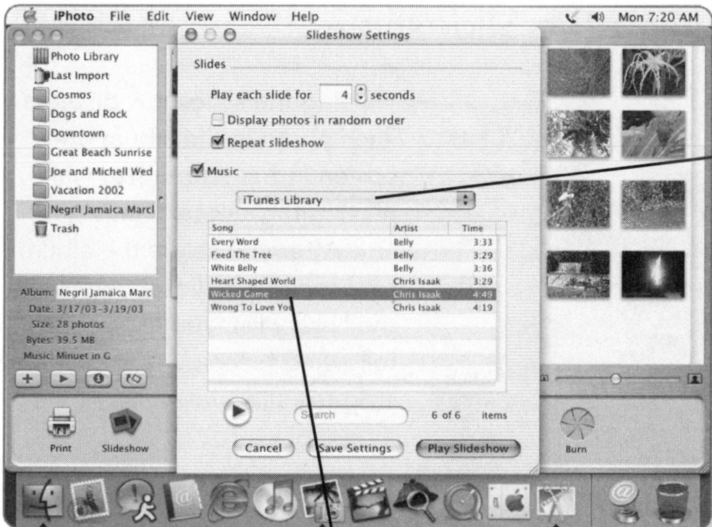


**6. Select iTunes Library**, if needed, from the pop-up menu below the Music check box. The songs you previously added to the iTunes library will appear in the list of songs.

> **NOTE**
>
> To set up the slideshow to run without music, click on the Music check box to clear the check.

**7. Click** on the **desired song**. The song will be selected.

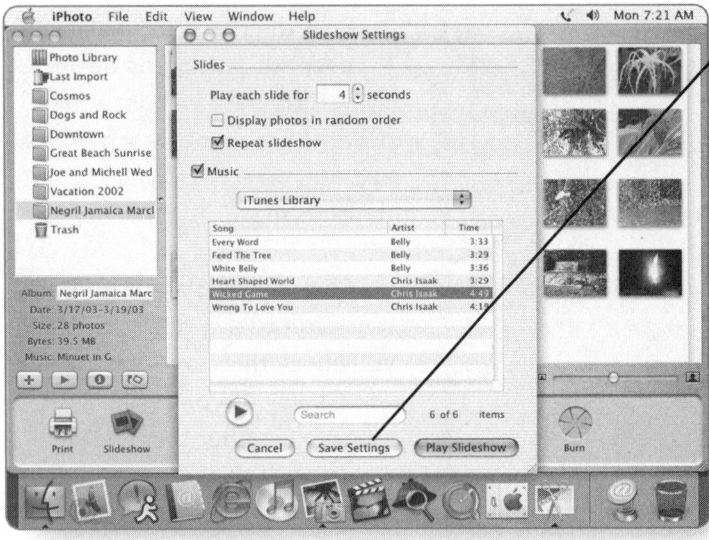


**8.** **Click** on **Save Settings**. The slideshow settings you specified will be applied to the album you selected in Step 1.

## Viewing the Slideshow

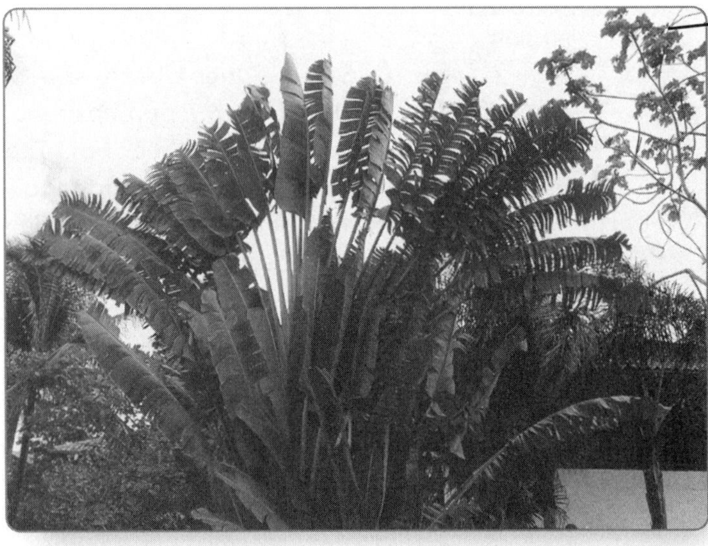

Viewing the slideshow displays each photo in the album on-screen at full-screen size while playing the selected music, if any. After you select the album to display as a slideshow from the library list, you can use the following techniques to play and stop the slideshow.

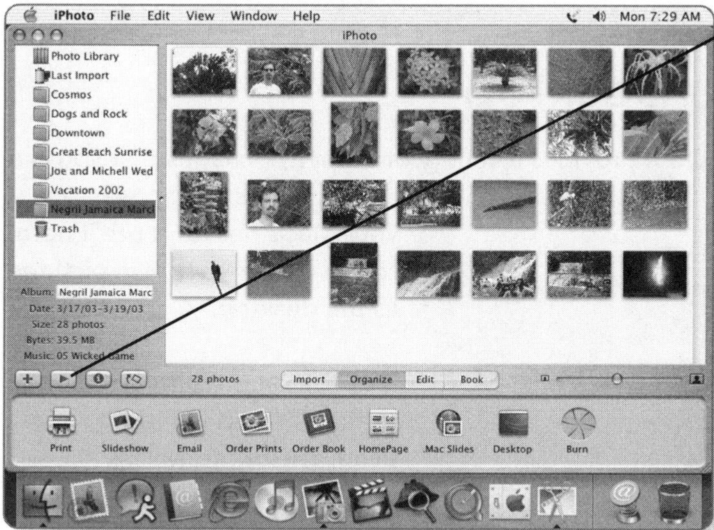


- **Click** on the **Play button** in the Organize pane to start the slideshow.

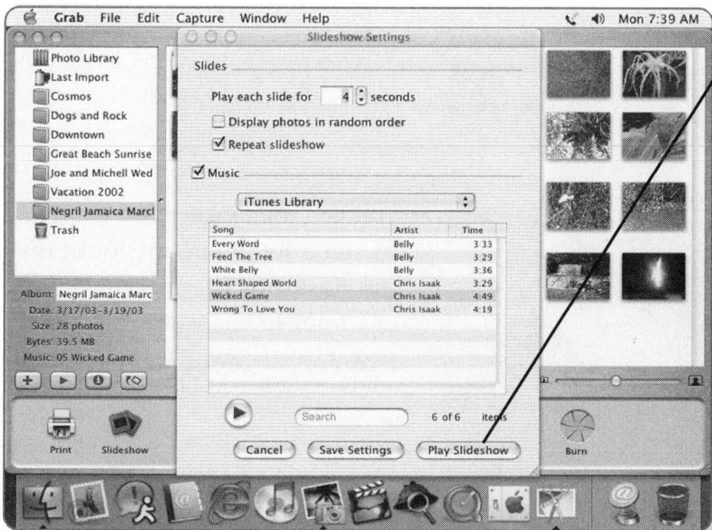


- Or, if you're working in the Slideshow Settings window, click on Play Slideshow to start the playback.
- To pause and restart the slideshow, press the Spacebar on the keyboard. Pausing stops on the current photo. The slideshow music continues playing while the photo playback is paused.
- To stop (exit) the slideshow, press the Esc key on the keyboard.

# Applying a Photo to the Desktop

Mac OS X provides a variety of attractive images that you can apply to the desktop. To render a *really* custom appearance to your Mac's desktop, use iPhoto to use one of your own pictures as the desktop.

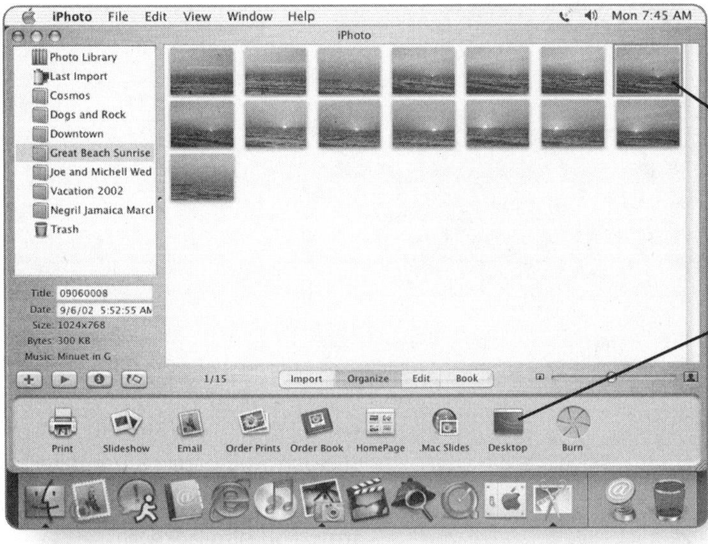


1. **Click** on the **photo** to apply to the desktop in the Organize pane. The photo will be selected.

2. **Click** on **Desktop**. iPhoto will immediately apply the photo to your desktop.

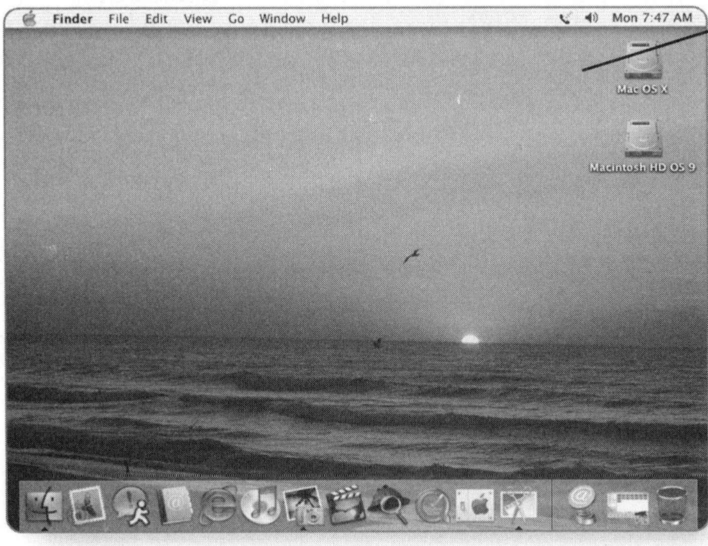


You can minimize open windows to see how the image looks on the desktop. Then, restore the windows to the prior size so that you can continue working.

**NOTE**

To change back to one of the Mac OS X backgrounds, Control+click on the desktop, and then click Change Desktop Background. Select the desired background image in the Desktop pane of System Preferences, and then choose System Preferences, Quit System Preferences.

# Rotating an Album's Images on the Desktop

You can use System Preferences to select an album of images to use on the desktop. System Preferences will display another image from the album on the desktop after the designated time frame. For example, it will display the first image for 15 minutes, switch to the next image and display it for 15 minutes, and so on. iPhoto need not be open for this process.

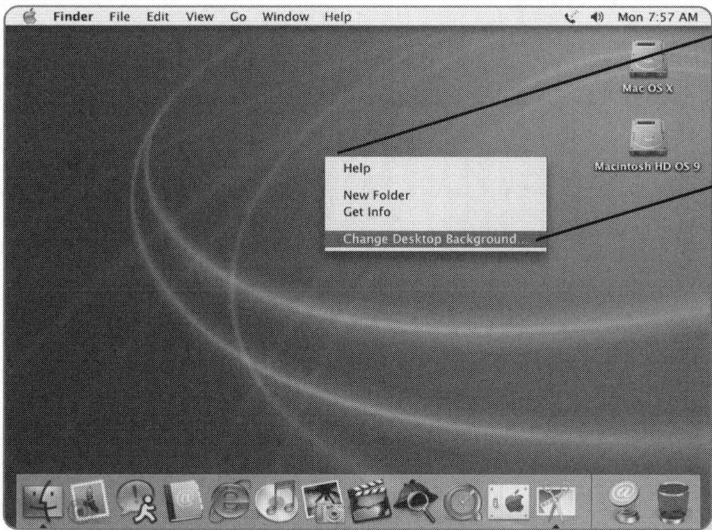


1. **Control+click** on the **desktop**. The contextual menu will open.

2. **Click** on **Change Desktop Background**. The Desktop pane in System Preferences will open.

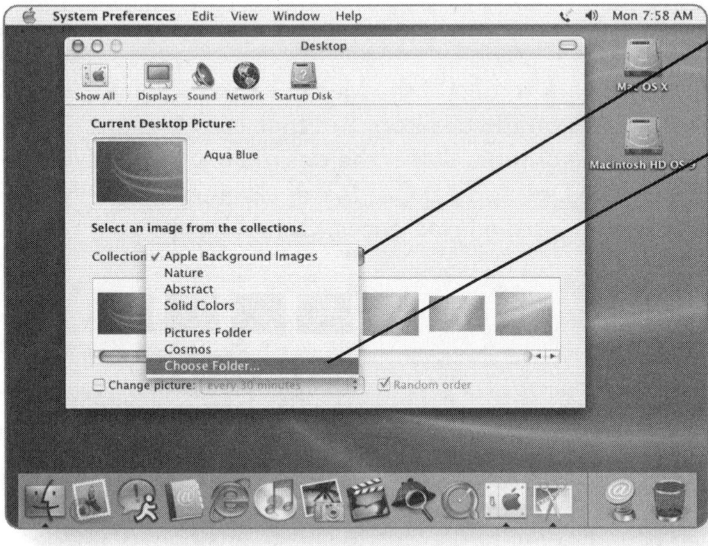


**3. Click** on the **Collection pop-up menu**. The menu will open.

**4. Click** on **Choose Folder**. A sheet for choosing a folder will open from the Desktop pane menu bar.

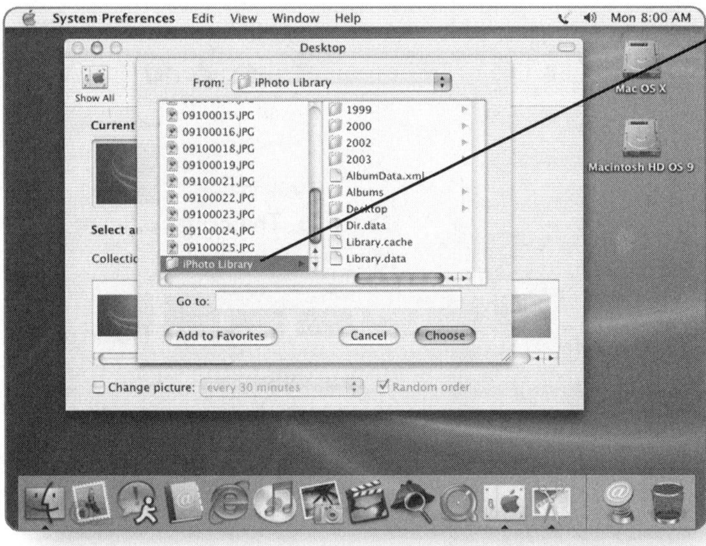


**5. Navigate** to the **iPhoto Library subfolder** in your Pictures folder. The Albums choice will appear in the list of folders.

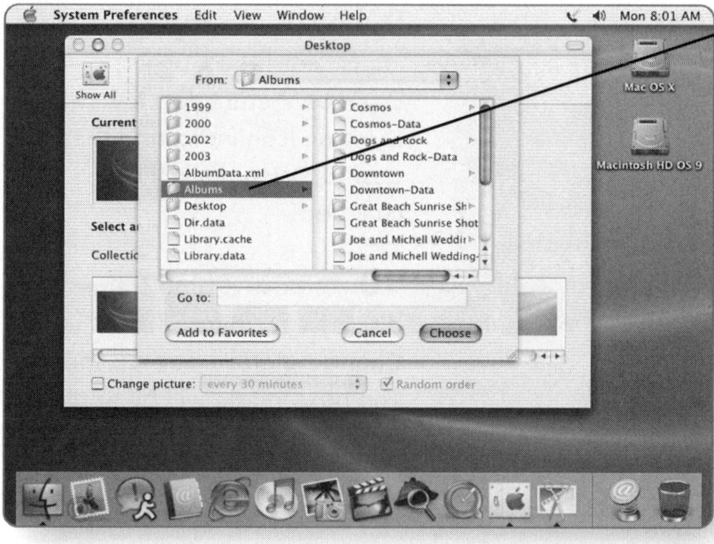

**6. Click** on the **Albums subfolder**. The available albums will each appear as a subfolder in the list of folders.

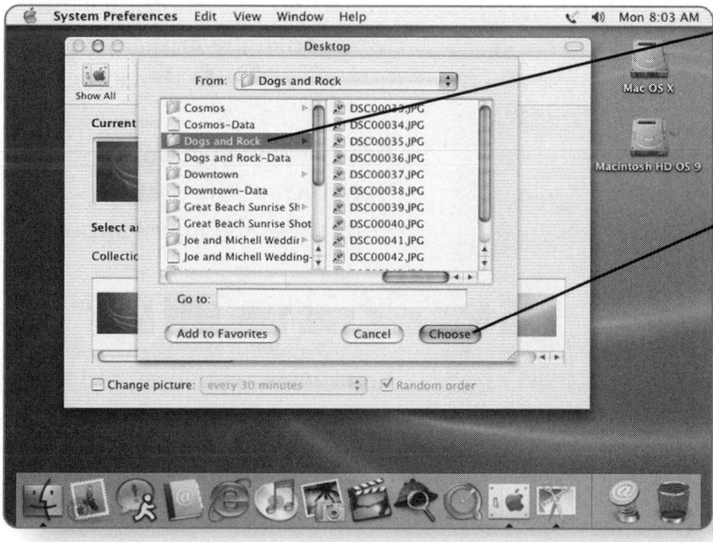

**7. Click** on the desired **album subfolder**. The icons for the shortcuts to the album's image files will appear.

**8. Click** on **Choose**. The images in the album will be loaded as the images available for the desktop in the Desktop pane.

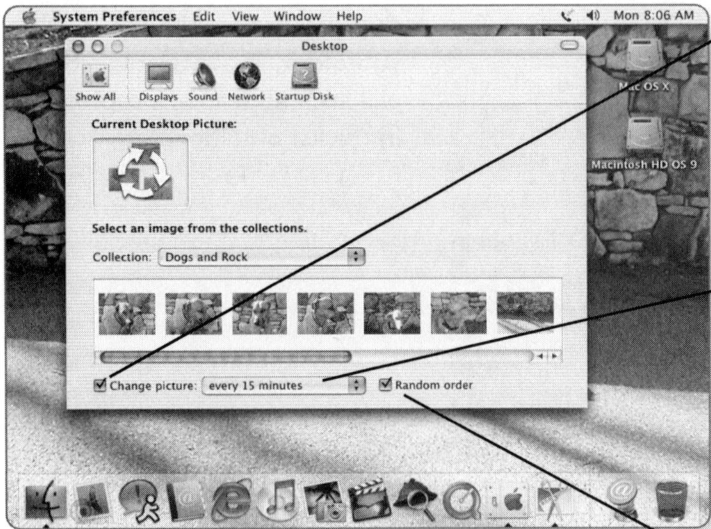


**9. Click** on the **Change picture check box**. The Current Desktop Picture preview will show an icon indicating that desktop pictures will be changed.

**10. Choose a time frame** to display each photo from the **Change picture pop-up menu**. The next image will be applied to the desktop, and the specified time setting will appear.

**11. Click** on **Random order**, if desired. When this option is unchecked, the photos will be displayed in the order in which they are stored in the album.

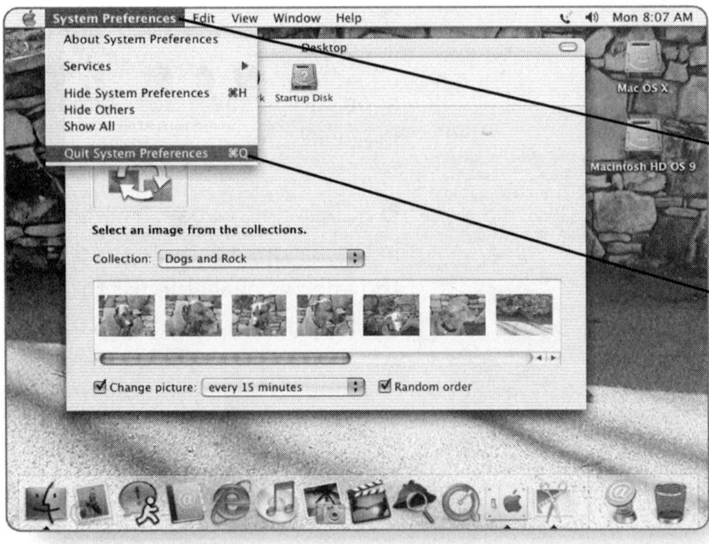


**12. Click** on **System Preferences**. The System Preferences menu will appear.

**13. Click** on **Quit System Preferences**. System Preferences will close, and the specified album's photos will be displayed one at a time on the desktop.

# Using an Album as Your Screen Saver

Similarly, you can display the photos from an album as your screen saver. Because you use System Preferences to choose a screen saver, iPhoto need not be open for this process.

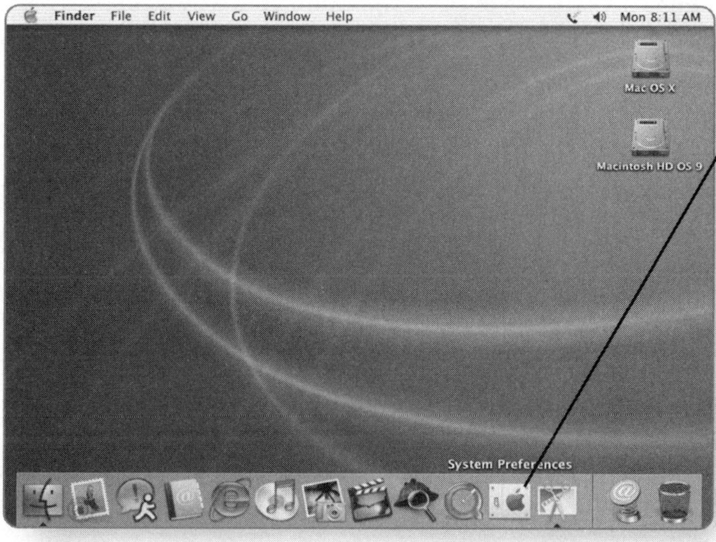


1. **Click** on the **System Preferences icon** on the Dock. The System Preferences application window will open.

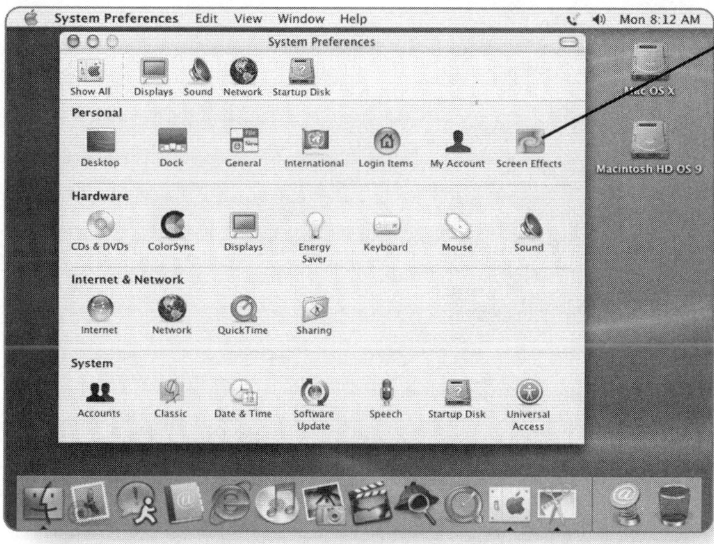


2. **Click** on **Screen Effects**. The Screen Effects pane will open.

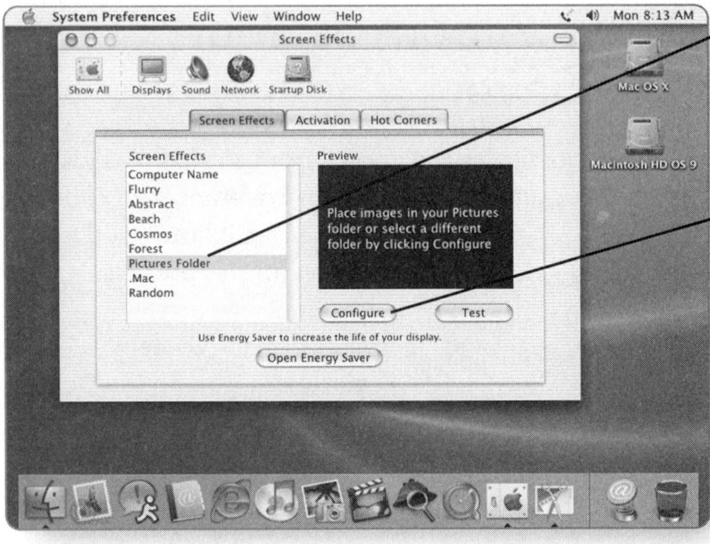


**3. Click** on **Pictures Folder** in the Screen Effects list. The Preview will explain how to start selecting a folder.

**4. Click** on **Configure**. A sheet will open so that you can choose the album folder.

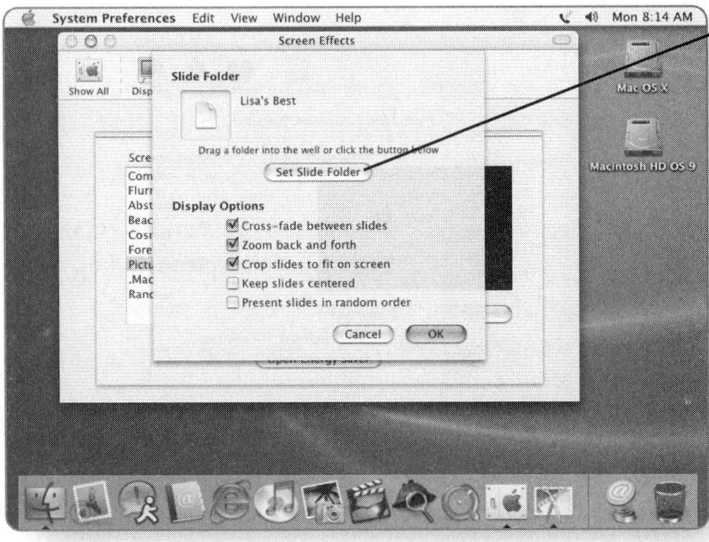


**5. Click** on **Set Slide Folder**. The Open dialog box will open.

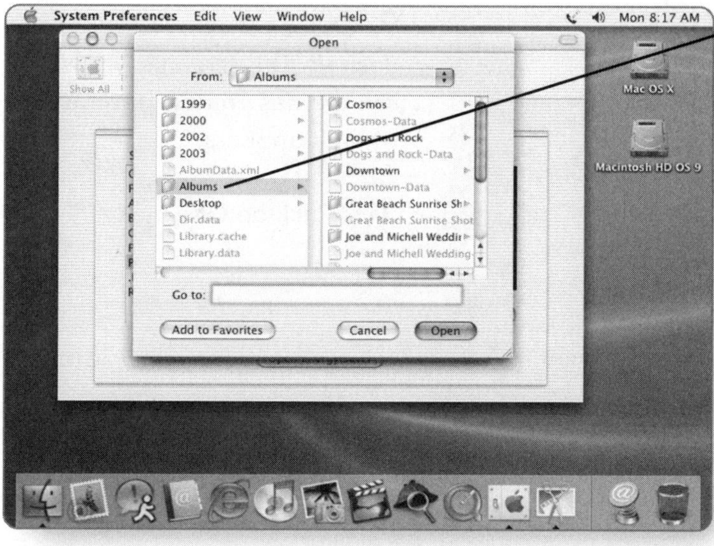

**6. Navigate** to your **Pictures: iPhoto Library: Albums subfolder**. The album subfolders will be listed in the dialog box.

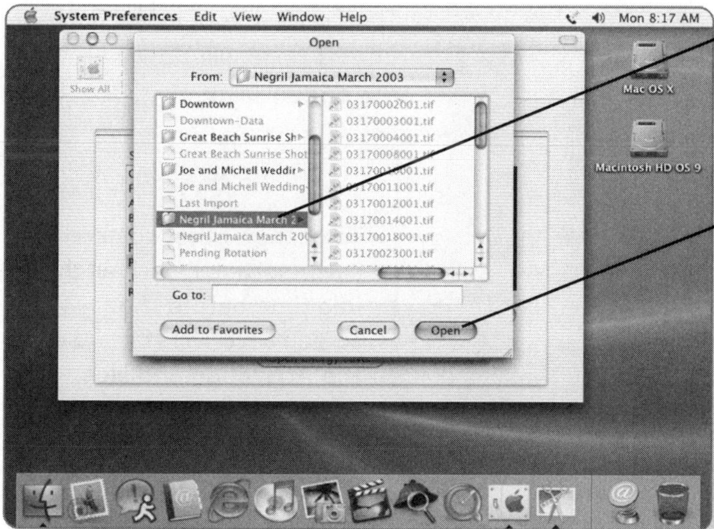

**7. Click** on the desired **album subfolder**. The icons for the shortcuts to the album's image files will appear.

**8. Click** on **Open**. The album will be listed as the Slide Folder in the Screen Effects sheet.

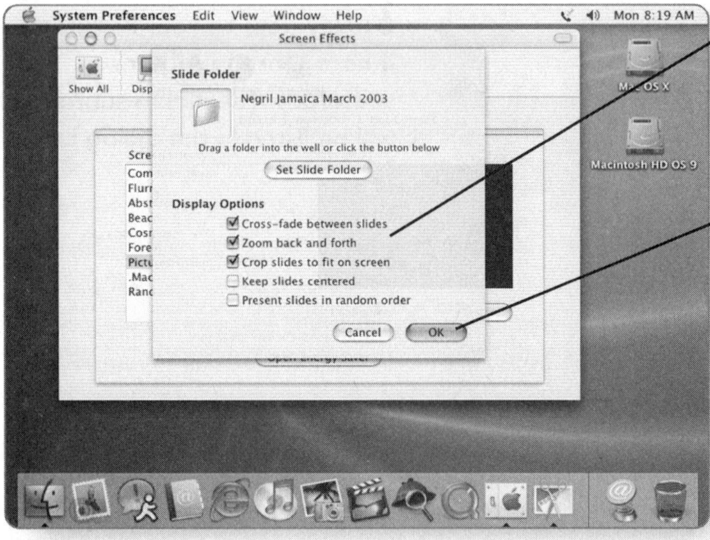


**9. Choose Display Options** as desired. The screen saver will use the designated settings when it appears.

**10. Click** on **OK**.

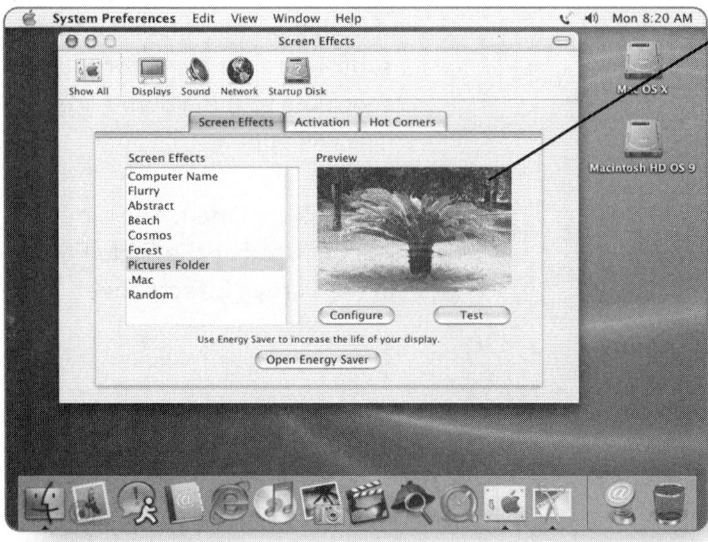


The Preview area in the Screen Effects pane will slowly preview the screen saver.

## NOTE

To change other screen saver settings, such as the idle time before the screen save will start, use the Activation and Hot Corners tabs of the Screen Effects pane in System Preferences.

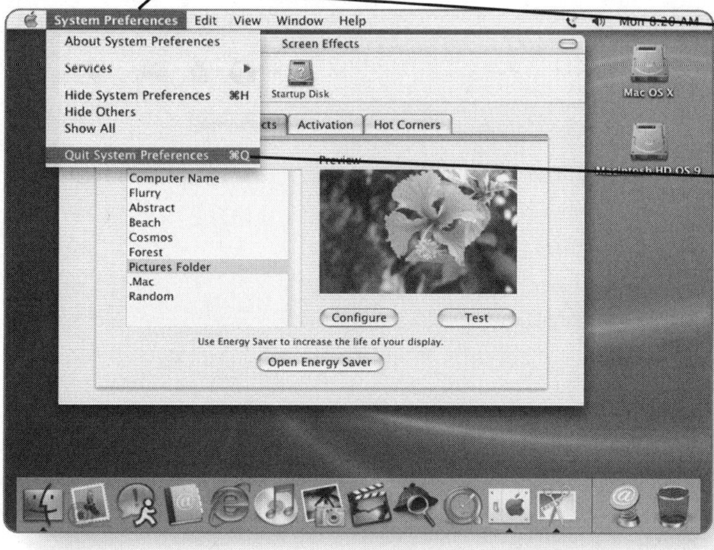


**11.** Click on **System Preferences.** The System Preferences menu will appear.

**12.** Click on **Quit System Preferences.** System Preferences will close, and the specified album's photos will be displayed one at a time on the desktop.

# 12

# Exporting Your Photos

Most users start exploring new programs as their computer skills increase. For that reason, iPhoto 2 enables you to export one or more photos in different ways, so that you can use those photos more effectively in other applications. In this chapter, you will learn how to:

- Export photos to make files in a new size or format.
- Create, edit, and post a Web page of photos.
- Create a QuickTime movie from an album.

# Exporting Images in Another Size or Format

Most digital cameras save images in either the JPG (JPEG) or TIFF file format. You may need to convert an image to another size or format for use in another application. For example, TIFF images often print more clearly in documents than JPEG images. As such, you may want to use iPhoto to convert a JPEG image into a TIFF. Or, you may want to convert full-sized photos to a smaller size, such as downsizing from 1152 x 864 pixels to 640 × 480 pixels. To perform such a conversion, you have to *export* the photos. iPhoto enables you to convert exported photos to the JPG (JPEG), TIFF, and PNG (a common format for Web graphics) formats.

> **NOTE**
>
> Each export operation can perform only one conversion. You can either export to a new file format or export to a new image size.

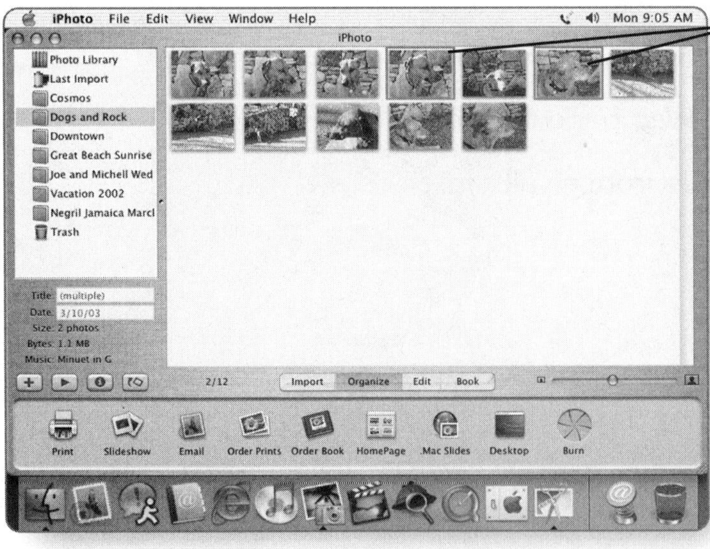


**1.** **Select** the **photo(s)** to export. A blue selection highlight will appear around the photo(s).

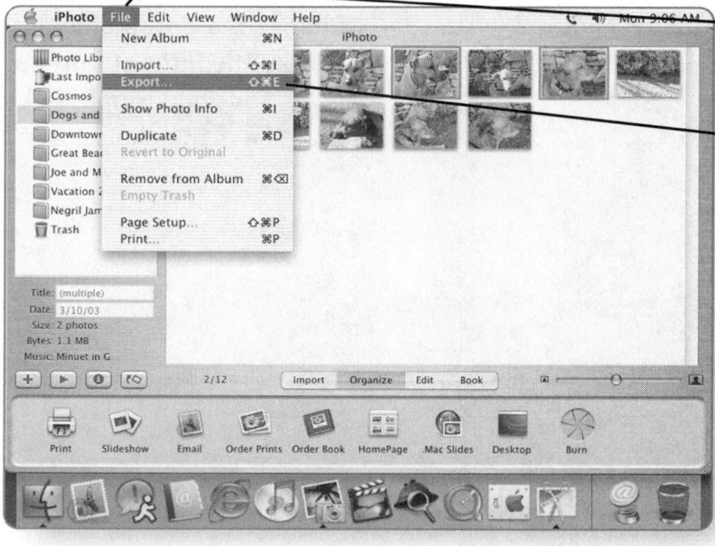

**2.** **Click** on **File**. The File menu will appear.

**3.** **Click** on **Export**. The Export Photos dialog box will open.

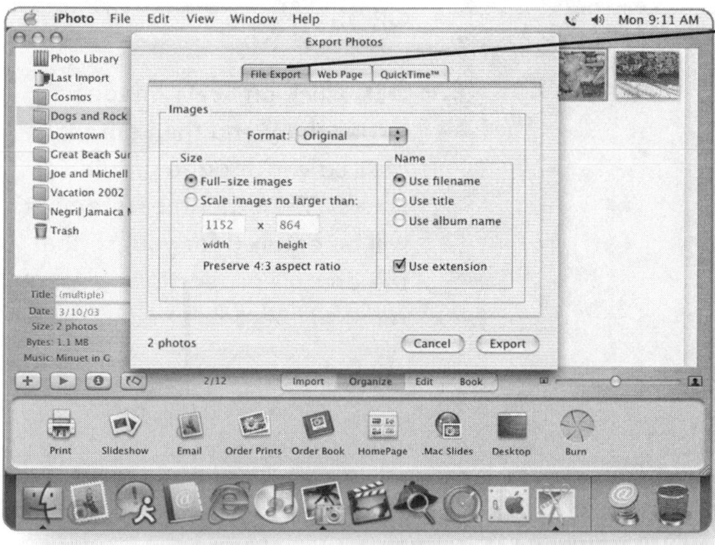

**4.** **Click** on the **File Export tab**. The options for exporting the selected photos to new files will appear.

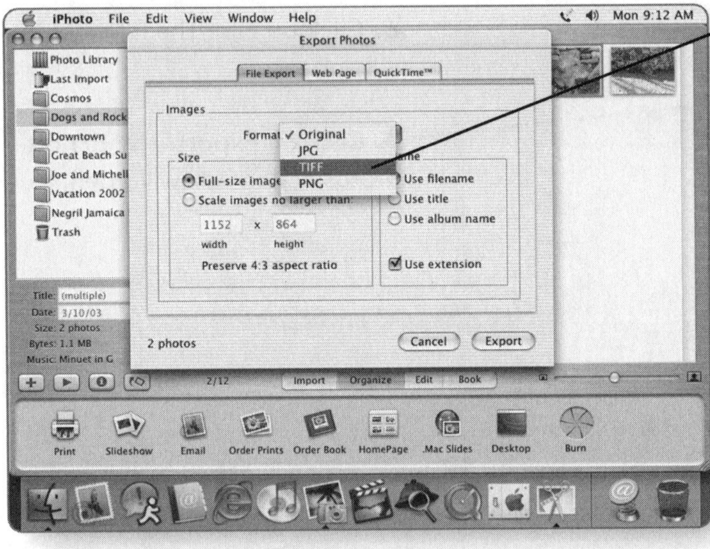


**5a. Choose** the desired **file format** from the **Format pop-up menu.** The specified format will appear as the menu choice.

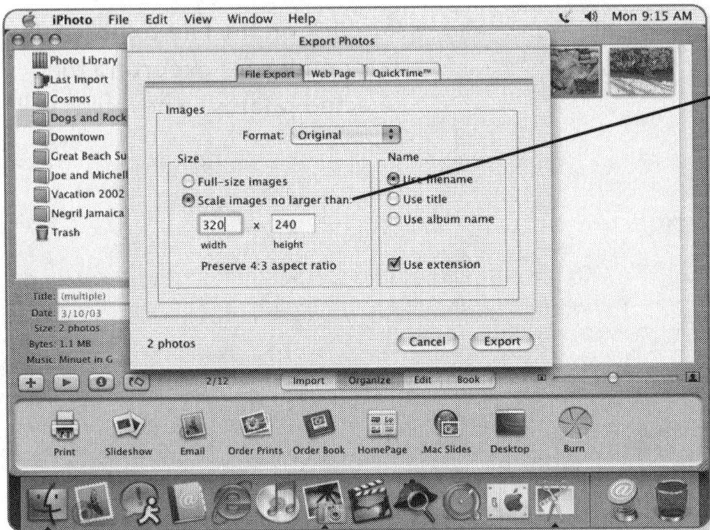


**OR**

**5b. Click** on **Scale images no larger than**, and then **enter** the desired **width** or **height** (in *pixels*). The other measurement will be entered for you, so that the photo's proportions (*aspect ratio*) will be preserved.

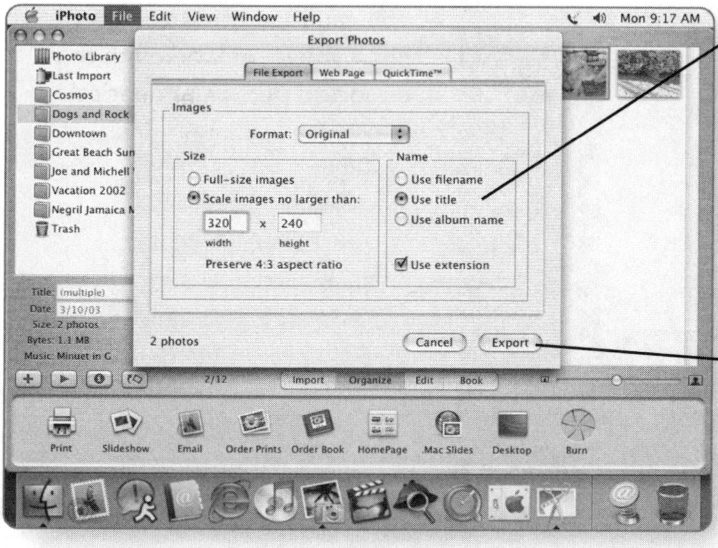


**6. Choose** the desired **Name settings** for the exported photos. The new files will be named using the current file name, a title you've entered, or the album name. The file name extension will be included if specified.

**7. Click** on **Export**. A sheet will open so that you can specify a folder in which to save the exported photos.

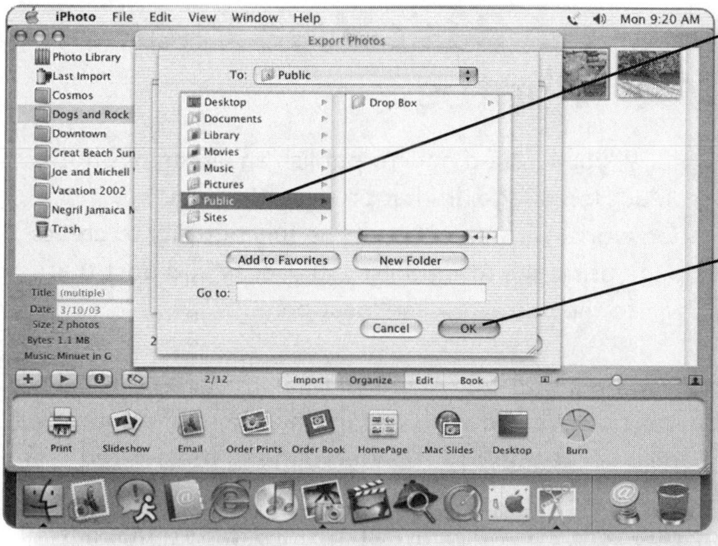


**8. Select** the **disk and folder** where you want to save the exported photos. The sheet will show any files already in that folder.

**9. Click** on **OK**. The images will be exported, and the Export Photos dialog box will close.

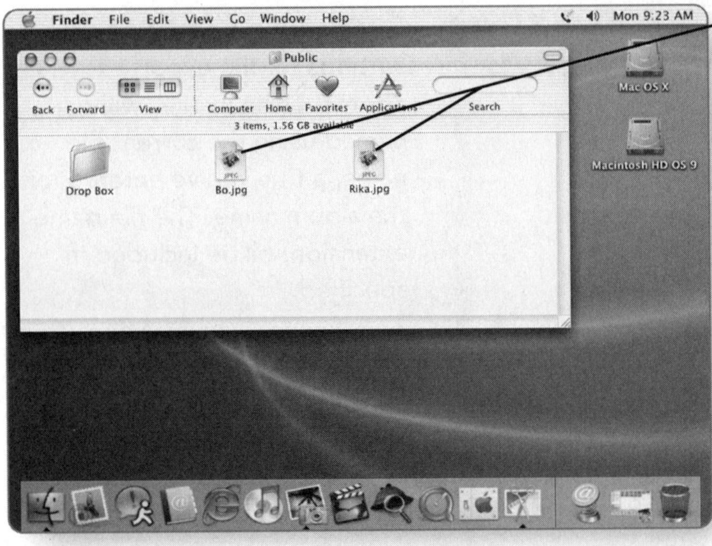


You can then use the Finder to copy, move, or work with the exported photos as needed.

# Creating a Basic Web Page of Your Photos

In Chapter 9, you learned how to publish an album of photos as your .Mac HomePage. In that process, the iPhoto application works with the .Mac online functionality to create a homepage using the formatting you specify and post that homepage to the correct online location.

You are not limited to publishing your photos as a .Mac homepage, however. You can export any album of photos as a Web page and then upload the Web page to the desired Web location, such as the Web page space you receive from your ISP for your Internet account. You use an export process from within iPhoto to create a Web page from your album. From there, you can use other applications to refine the Web page and post it to the desired location online.

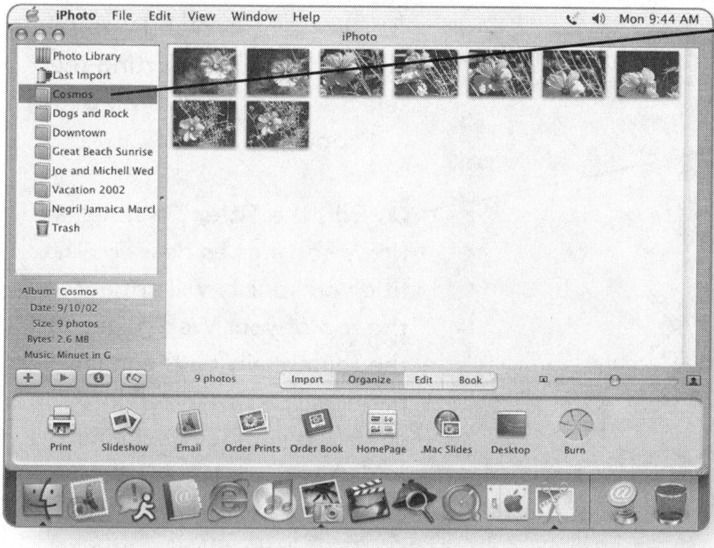


**1. Select** the **album** to export. The album's photos will appear in the photo viewing area.

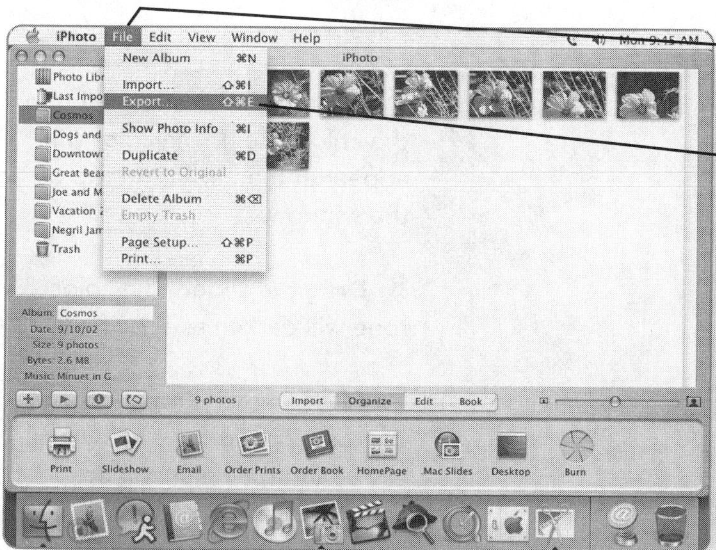


**2. Click** on **File**. The File menu will appear.

**3. Click** on **Export**. The Export Photos dialog box will open.

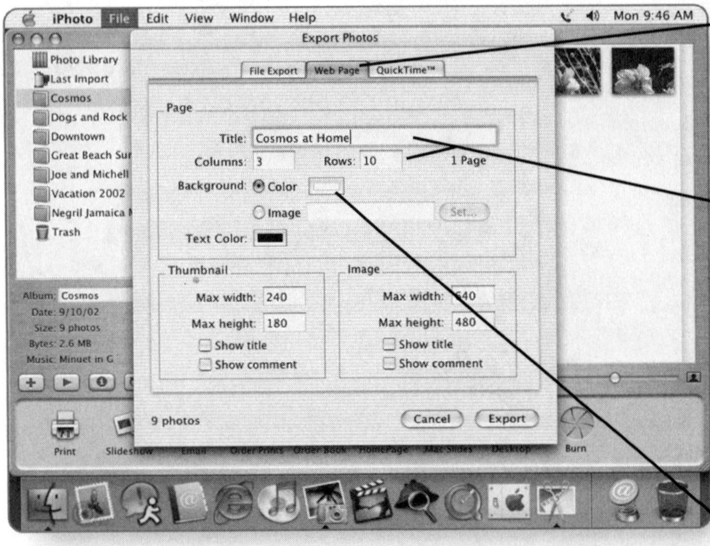


**4. Click** on the **Web Page tab**. The options for exporting the selected album to a Web page will appear.

**5. Edit** the **Title, Columns,** and **Rows settings** as desired. The title you specify will appear at the top of your Web page, and the thumbnails on the main page will be organized into the specified number of columns and rows.

**6.** To specify a Web page background color, **click** on the **Color icon**. The Colors window will appear.

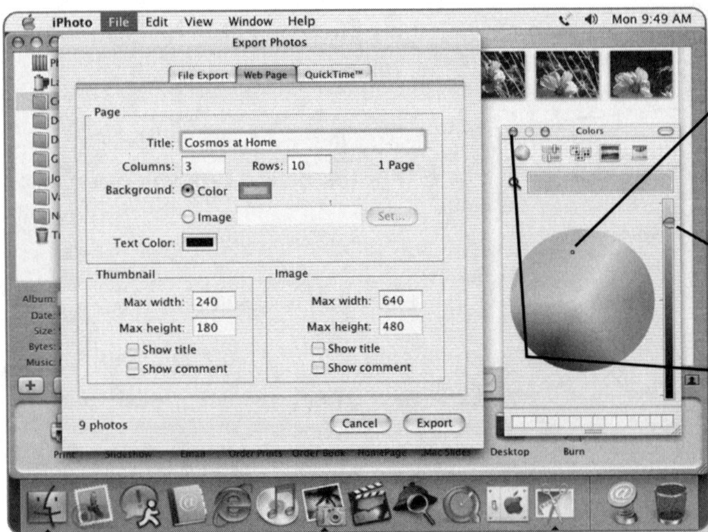


**7. Click** on the desired **color** in the color wheel. The color will appear in the bar at the top of the window.

**8. Drag** the **slider**. The color tone will darken as specified.

**9. Click** on the **window close button**. The Colors window will close, and the color will be specified for the Web page background.

**TIP**

To change the color for text, click on the Text Color icon, and then use the Colors window to choose a text color as described in Steps 7 through 9.

**10. Enter** the desired **Max width** or **Max height** values (in pixels) for each Thumbnail and Image. (The other dimension will be entered automatically.) The Thumbnail values will determine the size of each image thumbnail on the main Web page, and the Image values will determine the display size the image appears in after the viewer clicks on a thumbnail.

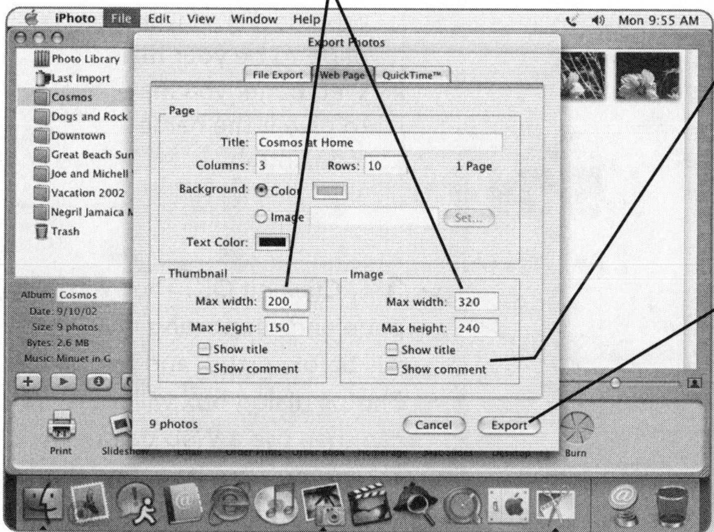


**11. Check** the **Show title** or **Show comment check box** as desired. The specified information will appear below the thumbnail or full image in the Web page.

**12. Click** on **Export**. A sheet will open so that you can specify a folder in which to save the exported Web site.

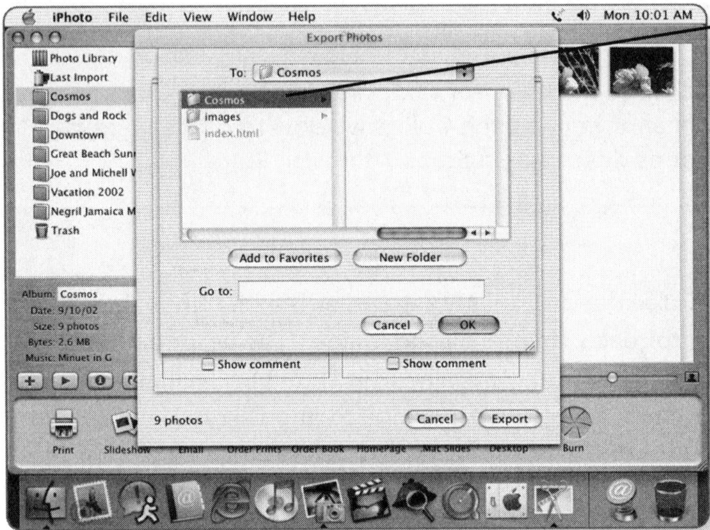

**13. Select** the **disk and folder** where you want to save the exported Web page. The sheet will show any files already in that folder.

## TIP

The exported Web page and subfolders will use the name of the specified folder, so you may want to create the folder to use in the Finder before completing the export process. If you want the page to be your main Web page, you may have to give it the name Index.html.

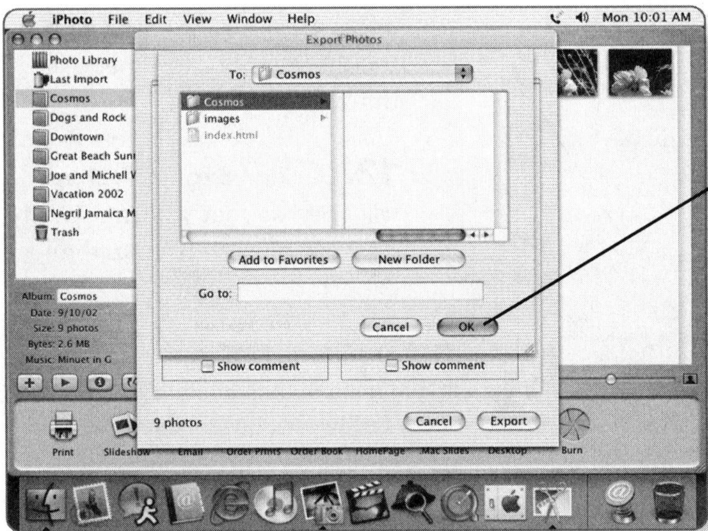

**14. Click** on **OK**. The Web page and supporting image files will be exported, and the Export Photos dialog box will close. You can then use a Web page editing program to refine the Web page, if desired.

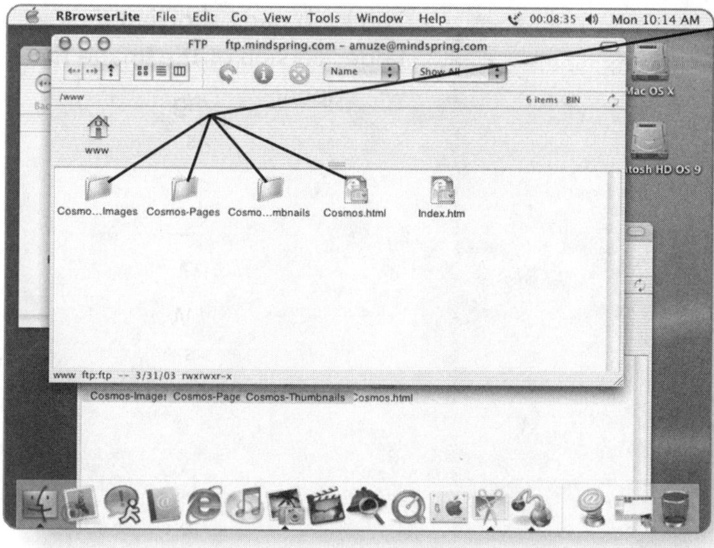


Connect to the Internet, and use an FTP utility such as RBrowserLite (shown here) to transfer the HTML file and subfolders created by the export process. The process creates three subfolders—one to hold the thumbnails for the initial Web page, one to hold the HTML file for each large image, and one to hold the large image files. You must be sure to transfer all the folders and their contents. Do not rename the folders. Doing so will impair the functionality of the finished Web page.

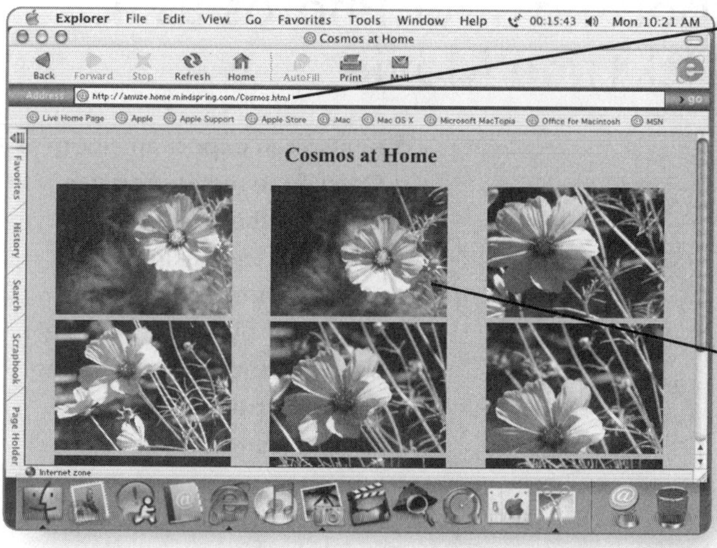


To view your new Web page, connect to the Internet, and use your Web browser to navigate to its URL. (Capitalization may count, so be sure to enter the file name for the main HTML file exactly when you enter the URL).

To see the larger-sized version of an image, click on the image thumbnail.

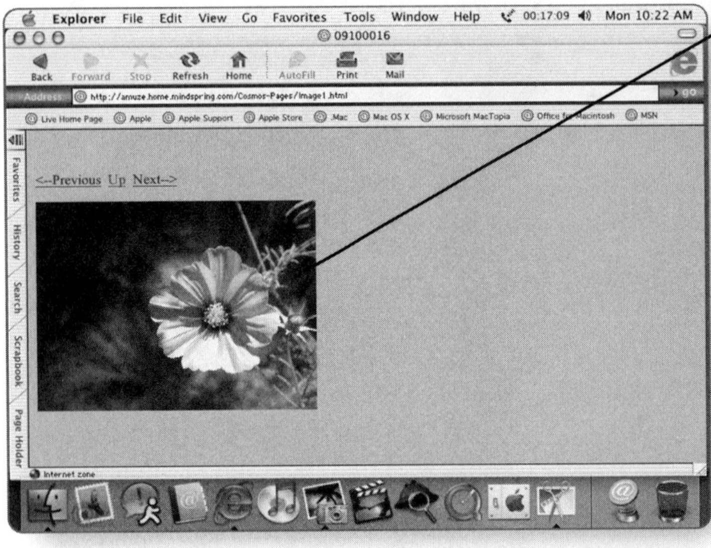

The Web page showing the larger version of the image file will appear.

# Exporting Your Photos as a QuickTime Movie

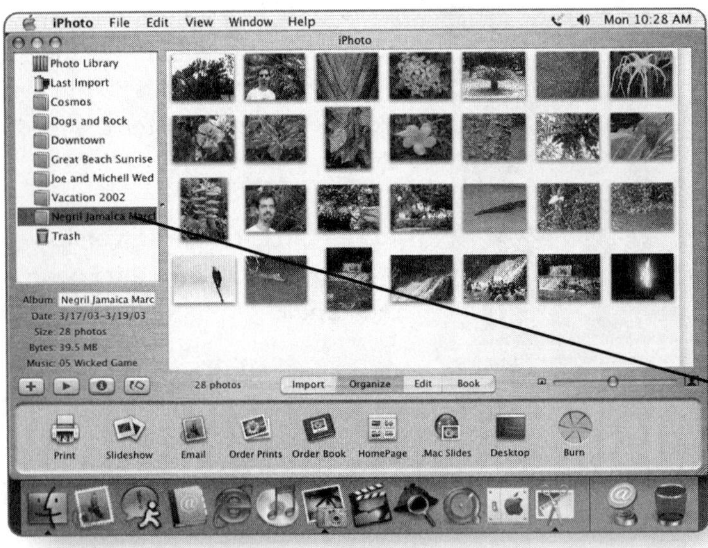

You also can export an album as a QuickTime movie. You can then share the QuickTime movie with others by making it available for download via a Web site or by burning it to a CD-R. This technique provides you more options for sharing your photos with others.

**1. Select** the **album** to export. The album's photos will appear in the photo viewing area.

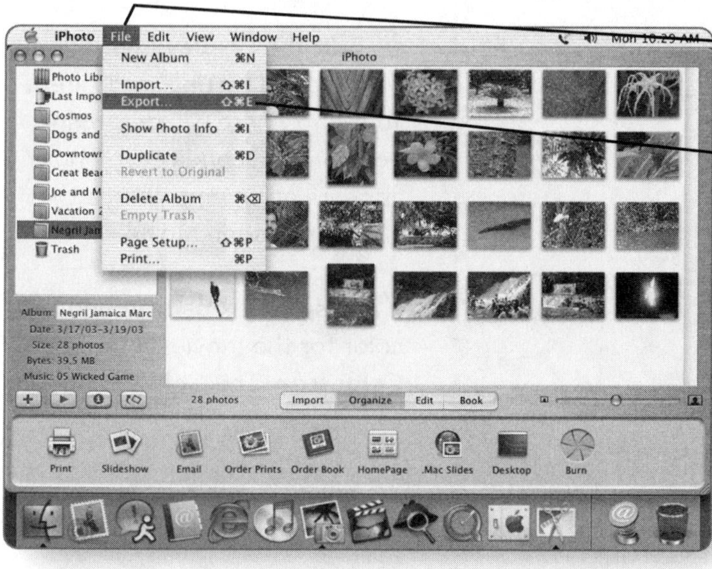


**2.** **Click** on **File**. The File menu will appear.

**3.** **Click** on **Export**. The Export Photos dialog box will open.

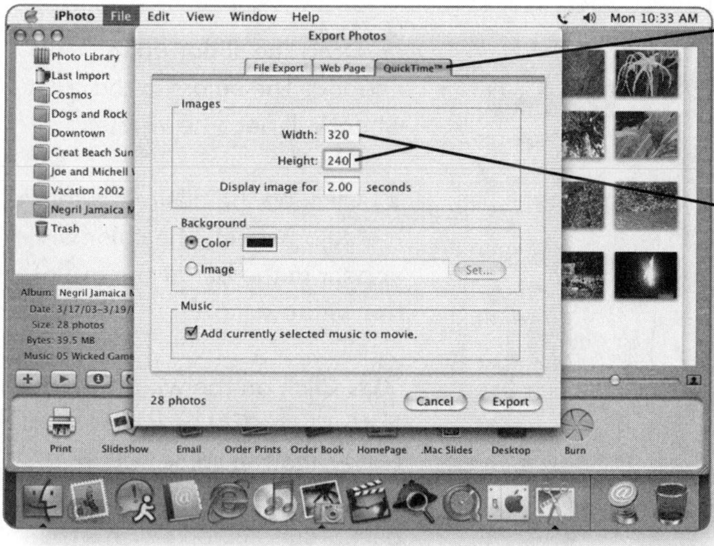


**4.** **Click** on the **QuickTime tab**. The options for exporting the selected album to a movie will appear.

**5.** **Enter** the desired **Width** and **Height** values (in pixels). The values will determine the size of the movie during playback.

### TIP

As video files tend to be quite large, enter smaller values for movies that you want to post for download or that will be shared with users who have older, slower computers.

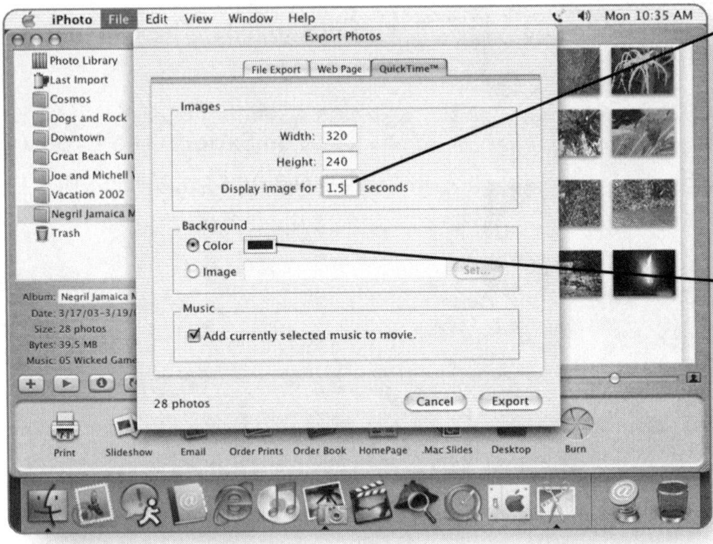


**6.** **Edit** the **Display image for (X) seconds setting** as desired. Your entry here will determine how many seconds each photo appears on screen when a viewer plays the movie.

**7.** To specify a background color for the movie, **click** on the **Color icon**. The Colors window will appear.

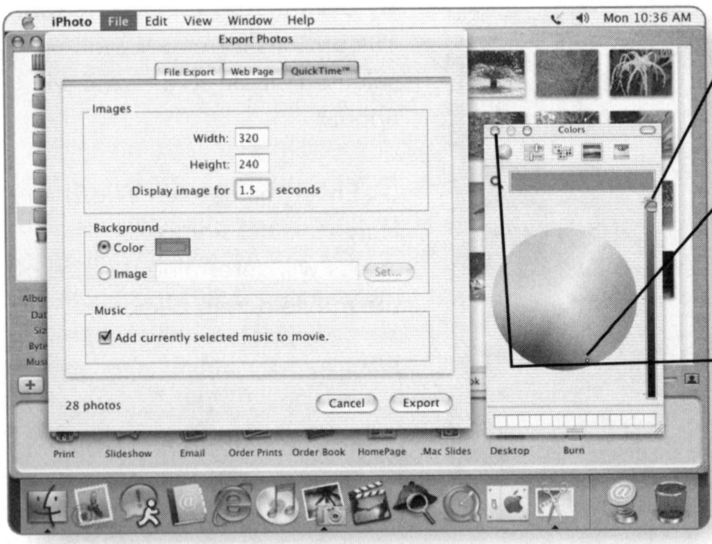


**8.** **Drag** the **slider up**, if needed. The colors in the color wheel will become visible.

**9.** **Click** on the desired **color** in the color wheel. The color will appear in the bar at the top of the window.

**10.** **Click** on the **window close button**. The Colors window will close, and the color will be specified for the movie background color, which appears on the initial screen and beside images with a vertical orientation.

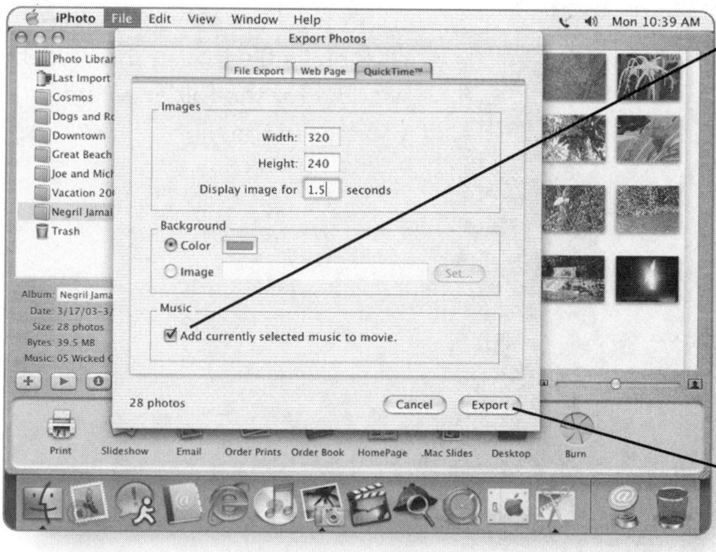


**11.** **Click** on **Add currently selected music to movie**, if desired. When this option is checked, the music currently selected for the album slideshow will be included in the QuickTime movie. See "Setting Slideshow Preferences for an Album" in Chapter 11 to learn how to choose a song for a slideshow.

**12.** **Click** on **Export**. A sheet will open so that you can specify a folder in which to save the exported QuickTime movie.

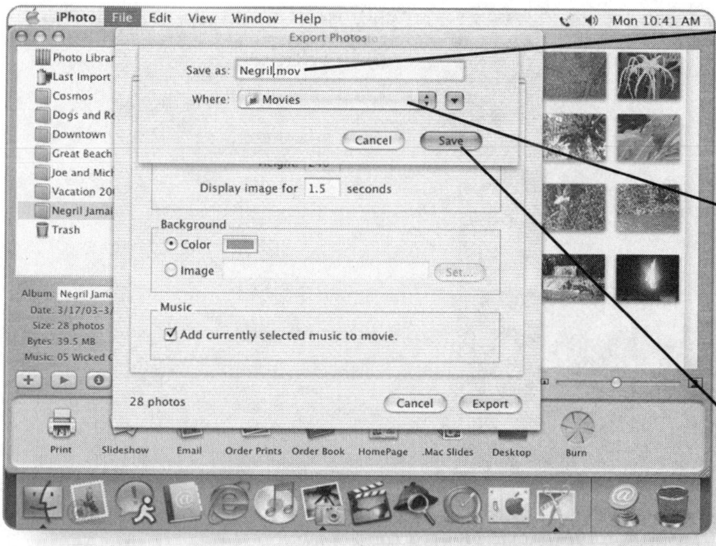


**13.** **Type** a **file name** for the movie in the Save as text box. The name will replace the placeholder text.

**14.** If needed, **select** an alternate **disk and folder** where you want to save the exported movie. The Where box will show that location.

**15.** **Click** on **Save**. The QuickTime movie will be exported, and the Export Photos dialog box will close.

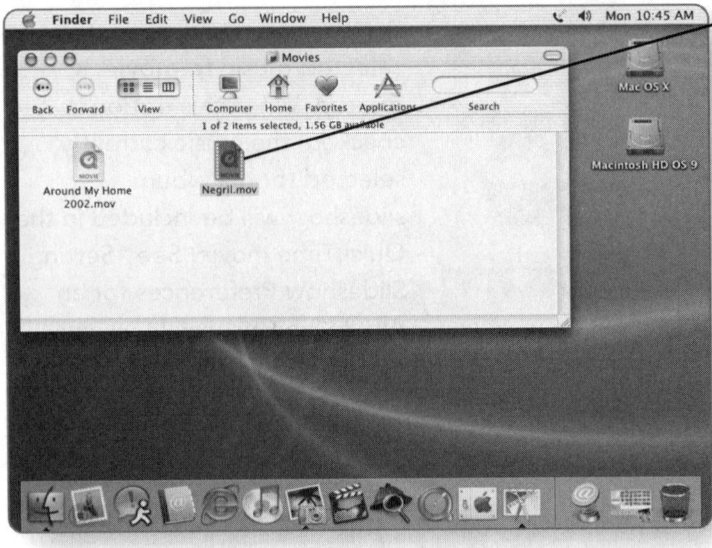


To preview the movie, double-click on its file icon in the Finder window for the folder where you stored the file.

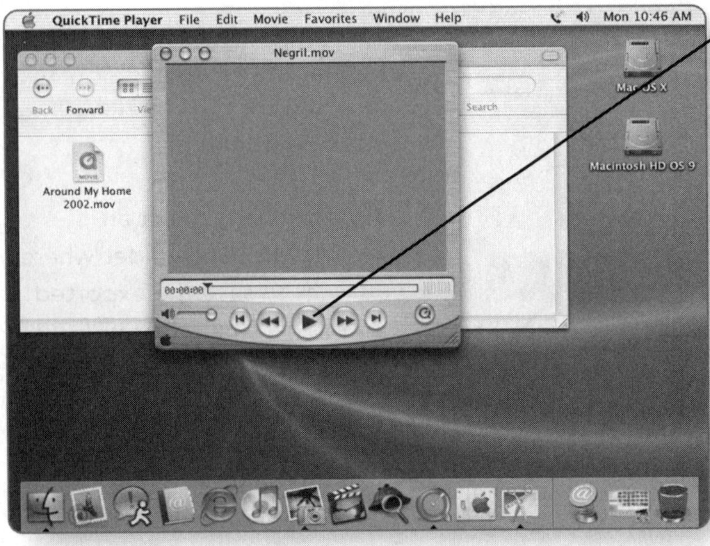


Click on the play button in the movie window…

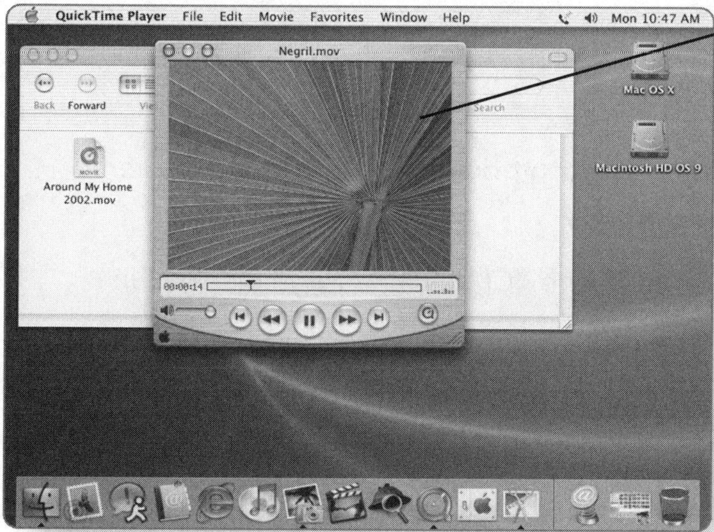


...and then enjoy!

## Part III Review Questions

1. How do I choose a look for a photo book? *See "Choosing a Theme and Page Contents" in Chapter 7.*
2. How do I set up a book page? *See "Choosing a Page Design" in Chapter 7.*
3. How do I make sure my photo book prints correctly? *See "Changing Print Settings" in Chapter 8.*
4. What's an easy way to share an album online? *See "Publishing Photos to Your .Mac HomePage" in Chapter 9.*
5. I want to print on 4 × 6 photo paper. What settings do I use? *See "Printing a 4 × 6 Photo" in Chapter 10.*
6. Is any type of professional printing available? *See "Ordering Prints" and "Ordering a Photo Book" in Chapter 10.*
7. How do I run an on-screen slideshow? *See "Viewing the Slideshow" in Chapter 11.*
8. How do I set up an album as a screen saver? *See "Using an Album as Your Screen Saver" in Chapter 11.*
9. Can iPhoto convert image file formats? *See "Exporting Images in Another Size or Format" in Chapter 12.*
10. How do I make a movie of my images? *See "Exporting Your Photos as a QuickTime Movie" in Chapter 12.*

PART IV

# Managing Your Digital Images

# 13

# Archiving Your Photos

Despite the fact that computers ship with larger and larger hard disks each month, you may accumulate photos so quickly that your hard disk becomes clogged and the size of your photo library becomes unmanageable. Fortunately, iPhoto 2 can work with features in Mac OS X version 10.2 (or later) to enable you to move images to external storage media. In addition, you can create and work with various photo libraries for your convenience in iPhoto. In this chapter, you will learn how to:

- Burn images, an album, or an entire library to CD-R or DVD-R.
- Open a photo library stored on CD-R.
- Create a new photo library.
- Switch between photo libraries on your hard disk.

# Prepping for the Burn

To be able to copy your images, albums, or libraries to removable storage media, your system must be equipped with an internal CD-R, Combo (CD-R/DVD), or SuperDrive (DVD-R) drive, or an external CD-R or DVD-R drive connected via USB or FireWire. You also must have Mac OS X version 10.2 or later installed on your system.

**1.** If you're using an external drive, connect it and turn it on.

**2. Insert** a **blank CD-R or DVD-R** into the drive. A message box prompts you to specify what to do with the CD-R.

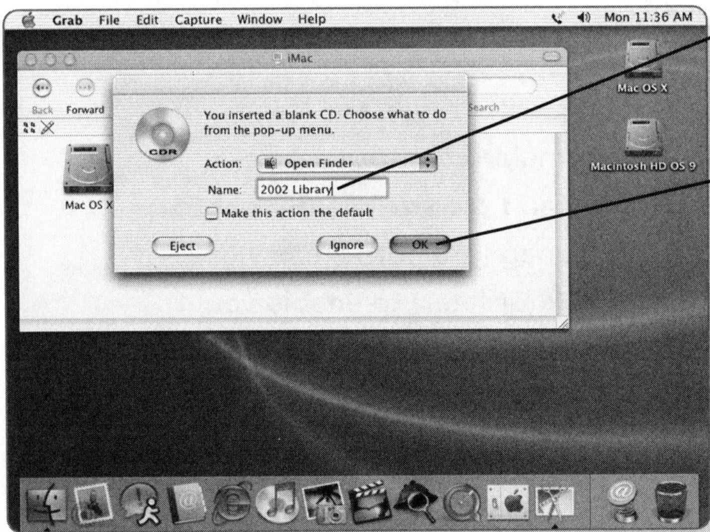


**3. Type** a **name** for the disc in the Name text box. The name will appear.

**4. Click** on **OK**. An icon for the disc will appear on the desktop.

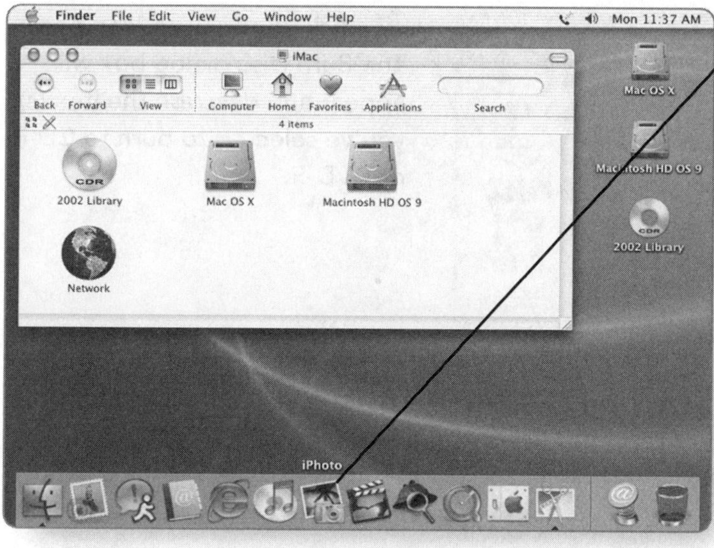


**5.** **Click** on the **iPhoto icon** on the Dock. The iPhoto application will start.

> **NOTE**
>
> If you're already working in iPhoto, insert the blank media and then perform Steps 3 and 4.

# Burning a CD or DVD

Once you've prepped the disc and have launched iPhoto, you're ready to select the information to copy (archive) to CD-R or DVD-R and then perform the burn. Work in the Organize pane (or view) to perform the following steps.

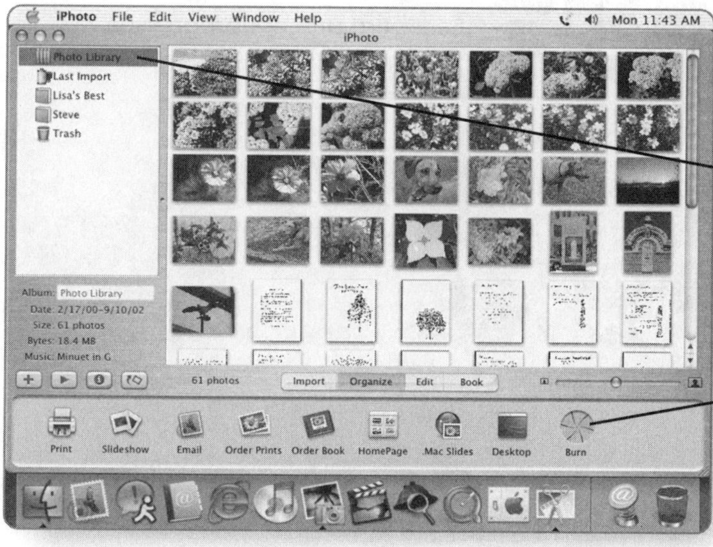


**1.** **Select** the **Photo Library,** an **album,** or **individual photos** as desired. The name will appear. The items will be selected for the burn operation.

**2.** **Click** on **Burn**. The Burn icon will "open" and pulse in yellow and red.

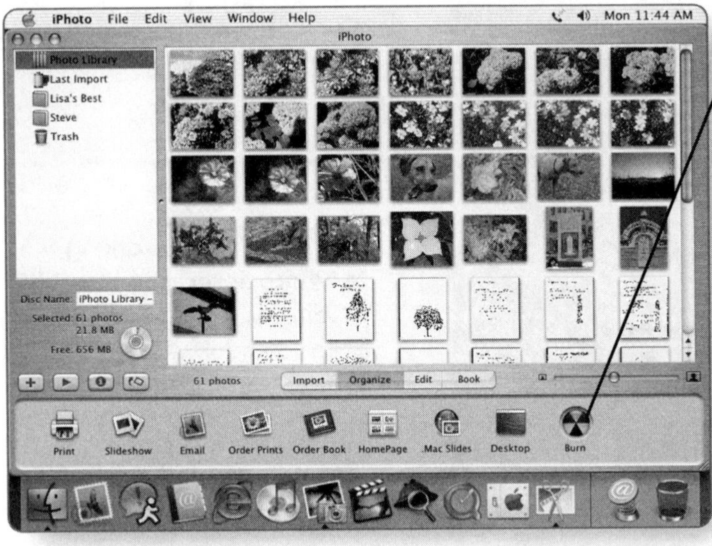


**3. Click** on the **Burn icon** again. The Burn Disc dialog box will appear and describe the item(s) you've selected to burn to CD-R or DVD-R.

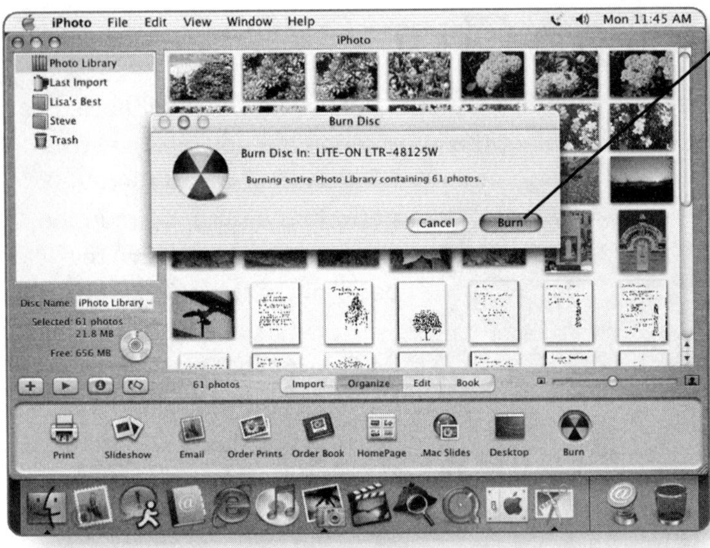


**4. Click** on **Burn**. Mac OS X and iPhoto will work together to burn the information to the removable media. Message boxes will inform you as the burn process progresses.

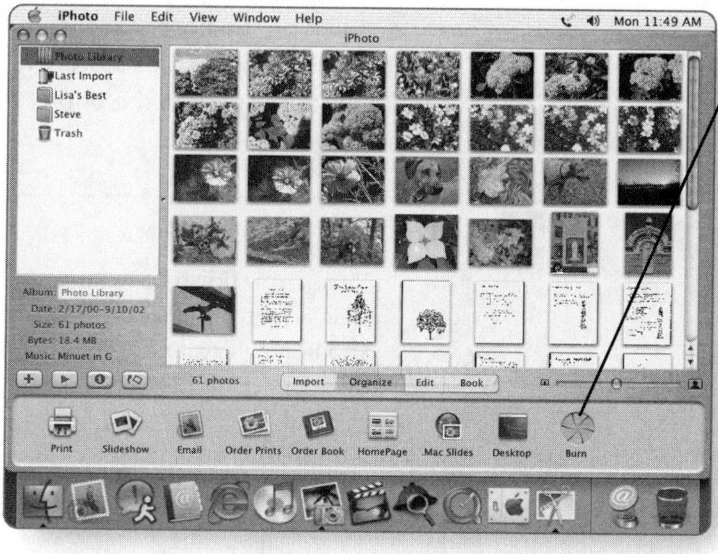


When the burn finishes, the drive will eject the disc, and the Burn icon will "close."

# Viewing a Library from a CD-R

If you've burned an entire photo library, an album, or selected images to a CD-R or DVD-R, iPhoto treats that CD-R or DVD-R as a photo library. You can view that library directly from the media without having to reimport the images or switch between libraries. This gives you access to the images stored on the CD-R or DVD-R.

**1.** **Insert** the **CD-R or DVD-R** into the drive. iPhoto will recognize the library (the CD-R or DVD-R) and load it into the library list.

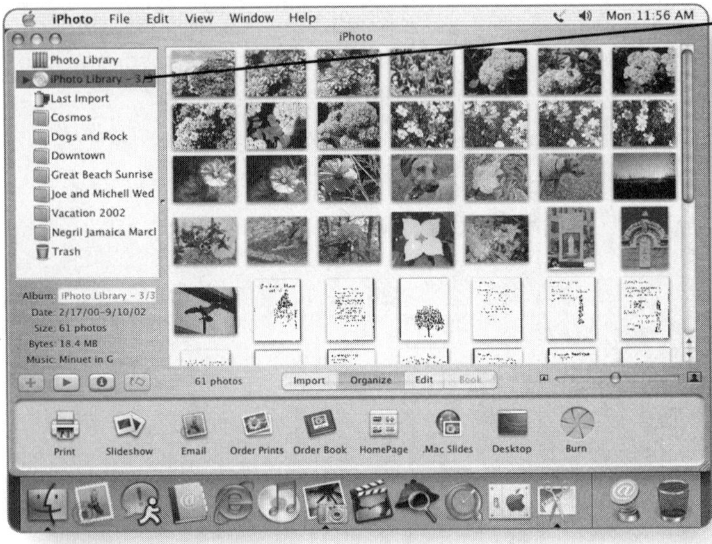


**2. Click** on the **library** in the library list. The images stored in the library appear in the photo viewing area.

> **NOTE**
>
> When you finish using the disc, Control+click on it in the library list, and then click on Eject.

# Creating a New Library

When a library has become so full of images and albums that it becomes difficult to use, you can create a new library. In this way, you can further organize your image files for ease of use. How you organize libraries is up to you. You can create a library for each year, you can create separate personal and business libraries, and so on.

**1. Quit iPhoto** if you're currently working in it. iPhoto will prompt you to create a new library when you restart the program later in the process.

> **TIP**
>
> If you haven't previously created an alternate library, the current library folder will be the Pictures: iPhoto Library folder in your Home folder by default.

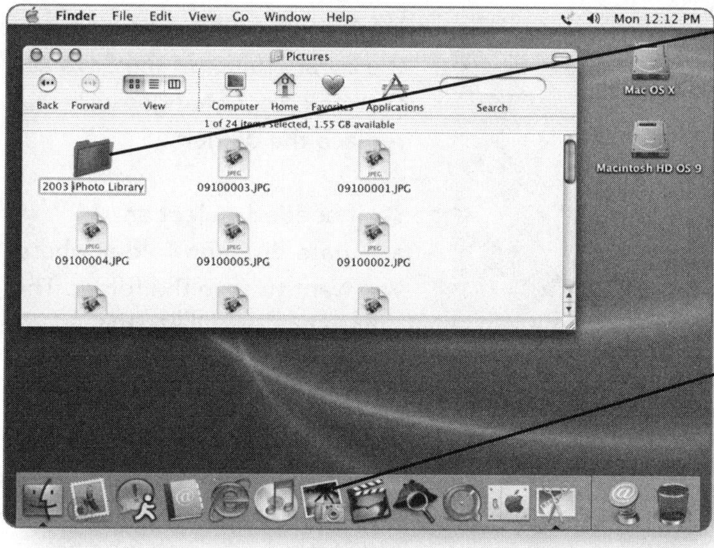


**2.** Use the Finder to **move or rename** the current library folder. (Moving the library folder moves all of its contents, as well.) Renaming or moving the library folder will cause iPhoto to prompt you to create or select another library.

**3. Click** on the **iPhoto icon** on the Dock. A dialog box will inform you that the Photo Library was not found.

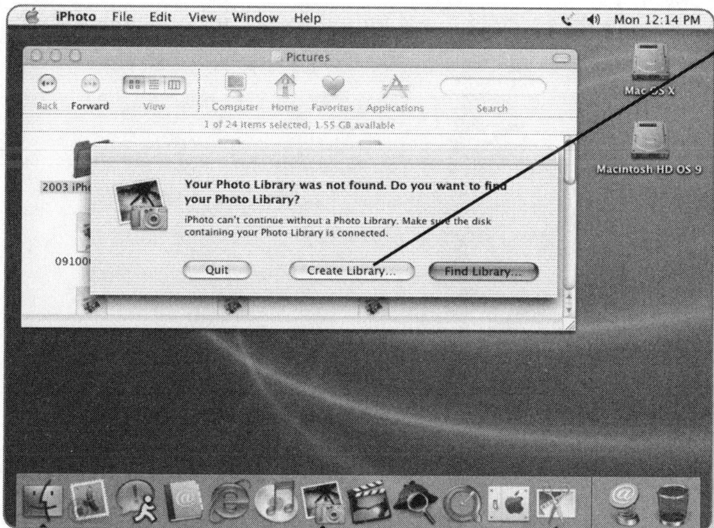


**4. Click** on **Create Library**. The New Photo Library dialog box will open.

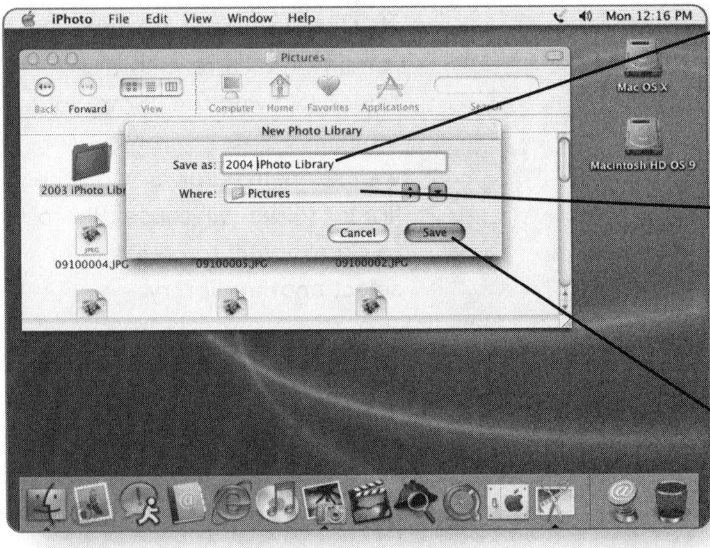


**5. Type or edit the name** for the library folder in the Save as text box. Your changes will replace the default.

**6.** If needed, **select** an alternate **disk and folder** where you want to save the folder. The Where box will show that location.

**7. Click** on **Save**. The new photo library folder will be created, and the iPhoto application will finish loading.

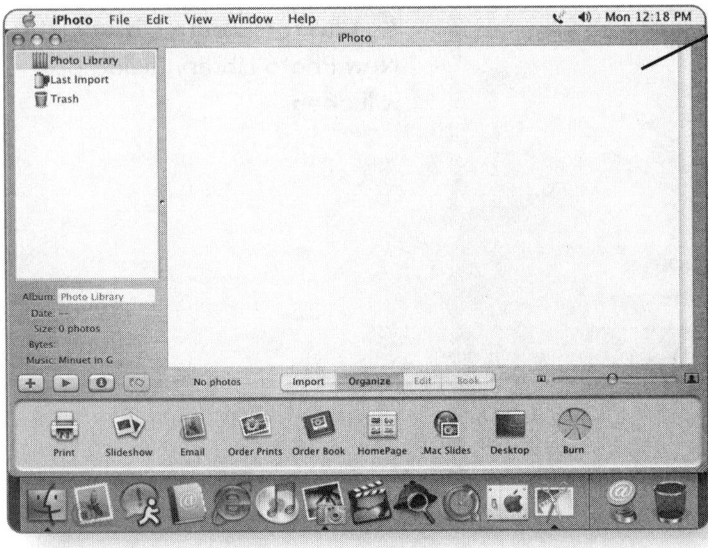


Once it loads, iPhoto will display the new, empty library.

# Selecting a Library

Once you've created and started using a new library, you can switch back to an older library at any time.

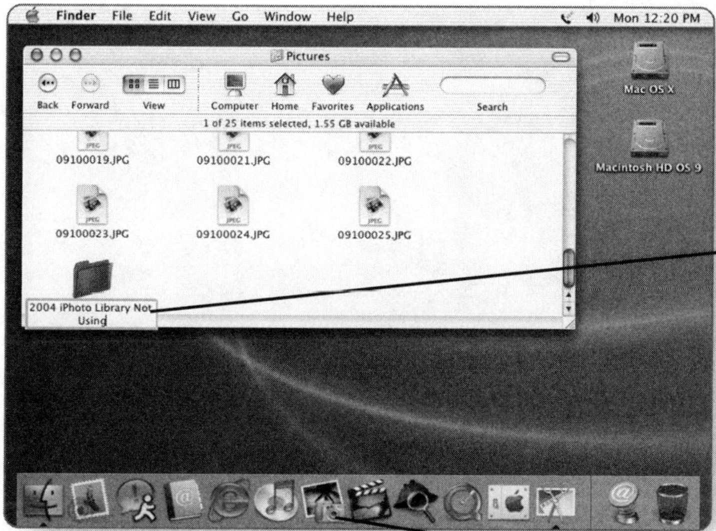


**1. Quit iPhoto** if you're currently working in it. iPhoto will prompt you to create a new library when you restart the program later in the process.

**2.** Use the Finder to **move or rename** the current library folder. (Moving the library folder moves all of its contents, as well.) Renaming or moving the library folder will cause iPhoto to prompt you to create or select another library.

**3. Click** on the **iPhoto icon** on the Dock. A dialog box will inform you that the Photo Library was not found.

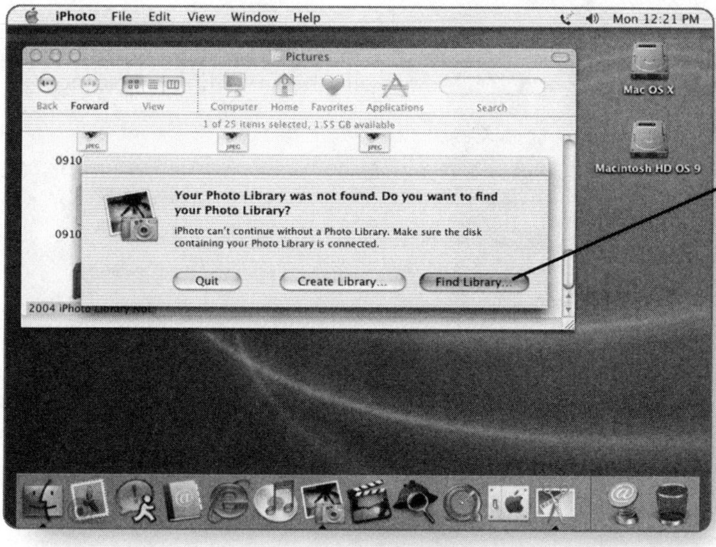


**4. Click** on **Find Library**. The Open Photo Library dialog box will open.

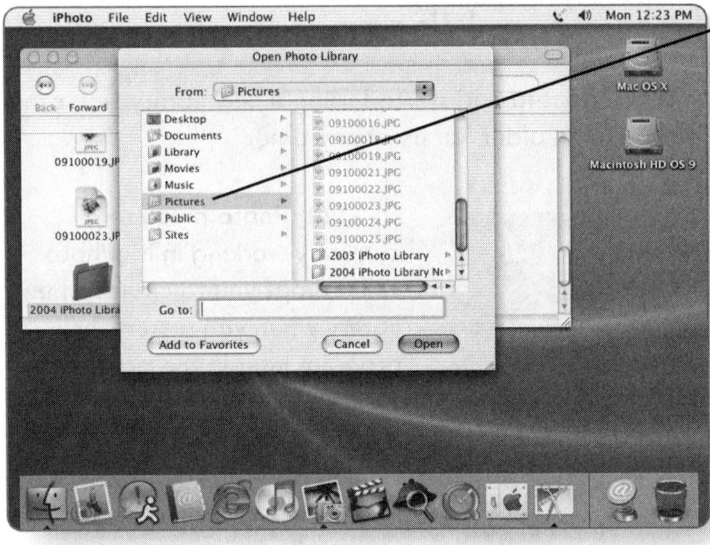


**5.** **Select** the **folder** that holds the library folder to open. The files and folders in the selected folder will be listed in the dialog box.

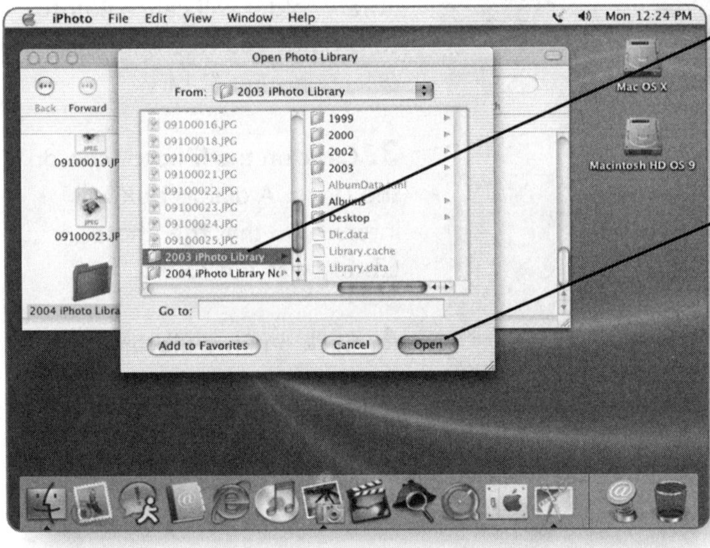


**6.** **Click** on the desired **photo library folder**. The subfolders within the photo library will be listed.

**7.** **Click** on **Open**. The iPhoto application will finish loading.

> **NOTE**
>
> If the library you select was created in a previous version of iPhoto, you will be prompted to upgrade the library so that iPhoto 2 can use it. This process is not reversible, so if needed, make a copy of the library folder first. Click on Upgrade to complete the upgrade.

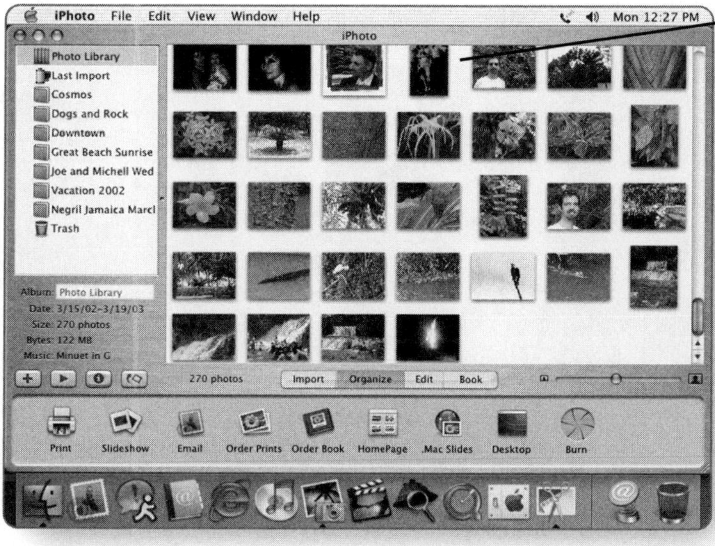


When it opens, iPhoto will display the photos from the selected photo library folder in the Photo Library.

# 14

# Publishing an Online Slideshow

If you opened a .Mac account as described in Chapter 9, then iPhoto provides you with one last method for sharing your photos online. You can publish them as a .Mac slideshow. In this chapter, you will learn how to:

- Publish the slideshow to your .Mac account.
- Send an e-mail announcing the slideshow.
- View the slideshow.

# Publishing and Announcing the .Mac Slideshow

When you create a .Mac slideshow, iPhoto publishes it to your iDisk (the storage area for your .Mac account). You must select the specific images to publish as the slideshow in order for this process to work.

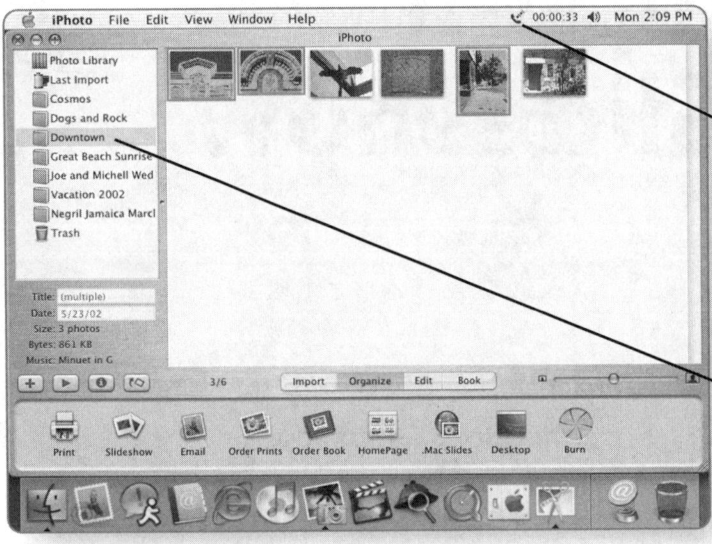


**1. Connect** to the **Internet,** if your system doesn't have an always-on connection. See Appendix C, "Dialing the Internet If Needed" to learn how.

**2.** In the Organize pane, **select** the **album** that holds the photos to publish. The album's photos will appear in the photo viewing area.

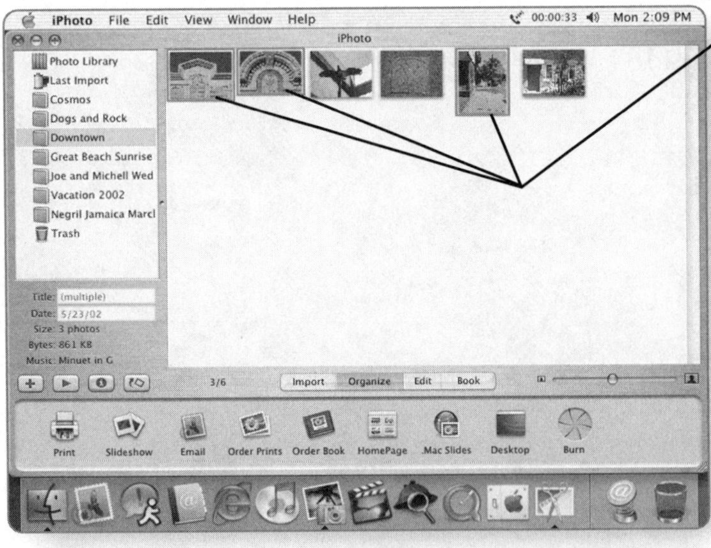


**3. Select** the **photo(s)** to include in the slideshow. A blue selection highlight will identify the selected album or photos.

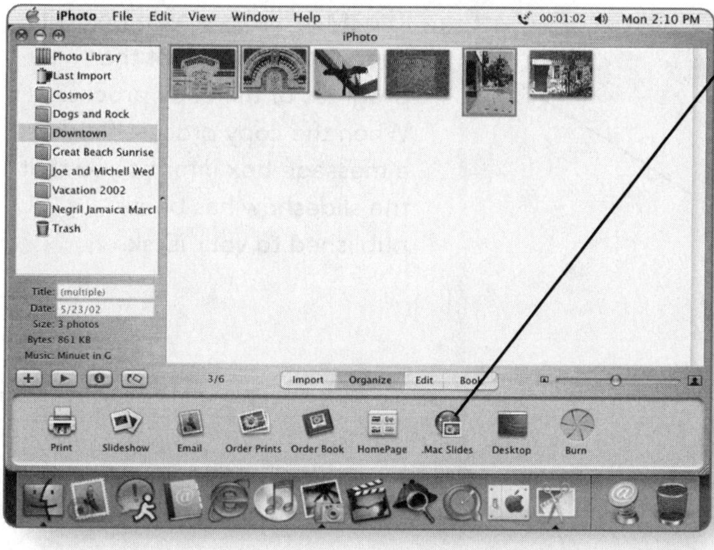


**4. Click** on **.Mac Slides**. iPhoto will connect to your .Mac account and prompt you to verify slideshow publication.

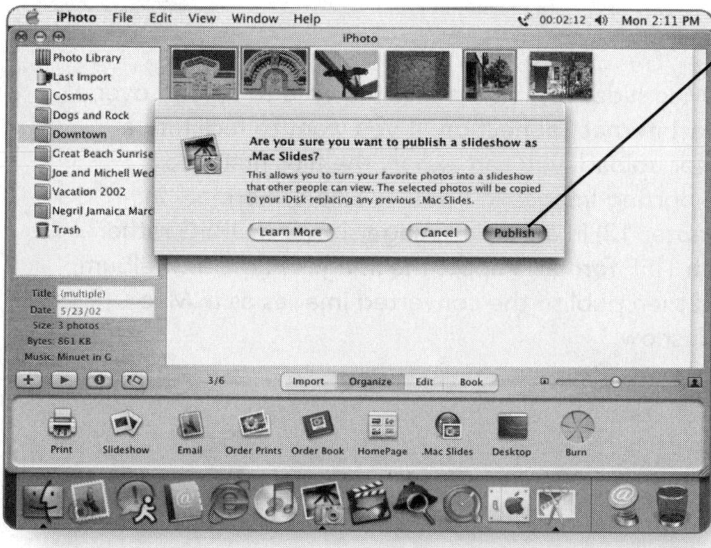


**5. Click** on **Publish**. iPhoto will copy the selected images to your iDisk as slides in the slideshow.

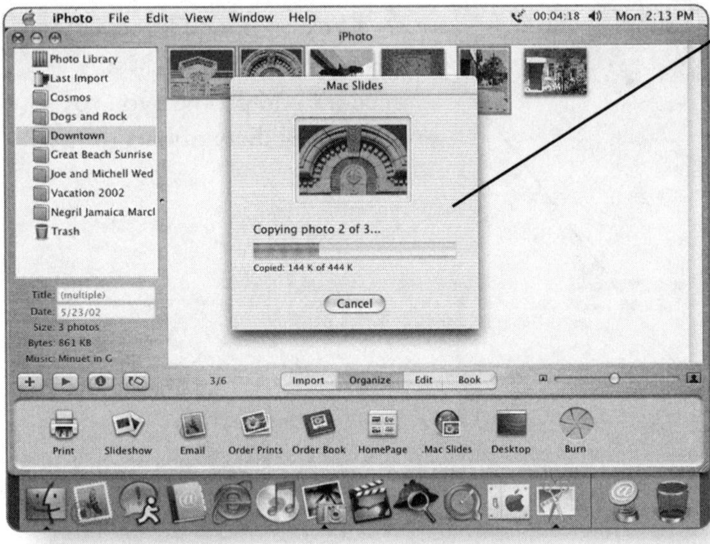


The .Mac Slides dialog box will keep you informed of the progress of the copy process. When the copy process finishes, a message box informs you that the slideshow has been published to your iDisk.

## NOTE

A .Mac slideshow can take some time to upload over a slow Internet connection. If you want to facilitate a faster upload, you can export the files first (see "Exporting Images in Another Size or Format" in Chapter 12) in a smaller image size or in JPEG rather than TIFF format, import the images into a new album, and then publish the converted images as a .Mac slideshow.

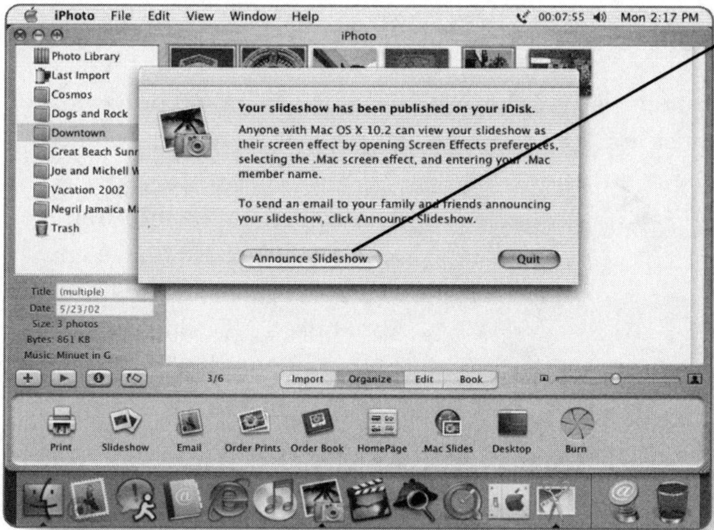


**6. Click** on **Announce Slideshow**. iPhoto will launch your e-mail application (Mail by default), and compose a new message explaining how to view the .Mac slideshow.

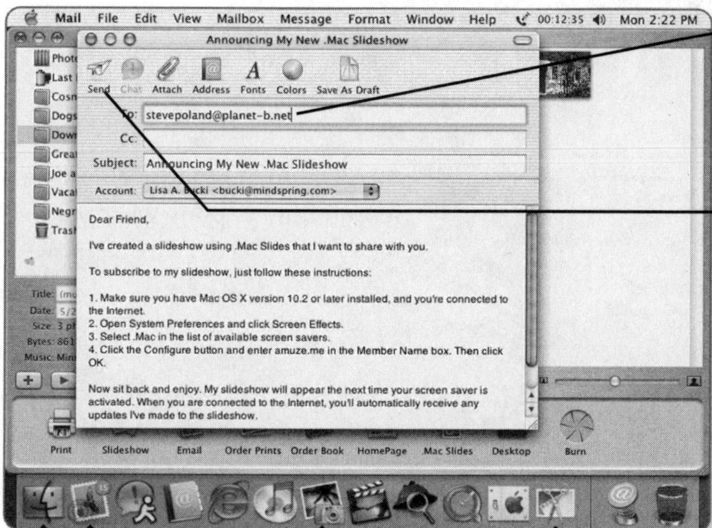


**7. Type** a recipient's **e-mail address** in the To: text box. The address will appear in the text box.

**8. Click** on **Send.** The e-mail message announcing the slideshow and providing instructions for viewing it via Mac OS X will be sent. You can then close your e-mail application and disconnect from the Internet.

# Viewing an Online Slideshow

Rather than viewing the .Mac slideshow in a Web browser, a user must use the Screen Effects pane in System Preferences.

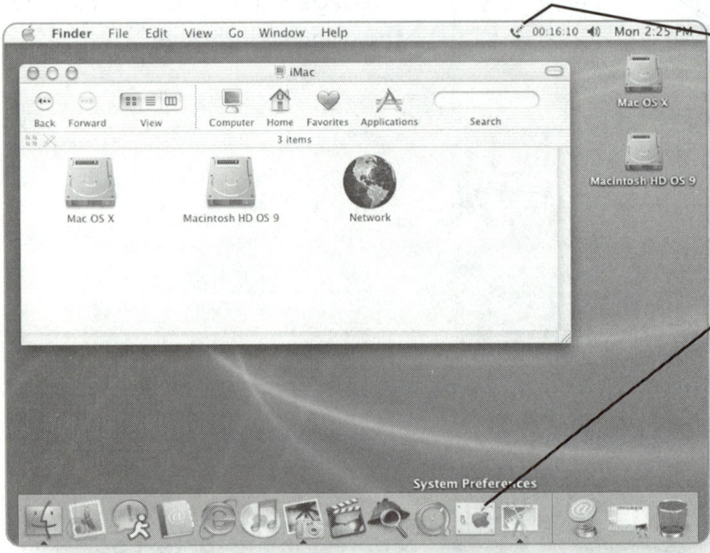


1. **Connect** to the **Internet,** if your system doesn't have an always-on connection. See Appendix C, "Dialing the Internet If Needed" to learn how.

2. **Click** on the **System Preferences icon** on the Dock. The System Preferences application will open.

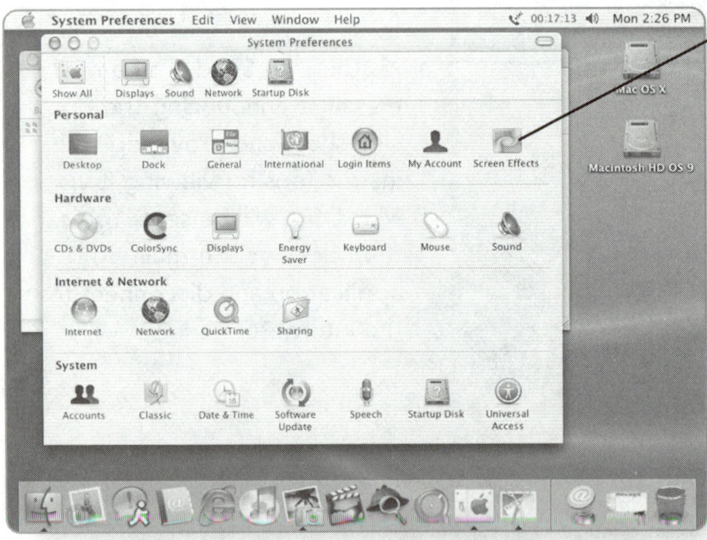


3. **Click** on **Screen Effects.** The Screen Effects pane will open.

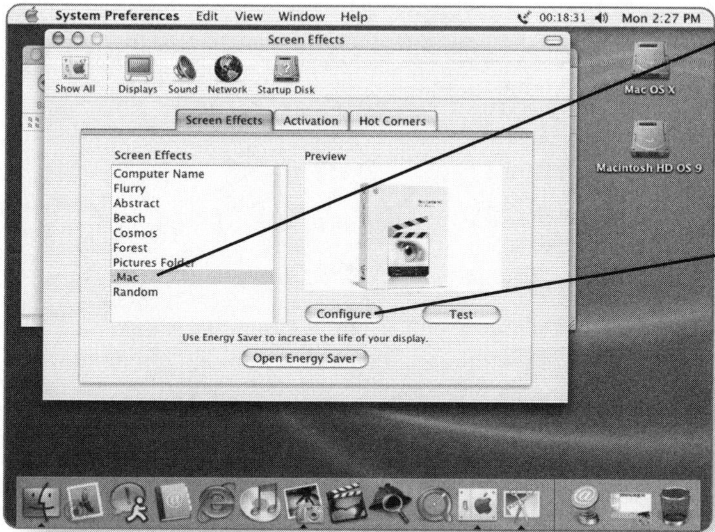


**4.** **Click** on **.Mac** in the Screen Effects list. The Preview will go blank, and then start showing images of Apple product packaging.

**5.** **Click** on **Configure**. A Subscriptions sheet will open so that the viewer can enter your .Mac member name to gain access to the slideshow.

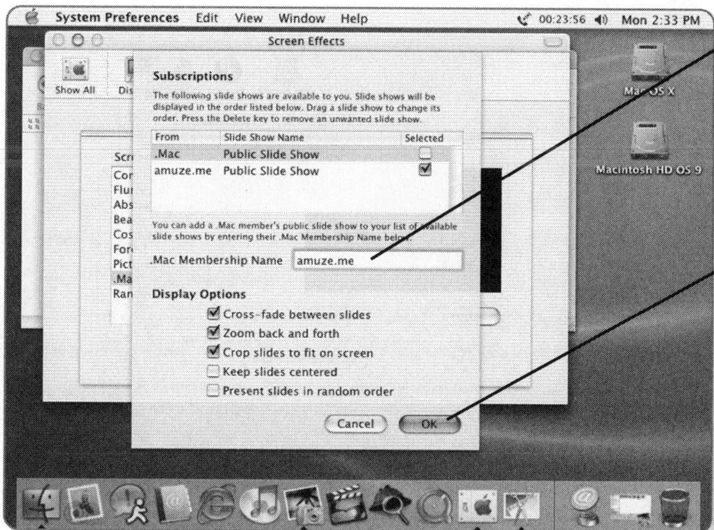


**6.** **Type** the **.Mac member name** (as noted in the announcement e-mail) in the .Mac Membership Name text box. The name will appear.

**7.** **Click** on **OK**. The Subscriptions sheet will close and the slideshow will download and play the next time your screen saver starts.

You can then quit System Preferences by choosing System Preferences, Quit System Preferences.

# 15

# Processing Photos with Scripts

If you're lazy like me, you're always looking for shortcuts even though today's programs make once tedious jobs a snap. This chapter shows you how you can take advantage of AppleScript automation to make even quicker work of certain tasks. In this chapter, you will learn how to:

- Download example scripts.
- Play scripts, including the examples you've downloaded.
- Create a very simple script.

# Understanding AppleScript

AppleScript enables you to automate repetitive actions in Mac OS X and Mac OS X applications using a simple command structure. Once you save a script that you've written as an AppleScript application, using the script can be as simple as double-clicking on the application icon or dragging and dropping one or more selected files onto it.

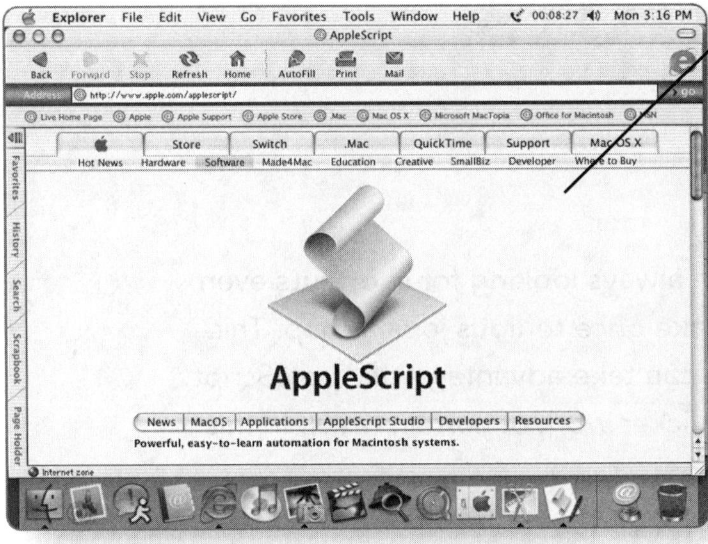


AppleScript originated in 1992. As such, the Web and book publishers offer a variety of resources that you can consult if you want to grow into an AppleScript guru. For example, you can consult the main AppleScript Web site at http://www.apple.com/applescript.

This chapter presents the absolute basics to help you start using AppleScript with iPhoto.

# Downloading Example Scripts

The idea of scripting makes some users run screaming (myself included). Luckily, you can take advantage of example scripts that have already been written for iPhoto. Download the sample iPhoto scripts collection from Apple's Web site using the following steps.

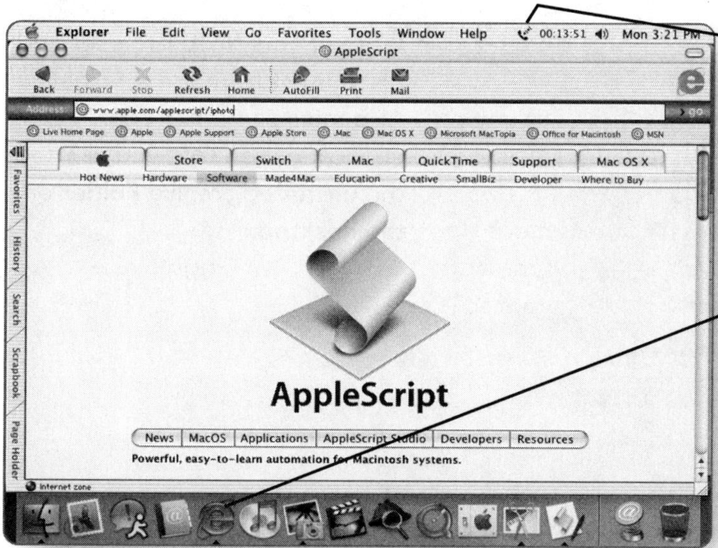


**1. Connect** to the **Internet,** if your system doesn't have an always-on connection. See Appendix C, "Dialing the Internet If Needed" to learn how.

**2. Launch** your **Web browser.**

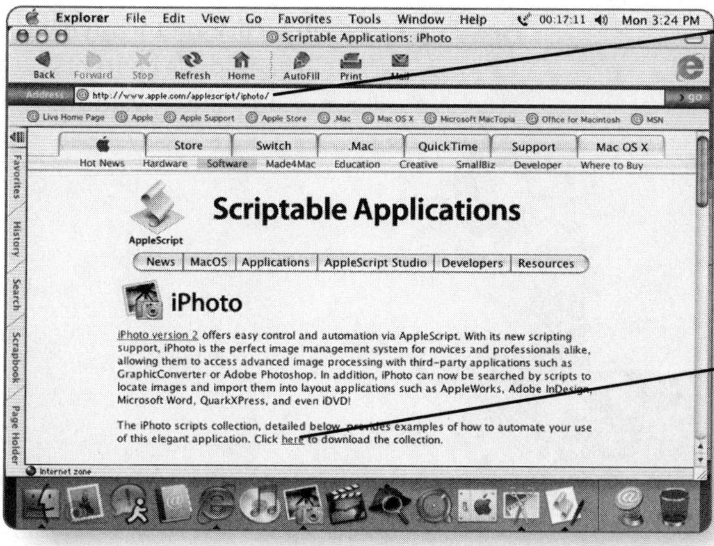


**3. Type www.apple.com/ applescript/iphoto** into the Address text box, and **press Return**. The AppleScript page for iPhoto 2 will open. This page describes the scripts in the collection and enables you to download the collection.

**4. Click** on the **download link.** The Download Manager window will open and show you the download progress. By default, the file will download to the desktop and unstuff automatically.

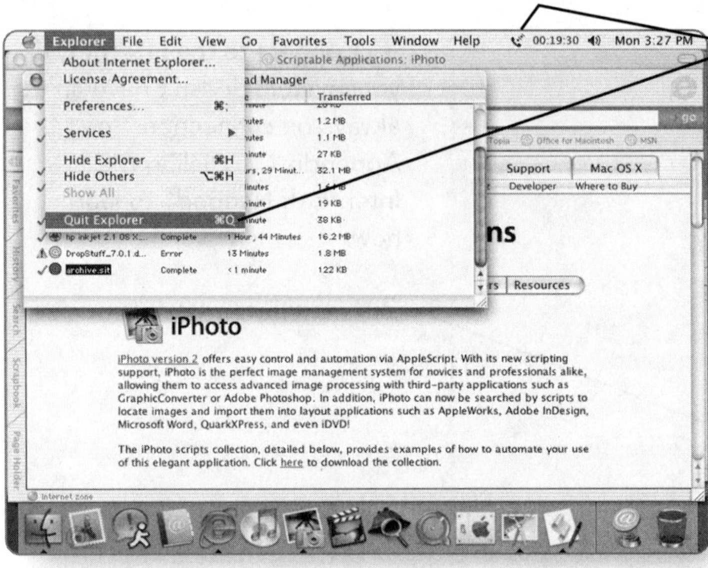


**5. Quit** your **Web browser** and **disconnect** from the **Internet.** Also minimize other open applications so that you can see the unstuffed archive Folder on the desktop.

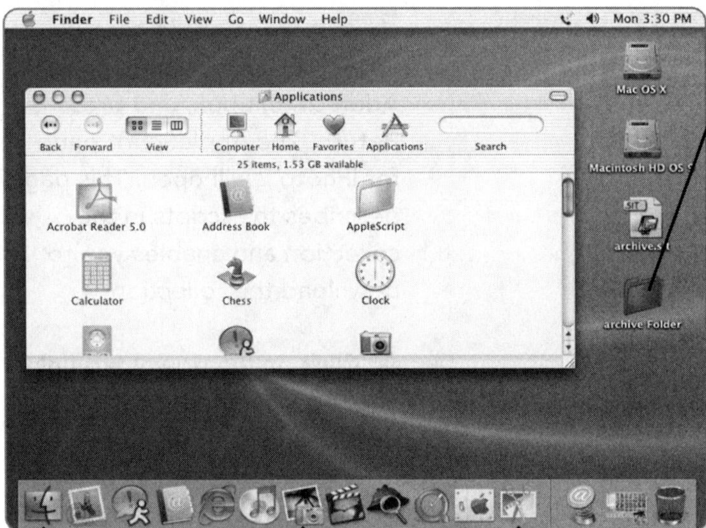


**6. Double-click** on the **archive Folder**. The folder's contents will open in a Finder window.

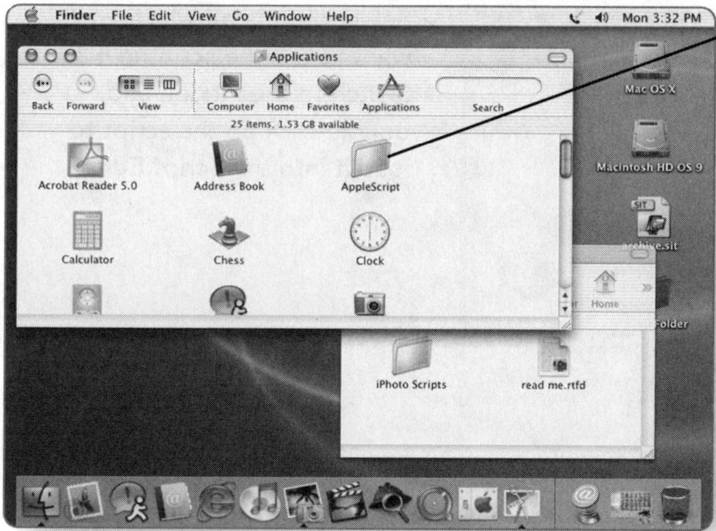


**7. Use Finder** to **move or copy** the folder contents to the desired location, such as within the AppleScript folder. The folder's contents will move or be copied to the specified location.

> **NOTE**
>
> The read me.rtfd file in the archive folder explains how to make the iPhoto scripts available via a Scripts menu that you can install.

# Running a Script

AppleScript generally gives you two ways to run a script, depending on how the script was written and saved.

Drag the file (in this case the image file) to process and drop it on the script droplet (a script saved as a stand-alone application). This is how you use the example scripts that you've now downloaded.

Use this latter method for the example scripts you downloaded.

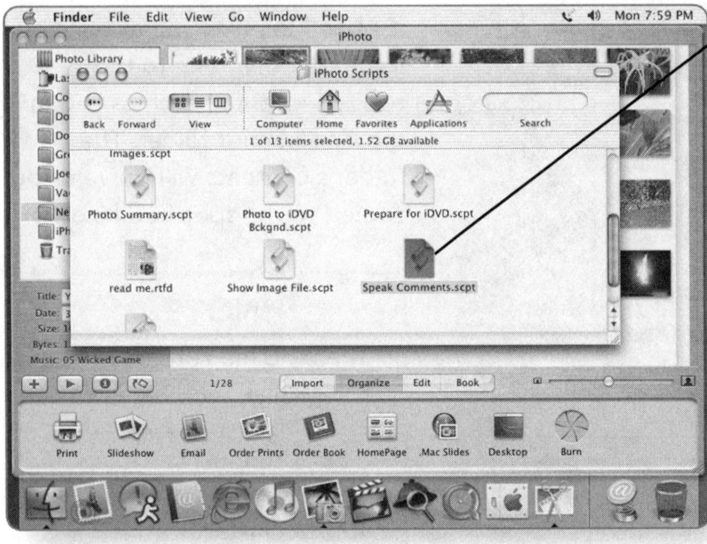


Select photos on which you want to run the script in iPhoto. Switch to the Finder, and double-click on the script to load it into the Script Editor.

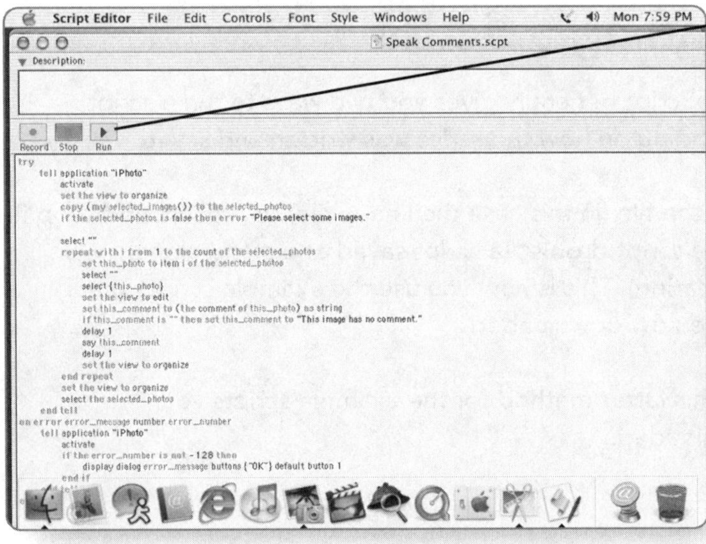


Then click the Run button. The script will run and prompt you for information, as needed.

**NOTE**

Even though scripting iPhoto is a challenge, there are experienced scripters out there who are writing iPhoto scripts and offering them to other users. For example, you can download a script called iPhotoSerialName 0.2 from http://www.versiontracker.com. You can use this script to rename and assign sequential numbers to photos you select in iPhoto. Check Web sites like http://www.versiontracker. com and http://www. MacUpdate.com periodically for additional scripts you can download, use, and examine to learn more about scripting in iPhoto.

# Creating a Basic Script

Unfortunately, iPhoto 2 does not offer the convenience of enabling you to use the Script Editor to record a script. However, you can create your own basic scripts in the Script Editor by studying existing scripts to copy and modify what you see in them.

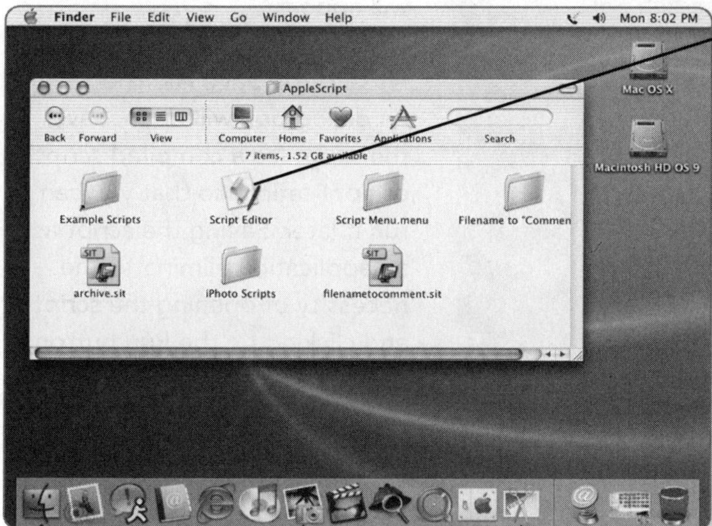


**1. Double-click** on the **Script Editor icon** in a Finder window for the Applications: AppleScript folder. The Script Editor will open.

**2.** **Type** the **script code** in the untitled script window. The code will appear. The commands in this example script will (refer to the code listing after the steps if you find the figure difficult to read):

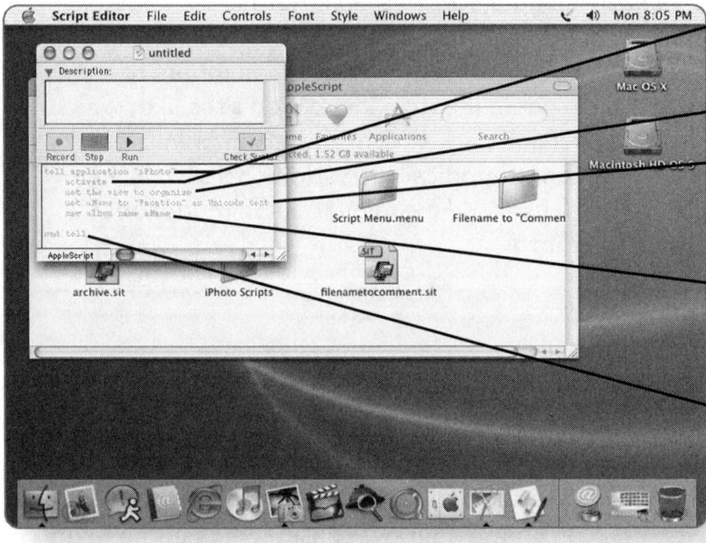


- Activate the iPhoto application.
- Change to the Organize view.
- Store the album name Vacation as the aName variable.
- Create a new album and name it using the contents of the aName variable.
- End the script.

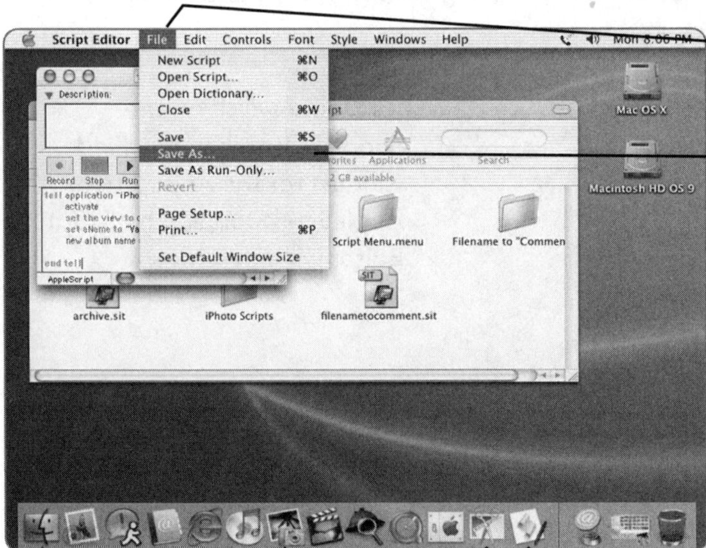


**3.** **Click** on **File**. The File menu will appear.

**4.** **Click** on **Save As**. The Save As dialog box will open. Save the script (as a compiled script or application) so that you can run it later. Saving the script as an application eliminates the necessity of opening the script and clicking on the Run button.

Here's the text of the example script one more time, in case you couldn't read it in the figure:

```
tell application "iPhoto"
    activate
    set the view to organize
    set aName to "Vacation" as Unicode text
    new album name aName
end tell
```

# 16

# Choosing iPhoto Preferences

We each have a unique working style, and iPhoto 2 offers a number of preferences that you can set to accommodate your style. In this chapter, you will learn how to:

- Choose a look for the photo viewing area.
- Specify editing behaviors.
- Choose the email program to use for mailing photos.
- Change slideshow defaults.

# Setting Viewing, Editing, and Mailing Defaults

You can choose most preference settings in iPhoto's Preferences window. That dialog window offers settings for adjusting the photo viewing area, choosing certain editing behaviors, and choosing the mail program to use for mailing photos.

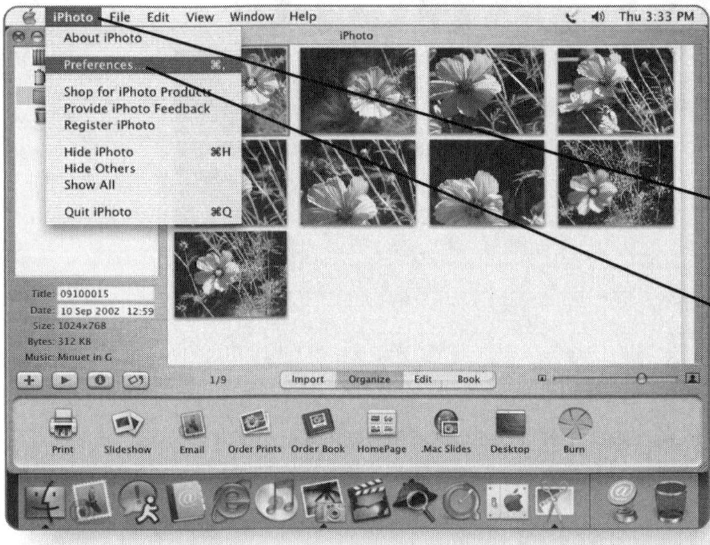


**1.** **Click** on **iPhoto**. The iPhoto menu will appear.

**2.** **Click** on **Preferences.** The Preferences window will open.

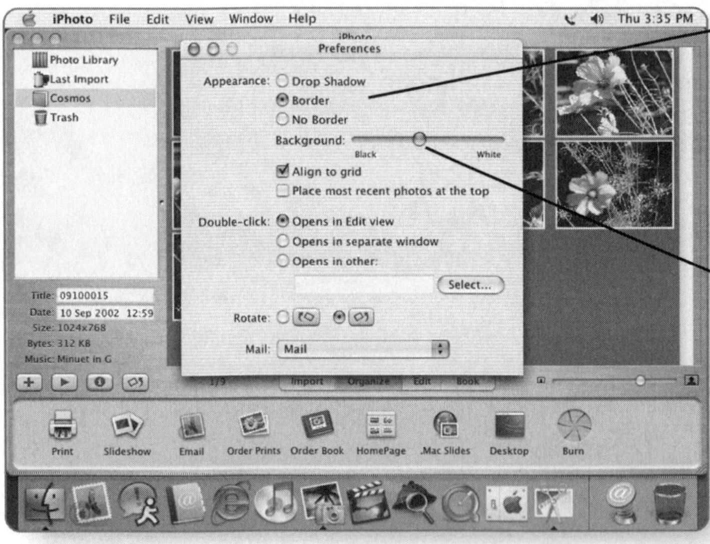


**3.** **Click** on an **Appearance option**. Your choice will designate whether or not each photo will have a Drop Shadow, Border, or No Border behind it in the photo viewing area.

**4.** **Drag** the **Background slider** as desired. The slider setting will determine the background color for the photo viewing area: black, white, or a shade of gray in between.

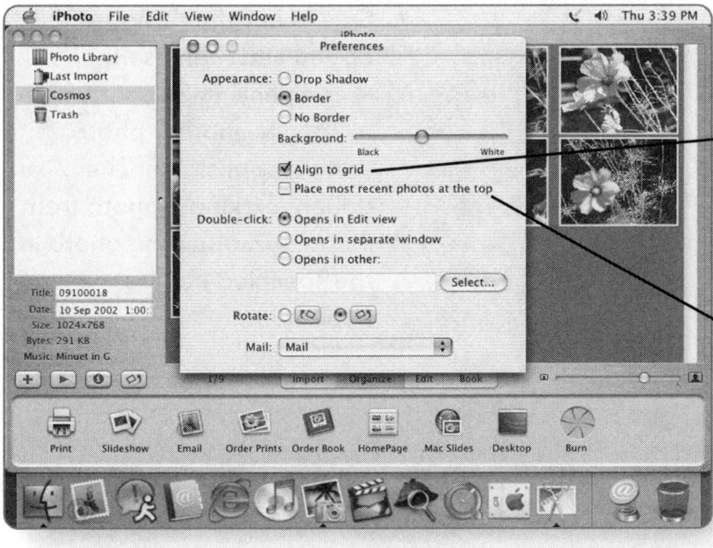


**5. Adjust** additional **Appearance options** as needed.

- **Align to grid.** When this option is checked, photos will align to a horizontal and vertical grid in the photo viewing area.
- **Place most recent photos at the top.** When this option is checked, iPhoto will place the most recent photos added to the album at the top of the album.

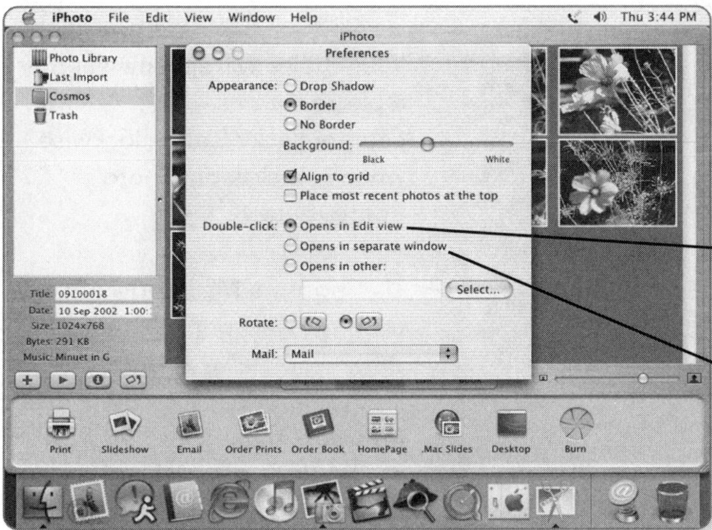


**6. Click** on a **Double-click option**. Your choice will designate what happens when you double-click on an image in the library or an album.

- **Opens in Edit view.** Choose this option to display the photo in iPhoto's Edit view.
- **Opens in separate window.** Choose this option to open the photo in a separate editing window in iPhoto. The editing window includes its own toolbar with editing tools.

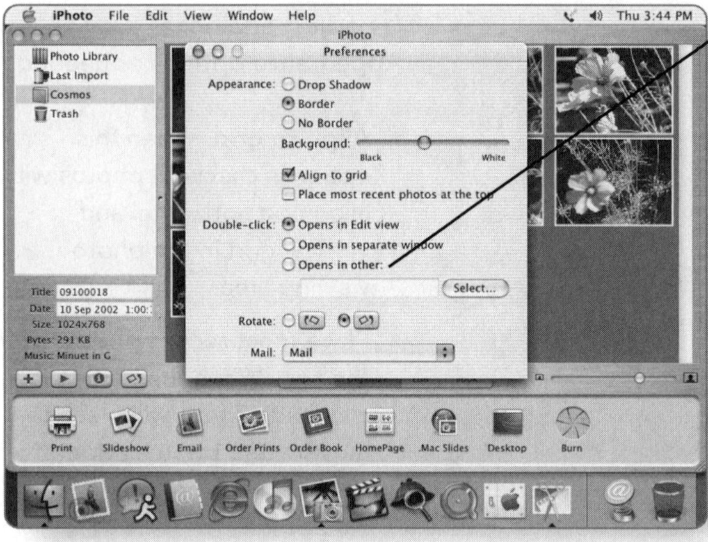

- **Opens in other.** Choose this option and then use the accompanying Select button to specify another photo editing application. Then, double-clicking a photo from iPhoto will open the photo in the specified editing application.

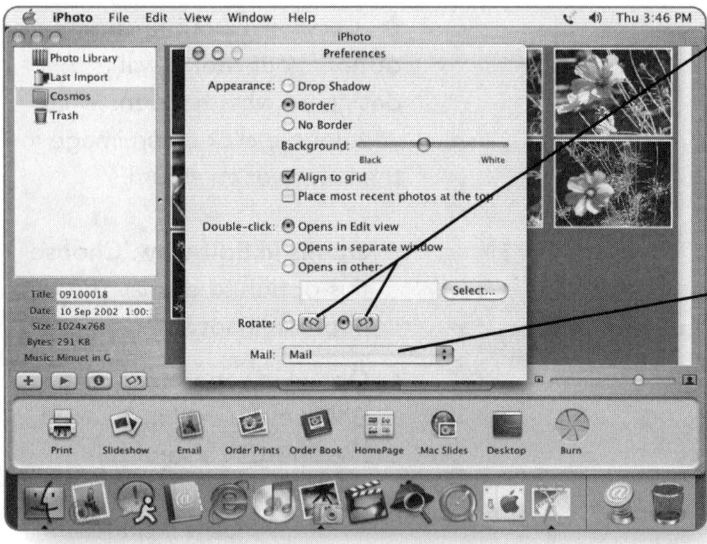

**7. Click** on a **Rotate option**. Your choice will specify whether a photo rotates counterclockwise or clockwise when you click on iPhoto's Rotate button.

**8. Choose** a **Mail application** from the Mail pop-up menu. When you mail a photo from iPhoto, iPhoto will create a mail message in the specified mail application, attach the photo to the message, and start the mail application so you can address and send the message. (See "E-Mailing Your Photos" in Chapter 9 to learn more.)

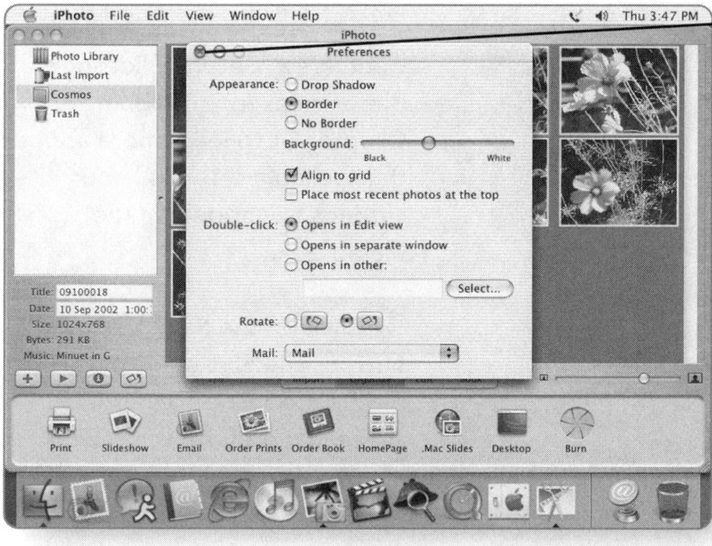


**9. Click** on the Preferences window **close button**. The Preferences window will close, and your settings will take effect.

# Setting Slideshow Defaults

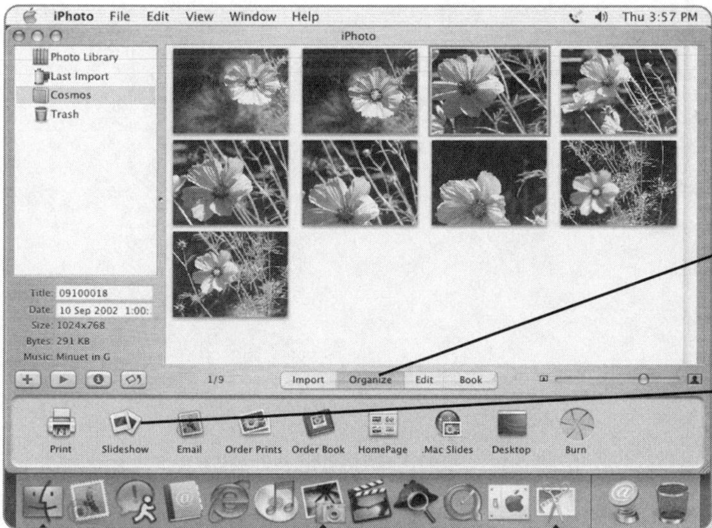


If you've come to prefer a particular collection of settings for onscreen slideshows, you can designate those settings as the slideshow defaults.

**1. Click** on the **Organize** button. The Organize view will appear.

**2. Click** on the **Slideshow icon**. The Slideshow Settings dialog box will open.

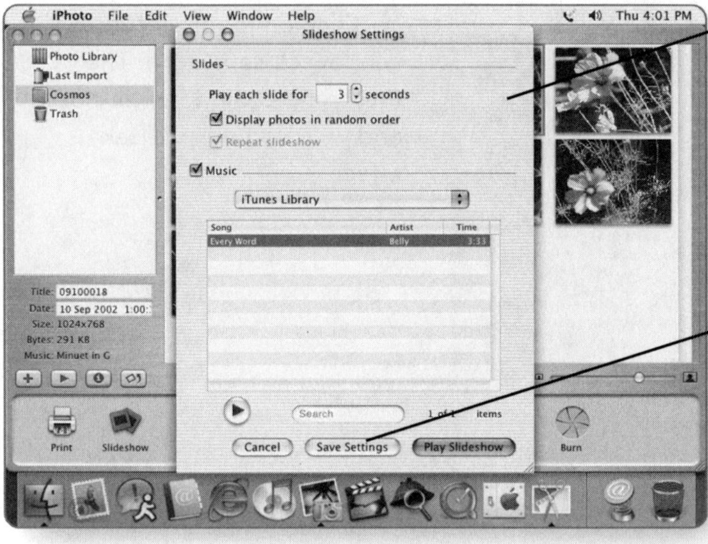


**3. Choose** the **settings** you want. (See "Setting Slideshow Preferences for an Album" in Chapter 11 to learn more about the available settings.) Your settings will appear in the dialog box.

**4. Click** on the **Save Settings** button. The Slideshow Settings dialog box will close, and your slideshow preferences will take effect.

# Part IV Review Questions

1. How do I preserve photos? *See "Burning a CD or DVD" in Chapter 13.*
2. Can I view CD-R Images? *See "Viewing a Library from a CD-R" in Chapter 13.*
3. How do I choose another library? *See "Selecting a Library" in Chapter 13.*
4. How do I share a slideshow online? *See "Publishing and Announcing the .Mac Slideshow" in Chapter 14.*
5. Are example scripts available? *See "Downloading Example Scripts" in Chapter 15.*
6. How do I run a script? *See "Running a Script" in Chapter 15.*
7. Can I write a basic script? *See "Creating a Basic Script" in Chapter 15.*
8. How do I set up basic iPhoto defaults? *See "Setting Viewing, Editing, and Mailing Defaults" in Chapter 16.*
9. How do I set slide show preferences? *Trick question! The details are covered in Part III.*

PART V

# Appendixes

# A

# Downloading and Installing iPhoto 2

After Apple introduced Mac OS X, it introduced the iPhoto software for managing digital images. Your Mac or Mac OS X version may have shipped without the iPhoto software, or you may have an older version of the software. In either case, you can obtain iPhoto 2 from the Apple Web site and install it at any time. In this appendix, you'll learn how to:

- Download iPhoto 2 from Apple.
- Install iPhoto 2 on your Macintosh.

# Downloading iPhoto 2 from Apple's Web Site

You can download iPhoto 2 from Apple's Web site free of charge. To run iPhoto 2, your system must be running Mac OS X version 10.1.5 or later. If you're currently using an older version, run Software Update in System Preferences to upgrade the operating system. Your Mac also must have a G3 or G4 processor running at 400MHz or faster. If your Mac has only 128M of RAM, upgrading to 256M or more will be useful, because photo files tend to be large, so processing multiple photos requires quite a bit of memory. The large iPhoto 2 download (over 32M) will take some time to download over a slow connection. If your Internet connection is slow, it's best to start this process when you've finished your work for the day.

> **TIP**
>
> iPhoto also can be purchased as part of the iLife suite, which includes iMovie 3, iDVD3, and iTunes 3. iLife costs $49, and you can buy it online in the Apple Store (http://store.apple.com).

**1.** **Connect** to the **Internet**, if required. Your Internet connection will become active. (See Appendix C, "Dialing the Internet If Needed," to learn how to start your dial-up Internet connection.)

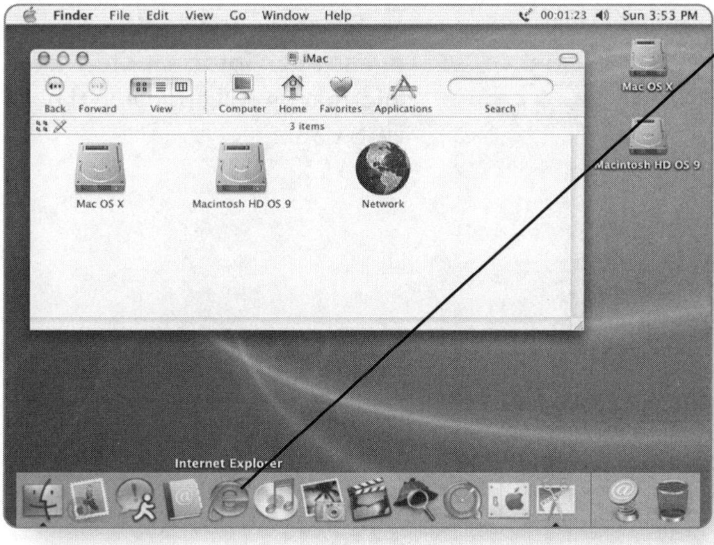


**2.** **Click** on the **Internet Explorer icon** on the Dock. Internet Explorer will open and display the home (start) page that you've specified.

> **NOTE**
>
> Of course, if you've installed another Web browser, launch it, instead.

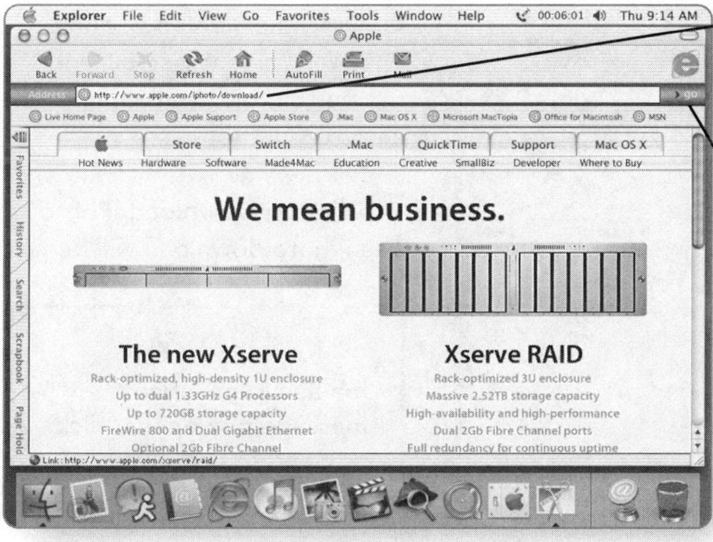


**3.** **Enter www.apple.com/iphoto/download** in the Address box. The Web address will appear in the box.

**4.** **Click** on **Go** or press Return. The iPhoto 2 download page will load.

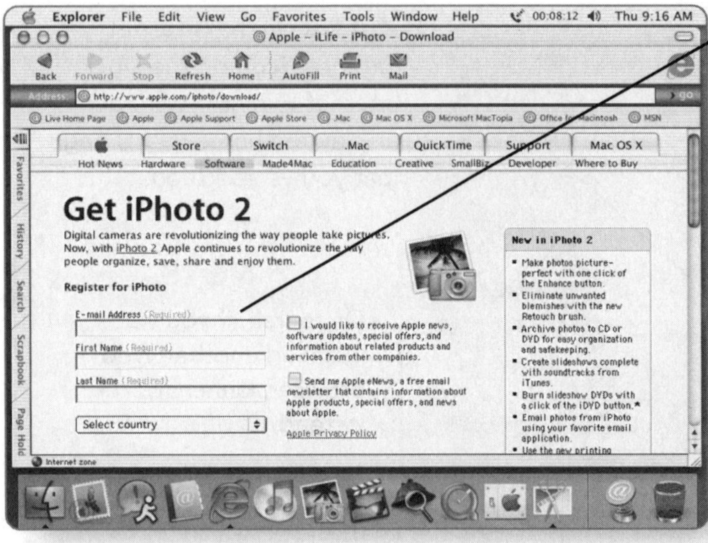


**5. Enter** the required **registration information.** The information will appear in the Web page.

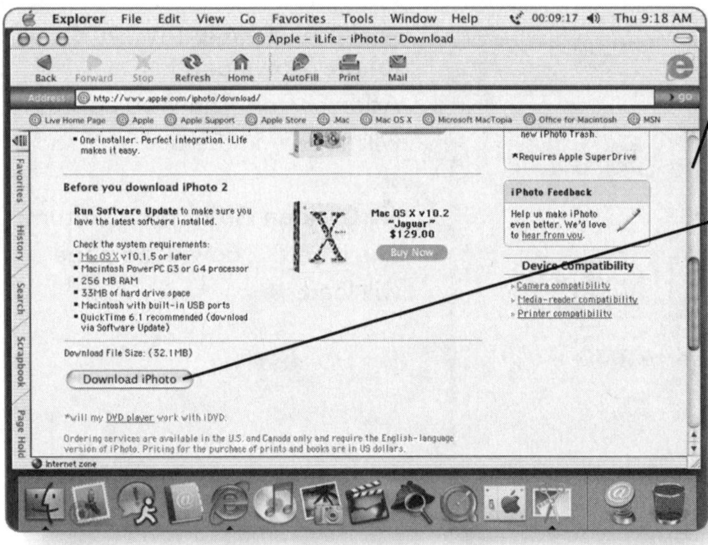


**6. Drag** the **scroll box** down. The Web page will scroll, and the button for downloading iPhoto 2 will appear.

**7. Click** on **Download iPhoto.** The iPhoto download will begin.

**NOTE**

If a Security Notice message box opens, click on Send to continue.

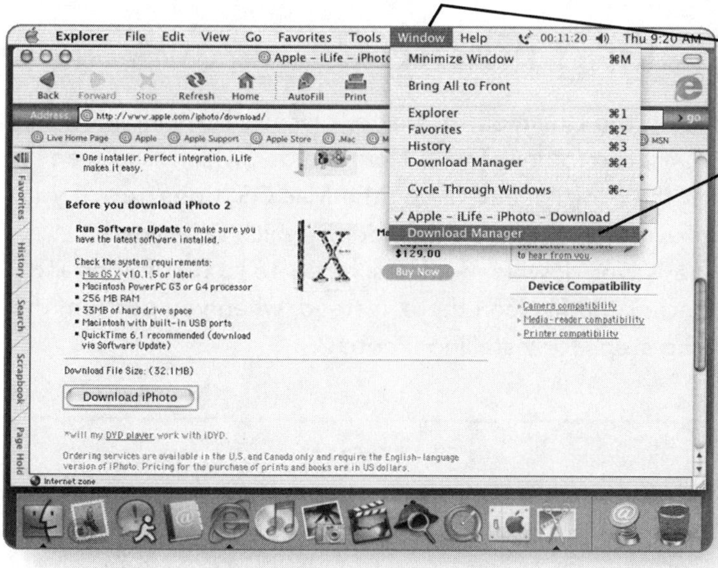


**8. Click** on **Window**. The Window menu will appear.

**9. Click** on **Download Manager**. The Download Manager window will appear, enabling you to track the progress of the iPhoto download.

## NOTE

To the right and slightly below the Download iPhoto button, the Web page offers a Device Compatibility section. Click one of the links there to identify whether your digital camera, card, media reader, or printer is compatible with iPhoto 2.

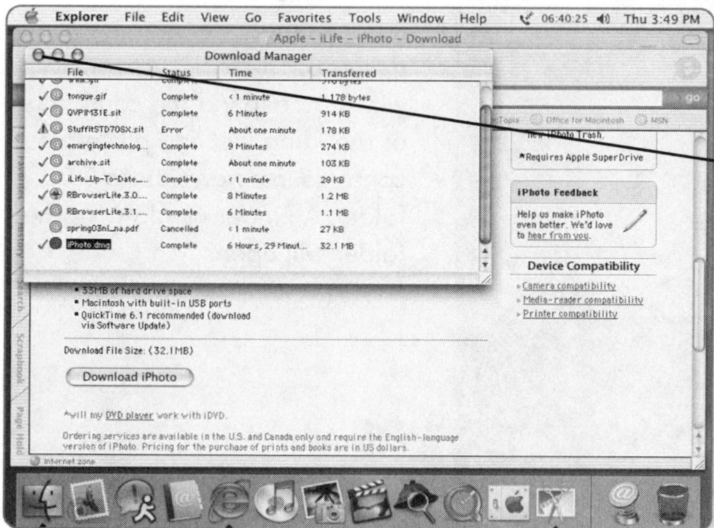


**10.** When the download finishes, **close** the **Download Manager** window, **exit Internet Explorer**, and **disconnect** from the **Internet**. The download process will be complete.

# Installing iPhoto 2

By default, the Download Manager places all downloaded files in the Desktop folder of your Home folder, which places an icon for the downloaded file on the Mac OS X desktop. If you have previously changed the folder in which Download Manager saves downloaded files, navigate to that folder and double-click the file icon there, instead, when you perform the following steps for installing iPhoto 2.

> **CAUTION**
>
> Installing iPhoto 2 converts the photo library to a format not compatible with older iPhoto versions, so back up the Pictures:iPhoto Library folder in your Home folder to preserve the old format before installing the new version, if required.

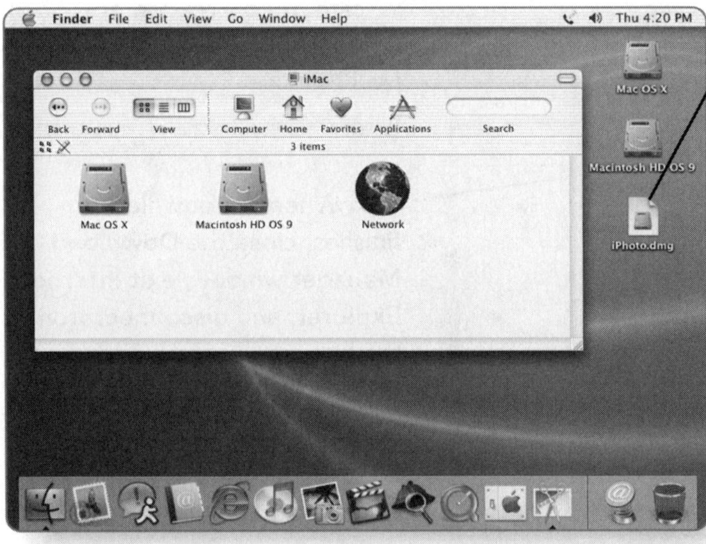


**1. Double-click** on the **iPhoto.dmg icon** on the desktop. The Disk Copy utility will start, expand the contents of the .dmg file, and place those contents in a new iPhoto 2.0 folder. A Finder window for the folder will open.

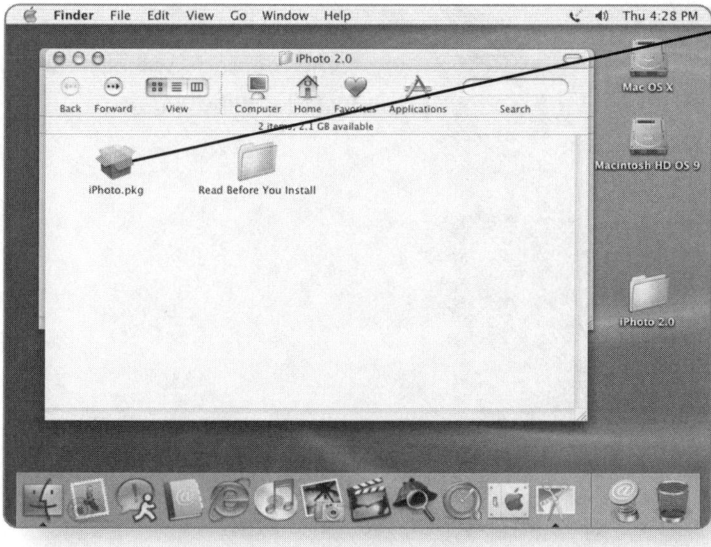


**2. Double-click** on the **iPhoto.pkg icon.** The Installer application will start and will prompt you to enter an administrator password.

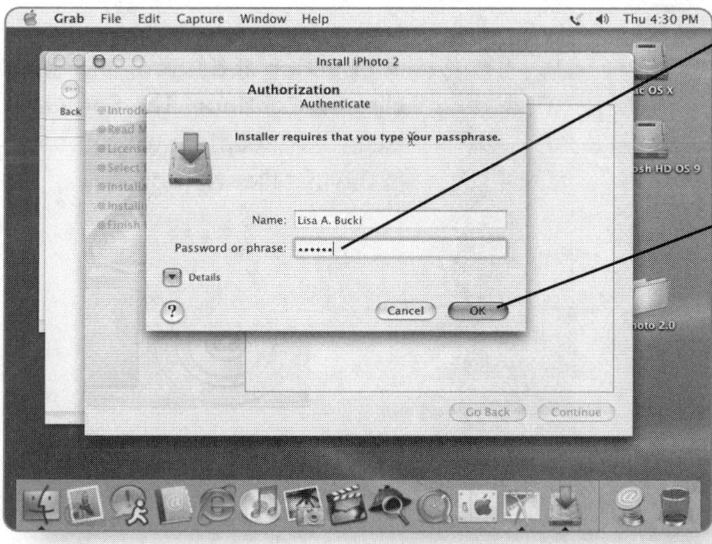


**3. Type** the **password**. An asterisk for each character will appear in the Password or phrase text box.

**4. Click** on **OK**. A welcome message will appear in the Installer window.

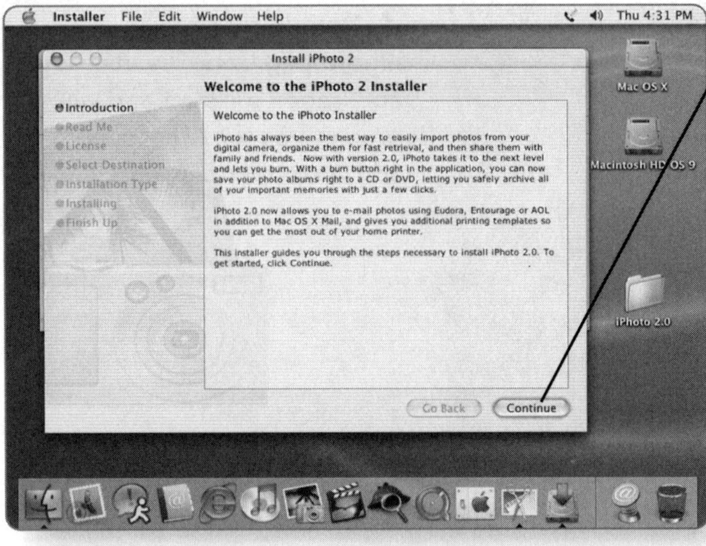


**5. Click** on **Continue**. A welcome message will appear in the Installer window.

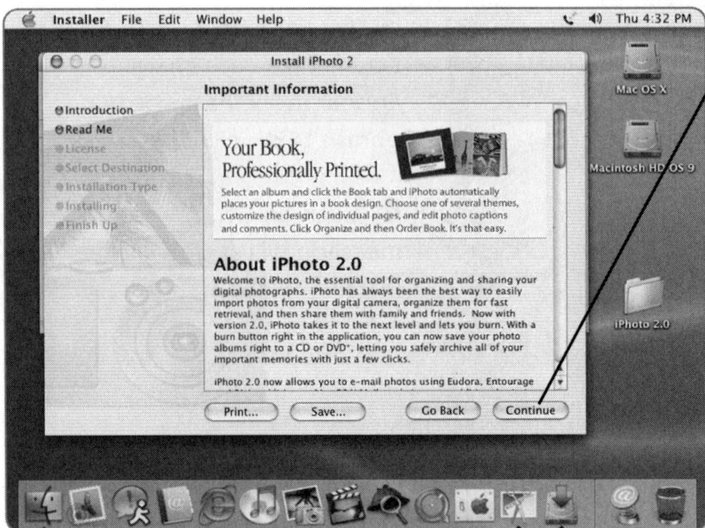


**6.** Review the Read Me information, if desired, and then **click** on **Continue**. The Software License Agreement will appear in the Installer window.

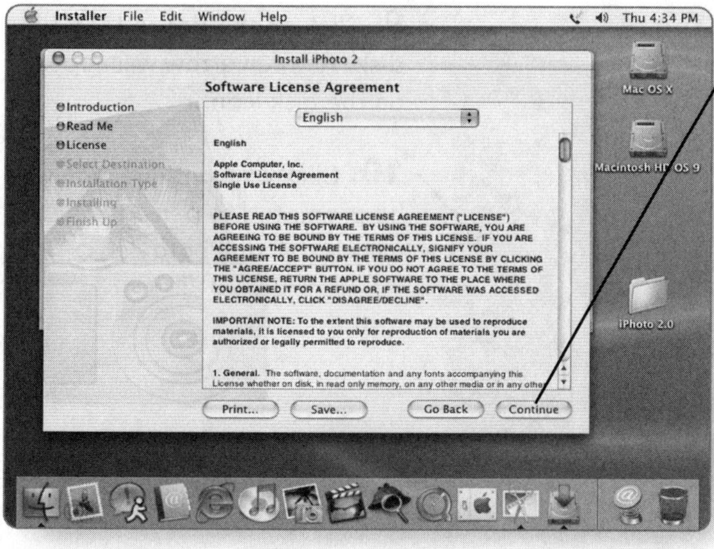


**7.** Review the Software License Agreement, and then **click** on **Continue**. A prompt to agree with the license information will appear.

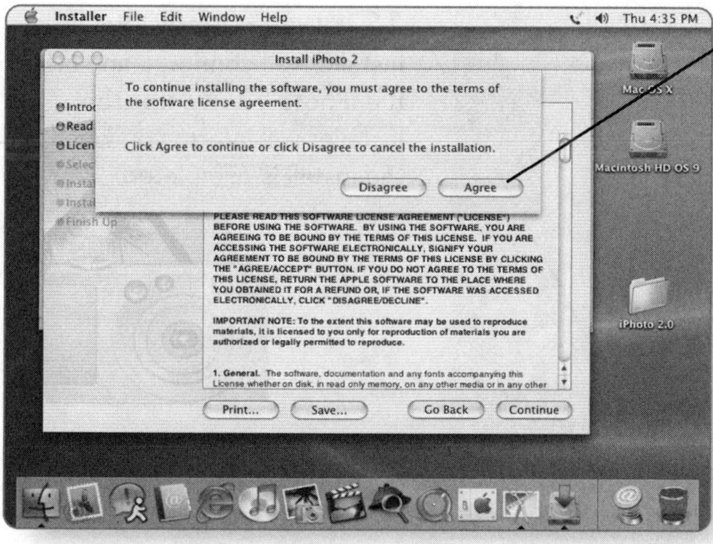


**8. Click** on **Agree**. The Installer will prompt you to select a destination disk for installing iPhoto (if your system has multiple hard disks or disk partitions).

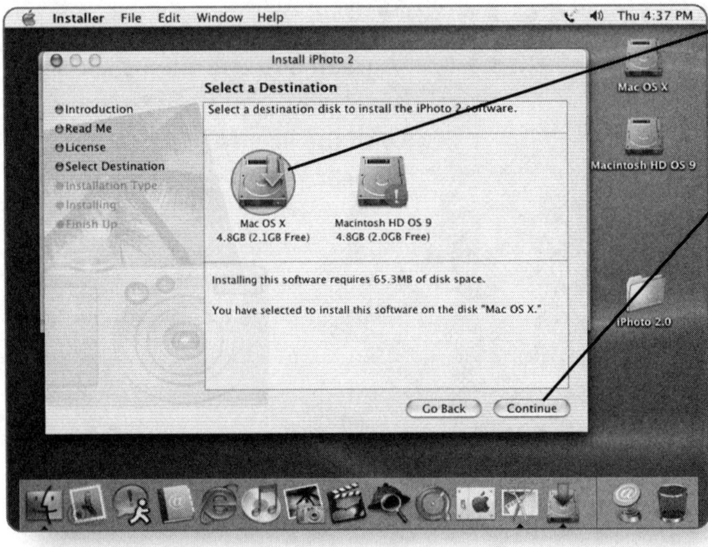


**9. Click** on the **desired install disk**. A green arrow will appear on the disk icon.

**10. Click** on **Continue**. You will be prompted to perform an easy install of iPhoto 2.

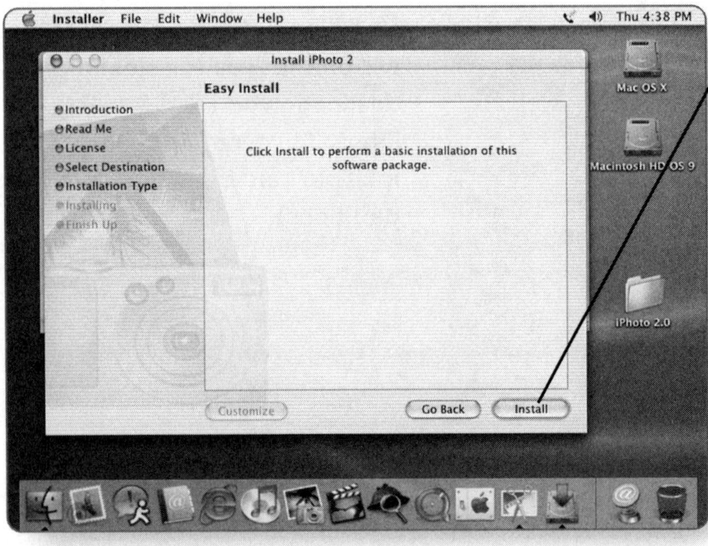


**11. Click** on **Install**. The Installer will configure and install the iPhoto 2 software. The Installer will inform you when the install is completed.

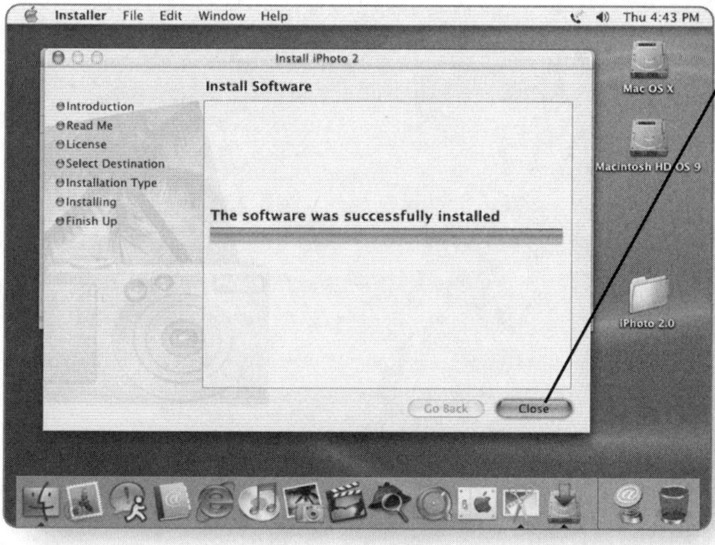


**12.** **Click** on **Close**. The Installer window will close.

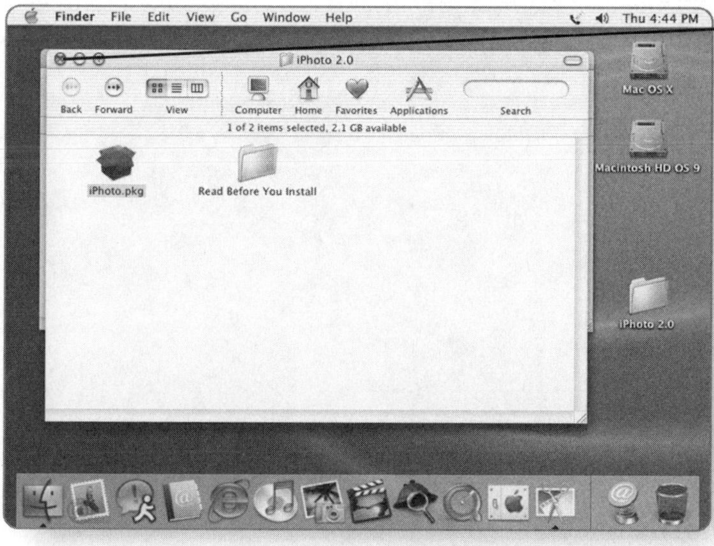


**13.** **Click** on the **window close button** for the iPhoto 2.0 window. The window will close.

> **TIP**
>
> It's a good practice to make a backup copy (preferably on CD-R) of any downloaded software installers such as the iPhoto 2 software. Then, if you ever have to reinstall the Mac OS X system, you can install the software from the backup copy rather than having to repeat a lengthy download.

# B

# Taking and Making Better Photos

Many of us are far from having the talent of famous photographers like Ansel Adams. Still, there are things each of us can do to enhance the quality of our digital photos, both while we're taking them and when we're enhancing them in a program like iPhoto. This appendix presents several pointers to help you expand your photographic limits.

**TIP**

Many colleges and community colleges offer photography courses as part of their media, art, or adult education programs. Check one out in your area if the tips herein only whet your appetite!

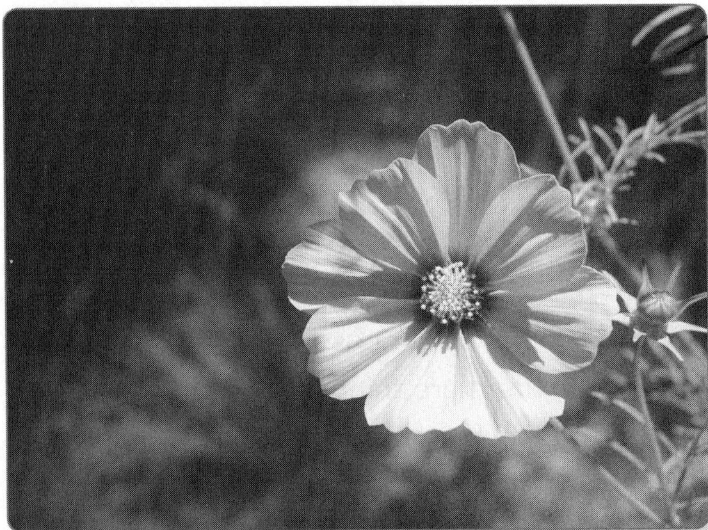

- **Framing your subject.** Probably the epitome of a boring shot is the typical "mug shot" of a person centered in the photo. You can add more interest to a photo by shooting or cropping so that the subject is off center. In fact, you can remember the "rule of thirds." Think of the photo as being divided in thirds both horizontally and vertically. Frame the photo so that the subject is approximately in the upper left (the far left and upper thirds) or lower right (the far right and lower thirds) for maximum punch.

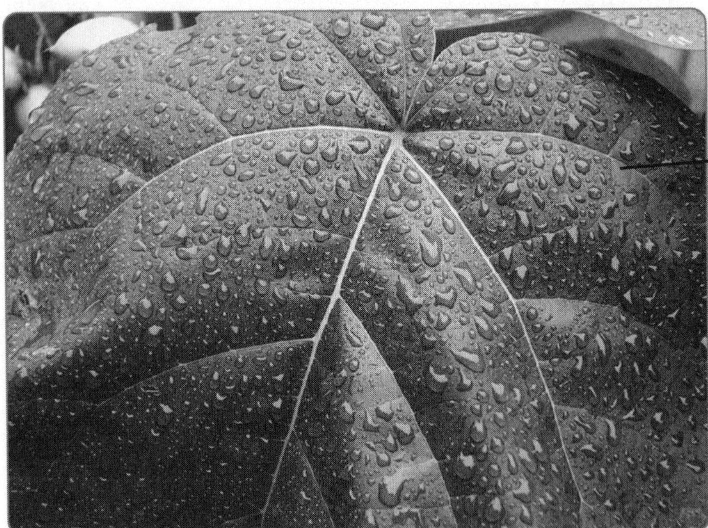

- **Try an extreme close-up.** If your digital camera has a macro (close-up) lens or mode, experiment with it. You can get stunning, detailed shots.

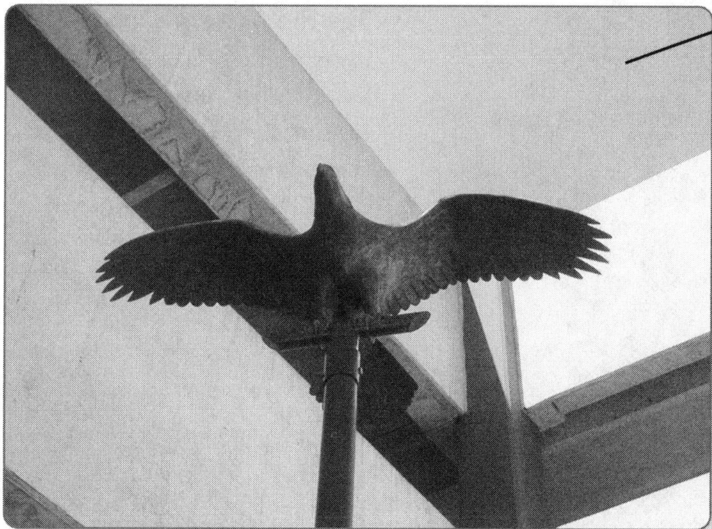

- **Consider all the angles.** Take a shot from an unusual angle or look for subjects positioned at interesting angles to other background objects. When shooting children or pets, kneel or lie down on the floor so that you can adjust the photo's aspect. Or, try to position yourself at an extreme angle to your subject for dramatic impact.

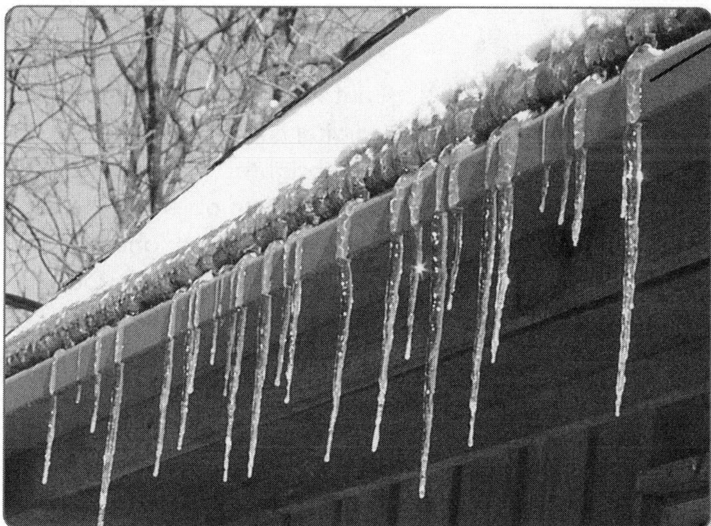

- **Repeat after me: Rhythm is good.** Repeating objects like these establishes a desirable visual rhythm, especially for photos that you want to use on the desktop or as a background for a document.

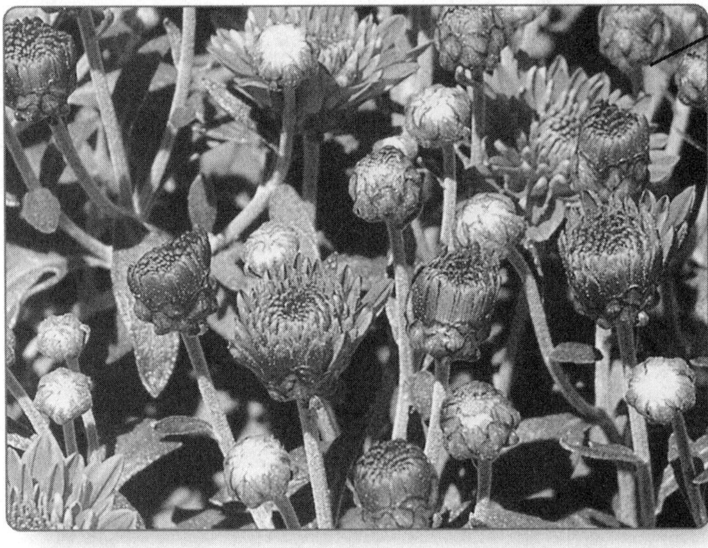

- **See the pattern.** Don't just think of individual subjects. Look for interesting shapes, textures, and patterns. Again, these look great on the desktop and are useful for decorating documents.

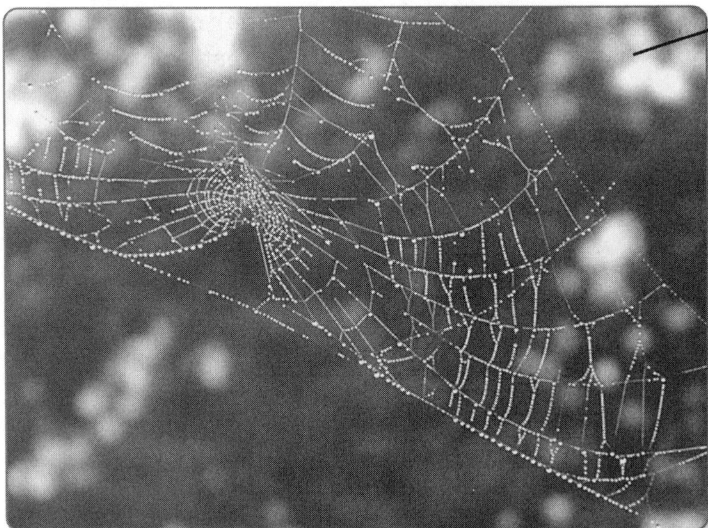

- **Lighting.** Pay attention to the lighting of your shots. The automatic mode for most digital cameras focuses on the brightest part of the image. If an object in the background is brighter than an object in the foreground, then the camera may focus on the background, resulting in a foreground that's out of focus. Likewise, if the sun or light source is behind your subject, called backlighting, the subject will likely appear too dark. Learn how to set the lighting (aperture and shutter) settings manually for your camera so you can correct lighting issues—or go for more dramatic lighting effects.

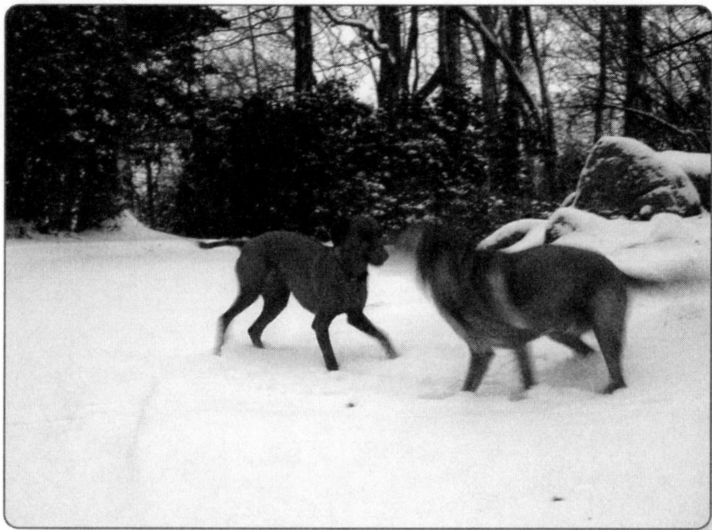

- **Go for the moment.** When shooting people, in particular, don't always settle for a posed shot. Shoot even at casual moments. You'll catch your subjects at their best, and your photos will have a pleasing spontaneity. Motion also can add drama to some subjects.

- **Shoot some more. And then some more.** Large storage cards and rechargeable batteries give you the ability to shoot dozens of photos, virtually for free. Take advantage of this abundance. You'll have more source material for your photo projects, and will often capture some surprising, interesting shots.
- **Break the rules.** You are the arbiter of what's cool or not in your mind's eye. Follow your artistic muse, disregard the rules, and you'll take photos that you love.

C

# Dialing the Internet if Needed

For certain iPhoto 2 operations, such as ordering a photo book or photo prints online, your system needs to be connected to the Internet.

Users with cable modem and DSL connections need not worry about connecting to the Internet, because those connections are always on. That's not true for users dialing in with a modem. Even if you configured Internet Connect to dial your Internet connection automatically (via the Network pane in System Preferences), you still may encounter times when you want to connect on demand. Further, since Internet Connect won't automatically disconnect, it's a good practice to always check for an active connection and disconnect it if needed.

# Connecting and Disconnecting with the Modem Status Icon

By default, a modem status icon appears at the far right end of the Finder menu bar, near the time. You can use this icon to dial your Internet connection.

> **NOTE**
>
> To show or hide the modem status icon, start System Preferences, click on the Network icon, and then choose Internal Modem from the Show pop-up menu. Click on the Modem tab in the window, and then check or uncheck the Show modem status in the menu bar check box.

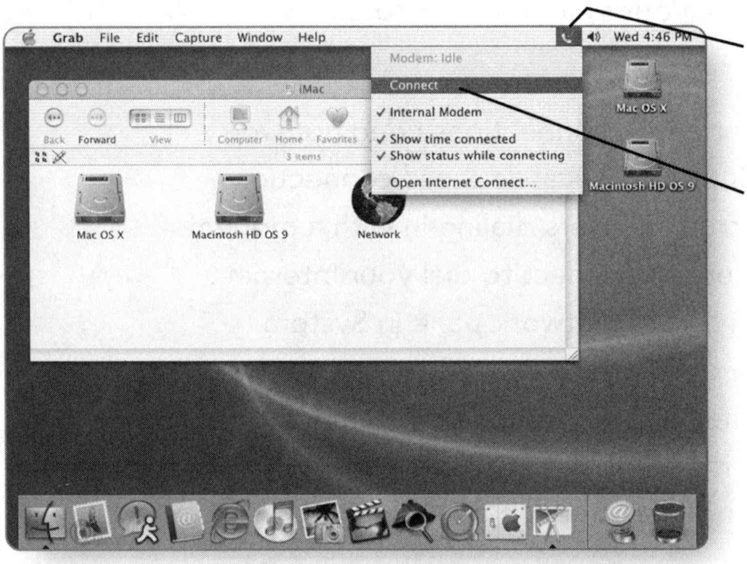


1. **Click** on the **modem status icon**. The modem status menu will appear.

2. **Click** on **Connect**. The modem will dial the Internet and log on to your account.

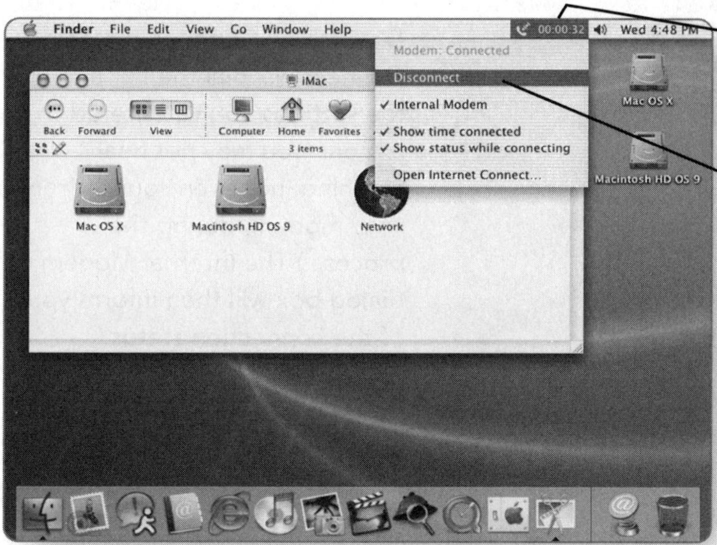


**3. Click** on the **modem status icon**. The modem status menu will appear.

**4. Click** on **Disconnect**. The modem will disconnect from the Internet, which may take slightly longer than making the connection.

# Using Internet Connect

If you've hidden the modem status icon or want to work with Internet Connect settings, you can use Internet Connect to dial your Internet connection and disconnect when needed.

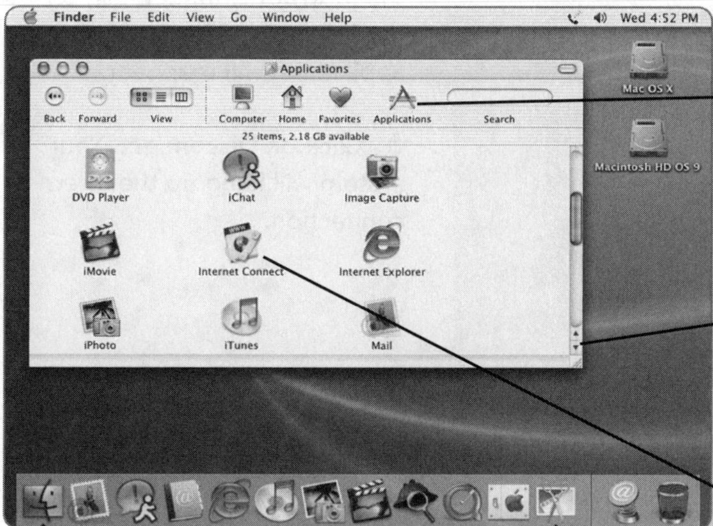


**1. Click** on the **Applications icon** on a Finder window toolbar. The contents of the Applications folder will appear in the window.

**2. Click** on the **down arrow** of the vertical scroll bar as needed. The Internet Connect icon will scroll into view.

**3. Double-click** on **Internet Connect**. Internet Connect will open.

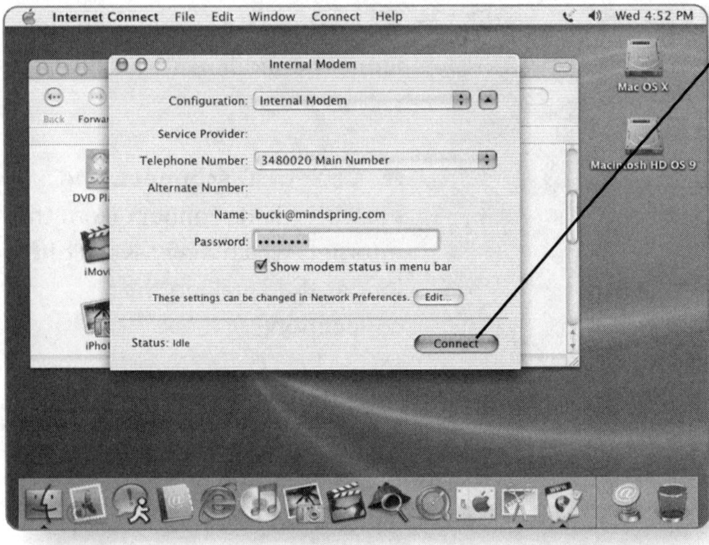


**4. Click** on **Connect**. Internet Connect will dial the ISP and use the settings you've entered to log on. (You may not hear anything, not even sounds from your modem, during the process.) The Internal Modem dialog box will then inform you of the connection status.

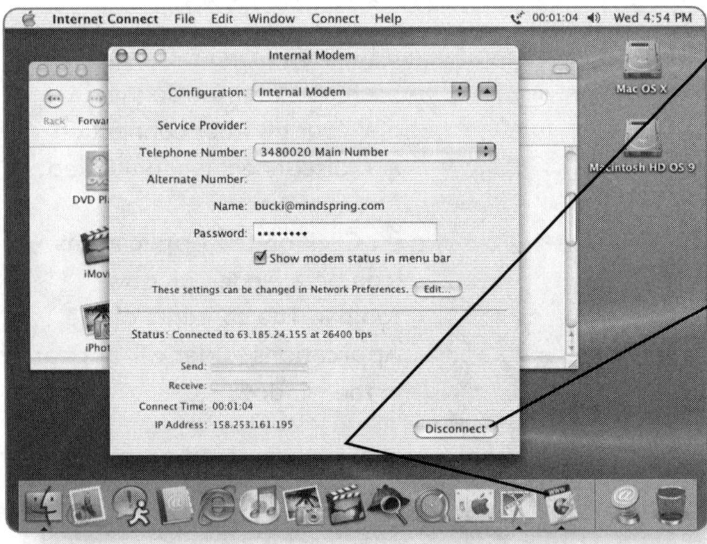


**5.** After you've finished your iPhoto Internet task and have closed iPhoto if needed, **click** on the **Internet Connect** icon on the Dock. The Internet Connect application will reappear.

**6. Click** on **Disconnect**. Your system will hang up the Internet connection.

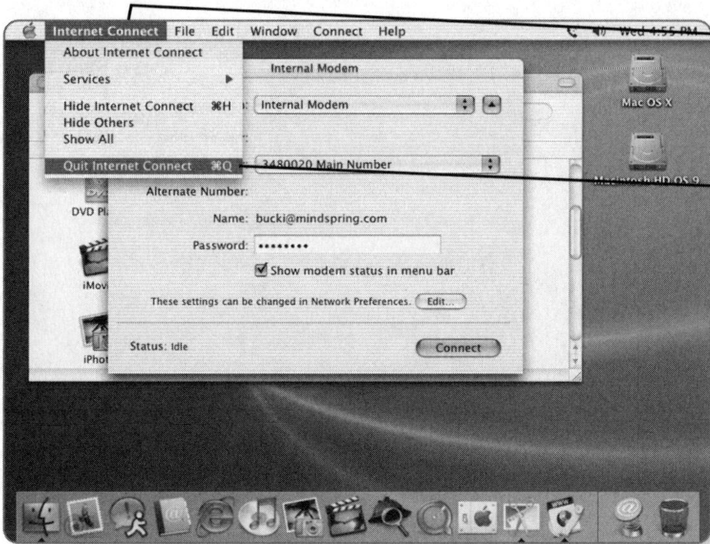


**7.** **Click** on **Internet Connect**. The Internet Connect menu will open.

**8.** **Click** on **Quit Internet Connect**. Internet Connect will close.

## NOTE

You can quit Internet Connect without clicking on the Disconnect button. This removes Internet Connect from your system's memory without hanging up the connection. Repeat Steps 1-3 to redisplay Internet Connect when you need to disconnect from the Internet.

# Glossary

**.Mac.** An Apple service that offers users a variety of convenient online features, including a .Mac e-mail address and 100M of storage accessible from any computer connected to the Internet, as well as the ability to publish photos online via iPhoto, and more.

**1-Click Ordering.** A secure Apple service that streamlines photo print and book ordering by entering your shipping and billing information for you.

**Album.** A collection of digital images in iPhoto to which you assign a particular name. Each digital album can hold as many images as you desire.

**Apple ID.** A secure online ID that Apple uses to store shipping, billing, and order information.

**Aspect ratio.** The relationship (proportions) between image width and height. Most images captured with a digital camera have a 4 to 3 aspect ratio.

**Automatic resolution enhancement.** A feature offered by some printers. When enabled, this feature automatically smoothes angles, curves, and edges.

**Bleed.** Printing an image or images on a page so that the page has no blank margins and the edges of the image reach the edges of the page.

**Book.** A digital layout for the images in an album. Specify a theme for the book and a design for each page.

**Brightness.** The relative overall tone of an image, from very dark to very light.

**CMYK color.** A color mode whereby an image is composed of Cyan, Magenta, Yellow, and blacK colors, the colors used by the four-color printing process. By default, digital camera and scanner images use the RGB (Red Green Blue) color mode. Those three colors of light combine on-screen to create the colors in an image file.

**Constrain ratio.** When you want to crop an image in iPhoto, you specify a constrain ratio to fix the aspect ratio of the cropped image. For example, you can choose one of the 5 x 7 Constrain choices to ensure an image will be cropped to the correct proportions to be printed as a 5 x 7 photo.

**Contrast.** The overall difference between the lightest and darkest tones in an image. An image with great difference between light and dark areas has high contrast and is said to "pop." An image with little difference between light and dark areas has low contrast and is called "flat."

**Crop zone.** After specifying a constrain ratio in iPhoto's Edit pane, drag on the image to specify the crop zone—the area that will remain after you click on the Crop button.

**Cropping.** Removing part of a photo to resize the photo's dimensions or focus on the most important photo content.

**dpi.** Dots per inch. The number of dots a printer can print per inch, or the number of pixels a photo includes per inch. Higher dpi values yield a better quality printout or image.

**Duplex printing.** Printing on both sides of each piece of paper. Not all printers offer duplex printing capabilities. Unless the printer is equipped with a duplex feeder, you must manually print one side of the pages, and then turn the paper over to print the other side.

**Enhance feature.** A new feature in iPhoto 2 that automatically corrects image color. Click on the Enhance button in the Edit pane to apply this feature.

**EXIF data.** The **Ex**changeable **I**mage **F**ile data format used to store information about exposure, shutter speed, flash, camera model, and so on in a JPEG image taken by a digital camera. Many image editing and publishing applications, such as iPhoto, can read the EXIF data stored in the file.

**Export.** To convert images from one file format to another for different uses. In iPhoto, you can export images to a new graphic file format or size, export images as a Web page, or export images as a QuickTime movie file.

**Film Roll.** *See Roll.*

**Font.** A full set of characters (a through z, numbers, etc.) in a particular size and style, such as the full set of Helvetica characters in the 10-point size.

**iCard.** A .Mac feature that enables you to send online greeting cards.

**iTunes library.** The songs that you've added to iTunes by converting them to the MP3 format. You also can add files that have already been converted to the library.

**Keywords.** Identifying categories you assign to photos. You can use keywords to more quickly display images in a particular category.

**Library.** Also called photo library. The central location that stores all of the photos you've imported into iPhoto. By default, the photo library is stored in the Pictures: iPhoto Library folder of your Home folder.

**Library list.** The pane at the left side of the iPhoto window that lists the Photo Library and each of the Albums you've created.

**Lock (page).** To prevent changes to the page design applied to a particular page in a photo book.

**Page design.** When creating a photo book, choose a page design to designate how many images should appear on each page, or whether the page should use the Introduction or End page design.

**PDF.** The Adobe Portable Document Format file format extension. PDF files can include text and graphics, and can be viewed in the Mac OS X Preview application or in Adobe's free Acrobat Reader application. You can save a photo book as a PDF file in iPhoto.

**Photo viewing area.** The area at the left side of the iPhoto window that shows the photos in the Photo Library or currently-selected album (Organize pane or view), the photo to be edited (Edit pane or view), or the currently-selected book page (Book pane or view).

**Pixel.** Another name for *picture element*—a single dot of light or color in an image. Smaller pixels (more pixels per inch) yield a higher-quality image.

**Preset.** A collection of print settings that you've saved. Selecting the preset for a new print job applies all the settings in the preset.

**Red eye.** An undesirable effect in a photo in which a subject's eyes appear red or in some cases green. This condition results from flash light bouncing off the interior of the subject's eyes. iPhoto 2 offers a feature in the Edit pane for correcting red eye.

**Resolution.** The size of an image in pixels. For example, an 800 x 600 image is 800 pixels wide by 600 pixels tall. Because higher resolution images contain more pixels, you can print them at larger sizes without loss of quality or graininess.

**Retouch feature.** A new feature in iPhoto 2's Edit pane that enables you to eliminate spots, scratches, and other small imperfections.

**Revert.** To discard all changes to an image file.

**Roll (film roll).** A number assigned when you import a set of photos into iPhoto, as in "Roll 3."

**Sort.** To place the images in the library or an album in a new order.

**Theme.** When designing a book in the Book pane (view), choose a theme to determine the overall look, size, and arrangement of the photos on the pages.

**Typeface.** The overall design for a set of characters. A font is a more specific subset of a typeface.

**URL.** The address for a Web page on the Internet.

**View.** A pane within iPhoto that provides particular features or capabilities. For example, use the Organize pane to change the order of images within the Photo Library or a selected album. Use the Edit pane to crop and correct a photo.

# Index

# Q



# R



# S